GERARD DAVID

Purity of Vision in an Age of Transition

GERARD DAVID

Purity of Vision in an Age of Transition

MARYAN W. AINSWORTH

Winner of the 1998 C.I.N.O.A. Prize

THE METROPOLITAN MUSEUM OF ART, NEW YORK
DISTRIBUTED BY HARRY N. ABRAMS INC., NEW YORK

This publication is made possible by the Samuel I. Newhouse Foundation and
the Samuel H. Kress Foundation.

For J. C., Rachel, Chuck, and Clark
in celebration, and with deep gratitude and love

Published by The Metropolitan Museum of Art

John P. O'Neill, *Editor in Chief*
Patricia Godfrey, *Copy Editor*
Margaret Davis, *Design and Typesetting*
Merantine Hens, *Production*

Metropolitan Museum of Art (New York, N.Y.)
Gerard David: purity of vision in an age of
transition/ Maryan W. Ainsworth
p.   cm.
Includes bibliographical references and index.
ISBN 0-87099-877-3 (HC). — ISBN 0-8109-6523-2 (Abrams)
1. David, Gerard, ca. 1460–1523—Criticism and
interpretation. I. Ainsworth, Maryan Wynn.
II. David, Gerard, ca. 1460–1523. III. Title.
ND673.D3M48   1998
759.9493—DC21   98-30075
                                       CIP

Printed and bound in Belgium

Jacket: Detail of Cervara Altarpiece, Figure 174

Frontispiece: Detail of Nativity Triptych, Figure 200

CONTENTS

The Metropolitan Museum of Art is extremely fortunate to house the most comprehensive collection of early Netherlandish paintings in this hemisphere. Comprising examples from nearly every leading artist of the period, the collection's greatest strength lies in works by masters of the Bruges school—among them Jan van Eyck, Petrus Christus, Hans Memling, and Gerard David. This book celebrates the major holding within that group—that is, the largest collection in this country or abroad of individual panels by Gerard David, the preeminent painter in Bruges from 1484 to 1523.

All of these rare works came to the Metropolitan Museum through the extraordinary generosity of New York collectors who bequeathed paintings or provided funds specified for their purchase. The earliest acquisition, David's poignant *Crucifixion* with Saint Jerome, was made possible by the Rogers Fund and the discriminating eye of the curator Roger Fry in 1909, not long after the momentous 1902 exhibition in Bruges that had featured David's works. Subsequent additions, including the *Annunciation* panels from the artist's monumental Cervara Altarpiece, entered the collection by bequest from Mary Stillman Harkness, Jules Bache, Michael Friedsam, Benjamin Altman, and Robert Lehman. The most recent acquisition of a painting by David, whose works are increasingly difficult to come by, was in 1977 through the kindness of Charles and Jane Wrightsman. This is the jewel-like *Virgin and Child with Four Angels*, which joins the sublime *Rest on the Flight into Egypt* as a crowning achievement of David's mature phase.

Now including sixteen panels and one manuscript illumination, which range in date from David's earliest endeavors to those of his late period, the Metropolitan's treasure trove tells the story of one of the leading art centers in western Europe during a period of transition from the courtly culture of the dukes of Burgundy in late Medieval times to the expanding world of the upwardly mobile and newly wealthy bourgeoisie. Indications of this transitional period are evident in David's paintings, which show the results of his increasingly astute assessment of the evolution of devotional practices and the transformation of taste among both his local and his foreign clients. New developments in the genres of landscape and still life, as well as the gradual assimilation of Italian art into David's paintings, illustrate his progressive tendencies.

The approach taken by the author of this volume, Maryan Ainsworth, is to consider the Museum's paintings not in isolation, but in the context of a broader study of David's oeuvre. Moreover, as with the ground-breaking exhibition and catalogue on Petrus Christus presented here just four years ago, she has pursued an interdisciplinary method in the investigation of these paintings, fostered by our Sherman Fairchild Paintings Conservation Center, which fully integrates art-historical and technical investigations. In close collaboration with the department's paintings conservators, she has reexamined the state and condition of these works and analyzed the artist's working procedure in creating them.

Preparing this in-depth study of David's working methods, the author has been able to rediscover the relationship to our own paintings of some of his exquisite silverpoint renderings of male and female heads and of plein-air studies from nature. Furthermore, with the new information provided by previously unknown details about the physical characteristics of these works, we have been able to reassess the original format of the Museum's panels—in some cases finding evidence to deconstruct former triptychs and in other cases to reconstruct our panels with others that originally formed part of the same altarpiece. Apart from these individual findings, the broader benefit has been a far greater understanding of the workshop practice of early Netherlandish painters, and of David's aims and achievements in a transitional period from the late

Medieval craft tradition to the new self-awareness of artists in the Renaissance age. The interdisciplinary approach of this book aims not only to provide a fresh look at the artistic production of Gerard David but also to launch a method of study that we hope will encourage others to ask new questions in the ongoing examination of early Netherlandish painters and their working methods.

This publication is made possible by the generosity of the Samuel I. Newhouse Foundation and the Samuel H. Kress Foundation. The book has also been honored as the recipient of the 1998 C.I.N.O.A. prize, awarded by the Confédération Internationale des Négociants en Oeuvres d'Art. We are pleased to be able to publish it as a companion volume to *From Van Eyck to Bruegel: Early Netherlandish Painting in The Metropolitan Museum of Art*, which accompanies our fall exhibition.

Philippe de Montebello
Director, The Metropolitan Museum of Art

ACKNOWLEDGMENTS

This book is the result of a number of years of research devoted to an ongoing investigation of the oeuvre of Gerard David, and it is a great pleasure at this time to thank those individuals and institutions who contributed to this work and supported it in so many different ways. Without the interdisciplinary approach of the Sherman Fairchild Paintings Conservation Center at The Metropolitan Museum of Art, whose vision includes a position for an art historian as an integral part of the staff of paintings conservators and scientists, such a project would never have come to fruition. For this and for countless valuable discussions on a variety of issues, I am most indebted to Hubert von Sonnenburg, Sherman Fairchild Chairman, and to the members of the department with whom I have worked closely, namely Dorothy Mahon, Charlotte Hale, Christopher McGlinchey, George Bisacca, Nicholas Dorman, and Katherine Blaney-Miller, who provided key assistance for numerous administrative details. The last stages of a book are invariably the most frenetic; for their remarkable resilience and for helping to keep production going on a steady path, I am especially grateful to Lisa Murphy, Art Historian Intern, and Alison Gilchrest, Research Assistant, whose help with text and image revisions respectively, can be appreciated on almost every page of this book. Over the course of this research, I have been blessed with a succession of talented art historian interns of boundless curiosity and keen intellect who have participated in this endeavor, and I gladly share the final result with them all: Chiyo Ishikawa, Katherine Crawford Luber, Ronda Kasl, Jeffrey Jennings, Cynthia Anderson, Jennifer Milam, Yvette Bruijnen, Jacob Wisse, Stephanie Buck, Sarah Ganz, Margaret Koster, and Aileen Wang. I am especially grateful to Ronda Kasl for a critical reading of the text in its first draft.

Many individuals freely gave their time and expertise and generously shared information. For this I owe my sincere thanks to Noël Geirnaert, J. R. J. van Asperen de Boer, Rachel Billinge, David Bomford, Claudia Goldstein, Françoise Viatte, Martin Wyld, Lorne Campbell, Susan Foister, Alistair Smith, Jean Wilson, Marigene Butler, Joseph Rishel, Mark Tucker, Joe Mikuliak, Patrick Le Chanu, Philippe Lorentz, Dan Ewing, Robert Noordtman, Micheline Comblen-Sonkes, Jacqueline Folie, Roger Wieck, William Voelkle, Dirk De Vos, Molly Faries, Liliane Masschelein-Kleiner, Henri Pauwels, Emil Bosshard, Erik Vandamme, Rainald Grosshans, Lynn Jacobs, Laurence B. Kanter, Jacques Foucart, Carmen Bambach, John Hand, Catherine Metzger, Sarah Fisher, Kristi Dahm, Laura Tagliaferro, Fritz Koreny, Maria Fontana Amoretti, Clario di Fabio, Helen Hyde, Mary Howard, Father Kilian McDonnell, O.S.B., Clifford LaFontaine, Deirdre Larkin, Susan Moody, Nadine Orenstein, Edwin Buijsen, Michel Jonker, Jørgen Wadum, Wolfgang Prohaska, Gerald Kaspar, Karl Schutz, Everett Fahy, Maria del Carmen Garrido, Juan Martinez, L. M. Goegebuer, Guido van de Voorde, Maurits Smeyers, Roger Van Schoute, Hélène Verougstraete, Alphonse Dierick, Konrad Renger, Christiane Andersson, John Brealey, Peter Eikemeier, Hélène Mund, Cyriel Stroo, Hilde Lobelle-Caluwé, Arnout Balis, Nico Van Hout, Margaret Scott, Giuseppina Angelantoni Malfatti, François Bergot, Helena Bussers, Françoise Robert-Jones, Bernice Davidson, Edgar Munhall, M. Serra de Alzaga, Sarah Staniforth, Oliver Lane, Marina Cano, Theo Jülich, A. Wiesman-Emerling, Gerald Stiebel, Eliane de Wilde, Thomas Kren, Martha Wolff, A. W. F. M. Meij, Geroen Giltaij, Michael Pächt, Marcia Steele, Margret Stuffmann, Susan Urbach, Peter Waldeis, Pierrette Jean-Richard, and Hans Mielke. Others are thanked within the endnotes; my sincere apologies for any inadvertent omissions.

The Museum alone could not provide the resources necessary to expand this research into the contextual study that it became. For additional support

I am extremely grateful to the Rowland Foundation for their long-standing commitment, to the J. Paul Getty Visiting Scholar Program, the National Endowment for the Humanities, and my dear friend Hester Diamond. The Samuel I. Newhouse Foundation and the Samuel H. Kress Foundation, as well as the award of the 1998 C.I.N.O.A. Prize, enabled us to publish this study in its present form.

The text benefitted from the careful editing of Patricia Godfrey and Barbara Burn, who with cheerful encouragement and great diligence saw this volume to its completion. Meg Davis designed the book, which was smoothly taken through various production stages by Merantine Hens with the assistance of Ann Lucke and Robert Weisberg; Connie Harper gave attention to administrative details. Barbara Bridgers and her staff in the Photo Studio, especially Bruce Schwarz, Juan Trujillo, and Susanne Cardone, provided an invaluable service on many occasions for new photography. Katria Czerwoniak efficiently facilitated interlibrary loan requests.

I am particularly grateful to Philippe de Montebello, Director, for his support of this book, and to Emily Rafferty, Senior Vice President for Development, and Chris Scornavacca for their efforts in seeking the funding for its publication.

To my family and friends who have buoyed me up and endured the long journey, a simple thank you is completely inadequate. I look forward to opportunities to return in kind all that I have received.

Maryan W. Ainsworth

NOTE TO THE READER

In all captions the measurements of works are given in centimeters; height precedes width. **Attributed to** suggests a lack of absolute certainty about attribution. **Workshop of** assumes that the painting was executed in the atelier of the artist, most likely during his lifetime. **Assistant** indicates the participation of another artist in the workshop. **Follower of** signifies proximity in style to the work of the artist named, but execution of a certain distance in time or place. **Copy after** notes that the painting is based on a prototype by the named artist.

Throughout the text IR stands for infrared photography, while IRR means infrared reflectography.

Infrared reflectography of Metropolitan Museum paintings, as well as those in other museums, was undertaken using a Hamamatsu C-2741-03 vidicon camera. The images were initially documented by photography from the monitor screen; more recently they were digitized and documented on computer, where they were processed using Adobe Photoshop. For this book it has been possible to digitize some of the earlier photographic images, so that new seamless assemblies could be produced for easier reading. The latter procedure was undertaken by Alison Gilchrest, with the assistance of Nicholas Dorman.

The modern rediscovery of Gerard David is largely due to the efforts of the Englishman James Weale, who—totally captivated by Bruges and its treasures—moved there in 1860 and began to comb the archives in search of names and dates that could be matched with the works of art he found in the churches and museums of that city.[1] Though considered by local historians and antiquarians at the time as somewhat of an irksome aficionado, Weale was responsible for laying the groundwork for the reconstruction of the lives and oeuvres of Gerard David, Hans Memling, Jan Provost, and Adriaen Isenbrant, among others. His initial findings concerning David's paintings were first published in the 1861 catalogue of the Musée de l'Académie à Bruges; further conclusions appeared in the first monograph on the artist, in 1895, wherein Weale was able to establish the two most securely documented works, the *Justice of Cambyses* panels completed for the Bruges town hall in 1498 (Figures 65 and 66) and the *Virgin among Virgins* donated to the Convent of Sion in Bruges in 1509 (Figure 79). As the accounts of Vasari (1566) and Guicciardini (1567) mentioning a certain "Gherardo" along with the miniaturists Simon Bening and Lucas Horenbout may refer to the illuminator Gerard Horenbout rather than to Gerard David, and the passages by Karl van Mander (1604) and A. Sanderus (1641–44) are brief notices at best, it is the archival work of Weale that is the foundation of our modern appreciation of the artist.[2] Building upon Weale's pioneering efforts, Eberhard Freiherr von Bodenhausen produced the first major monograph on the artist and his workshop in 1905.[3]

From David's epitaph on his grave in the Onze-Lieve-Vrouwekerk, as well as from the short account of Sanderus, we know that David originated in the north Netherlands, specifically Oudewater, near Gouda. Although it is likely that he was trained in the main artistic center of nearby Haarlem, there is no documentation of this, nor of any apprenticeship he carried out with painters there before his arrival in Bruges as a full-fledged master himself. He joined the Corporation of Imagemakers and Saddlers (which included panel painters) as a free master in 1484.

David's earliest paintings appear to show a blending of north and south Netherlandish styles and, above all, to have been influenced principally by the art of Dieric Bouts in Leuven and not of Hugo van der Goes in Ghent, as has been supposed.[4] The new visual evidence presented in this book—based on the technical investigation of David's works—indicates that when David departed for the southern territories, he was initially attracted to the workshop of his compatriot Dieric Bouts of Haarlem, who settled in Leuven by 1457 and was the official city painter there in 1468. Even if David never personally met Bouts, who died in 1475, he became intimately acquainted with the artist's work, probably through participation in Bouts's Leuven workshop, which continued under the management of his sons, Dieric the Younger and Aelbert.

When David arrived in Bruges in 1484, Hans Memling was fully ensconced as the leading artist in a city rich with the legacy of Jan van Eyck. But David had no sooner settled there than the political upheaval of the times wreaked havoc on the town. The death of Charles the Bold at the battle of Nancy in 1477 precipitated the substantial weakening of the Burgundian empire, due not only to a significant loss of territory but also to domestic revolts. His daughter and heir, Mary of Burgundy, married Maximilian of Austria, thus launching the Hapsburg era and Maximilian's efforts to act as regent over the northern territories at Mary's untimely death in 1482. Flanders rejected Maximilian's advances, and his plans to recapture the French territories that had been lost, and revolted against him. A series of bloody insurrections ensued, and Maximilian was captured and imprisoned in

Detail of Figure 79

Bruges in 1488 for two months while his supporters and sympathizers were tortured and executed. Maximilian's German troops finally succeeded in forcibly restoring their leader's authority, and Bruges was severely punished for insubordination, with disastrous economic effects, notably the banishment of the large community of foreign businessmen to Antwerp. This, as well as the gradual silting up of the Zwin River, Bruges's main artery to the Atlantic Ocean and an easy point of access to international trade, eventually led to Antwerp's superseding Bruges as the economic center of western Europe during David's lifetime.

Somehow David weathered the political storm, even managing to be elected in 1488, the very year of Maximilian's imprisonment at the Craenenburgh house on the Markt, as *tweede vinder,* or second assistant, to the dean of the Corporation of Imagemakers. In these early years in Bruges, David must have had contact with his leading competitor there, Hans Memling. But the aesthetic sensibilities of the two were completely different. The kind of tangible realism David presented in his works was contrary to Memling's more courtly elegance. The two served different clients and probably did not often cross paths socially. David was apparently relatively civic minded, having early on received the important commission for the *Justice of Cambyses* panels to hang in the aldermen's chambers in the town hall. He joined the prestigious religious Confraternity of Our Lady of the Dry Tree in 1507 and donated a sumptuous altarpiece, the *Virgin among Virgins,* which prominently featured his wife, Cornelia Cnoop, and himself as donors, to the Convent of Sion in 1509. Memling, on the other hand, worked almost exclusively for the wealthy bourgeoisie and had a thriving business in independent portraiture, especially for his Italian and English clients. While Memling's day-to-day life is difficult to reconstruct from documentary sources, David's name appears with a certain regularity in the guild records, where he is mentioned in a number of positions of authority (second and first assistant to the dean of the Corporation of Imagemakers and Saddlers, and eventually dean himself),[5] and also in court cases as both plaintiff and defendant.

These differences between Memling and David notwithstanding, David was not unaffected by Memling's art and reputation. The Sedano Triptych (Figures 149 and 150), for example, which David produced for the Castilian merchant Jan de Sedano and his wife, derives from a compositional formula and decorative effects made popular by Memling, joined with figures inspired by the works of Jan van Eyck. David's obvious reference to his two most eminent predecessors in Bruges was made at a time (in the 1490s) when he was eager to establish his position as their likely successor. Perhaps an indication of David's savvy business acumen, even opportunism, is that he moved his atelier across the Vlamijncbrugghe (Flemingbridge) to occupy a property near the workshop that Hans Memling had vacated at his death in 1494.[6] Following close on the heels of this seemingly deliberate career move, David was elected *eerste vinder,* or first assistant, to the dean of the painters' corporation in 1495.

During this last decade of the fifteenth century, David completed his first major civic commission, the *Justice of Cambyses* panels, in 1498, and in that same year was again appointed *eerste vinder.* Not long after, in 1501, he became dean of the corporation, in a period when the Corporation of Booktrades (Librariërsgilde, including illuminators) and the Corporation of Imagemakers were closely allied. Although panel painters and illuminators were never part of the same corporation in Bruges, the former repeatedly attempted to control the production of the latter. Regulations instituted in the fifteenth century required illuminators to register their marks officially and to pay a fee to the painters' corporation in order to work in Bruges.[7] The physical evidence of this association can be found in the increased exchange of patterns for compositions and figures between manuscript illuminators (especially Simon Bening) and Gerard David in the first two decades of the sixteenth century.

The opening decade of the new century marked David's most successful period. He received commissions for major altarpieces to be installed in Bruges's churches and to be sent abroad. The remarkable panel of Canon Bernardinus de Salviatis, with Saints Bernardinus, Martin, and Donatian (National Gallery, London), which Lorne Campbell has convincingly suggested is the left half of a diptych including the great *Crucifixion* in Berlin (Gemäldegalerie),[8] was probably begun after 1502. It was destined for Sint Donaaskerk (Saint Donation's), as was the *Virgin and Child with Saints and a Donor* (Figure 23), commissioned by Richard de Visch van de Capelle at approximately the same time. With workshop assistance, David produced a *Marriage at Cana* (Musée du Louvre, Paris) to hang in the Basiliek van het Heilig Bloed, just across the Burg square from Sint Donaaskerk.[9] He must have been occupied with the sumptuous Baptism Triptych (Figures 213 and 214) for Jan des Trompes during the same period (ca. 1502–8) that he was working on his most ambitious project of these years, the 1506 Cervara Altarpiece (Figure 176), commissioned by Vincenzo Sauli to be installed on the high altar of the church of San Gerolamo della Cervara, the important Benedictine abbey near Santa Margherita Ligure.

These varied and ambitious projects show a new confidence in David's approach and a willingness, even eagerness, to experiment with novel modes of expression. It was most likely the commission for the Cervara Altarpiece that afforded David firsthand experience with Italian art and enabled him to develop progressive ideas for both the form and the technique of his subsequent paintings, especially the *Virgin among Virgins* of 1509 and the Nativity Triptych of about 1510–15 (Figures 79, 199, and 200). The lessons that David apparently learned through an exposure to the art of Liguria and Lombardy were formative for him. In his rapid assimilation of Italianate features into his paintings, David was a forerunner, not a follower, of the new mode quickly gaining popularity in Antwerp.

The growing importance of Antwerp as an art market and its supplanting of Bruges in the early sixteenth century obliged David to reexamine his formal affiliations as well as his habitual working methods. Although he never moved to Antwerp, David joined the Antwerp Painters Guild in 1515

and began to initiate methods of streamlining the production of his works in order to supply more efficiently the demand for paintings. Mindful of the changing tastes of the increasingly numerous and wealthy bourgeoisie, he subtly adjusted the thematic content of his paintings, as, for example, in the *Virgin and Child with the Milk Soup* (Figures 284–287), from purely religious to the more secular concerns of the sixteenth century. Indeed, a fresh look at David's oeuvre indicates that he worked in a progressive manner, abandoning his late Medieval heritage and proceeding with a certain purity of vision in an age of transition.

The modern critical review of David's life and works has passed over his innovations and his pivotal position as not only a transitional figure, but even a forerunner in his introduction of new themes in paintings and workshop methods of producing them. In the considerable contributions of Max J. Friedländer and Erwin Panofsky to our knowledge of early Netherlandish painting, David gets short shrift. He is deemed by them as the last member of the old guard, part of the "last flowering of the [Flemish] tradition."[10] Friedländer's stinging evaluation describes him thus: "Slow-moving and barren of ideas, David's imagination failed to encompass the process of growth. Creative only in picturing the enduring scene, he was neither epic nor dramatic."[11] Panofsky dwells on the "archaism" of David and on his "striving for a new language without the benefit of a new vocabulary."[12]

More recently, the dissertations of Scillia (1975) and Mundy (1980) have focused on aspects of David's production and recognized greater versatility and innovation in his works but fail to solve questions of attribution and dating. Scillia ascribes a number of paintings in the oeuvre that exemplify an innovative spirit to other artists with newly created names, while Mundy attempts to elucidate thorny attribution and dating problems by categorizing them as part of David's "monumental or intimate style." In his monograph (1989), which conveniently pulls together all of the known documentary evidence, van Miegroet, like Mundy, dwells on the chronology and iconography of the paintings from a rather conservative viewpoint, in the vein of Panofsky.[13] While certain innovations in terms of subject matter and landscape development are acknowledged, they are not fully investigated for the precise nature of the innovation, either for David's methods of introducing them or for the effect they had on a subsequent age.

What these accounts have failed to take into consideration are the number of diverse factors that served as catalysts for change in David's art in the early years of the sixteenth century: shifting devotional practices, changing art markets and market strategies, the considerable draw of foreign markets, and the evolving demand for secular paintings by the buying public, to name only a few.

Also missing in all of these evaluations is a closer look at the work of art itself in order to define more clearly the nature of David's development and, indeed, of his contribution to the history of early Netherlandish painting. This study, which takes into account his drawings and his working methods as an integral part of the stylistic development of his paintings, offers further help in solving some traditional connoisseurship problems of attribution and dating. Such an inclusive method can also reveal the various stages of David's evolution as an artist and the formative influences on him in this process, in particular his assimilation of aspects of the art of Jan van Eyck, Dieric Bouts, and various Italian masters.

In order to recognize and understand the character and significance of shifts in David's working procedure, it has been essential to investigate as many works attributed to the artist as possible; this has been done by close physical scrutiny, using such technical means as X-radiography, infrared reflectography, and dendrochronology, as well as examinations of paintings under the microscope and occasional cross section and pigment analysis. These findings are not presented here as an end in themselves. Rather, as a result of the evaluation and interpretation of this material, it has been possible to reach conclusions about David's standard practice and the exceptions or deviations from his normal routine that show innovative solutions to problems.

The starting point for this line of inquiry has been the collection of paintings attributed to Gerard David at The Metropolitan Museum of Art. The repository of the largest number of individual paintings by this artist anywhere, this collection comprises nineteen panels by David or his close followers, some forming parts of the same altarpiece, as well as one illumination. In addition to the Metropolitan Museum collection, there are other important works nearby, namely the *Deposition* in the Frick Collection and the miniature of the *Virgin among Virgins* in the J. Pierpont Morgan Library. These works make up the core group for this study, which has been informed by the further investigation of about one hundred individual paintings attributed to David and his close followers in collections in the United States and abroad, thus providing a significant amount of comparative material.

Although the Metropolitan Museum owns no complete altarpiece by David, the important individual works in the collection span the artist's career from his earliest period to his late phase and include both panel paintings and manuscript illumination. It is a diverse group that raises the most significant questions concerning David's oeuvre. Among these are several queries either initiated for the first time or more fully discussed than previously because of the possibility of adding new information based on the investigation of David's working methods. The broad range of issues addressed encompasses the relationship of David's drawings to the underdrawings in his paintings, the poles of his style as revealed by the technical investigation of his securely documented works, the question of David's origins and early development, his varied approach to different commissions produced for export to Italy and Spain, the artist's innovations in the genre of landscape painting, and the nature of copies and David's development of methods to streamline production. The first two chapters introduce David's working methods and the interrelationship of the making and meaning of his drawings and paintings. In the following four chapters a painting or group of paintings in the Metropolitan Museum introduces the main issue to be discussed; here abundant comparative material is provided in order to clarify the place of the work or works within the larger context of David's oeuvre.

The virtue of the method followed in this study lies in the combination of technical investigations with stylistic and iconographic analyses for an evaluation of the work in its totality. The details of the production of each painting are thus inextricably bound to its meaning. It is hoped that through such a method we might come closer to understanding the unique contributions of Gerard David to the development and history of early Netherlandish painting.

NOTES

1. Biervliet 1991, esp. pp. 146–50.

2. Vasari (Milanese ed.) 1906, p. 587, nn. 2 and 4; Guicciardini 1567, p. 128; van Mander 1604, fol. 205; Sanderus 1641–44, p. 154.

3. Bodenhausen 1905.

4. Van Miegroet 1989, pp. 35–93.

5. Ibid., docs. 3, 7, 10, 13 on pp. 332–36.

6. David lived there from 1494 to 1523, at an address that he shared with one Antheunis Huyghe, not mentioned in the guild records, who may or may not have been David's journeyman or assistant for a decade or more.

7. The corporations of the painters and illuminators (the latter also known as the Guild of Saint Luke and Saint John) were never consolidated as has been stated by Scillia (1975, p. 195), followed by van Miegroet (1989, pp. 24–25) and Alexander (1992, p. 31 and n. 159). For a correct reading of the documents, see Weale 1864–65, pp. 298–319; 1872–73, pp. 111 19, 238–337. I am grateful to Noel Geirnaert for clarification of this issue (personal communication, April 13, 1998).

8. Personal communication (Sept. 12, 1997). This material will be discussed in Campbell's forthcoming catalogue of the early Netherlandish paintings in the National Gallery, London.

9. For illustrations of the paintings mentioned, see van Miegroet 1989, pp. 72, 197, 200, and 207.

10. Panofsky 1953, vol. I, p. 352.

11. Friedländer 1967–76, vol. VIb (1971), p. 98.

12. Panofsky 1953, vol. I, p. 352.

13. See Ainsworth 1990, pp. 649–54 and Campbell 1991, pp. 624–25.

CHAPTER ONE

CHAPTER ONE

Designing Solutions:
David's Drawings and Workshop Practice

Only vague hints remain about the specific workshop practices of Netherlandish artists of the late fifteenth and early sixteenth centuries.[1] There is little surviving written documentation and a relative scarcity of drawings that provide clues to methods of working. What can be reconstructed about artists' working procedures, then, must be gleaned from scrutiny of the remaining sheets and a comparison of them with the given artist's underdrawings on paintings and the paintings themselves.[2] Insofar as the drawings of this period were not conceived as autonomous works of art, but as aides-mémoires for use in the production of paintings, they ought not to be considered independently. In this regard, the relationship of drawings to underdrawings in paintings is a too-often-neglected but very revealing area of research that provides a key to an understanding of the fundamental concerns of artists in the Netherlands in the fifteenth and sixteenth centuries.

In the case of Gerard David, the sole documentary mention of drawings is a rather negative one, found in records of litigation of 1519–20 between Gerard David and his *compagnon,* a journeyman painter from Lombardy named Ambrosius Benson.[3] When Benson departed from David's workshop, after serving as his assistant there for an unknown period of time before joining the Bruges painters' guild as a master on August 21, 1519, he left behind two trunks. David apparently opened them, discovering among the contents various projects and *patrons* (or patterns) having to do with panel painting and manuscript illumination, a small sketchbook full of studies of heads and of nudes, a painting of

the Virgin made for Benson's father, a small, finished Pietà, a Magdalene begun in dead coloring (that is, the underpainting), a box of pigments, diverse patterns that David had taken from the house of Adriaen Isenbrant but that, in fact, belonged to Benson, as well as some additional patterns that Benson had borrowed from a certain Aelbrecht (probably Albrecht Cornelis) for the fee of two florins *philippus.*

David acknowledged that he had the two trunks, but pleaded that he had found unfinished patterns therein which belonged to him. The matter was further complicated by the fact that Benson owed David the large sum of seven *livres de gros,* an amount he had agreed to work off three days a week until the debt was repaid; but he had not done so. The trunks were being retained, therefore, as security. In the meantime David promised to return certain materials to Benson and to Albrecht (Cornelis). Eleven months later, however, he still had not complied and was thrown into prison as a result of Benson's protestations.

This record of litigation provides not only an inventory of the artist's materials and works in progress, which were all kept together, but also places particular emphasis on the right of ownership. "Diverse patterns" are cited more than once, as is their exchange through borrowing or renting, but whether these were model drawings or pricked cartoons used for the transfer of repeatedly used designs is not clear. The mention of a sketchbook including head studies is evidenced in David's own surviving sheets (Figures 1 and 2). Drawings of nudes, however, are more of a surprise, for aside from infrequent renderings of Adam and Eve, the torso of the adult Christ in scenes from the Passion, or the body of the flayed Sisamnes in his *Justice of Cambyses,* David's

Detail of Figure 19

1. Gerard David, *Study of Sixteen Heads and Hands*, ca. 1490. Metalpoint on prepared paper, dimensions unknown. Location unknown

2. Gerard David, *Study of Ten Heads*, ca. 1490. Metalpoint on prepared paper, dimensions unknown. Location unknown

paintings do not feature nudes. The authorship of these particular sheets is not mentioned; they could have been by David, but just as well by Isenbrant, whom Sanderus praised for his nudes;[4] or they may have been brought by Benson from his native Italy, where studies of nudes were a more standard feature of workshop paraphernalia.[5] In any event, the court record clearly indicates that the four artists—Gerard David, Adriaen Isenbrant, Ambrosius Benson, and Albrecht Cornelis—were exchanging patterns and designs, a fact that is apparent from their extant paintings.

There are about fifteen remaining drawings (some of them on two sides of a single sheet) that can be attributed with assurance to Gerard David himself. Though few in number, this is comparatively abundant evidence of David's drawing style. Other artists of the period—such as Jan van Eyck, Rogier van der Weyden, and Dieric Bouts—are represented by only one or two known sheets each.[6] Given the fact

that David's drawings are mostly sketches of heads and hands, drapery studies, and landscape motifs—that is, the types of drawings routinely used in the atelier and consequently often damaged and discarded as a result of repeated handling—it is exceptional that so many have survived. Several of these sheets appear to have belonged to the same sketchbook, as they share a similar water damage at their lower edges, and some are numbered in a fifteenth- or early-sixteenth-century hand, which perhaps indicates their order within a book or a portfolio.[7]

The sketchbooks of David's time were a development beyond late Medieval model books, in which more conventionally arranged and finished-looking drawings provided a stock of motifs for use in paintings.[8] Though few sketchbooks from the northern Renaissance remain, most surviving examples show a more haphazard placement of figures and motifs than is generally found in model books. Some sheets are minimally used, even blank; others are crammed full with head and hand studies, as is the case with selected drawings by David (Figures 1 and 2). There is seldom any order to these sketches—subject matter, scale, and handling on an individual sheet may differ significantly. Essentially, the artist's sketchbook was used like a memo pad, with certain motifs carried out further than others, which remained as mere notations.

In general, David seems to have followed the kind of advice offered by Leonardo da Vinci in his *Notebooks* on the practice of painting: "be sure to take with you a little book with pages prepared with bone meal, and with a silverpoint briefly note the movements and actions of the bystanders and their grouping. . . . When your book is full, put it aside and keep it for your later use, then take another book and continue as before."[9] On the manner and function of these summary notations, Leonardo said: "these are not things to be erased but preserved with great care, because these forms and actions are so infinite in number that the memory is not capable of retaining them, wherefore keep your sketches as your aids and teachers."[10]

It is in this context that the drawings by David should generally be considered. Up to this point, however, attention has been directed solely to identifying the similarities of the attributed sheets in order to establish a secure authorship for them; the subtle differences have been ignored. By disregarding these differences in the drawings, scholars have overlooked a fundamental issue—how the medium and technique indicate the function these drawings served in David's atelier.

Drawings Mostly of Heads and Hands

Unlike his predecessors Jan van Eyck and Rogier van der Weyden, who employed the metalpoint to produce highly finished drawings composed of delicate, fixed strokes (for example, Figure 3), David used the tool to sketch freely, with a more fluid line, and reworked contours of forms to create subtle transitions and blending of tone.[11] In this approach David was preceded and probably influenced by the workshop practices of Dieric Bouts, whose *Portrait of a Man*

3. Rogier van der Weyden, *Head of the Virgin*, ca. 1460. Silverpoint on prepared paper, 12.9 × 11 cm. Cabinet des Dessins, Musée du Louvre, Paris (Photo © RMN)

4. Attributed to Dieric Bouts, *Portrait of a Man*, ca. 1467. Metalpoint on prepared paper, 14 × 10.7 cm. Smith College Art Museum, Northampton, Mass. Purchased, Drayton Hillyer Fund, 1939

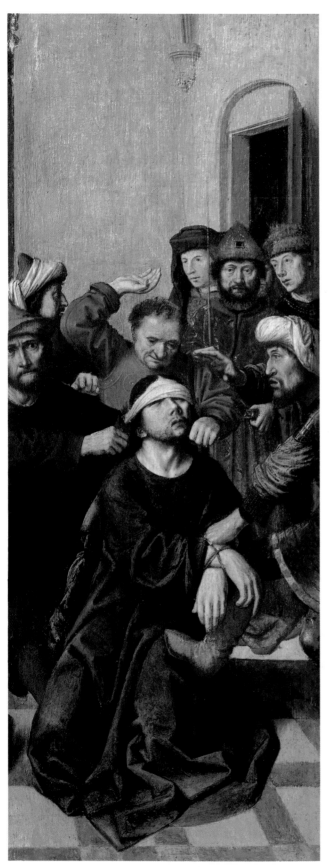

5. Gerard David. *Mocking of Christ* (fragment), ca. 1490. Oil on oak, original portion: 39 × 14.3 cm. Private collection

(Figure 4) exhibits a similar heightened flexibility in the handling of the tool.[12]

Most of David's drawings were begun as sketches from life. Some were then further worked up as studies for various purposes. Only a few reflect his interest in recording motifs from the works of other artists in order to incorporate them into his own compositions. Although the sketchbook pages are primarily studies of heads and hands, David's method and purpose differ from sheet to sheet. Some drawings, such as the two now lost pages last seen at the Klinkosch sale in Vienna in 1889 (Figures 1 and 2), are clearly notations made from life.[13] His aim was to assemble a stock of diverse attitudes and poses of his subjects for later use in his paintings. Certain heads appear to be captured more than once, in different positions and at a seemingly feverish pace; all are crammed onto the sheet without concern for issues of composition. In this way he forged a link with the contemporary viewer and enlivened his paintings with a host of interested bystanders or secondary figures witnessing a significant event, like those of the left wing of the triptych *Christ Nailed to the Cross* (Figure 92), the torturing soldiers in the *Mocking of Christ* (Figure 5),[14] the assembled multitude at the *Adoration of the Magi* (Figure 6), or even the bystanders in the *Justice of Cambyses* panels (Figures 65 and 66). In particular, two of the favored profile views of men's heads at the far right edge of one sheet (Figure 1), which David often used to close off his compositions, are again found at the upper left and the lower right of the *Mocking of Christ*. These paintings, all of which were produced within the last decades of the fifteenth century, suggest a date of about 1490 for the two sheets of multiple head studies.

It is a characteristic feature of most of David's drawings that the subjects were often first summarily captured, usually in black chalk and sometimes in metalpoint.[15] Subsequently, perhaps back in his

6. Gerard David. *Adoration of the Magi*, ca. 1490. Oil on oak, 84 × 68 cm. Musées Royaux des Beaux-Arts de Belgique, Bruxelles-Koninklijke Musea voor Schone Kunsten van België, Brussels

7. Gerard David, *Four Heads* (recto), ca. 1495. Metalpoint over traces of black chalk on prepared paper, 12.8 × 9.2 cm. Städelsches Kunstinstitut, Frankfurt (Photo U. Edelmann, Frankfurt)

atelier, selected ones were brought to a more finished state in metalpoint. This is most readily apparent in a double-sided drawing in the Städelsches Kunstinstitut, Frankfurt (Figures 7 and 10).[16] Always ignored in any discussion of the sheet usually entitled *Two Heads* (Figure 7) is the fact that there are actually four heads on the recto of the sheet. Two heads that were abandoned as light sketches are at the right and left of the exquisite head of a girl in an elaborate headdress. The manner in which David continued to work up the sheet indicates the purpose he had in mind. For example, of the four heads on the Frankfurt sheet, two appear to be the same male head, though in slightly different poses: the light sketch at the far left edge of the sheet studies the head angled downward, while the one at the upper right represents a full-face, nearly frontal view.

David abandoned the former, choosing to develop the latter pose. This in turn served as a model for a centrally placed portrait head in the *Flaying of Sisamnes* (Figure 66), one of the two paintings constituting the *Justice of Cambyses,* dated 1498 (compare Figures 7 and 9).[17] The small sketch apparently provided David with sufficient information about the details of the man's physiognomy, for the underdrawing of this head on the panel (Figure 8) barely indicates the location of the facial features and the suggested illumination of the head. The study of the head of a girl, produced with lightly feathered strokes that form the subtle modeling of her face, was doubtless captured from life. It provided a model for the female types of David's religious paintings, such as the Saint Catherine in the *Virgin among Virgins* (Figure 79).

On the verso of the Frankfurt sheet is a drapery study (Figure 10) that David began as a rough black-chalk sketch for the ermine-cloaked King Cambyses in the *Arrest of Sisamnes* (Figure 65). This time, however, he deliberately chose a different technique— that is, pen and ink rather than metalpoint—because of the possibility of achieving more pronounced effects of light and dark, so as to approximate the depiction of the drapery folds in painted form. David tried out his tool first, testing its precision of handling and the flow of ink in short staccato strokes to the right of the figure. He then proceeded from his summary sketch to the fully worked-up study with a specific use in mind, and he chose the appropriate technique to produce the desired effect. This drawing technique—a pen-and-ink drapery study over a rough black-chalk sketch of the figure—again follows examples associated with the workshop of Dieric Bouts, such as the study of a kneeling donor (Figure 11).[18]

That the Frankfurt drawing is a preparatory sketch rather than a copy after the figure in the painting is readily apparent by a comparison of it with the underdrawing of the king's draperies and the final painted forms (compare Figures 10, 12, and 13).[19] The underdrawing exactly follows the configuration of folds found in the ermine cloak gathered at

8. IRR detail of head of man in Figure 66

9. Detail of head of man in Figure 66

the king's right shoulder in the Frankfurt drawing. The painted form alters this design slightly for the final solution by simplifying the arrangement of folds for a more natural fall of the heavy cloak.

David drew *Four Girls' Heads and Two Hands*[20] (Figure 14) and the study of *Three Female Heads*[21] (Figure 15) first in black chalk (traces of which can be seen only with magnification), further working up the heads in silverpoint. The black chalk is essentially effaced by the reworking of each head with the silverpoint, but an example of how these initial sketches appeared is provided by a female head on the verso of the Kraków sheet (Figure 16), apparently abandoned at this preliminary stage.[22] Although the initial drawing of the heads was doubtless recorded from life, David probably completed the drawings under studio conditions, for the illumination uniformly comes

from the left, so that the right side of the heads is cast into shadow. Among David's drawings, the only exceptions to this routine practice are found in the already discussed sheets of multiple heads (Figures 1 and 2), which are notations and jottings of fleeting images from life, and in a drawing David made after four heads from the group of the elect in the Ghent Altarpiece (discussed below, Figures 33 and 34), where he respected the original lighting schemes of the work by Hubert and Jan van Eyck.

The subtle differences in pose and expression of the heads studied on the Louvre and Kraków sheets provided David with models for animating otherwise generally static scenes, such as the *Virgin among Virgins* (in both David's miniature and panel painting, Figures 27 and 79) or the right inside wing of the Baptism Triptych of 1502–8 (Figure 213).[23] In the

10. Gerard David, *Standing Man* (verso), ca. 1495. Pen and ink over black chalk on paper, 12.8 × 9.2 cm. Städelsches Kunstinstitut, Frankfurt (Photo U. Edelmann, Frankfurt)

gled out as an expressive feature of the painting and used to help communicate the mood of the figure within the spirit of the painting, as well as to add a sense of life and movement to otherwise staid devotional scenes.

Examples of independent portrait drawings made on commission or as substitutes for paintings are not generally found in northern art before the middle of the sixteenth century. Likenesses of particular individuals were recorded, of course, but these were made in preparation for paintings, in order to capture specific traits of the sitter's physiognomy (for example, Figures 7 and 19). Few of these drawings have survived, and none, in fact, for David's predecessor and chief competitor, Hans Memling, who

latter a variety of expressions in the daughters of Elisabeth van der Meersch (left to right)—pious, apprehensive, and mischievously smiling—individualizes the girls in a way never attempted by David's predecessor in Bruges, Hans Memling (as, for example, in the Moreel Triptych, Groenigingemuseum, Bruges, where the somber expressions of the daughters are unvaried). The close relationship of the heads and their modeling in both the drawings and the Baptism Triptych suggests proximity in date. Given the preliminary nature of these drawings, they were probably produced about 1500–1505.

Sharing the same side of the sheet with the four girls' heads are two hands (Figure 14). They demonstrate David's idiosyncratic interest in the skeletal structure of the form. With only the thinnest, glovelike skin pulled over the bones, these hands show an exaggerated articulation of the knuckles. It is a short step to the representation of such hands in painted form, for example, those of the Virgin in the Metropolitan Museum *Annunciation* (Figure 175). Here, as is characteristic of all of David's paintings, the hands are sin-

11. Attributed to Dieric Bouts, *Kneeling Donor*, ca. 1465. Pen and brown ink over black chalk, 26.2 × 17.5 cm. Rijksmuseum Prentenkabinett, Amsterdam

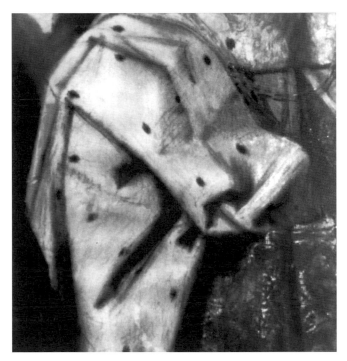

12. IRR detail of drapery of King Cambyses in Figure 65

13. Detail of King Cambyses in Figure 65

had a thriving business in portraiture in Bruges. David, on the other hand, more often incorporated portraits and highly individualized characters into his paintings rather than specialized in portraiture as an independent genre. In this regard, he is more closely allied with the tradition of his north Netherlandish compatriots, in particular Geertgen tot Sint Jans, whose altarpiece for the high altar of the church of the Order of Saint John in Haarlem (including the *Lamentation* and the *Burning of the Bones of Saint John the Baptist,* Figures 202 and 203) represents one of the first group portraits within a religious scene in early Netherlandish painting, and Dieric Bouts, whose *Justice of Emperor Otto III* panels (Musées Royaux des Beaux-Arts de Belgique, Brussels, Figure 68) likewise show a mixture of portrait heads and types fully integrated into the thematic treatment.

One of David's two independent portraits, the *Portrait of an Ecclesiastic* (Figure 18)[24] implies the prior existence of a detailed preparatory drawing, for the preliminary sketch on the panel (Figure 17) shows simple contour lines and limited parallel hatching for the system of lighting on the face and provides no

specific information regarding the physiognomy of the sitter.[25]

The type of preparatory drawing upon which the London portrait may have relied in order to accurately reproduce the sitter's true features can be found in the Rothschild Collection *Portrait of a Woman* (Figure 19).[26] This drawing differs from David's other head studies by the prominence given to the woman's three-quarter-length pose, isolated on and entirely filling the sheet, as well as her ingenuous confrontation of the viewer. In addition, though the hallmarks of David's execution are clearly evident here (particularly in comparison with the exquisite Frankfurt head of a woman, Figure 7), the seeming anonymity of his other head studies, with their more regularized rhythm of strokes, has given way to an individualized treatment. In the modeling of the face, David's usual evenhanded, curved strokes are modified;

14. Gerard David, *Four Girls' Heads and Two Hands* (recto), ca. 1500–1505. Silverpoint on prepared paper, 8.9 × 9.7 cm. Cabinet des Dessins, Musée du Louvre, Paris (Photo © RMN)

15. Gerard David, *Three Female Heads* (recto), ca. 1500–1505. Silverpoint on prepared paper, 9 × 6 cm. Czartoryski Museum, Kraków (Photo Ryszard Kubiczek)

16. Gerard David, *Girl's Head* (verso), ca. 1500–1505. Black chalk, 9 × 6 cm. Czartoryski Museum, Kraków (Photo Ryszard Kubiczek)

17. IRR detail of Figure 18

18. Gerard David, *Portrait of an Ecclesiastic*, ca. 1510. Oil on wood, 35.9 × 28.6 cm. National Gallery, London (Photo © National Gallery, London)

in this instance he employed the silverpoint for a fuller blending of tones as one would customarily do with charcoal or black chalk. As a result, the greater nuances of the modeling contribute to a more life-like expression, which is enhanced by the sitter's direct glance toward the viewer.

Although this was certainly a portrait study, not simply an exercise in attitude and lighting effects, the sitter cannot be positively identified. The woman bears some resemblance (although in reverse) to the probable portrait of David's wife, Cornelia Cnoop, who, along with the artist, is featured as a donor in the *Virgin among Virgins* (compare Figures 20, 21, and 79), which David donated to the Convent of Sion in 1509. Such an identification would account for the especially personal and nuanced treatment of the rendering of the sitter.

Particularly instructive for an understanding of the use of David's drawings as workshop models is the juxtaposition of the Rothschild portrait with the Louvre *Seated Girl with a Flowered Background*[27] (compare Figures 19 and 22). Though the preliminary sketch in black chalk of the latter was probably taken from life, the vitality of her image was significantly reduced as David further worked up the drawing in silverpoint, producing an idealized type. It is

significant that the flowers to the right and left of the sitter are in silverpoint alone, added when David reworked the drawing in a second stage, presumably with a specific plan in mind. This project may well have been the *Virgin among Virgins* (Figure 79), for the flowers suggest those in the millefleurs tapestry originally in the background of the painting, a feature that has irreversibly darkened to black over time and that was revealed only through the study of the painting with infrared reflectography (Figure 21).[28] In general, the seated three-quarter view, the head type, and the features of the young woman in the drawing recall those of various female saints in the Rouen painting (Figure 79), for which it may have served as a ready reference.

Whether or not the Louvre drawing was made initially as a study for the *Virgin among Virgins,* such drawings provided stock types for use in several different paintings. The model for the figure of Saint

19. Gerard David, *Portrait of a Woman* (recto), ca. 1505–10. Silverpoint on prepared paper, 9.1 × 6 cm. Rothschild Collection, Musée du Louvre, Paris (Photo © RMN)

Barbara in the *Virgin among Virgins,* for example, reappears again as Saint Barbara in the *Virgin and Child with Saints and a Donor* (Figures 23 and 24) in the same pose, angle of the head, and similar head-dress as well. Likewise, another model was used for the Virgin's head in both the outside left wing of the Baptism Triptych and the *Virgin and Child with the Milk Soup* (compare Figures 214 and 284). In the Louvre drawing, David's aim was to create an idealized female type in pose, somber expression, and lighting. In contrast to the treatment in the Rothschild portrait, the parallel hatching of the metalpoint is more controlled and evenly spaced, particularly in the shading of the neck and right side of the face, as if the image were recalled from memory without the benefit of the live model to refer to, or as a copy of another work. Perhaps as a result, the eyes have been

spaced unnaturally far apart, accentuated in their almond shape, and the far side of the face is less convincingly described in three-dimensional form than that of the Rothschild portrait. David has added long, diagonal strokes of shading to the left of the figure, a feature that enhances its three-dimensional aspect and indicates David's greater interest in the volume of forms and in chiaroscuro effects in his mature works.

Though only hinted at in the drawing, the painted forms dependent on studies of this type (especially the Mary Magdalene and Saint Barbara in the *Virgin and Child with Saints and a Donor,* painted between 1501 and 1511, and the Saint Barbara in the *Virgin among Virgins* of 1509) take on a new solemnity and monumentality in David's works. At this time, David adopted a facial type that accentuates sharp angles rather than soft contours—features that are found in contemporary Italian examples. The widely spaced and prominently almond-shaped eyes of our sitter, and particularly the transformation of this type into paint for David's female saints of the first decade of the sixteenth century, readily call to mind examples of the Lombard followers of Leonardo, such as Bergognone, whose female types bear a certain resemblance to David's (for example, Figure 25). It has been suggested that David traveled to Italy sometime during the first decade of the sixteenth century,[29] a period when the North experienced the apparent influx of drawings, prints, or even paintings, especially from northern Italy, apparently by Leonardo and his followers. Such examples were very much in vogue and were rapidly assimilated into the compositions and figure types of the Antwerp school of painting.[30]

The hypothesis that the technique David used and the degree of finish he brought to his drawings indicate their function for workshop practice may now be self-evident from the preceding discussion. There are, however, two remarkable sheets that stand out in this regard: the *Head of a Girl*[31] (Figure 26) and the *Head of a Young Man*[32] (Figure 30). Over a light black chalk sketch, David thoroughly worked up the *Head of a Girl* in point of the brush and black ink with a little body color. Several features

20. Detail of Cornelia Cnoop and Saint Lucy in Figure 79

21. IRR detail of Cornelia Cnoop and Saint Lucy in Figure 79

of this drawing suggest its primary function as a workshop model of an ideal type for repeated use in paintings and probably manuscript illuminations as well. There is nothing casual, unresolved, or experimental about this drawing. The head is viewed straight on, as are the majority of David's figures of the Virgin within his mature works. Its proportions are formed according to principles of ideal construction: the tip of the forehead to the eyebrows, the eyebrows to the tip of the nose, and the tip of the nose to the bottom of the chin each constitutes one-third of the total head. The system of shading establishes David's conventional lighting of his models from the left. Instead of the metalpoint that he used in his studies of the varied poses and expressions of female heads, however, David here used the point of the brush and black ink because of the possibility of creating greater chiaroscuro effects not easily produced with the metalpoint alone. He could also practice the manipulation of the brush for subtle gradations of tone by varying his brushstrokes in width and density for the sfumato effects that characterize the face of the Virgin, particularly in paintings

22. Gerard David, *Seated Girl with a Flowered Background* (recto), ca. 1505–10. Silverpoint on prepared paper, 9.5 × 6.5 cm. Cabinet des Dessins, Musée du Louvre, Paris (Photo © RMN)

23. Gerard David, *Virgin and Child with Saints and a Donor*, ca. 1506–10. Oil on oak, 106 × 144 cm. National Gallery, London (Photo © National Gallery, London)

that postdate the Cervara Altarpiece (Figure 176) of 1506. Among these are the *Virgin and Child with Saints and a Donor*, the *Virgin among Virgins*, the Metropolitan Museum version of the *Rest on the Flight into Egypt*, the *Virgin and Child with Four Angels*, the *Virgin and Child in a Landscape* (Museum Boijmans Van Beuningen, Rotterdam), and the *Virgin and Child with Four Saints* (Figures 23, 79, 234, 241, and 59).

Although David's activity as an illuminator as well as a panel painter has been questioned, the comparison of the details of handling and execution of the Hamburg drawing with those of the single-leaf miniature the *Virgin among Virgins* (Figure 27), makes the most convincing case for the attribution of the latter to David. Despite a difference in the angle of the head, the Virgin's physiognomy in both drawing and

24. Detail of Saint Barbara in Figure 79

25. Ambrogio Bergognone, *Presentation in the Temple* (detail), ca. 1500. Tempera and oil on wood, 138 × 96.8 cm. Santuario di Santa Maria Incoronata, Lodi

miniature is identical. Moreover, the modeling of the face, with its lightly feathered, but tightly controlled, even parallel hatching, which at once suggests volume and shading, is the same. For this exquisitely refined miniature, bold in its design and rich in its color effects, David has clearly made use of his other model drawings as well. The marvelously varied heads of the accompanying virgins—subtly

different in their attitudes and expressions—are closely linked to David's silverpoint studies, especially to the Louvre and Kraków sheets, and even to the newly introduced type of the young girl with the almond-shaped eyes (Figures 14, 15, and 22). The miniature, therefore, probably dates about 1505–10.

The practical function of the Hamburg drawing for David, as well as for members of his atelier, as a

26. Gerard David, *Head of a Girl* (recto), ca. 1505–10. Brush and black ink over black chalk, with some white heightening on paper, 14.2 × 10.2 cm. Hamburger Kunsthalle (Photo courtesy of Elke Walford, Hamburg)

pattern for the ideal modeling of a featured head is exemplified by its relationship to the head of the Virgin in the *Virgin and Child with Four Saints* (Figure 59), where a nearly identical grouping of strokes in the underdrawing establishes the volume of forms and the fall of light on the Virgin's head (compare Figures 26 and 28). Such a practice was not restricted to David's female types; the Philadelphia *Head of Christ* (Figure 29),[33] a considerably damaged painting probably of about 1505–10, also shows an underdrawing that carefully produces tonal effects similar to the pattern of the Hamburg drawing. The use of this

sheet as a workshop model is further indicated by the stylus marks that can be found at the right side of the face and at the mouth, where the lips meet. These were possibly used for tracing the exact form onto the sheet of paper before working it up in brush and ink or for tracing the pattern of the finished head to another sheet. The random brushstrokes to the left of the girl's head are trial marks David made in order to form a point on his brush or to check

27. Gerard David, *Virgin among Virgins*, ca. 1505–10. Tempera on vellum, 18 × 13.4 cm. Pierpont Morgan Library, New York

28. IRR detail of the Virgin's head in Figure 59

29. IRR detail of head in Gerard David, *Head of Christ*, ca. 1505. Oil on oak, 43 × 31 cm. John G. Johnson Collection, Philadelphia Museum of Art, Philadelphia

the flow of ink for making precise, continuous, even lines.

Like the *Head of a Girl,* the *Head of a Young Man* (Figure 30) is a remarkable study worked out in meticulous detail from a live model. Rubbed remnants of black chalk at the back of the head show that David initiated the drawing in his usual manner as a summary sketch. Over this he used the silverpoint in a similar way to that in which he manipulated the point of the brush for the *Head of a Girl*—to render with extreme precision the fall of light on the shaved head in nearly profile view. As in the *Head of a Girl,* the head of the young man has been established according to a system of ideal proportion: the measurements of the crown of the forehead to the eyebrows, the eyebrows to the tip of the nose, and the nose to the chin are all equivalent.

This drawing could have served multiple purposes when simply altered by a change of hairstyle or headdress. An example of a head that might have relied on this type of study is found at the far left of the *Virgin and Child with Four Saints* (Figure 59), where the underdrawing in brush matches the arrangement of obliquely placed, long parallel strokes across the forehead, at the inside of the right eye and upper cheek, and at the nostril and shorter hatching along the bridge of the nose, beneath the lower lip, and along the contour of the chin (compare Figures 30 and 31).

The pose recalls that of a male head (Figure 38) more casually sketched from life on the verso of the *Head of a Girl,* while the delicacy of handling of the silverpoint and the exquisite refinement of the head with almond-shaped eyes is similar to the Louvre study of a *Seated Girl with a Flowered Background* (Figure 22). Also typical for David's drawing style is the particular shape of the mouth and its soft modeling at the corners and below the lower lip, the decisive articulation of the nose and dark nostril, and the manner of rendering eyes with the sharp delineation of the upper lids and ambiguously undefined lower lids, and eyebrows of repeated dark strokes near the nose trailing off into light, wispy strokes at their outer edges. The directed gaze of the man conveys the same intensity as David's self-portrait in the *Virgin among Virgins* (Figures 79 and 86).

The attribution of the *Head of a Young Man* to David has not been unanimously accepted.[34] Among the other suggestions have been "School of Leonardo da Vinci" and "Pisanello," both of which apparently take into account the unusual feature for a northern drawing of a model in near-profile view with a shaved head. Like the *Seated Girl with a Flowered Background,* this *Young Man* has distinct connections with contemporary Italian drawings, particularly with the numerous sheets by Leonardo and his followers that study a male or female head in profile or near-profile view (for example, a study sheet, Figure 32).

David's drawing shares with these the three-quarter turned body in space, the sharply defined near-profile view, the accentuation of the features of the face, and the tightly controlled parallel hatching in the zones

30. Gerard David, *Head of a Young Man*, ca. 1505–10. Silverpoint over traces of black chalk on prepared paper, 11 × 8.5 cm. Cabinet des Dessins, Musée du Louvre, Paris (Photo © RMN)

31. IRR detail of Saint John the Evangelist in Figure 59

32. Leonardo da Vinci?, *Head of a Youth with Curly Hair, Almost in Profile to Left*. Metalpoint on prepared paper, 14.5 × 7.1 cm. Collection of Her Majesty Queen Elizabeth II, Windsor Castle (Photo The Royal Collection © 1998 Her Majesty Queen Elizabeth II)

sixteenth-century Lombard artists who worked in Leonardo's style). David's access to such drawings could have occurred through his possible travels in Lombardy in the first decade of the sixteenth century, or by way of drawings brought north by his Lombard assistant, Ambrosius Benson, who joined David's workshop in the second decade. However, evidence that Leonardo's head studies had already migrated early on to Antwerp is found in Quentin Massys's *Saint John Altarpiece* (Koninklijk Museum voor Schone Kunsten, Antwerp), painted between 1508 and 1511, in which two of Leonardo's physiognomic types appear as executioners. This was among the earliest manifestations of the enormous popularity of Leonardo's art in the north and its assimilation into Netherlandish painting. David was keenly aware of this new trend, and participated in its initial stages.[35]

Ricordi

Concurrent with David's progressive tendencies, namely his interest in Italian art, was a more conservative strain influenced by the powerful legacy in Bruges of Jan van Eyck. Like many artists of his day, David may have often journeyed to Ghent to see the renowned Ghent Altarpiece in the church of Sint Baafs (Saint Bavo), perhaps as much in homage to van Eyck, who had died more than forty years earlier, in 1441, as out of curiosity. It is impossible to say just how many drawings David made after details of the Ghent Altarpiece; only one tiny sheet remains, which records four heads from the group of the elect, popes and bishops in the right foreground of the central panel of the van Eyck brothers' masterpiece (compare Figures 33 and 34).[36] David doubtless felt immediate rapport with the remarkable display of head types, poses, and attitudes that showed the range of expression that he attempted in his own works. He recorded the four chosen heads in metalpoint, meticulously following the form, modeling, and system of lighting established in his predecessor's work. He carefully arranged the heads on the sheet (more in the manner of a model book than a sketchbook) for ready reference at a later time and

of shading. Leonardo's sojourn in Milan from 1482 to 1499 and then again from 1506 to 1513 had a major influence on the Lombard-Milanese school, and his drawings of profile heads, young men and women, grotesques, and caricatures were disseminated through copies made by the so-called *leonardeschi* (the early-

33. Gerard David, *Four Heads* (copy after details of the Ghent Altarpiece), ca. 1500. Metalpoint on prepared paper, 7.1 × 6.3 cm. National Gallery of Canada, Ottawa

34. Detail of popes and bishops from Figure 215

35. Gerard David, *Virgin and Child at the Fountain* (copy after Jan van Eyck, Figure 242), ca. 1510. Pen and brown ink, 19.6 × 13.1 cm. Kupferstichkabinett, SMPK, Berlin (Photo © Kupferstichkabinett–Sammlung der Zeichnungen und Druckgraphik)

assimilation into his own paintings. Though there is no surviving work in which David employed these specific heads, other known cases exist where he used Eyckian models. Adam and Eve again from the Ghent Altarpiece provided the source for the figures on the exterior wings of the Sedano Triptych (Figure 149), while David consulted van Eyck's works in Bruges, namely the *Virgin and Child with Saints and Canon van der Paele* (Figure 154), for the motif of the Sedano Virgin and Child (see chapter 4).

The figures in the upper left background of *Christ Nailed to the Cross* (Figure 92) were inspired by those found in Jan van Eyck's *Crucifixion* in The Metropolitan Museum of Art.[37] David's *ricordi* made from Eyckian paintings no doubt were kept readily accessible as workshop models in his atelier.

To these examples may be added a drawing in pen and ink (Figure 35) that copies Jan van Eyck's *Virgin and Child at the Fountain* (Figure 242). The dimensions of the Berlin sheet are equivalent to

36. IRR detail of Saint John in Figure 141

whose poses and draperies are copied in meticulous detail. The setting (fountain, grassy bench, cloth of honor) and angels are more summarily depicted. It is precisely the motif so carefully studied in the drawing, that is, the Virgin and Child, that David appropriated for the *Virgin and Child with Four Angels* (Figure 241), which he placed in a new setting, identified by its background buildings as Bruges (for further discussion, see chapter 6).

The association of the formerly anonymous Berlin drawing with Gerard David is based on the drawing's close relationship to the style of the autograph Frankfurt study for the standing King Cambyses (Figure 10) and on the underdrawings in David's paintings, such as the figure of Saint John in the Chicago *Lamentation* (Figure 36) or the Saint John the Baptist in the *Virgin and Child with Four Saints* (Figure 37). Common to all three are certain graphic idiosyncrasies—there are the same jagged contours of folds that are emphasized by short crossing lines, like stitching; shallow folds are marked by long, wispy parallel strokes, usually going from upper right to lower left; peaks of the folds show short, staccato parallel strokes angled uniformly to the left or to the right; and the deepest folds are indicated by cross-hatching arranged in a diamondlike pattern.

Added to these generally characteristic features of David's execution in his works ranging from the 1490s to about 1515 are certain aspects of his treatment in later works that show further idiosyncratic notations for the expression of forms. The even parallel hatching along the side of the face of the Virgin (at the viewer's right), in curved strokes that at once suggest the volume and the shading of the side of the face, is a feature common to David's later works (as discussed above): the Hamburg *Head of a Girl* (Figure 26) and the underdrawing in the head of the Virgin in the Norton Simon Museum *Virgin and Child with Four Saints* (Figure 28). The abbreviated strokes, almost like stippling, that describe shallow folds at the lower left side of the Virgin's draperies and the left-hand angel's draperies in the Berlin drawing are found serving the same function in the underdrawing of the Virgin's drapery in the

those of the Antwerp painting (ca. 19 x 13 cm), which it reproduces faithfully.[38] Clearly the draftsman studied the painting within its engaged frame, for the drawing stops where the painting meets the framed edge, truncating the forms of the angels' draperies and the left edge of the fountain basin, just as in the painting. The drawing concentrates above all on the motif of the Virgin and Child,

Frankfurt *Annunciation,* a painting that can be dated to the first decade of the sixteenth century.[39] The type of shorthand notation for plants on the grassy bench to the right and left of the Virgin is matched by similar deft strokes of minimal botanic description in the landscape study (Figure 40) on the verso of the Rothschild *Portrait of a Woman,* drawings that both relate to David's paintings of about 1509–10. These connections of the Berlin drawing with details of David's draftsmanship of about 1510 help to secure a date for the drawing, which must have been made close in time to the painting of the *Virgin and Child with Four Angels,* as a preparatory study for the commission.

The *Virgin and Child with Four Angels* by David (Figure 241), which assimilates Jan van Eyck's Virgin and Child motif, uncharacteristically for David reveals an underdrawing that is almost entirely restricted to the contours of the figures, with relatively little internal hatching or cross-hatching for the modeling of forms (Figure 250). This is probably due to the fact that the drapery folds and system of lighting had already been fully worked out in the Berlin drawing, and so little or no additional guide was required in the underdrawing.[40] The minimal strokes for the form and shading in the Virgin's right sleeve, nonetheless, are identical to those found in the corresponding area of the Berlin drawing (compare Figures 35 and 251). The few changes David made from the original Eyckian model for his own painting—the head of the Christ Child, who looks out at us rather than at the Virgin, and the free-flowing, rather than pulled-back, hair of the Virgin—were all made in the upper paint layers, not corrected in the preliminary stage of the underdrawing (see further discussion in chapter 6).

The function of the Berlin sheet for David's workshop practice, then, was twofold: it precisely recorded the desired motif of the Virgin and Child from Van Eyck's painting for assimilation into David's

own reworking of the theme, and it served as a model for the exact configuration of folds and modeling of the drapery in lieu of working out these features in further detail in the underdrawing. That is to say, the Berlin drawing provided a model in hand as the painting evolved.

Landscape Studies

A few surviving drawings reveal what is self-evident, especially in the painting of David's mature period: that he considered the setting and the figures portrayed as equally important. On the versos of two sheets are studies from nature of trees and landscape features. The simple and delicate silverpoint sketch of a tree shares the same side of the paper with a study of the head of a man (Figure 38, the verso of the *Head of a Girl,* Figure 26). David's interest in the portrayal of nature in his paintings focuses on these singular observations of the individual parts of a forest or landscape, most likely recorded *en plein air.*

He captured the manner in which the branches spring from the trunk of the tree, how the leaves obscure the specific structure of branches, how the effects of light and gentle breezes blur the individual forms themselves. For David the isolated tree was an often-used motif—even a trademark—in his paintings, one for which the art of Dieric Bouts must have been an inspiration.[41] Take, for example, the *Resurrection* (Figure 138b), where the underdrawing of the painting shows that David originally planned a towering single tree in the distance on the hill (Figure 39) quite similar to the rendering in the Hamburg study. In the painting David revised his plans and made two smaller trees nestled into the hillock. The underdrawings of the Frankfurt *Saint Jerome* (compare Figures 210 and 211) and of the Aurora Trust *Virgin and Child with the Milk Soup* (compare Figures 284 and 288) also feature solitary trees in the center distance, whose form and execution in the underdrawing are close to the Hamburg silverpoint study. The isolated tree study also served in the construction of vast forests, as in David's landscape wings (Figure 199) for the Nativity Triptych

37. IRR detail of Saint John the Evangelist, Saint John the Baptist, and the Virgin and Child, in Figure 59

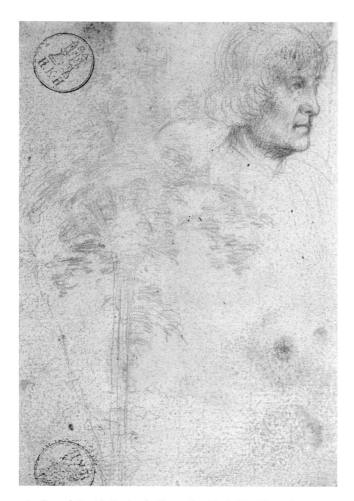

39. IRR detail of Figure 138b

38. Gerard David, *Study of a Tree and a Man's Head* (verso),
ca. 1505–10. Metalpoint on prepared paper, 14.2 × 10.2 cm.
Hamburger Kunsthalle (photo courtesy of Elke Walford, Hamburg)

or for the setting for the interior of the Baptism
Triptych (Figure 213), where the single tree stands
out against the darker mass of the forest. It is characteristic of David's art that he focuses on individual
details as a way of expressing the illusion of reality of
the whole.

Escaping notice since its rediscovery in 1959–60
on the reverse side of the Rothschild collection
Portrait of a Woman[42] (Figure 19) is a delicate landscape study with houses and a church tower (Figure
40). Though the exact site rendered in the drawing
cannot be determined, there are certain visual
parallels between the drawing and the numerous
flat-topped towers of churches in the countryside
around Bruges.[43] Executed in pen and ink (there are
a few slight traces of black chalk in the upper left in

the buildings) on unprepared paper, the drawing
possesses a liveliness and spontaneity of draftsmanship, which imply that this study was made *en plein
air* in a specific location.

The drawing represents a view of landscape as a
kind of collaboration between man and nature, the
intimacy of the view reflected in the easy accommodation of buildings by the trees. The specific
placement of the individual features on the page,
however, is telling for the function of this type of
drawing for David's work. Though the lower portion
of the sheet has been repaired, and we may assume
that it has been cut somewhat at the edges, much of
the original drawing remains. David deliberately
arranged the most descriptive forms of his landscape at the top of his page, leaving a significant
open plain in the middle distance, and filling in at
the foreground with grasses and plants viewed close-
up. It is an intimate, closed world of meditation,
remarkably similar to the landscapes of several versions of the Rest on the Flight into Egypt (Figure

40. Gerard David, *Landscape Study* (verso), ca. 1505–10. Pen and ink over traces of black chalk on prepared paper, 9.1 × 6.0 cm. Rothschild Collection, Cabinet des Dessins, Musée du Louvre, Paris (Photo © RMN)

234). One can imagine that David had such a composition in mind as he drew from nature and that he deliberately placed the wooded view on the upper part of the sheet, leaving an open area in the center foreground where, as in his paintings, a Virgin and Child would comfortably fill the space. The closest contemporary parallel to this type of study is to be found not in early Netherlandish but in Italian art, in the exquisite renderings of landscape vignettes by Fra Bartolomeo, which the artist incorporated into his paintings.[44]

Workshop Drawings for Paintings and Illuminations

Some two dozen or so additional drawings carry attributions to David that can no longer be maintained. Certain ones, like the Rotterdam *Man with a Turban*[45] or the Louvre *Portrait of a Woman*[46] are simply too

41. Geertgen tot Sint Jans?, *Head of an Old Man*, ca. 1484. Brush and brown ink over metalpoint on prepared paper (touches of red on lips and nose), 9.1. × 6.7 cm. Cabinet des Dessins, Musée du Louvre, Paris (Photo © RMN)

42. Detail of head from Figure 202

weak in their execution and uncharacteristic of David's drawing style to be considered as by him. Others, such as the British Museum *Portrait of a Monk*,[47] are of higher quality and closely related in terms of date and subject matter (the *Monk* can be compared, for example, with David's *Portrait of an Ecclesiastic*, Figure 18) but show nothing of the graphic mannerisms we now recognize as typical of David's hand.

Other drawings that have been attributed to David must also be rejected on the basis of style and execution. Although by various hands, they all have some sort of connection to David's artistic development or workshop practice, and as such they merit brief discussion here because they provide further clues to the day-to-day routine of the atelier. An intriguing relationship to David is presented by five drawings,

four of which apparently originally shared the recto and verso of the same sheet. These are the Louvre *Study of a Head* (recto) and *Study of Hands* (verso),[48] the Albertina *Study of a Head* (recto) and *Study of Hands* (verso),[49] and the Louvre *Head of an Old Man* (Figure 41).[50] Lugt recognized early on that the verso of the Albertina sheet showed the fingertips of a hand cut off on the right side of the Louvre study of hands and thus identified two halves of the same sheet (reunited in Figure 44).[51] The reverse presents two male head studies back-to-back in an uncomfortably close arrangement on the sheet (Figure 43), which shows a portion of the headdress of the man at the left extending onto the shoulder of the man at the right.

Opinion is divided concerning the attribution of all five drawings. Despite the strong impression made by the boldly articulated features of the heads and the decisive handling of the pen and brush that conceive the forms in such a sculptural manner, the execution has little to do with David's characteristic handling as it has been described above. The hand studies, furthermore, do not display anything of David's interest in their skeletal structure.

Albert Châtelet is probably right in assigning these drawings to Geertgen tot Sint Jans, the Haarlem painter who has often been suggested as David's teacher, or at least an influential contemporary.[52] A comparison of the head studies with the only securely documented work by Geertgen, the altarpiece made for the church of the Order of Saint John in Haarlem, of which the *Lamentation* and the *Burning of the Bones of Saint John the Baptist* are the only two remaining parts (now in the Kunsthistorisches Museum, Vienna, Figures 202, 203), reveals notable connections. As Châtelet has observed, the servant behind Nicodemus in the *Lamentation,* whose individualized physiognomy suggests a portrait, bears a very close resemblance to the Louvre drawing (compare Figures 41 and 42). Although the drawing is not necessarily a study for the painted head, the rendering of the features is

closely allied: the direction of the gaze and the large, glassy irises of the deep-set eyes with pronounced contours of the lids, the prominent aquiline noses, the thin-lipped mouths with down-turned corners, and the square chins. Special attention as well is given in both heads to the character of age lines at the contours of sunken cheeks, bags under the eyes, wrinkled brows, and the tonal modeling of the head. The sculptural quality of the head in the drawing and the painting is enhanced by the emphasis on the meandering contour at the left side of the face and the deeply etched age lines that define the sagging flesh.

Favoring three-quarter and profile views of heads, Geertgen fashioned his "types" to look very lifelike,[53] just as Gerard David was to do in his own paintings, but with a different approach. The Paris and Vienna

43. Geertgen tot Sint Jans?, two drawings reunited: *Profile Head* (recto), ca. 1480–85. Silverpoint with brush and ink on prepared paper, 9.3 × 6.7 cm. Albertina, Vienna; and *Head Study* (recto). Silverpoint on prepared paper, 9.4 × 6.65 cm. Cabinet des Dessins, Musée du Louvre, Paris (Photo © RMN)

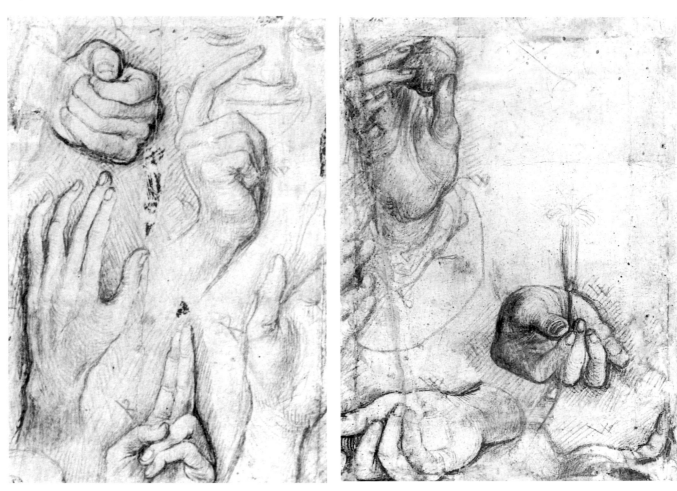

44. Geertgen tot Sint Jans?, two drawings reunited: *Head and Hand Studies* (verso), ca. 1480–85. Silverpoint on prepared paper, 9.4 × 6.65 cm. Cabinet des Dessins, Musée du Louvre, Paris (Photo © RMN); and *Hand Studies* (verso). Silverpoint on prepared paper, 9.3 × 6.7 cm. Albertina, Vienna

drawings, of course, cannot compare with David's quickly dashed-off metalpoint sketches (Figures 1 and 2) but instead resemble his carefully studied portrait types. David's modeling of these heads is more subtle than that of the drawings attributed to Geertgen, and the general impression is more painterly than sculptural. In this way David shed or altered his stylistic origins in the north Netherlands as he moved south to Brabant.

David and Geertgen also shared a pronounced interest in the expressive power of hand gestures. The Louvre-Albertina sheet (Figure 44) features studies of varied poses that are also found in Geertgen's paintings, for example, in the Louvre *Raising of Lazarus,* where a number of the hands reflect gestures similar to those found in the drawings (compare Figures 44 and 45), as well as Geertgen's idiosyn-

crasies of form. The fingers appear proportionately long and boneless but do not indicate any interest in anatomy, as was David's tendency.

One other head study suggests a direct connection with David's workshop. The *Portrait of a Man,* or *Study for the Portrait of the Duke of Suffolk* (Figure 46), was attributed by Friedländer to the Master of the Brandon Portraits, to whom he also assigned six other sheets of the so-called Klinkosch sketchbook.[54] It is the verso of the previously discussed *Four Girls' Heads and Two Hands* (Figure 14) by David. Friedländer based his attribution on the close relationship between the drawing and a painted portrait of the duke (Norbert Fischman collection, London). He further suggested that the anonymous master was likely a follower of David in England, either Gerard Horenbout or Jan Rave (Johannes Corvus). The former was appointed

45. Geertgen tot Sint Jans, *Raising of Lazarus*, ca. 1480. Oil on oak, 127 × 97 cm. Musée du Louvre, Paris (Photo © RMN)

court painter and illuminator by Margaret of Austria. The more likely suggestion, however, is Rave, who was listed with the Bruges painters' corporation beginning in 1512 and is said to have been connected with the Brandon household. He painted the portrait of the duchess (who was Mary Tudor, the widowed queen of France and sister of Henry VIII)[55] and signed it "Joannes Corvus Flandrus Faciebat."[56]

Unlike most of David's drawings, this likeness is executed entirely in black chalk and bears no relation otherwise to his style. As none of the other sheets by David shows the same details of handling and execution found in this drawing, it is likely that, as Lugt suggested,[57] the sketchbook passed into the hands of another artist associated with David, probably Jan Rave, who made use of a blank sheet for his own study of a man's head.

We know relatively little about the membership of David's workshop, but it is clear both from the documents of the 1519–20 litigation and from visual

46. Jan Rave?, *Portrait of a Man* (verso), ca. 1512–15. Black chalk on paper, 8.9 × 9.7 cm. Cabinet des Dessins, Musée du Louvre, Paris (Photo © RMN)

47. Workshop of Gerard David (Adriaen Isenbrant?), *Christ in the Garden of Gethsemane*, ca. 1515. Oil on canvas transferred from wood, 43 × 29.3 cm. Musées de la Ville de Strasbourg

evidence that at least two artists, Adriaen Isenbrant and Ambrosius Benson, had access to David's designs and patterns.[58] Indications of the procedures used by these artists to implement David's designs are apparent in the underdrawings of paintings attributed to them, but no known drawings on paper have survived.

One possible candidate for a drawing produced within the workshop of David is a fragment of the figure of Christ (Figure 48). The growing interest in

48. Workshop of David (Adriaen Isenbrant?), *Christ in the Garden of Gethsemane*, ca. 1515. Pen and brush in brown and black ink with white heightening on brown prepared paper, 22.1 × 8.1 cm. Museum Boijmans Van Beuningen, Rotterdam

49. Master of Mary of Burgundy, *Justice Scene*, ca. 1480. Black chalk on paper, 19.3 × 14.4 cm. Museum Boijmans Van Beuningen, Rotterdam

50. Simon Bening, *Christ before Pilate or Caiaphas*, from the *Prayer Book of Cardinal Albrecht of Brandenburg* (83.ML.115, Ms. Ludwig IX.19, fol. 143v), 1526–28. Tempera, gold paint, and gold leaf on vellum, 16.8 × 11.5 cm. J. Paul Getty Museum, Los Angeles

the early sixteenth century in greater tonal effects in paintings is evidenced in the sudden popularity of night scenes produced mostly by Antwerp artists. These included the Night Nativity, and certain scenes from the Passion of Christ, such as the Arrest of Christ or Christ in Gethsemane. Paintings of these subjects necessitated the study of dramatic lighting effects within the compositions through preparatory drawings on paper. An example attributed to David is the single chiaroscuro drawing of Christ (Figure 48) in the Museum Boijmans Van Beuningen made in pen and brush and brown and black ink with white heightening on brown prepared paper.[39] Although made in the style of David, it does not manifest his distinctive manner of hatching for the modeling of forms, nor the characteristic skeletal quality of the hands. This type of chiaroscuro study, so popular in the

second decade of the sixteenth century in Antwerp, when both David and Isenbrant were working there, can be directly associated with a *Christ in the Garden of Gethsemane* (Figure 47) attributed by Friedländer to the Isenbrant group.[60] This painting is perhaps closest in style to the Fogg Art Museum *Pentecost* (Figure 56), a relationship that merits further consideration.[61] The pose of the figure and the configuration of drapery folds in the drawing correspond closely with the figure of Christ in the Strasbourg painting— that is, except for small details such as the added visible thumb of Christ's left hand in the painting. The drawing is perhaps indicative of a type made by

51. Alexander Bening?, *Transfiguration* (recto), 1490–1500. Pen and brown ink over black chalk on prepared paper, 25.5 × 17.3 cm. Museum Boijmans Van Beuningen, Rotterdam

52. Simon Bening?, *Transfiguration*, from the *Grimany Breviary* (Cod. marc. Lat. I, 99, fol. 660v), ca. 1515. Tempera on vellum, 14.7 × 10.8 cm. Biblioteca Marciana, Venice

David for his own paintings that call for dramatic lighting effects, such as his *Night Nativity* in the Kunsthistorisches Museum, Vienna.

Most of the other drawings attributed to David have a link to an aspect of the workshop production not yet discussed, namely the connections between the practice of panel painting and manuscript illumination. Three drawings in Rotterdam, two on the recto and verso of the same sheet, are worth mentioning here because they are indicative of this close relationship at the time when Bruges was one of the leading centers of manuscript production.[62] In repeated battles and long periods of squabbles between practitioners of the two arts over the production, distribution, and sale of miniatures, the painters' corporation usually prevailed. It required that the illuminators in

the Librariërsgilde (Guild of the Book Trades, also known as the Guild of Saint John and Saint Luke) register their marks and pay a fee to the Corporation of Imagemakers so that the panel painters could maintain some control over what they considered as possible competition.[63] This helps to explain the connection to David's workshop of certain other drawings that are related to both manuscript illumination and panel-painting production, and it brings us back to the document with which we began this chapter—the account of the items within the trunk that David commandeered from Benson in the 1519–20 dispute—in which various projects and *patrons* (or patterns) having to do with panel painting

53. Gerard David, *Transfiguration*, ca. 1500–1505. Oil on wood, 174 × 120 cm. Onze-Lieve-Vrouwekerk, Bruges (Photo Copyright IRPA-KIK, Brussels)

55. Simon Bening or Gerard Horenbout, *Pentecost*, from the *Grimany Breviary* (Cod. marc. Lat. I, 99, fol. 205v), ca. 1515. Tempera on vellum, 14.7 × 10.8 cm. Biblioteca Marciana, Venice

54. Alexander Bening?, *Pentecost* (verso), ca. 1490–1500. Pen and brown ink over black chalk on prepared paper, 25.5 × 17.3 cm. Museum Boijmans Van Beuningen, Rotterdam

and manuscript illumination are discussed together as part of the same workshop paraphernalia.

Although attributed to the circle of Gerard David, the preparatory drawing in black chalk of a Justice scene (Figure 49) has been convincingly linked to the Master of Mary of Burgundy, who is considered to be the founder of the school of Ghent-Bruges illumination.[64] The right half of the drawing, including the centrally positioned king with arms akimbo, was used later by the leading illuminator of the sixteenth century, Simon Bening (son of Alexander Bening and a close associate of David's), about 1525–30 for a *Christ before Pilate or Caiaphas* in the prayer book of Cardinal Albrecht of Brandenburg (Figure 50).

A contemporary of the Master of Mary of Burgundy, Alexander Bening (also known as the

Master of the Older Prayer Book of Maximilian I) and his son Simon worked as illuminators in Ghent and Bruges. It is to both Benings as well as to Gerard David that the *Transfiguration* and *Pentecost* have been attributed (Figures 51 and 54).[65] The recto and verso of the same sheet, these drawings show the style of pen work common to illuminators; short strokes and stippling used to model the forms and surface characteristics are emphasized over the in-depth modeling of three-dimensional forms necessitated by larger-format panel painting.

Although most frequently used as models by Simon Bening in his illuminations, these drawings are

56. Follower of Gerard David, *Pentecost*, ca. 1515. Oil on wood transferred to wood, 95.3 × 67.3 cm. Harvard University Art Museums, Cambridge, Mass. Courtesy of the Fogg Art Museum, Gift of Mrs. Norton Peabody Prince

probably by his father, Alexander, whose elongated figures are closer to those found in the drawings. Figural motifs and compositions, however, are easily transformed from one medium to another. Thus the *Transfiguration*, so closely connected with David's painting of the same subject (compare Figures 51 and 53) in the Onze-Lieve-Vrouwekerk in Bruges, is also intimately related to miniatures in the *Grimany Breviary* (attributed to Simon Bening and Gerard Horenbout, Figure 52), and in the Mayer van den Bergh Breviary, and somewhat less so to another, attributed to Simon Bening, in the Chester Beatty Rosarium.[66] Likewise, the *Pentecost* (Figure 54), a drawing by the same hand as its reverse side *Transfiguration*, is linked both to a painting from David's workshop in the Fogg Art Museum (Figure 56) and more specifically to a *Pentecost*, again in the *Grimany Breviary*, attributed to Simon Bening or Gerard Horenbout (Figure 55), as well as to one in the Stockholm-Kassel Book of Hours from the workshop of Simon Bening.[67] These would not have been the only examples of the use of these particular compositions, and it is a difficult, if not futile, exercise to try to determine the exact origin of each design. Suffice it to say that among the drawings in David's workshop were patterns used by panel painters and manuscript illuminators alike[68] and that there was an ongoing exchange between the two arts. As we shall see, David's close association with the art of manuscript illumination is a recurring theme throughout the study of his works.

Lost Drawings and Underdrawings

The drawings by David that remain are but a small fraction of those that must have originally existed. The more recent opportunity to study a painting's underdrawing, however, allows us to consider those drawings that no longer remain but whose previous existence and workshop function are suggested by clues found in the underdrawings of David's paintings. Although there are some exceptions, David's drawings and underdrawings generally bear a direct relationship to one another in style and technique,

the characteristics of the one group helping to clarify those of the other.[69]

Just as in his drawings, where black chalk is often employed to work out the preliminary nature of the composition or motif, so too David used black chalk for the rough sketch of the composition and placement of individual forms on panels. In both drawing and underdrawing the more fixed design to be followed is made in pen or brush and ink. The consistent use by David in his mature works of two different underdrawing media is characteristic of his working procedure. In this, David was preceded by, or may even have been taught by, the example of his north Netherlandish compatriot Geertgen tot Sint Jans, who at least in his documented works used both black chalk and brush.[70] In the *Lamentation* and the *Burning of the Bones of Saint John the Baptist,* however, Geertgen appears to have worked in the reverse manner of Gerard David—that is, initially working out the composition and individual figures in brush, and subsequently, in a second stage, correcting these forms or augmenting them with parallel hatching for shading with black chalk. Although David's forerunner in Bruges Hans Memling also used both media on occasion in the same altarpiece (for example, the Last Judgment Altarpiece in Gdansk),[71] further study is needed in order to determine whether he regularly employed these different media together on the same panel as David did.[72]

It is also possible to draw some conclusions about the chronology of David's underdrawing style, which in turn leads to observations about his origins and influences on his later development. A parallel exists in the evolution of the technique of drawings on paper from the late fifteenth century to the early decades of the sixteenth century, where the preferred medium changed from the earlier metalpoint and pen or brush and ink to black chalk. Such an evolution is echoed in the underdrawings of the artists preceding and following Gerard David in the south Netherlands.

So far as we know at this point in our investigations, Dieric Bouts and Hugo van der Goes (both artists primarily active around the third quarter of the fifteenth century) commonly employed pen or brush and black pigment for underdrawings in their paintings.[73] Although he began by employing brush, Hans Memling changed to black chalk for the underdrawings of the paintings he produced in Bruges.[74] David, for his part, also began with a brush underdrawing, which evolved later into a mingling of the two techniques. It would be simplifying matters too much, however, to end the discussion with this generalized statement, for the issue is more complicated than that. An overview of the development of underdrawings in David's paintings helps to clarify their relationship to his drawings on paper and to lay the groundwork for the following chapters, which discuss David's technique as an integral part of the art-historical concerns raised by individual paintings.

Among David's earliest works, most likely produced before his first recorded presence in Bruges in 1484, are a triptych of *Christ Nailed to the Cross* (Figures 91–93) and various versions of the theme of the Nativity that show the influence of Dieric Bouts (to be discussed in greater detail in chapter 3). As the stylistic evidence shows, David probably spent some time in Leuven following in the footsteps of his compatriot from Haarlem, Dieric Bouts, on his way to settling in Bruges. It is not surprising, therefore, that the underdrawings of David's early works resemble those of the paintings produced in Bouts's workshop—free brushwork for the layout of the composition and setting, and tightly controlled hatching and cross-hatching in pen or brush and black pigment for the modeling of the figures and their draperies. Compare, for example, the preliminary sketch on one of the panels for the *Justice of Emperor Otto III* with that of the right wing of the triptych of *Christ Nailed to the Cross* (Figures 57 and 58).

Upon his arrival in Bruges, David was already a mature artist when he encountered the work of the city's then leading master, Hans Memling. Memling's own move to Bruges after a period of time in the Brussels studio of Rogier van der Weyden must have been a liberating experience, for we can begin to see developments in his style, among them the change from a tightly controlled brush underdrawing to a remarkably free sketch in black chalk.[75] David must

have been aware of Memling's activities in Bruges and perhaps was familiar with his working procedures for painting. Whether this is a specific case of influence from Memling to David or whether David was merely following general trends, he soon adopted a standard technique in his Bruges paintings that included a preliminary rough, free black-chalk sketch at the initial stage of work. The *Justice of Cambyses* panels (completed in 1498) and the *Virgin among Virgins* (donated in 1509), both of which will be discussed in the next chapter, are prime examples of this working technique, where David used black chalk to freely lay out the composition and brush and black pigment to work out the details of modeling and the system of lighting to be used in the painted layers.

During the first decade of the sixteenth century, David must have employed apprentices and assistants in his workshop, for there was a significant market demand in Bruges and a developing one in Antwerp that encouraged increased production. This would have provided the impetus for David to devise more efficient methods of producing paintings of standardized themes. Certainly the evidence of this is found in the evolution of the working techniques used in his paintings. That is to say, the underdrawings of this period begin to show that certain designs were underdrawn in an already fixed or finished form, while other features (the unusual or variable forms) continued to evolve in a freely sketched manner directly on the grounded panel. Furthermore, these later works begin to show the evidence of designs transferred from a pounced cartoon.

Extremely instructive in terms of understanding the standard working methods that David developed is a painting in which two different styles of underdrawing coexist side by side. This is the *Virgin and Child with Four Saints* (or *Maria in Sole*)[76] of about 1515 in the Norton Simon Museum (Figure 59). The underdrawing of the Virgin's drapery (Figure 37) is carried out entirely in a crumbly medium (probably black chalk), and its character is sketchy, with numerous forms in flux and the final design not at all fully resolved. Several changes between the underdrawing and the painting are evident in the folds of the

57. IR photograph of drapery of woman in Figure 68 (Photo Copyright IRPA-KIK, Brussels)

draperies and the placement of the moon sliver at the lower end of the Virgin's drapery. The underdrawing of Saints John the Evangelist and John the Baptist at the left, however, is extremely meticulous and carefully worked out, presenting a preestablished form and modeling in brush and a black pigment.

This latter underdrawing probably relied on a preliminary sketch on paper for the specific design of the draperies, while the Virgin's draperies continued to be adjusted in their configuration directly on the panel in the underdrawing, due in part to the repositioning of the crescent moon in the lower portion

58. IRR detail of Figure 93

ing.[78] If the specific characteristics of these paintings are considered, some interesting common features emerge. Though it sometimes appears as if the relative covering power of the color of upper paint layers has something to do with the complexity and finish of the underdrawing, this is not a standard determining factor. Of the fifteen individual panels in this grouping, except for the large-scale central panels of the Saint Anne Altarpiece and the Sedano Triptych (Figures 159 and 150), all are relatively small in size, that is, closer to the scale of a pattern drawing available in the workshop, and thus more easily copied by eye, detail for detail. This type of underdrawing is without exception made in pen or brush and a black pigment, that is, with the tools and medium David used for the final draft of his ideas, reserving black chalk or charcoal routinely for those compositions and forms he was still working out. Also without exception, the figures and forms of these paintings that share the same type of underdrawings are all from David's stock types: certain poses of the Virgin, saints, female mourners, and so on. In other words, they are exactly the subjects of model drawings that David would have had available in the workshop, ready to be incorporated into paintings.

A final type of underdrawing existing in David's paintings provides evidence of lost cartoons used for the transfer of motifs or compositions. Recalling David's legal battles with Ambrosius Benson, the court records state that David removed from the house of Adriaen Isenbrant certain patterns that Benson thought were his and that there were in the trunks Benson left behind some additional patterns, which were the property of a certain Albrecht. It is impossible to say whether these *patronen* were simply drawings on paper or whether they were actually cartoons used for the transfer of designs.

Although no pricked drawings from David's atelier have survived, we do have evidence from the underdrawings of the paintings themselves about which designs were duplicated and often how they were transferred.[79] Perhaps the best-known example among David's paintings is the *Adoration of the Magi* (Figure 60), which Johannes Taubert and Karl Arndt

of the painting. Another case that combines the two different media for an evolving as opposed to a fixed design is the *Annunciation* in Frankfurt.[77]

There are about fifteen paintings in David's oeuvre that, like the two saints in the Norton Simon Museum *Virgin and Child* show a fixed underdraw-

60. Gerard David, *Adoration of the Magi*, ca. 1500–1505. Oil on oak, 121 × 167 cm. Alte Pinakothek, Munich (Photo Artothek, Munich)

have discussed as a copy after Hugo van der Goes.[80] Both these scholars identified the telltale marks of pouncing from infrared photographs of the Munich painting. Arndt noticed what he considered to be a difference in the sizes of the dots used in the pricking for the background scene of horsemen and the foreground figures of the kings. This may be the clearest indication that not one complete cartoon, but several cartoons for discrete parts of the composition, were used to transfer the design of this relatively large painting. As can be proven by practical application of the process of pouncing, the carbon or chalk material of the pounce will adhere well only to a slightly tacky surface, that is, a ground

59. Gerard David, *Virgin and Child with Four Saints*, ca. 1515–20. Oil on oak, 70.8 × 54 cm. The Norton Simon Foundation, Pasadena, California

preparation that has been wetted or oiled.[81] After transferring the design, David kept the upper left background scene as a series of dots (Figure 61). For the major portions of the composition, however, he went back over the dots, connecting them with a brush and black paint (Figures 62 and 63). That he did this rather soon after the design was transferred is evident by the way the brushstrokes adhere to the surface of the painting. Where the surface was still tacky, the brushstrokes beaded up with the meeting of the aquaeous and oil media. This effect may be seen in the figures of the three kings. By the time David (or an assistant carrying out this manual task) reached the figures of Mary, Joseph, and the Christ Child, however, the surface was apparently dry, and the brush connecting the pounced dots covered them evenly, in fluid, uninterrupted strokes. The

61. IRR detail of upper left of Figure 60

only indication that there was pouncing here at all is found in the feet of the Christ Child, where the connecting brushstroke goes inside the pattern of the pounced dots, and in the left forearm of the Child, where the dots can still be seen.

We are at a disadvantage regarding this composition, for we don't know exactly what the supposed prototype design by Hugo van der Goes looked like. Other versions of the composition—a copy in Berlin and one in Princeton, as well as several versions in manuscript illumination—seem to follow the same design with minor adjustments in the spacing of figures.[82] The only area of the composition where there is even a slight indication that David may have

deviated from Hugo's design is in the angels hovering over the Virgin and Child. Here there is no evidence of a pounced design. Instead, David used his habitual sketching tool—black chalk—to draw the forms of the two angels, presumably after the surface of the ground preparation was dry, for the lines are distinct and unsmudged (Figure 64). That he used black chalk after the surface was dry may have been prompted by the less usable form-defining lines of the angel at the right. This area may have been oiled out or rewet, which would cause the application of the underdrawing in brush to bleed out from the applied lines. It may have been because of this undesired effect that David waited for the area

62. IRR detail of king and shepherd in Figure 60

63. IRR detail of Holy Family in Figure 60

to dry and then employed black chalk for the pre-liminary design.

David seems to have used pouncing as a technique for transferring designs relatively infrequently. In fact, the only other obvious example of David's use of a pounced design is in his series of the *Virgin and Child with the Milk Soup* paintings, of which there are numerous versions now belonging to the Aurora Trust; the Musées Royaux des Beaux-Arts de Belgique, Brussels; the Deutz collection; and the Palazzo Bianco in Genoa, among others (Figures 284–287).[83] The relationship of these paintings to one another and the possible conclusions to be reached about them will be discussed in chapter 6.

From time to time David made use of other methods of transfer, which are not so readily visible. A tracing made on Mylar (from the X-radiograph) of the major motif of the Virgin and Child from the Sedano Triptych (Figure 150) and its exact corre-spondence, in a flipped version, with the Phila-delphia Museum of Art *Virgin and Child Enthroned with Two Angels* (Figure 280) prove that some kind of now invisible method of pattern transfer took place.[84] Likewise, a survey of the correlation between similar features in numerous paintings (for example, the head of Mary Magdalene in the London *Virgin and Child with Saints and a Donor* and in the *Virgin among Virgins,* or the Virgin in the outside left wing

64. IRR detail of angels in Figure 60

of the Baptism Triptych and in the *Virgin and Child with the Milk Soup*) clearly indicates a rather consistent dependency upon the use and reuse of pattern drawings as a standard practice in David's workshop.

The artists who followed David, chiefly those assembled in the group around Adriaen Isenbrant, employed pricked cartoons as a standard working technique.[85] This accomplished the proliferation of David's designs in countless works produced toward the end of his life and thereafter, extending his legacy well into the sixteenth century, in a new era of the mass production of paintings.

NOTES

1. This chapter is a much-revised version of an inaugural lecture delivered at Colloque IX of "Le dessin sous-jacent dans la peinture" and first published in Ainsworth 1993a. For a review of workshop practice in general and helpful bibliographies, see the section "Le Peintre et son métier," in Patoul and Schoute 1994.

2. The literature on underdrawings in panel paintings is now considerable. The reader is directed to the proceedings of the colloques of "Le dessin sous-jacent dans la peinture" published every two years since 1971 under the editorship of Hélène Verougstraete and Roger Van Schoute. For the methodology of comparing drawings and underdrawings, see Ainsworth 1989b.

3. The documents were first published by Parmentier (1937, pp. 92–93) and subsequently transcribed and discussed by Georges Marlier (1957, pp. 15–19 and 41–42) and van Miegroet (1989, pp. 345–46). For a discussion of various levels of workshop assistants and their particular obligations, see Campbell 1981a, pp. 43–61.

4. For a review of the Sanderus quotation and other documents concerning Isenbrant, see Wilson 1995a, pp. 1, 15 nn. 1, 2.

5. For a general study of types of workshop drawings existing during the Renaissance in Italy, see F. Ames-Lewis, *Drawing in Early Renaissance Italy* (New Haven and London, 1981), and F. Ames-Lewis and J. Wright, *Drawing in the*

Italian Renaissance Workshop, exh. cat.,Victoria and Albert Museum (London, 1983).

6. Sonkes 1969b, pp. 1–5; for Dieric Bouts, see Brussels 1957–58, nos. 32, 33, pp. 92, 94.

7. Waagen first published certain of these drawings in the Klinkosch collection,Vienna, as Holbein (Waagen 1867, p. 196). They were sold as such in the Klinkosch sale: *Katalog der reich-haltigen und vorzüglichen Sammlung von alten Handzeichnungen, Miniaturen, alten Kupferstichen, Radirungen, Holzschnitten, Büchern Bildwerken, etc. aus dem Nachlasse des Herrn Josef C. Ritter von Klinkosch* (April 15, 1889,Vienna), pp. 43–44, nos. 468–473 (wherein the accompanying text suggests that they may instead be by Rogier van der Weyden); Conway (1908, p. 155) attributed them to David, and Meder (1908, no. 1407) agreed, although Leprieur (1910, pp. 161–75) considered one of the Louvre drawings to be French.Winkler (1913, pp. 273–74; 1929, pp. 271–75) regarded the assembled six sheets as part of the same sketchbook, dating them to between 1500 and 1515. After first accepting the idea of the Klinkosch sketchbook, Friedländer (1937, pp. 5–18) discovered the relationship between one of the drawings, a *Portrait of a Man* on the reverse of the Louvre study of *Four Girls' Heads and Two Hands,* and a painted portrait of Charles Brandon, duke of Suffolk, and renamed the artist of all of the assembled drawings the Master of the Brandon Portraits.This attribu-tion has never been accepted in the literature, the most recent of which (Lugt 1968, p. 20; Mundy 1980a, p. 58, and 1980b, p. 125; Hand and Wolff 1986, p. 131 n. 7; Ainsworth 1988, pp. 528–30; Ainsworth 1989a, pp. 53–60; 1989b, pp. 9, 22–34; and 1993, pp. 11–33; and van Miegroet 1989, pp. 321–26 [who misidentifies the medium of many of the drawings and must be read with caution as to reliability of the text]) have securely established these drawings as by David.

8. On the development of model books and workshop practice, see P. W. Scheller, *Exemplum Model-book Drawings and the Practice of Artistic Transmission in the Middle Ages, ca. 900–ca. 1470,* trans. M. Hoyle (Amsterdam, 1995), esp. pp. 1–88.

9. Leonardo da Vinci 1956, par. 249, p. 105.

10. Ibid., par. 258, p. 107.

11. Benesch 1957, pp. 12–13.

12. Brussels 1957–58, p. 92, no. 32.The relationship between Gerard David and the workshop of Dieric Bouts will be discussed more thoroughly in chap. 3.

13. Fritz Koreny (Albertina,Vienna) has kindly notified me that the sheet with ten heads (Figure 2) was subsequently mentioned in a 1908 inventory of objects in Viennese collec-tions (*Österreichische Kunsttopographie,* vol. 2, *Die Denkmale der Stadt Wien, XI–XXI Bezirk* [Vienna, 1908], p. 224; fig. 241, p. 220). Richard Day Ltd. (letter of March 3, 1993) has informed me that the drawing was formerly in the Kuffner collection,Vienna, and later in the Mrs.V. Eberstadt collec-tion, New York.The sheet cannot at present be traced.

14. Ainsworth 1997b.

15. This determination of medium cannot be made by photographs, and in most cases the black-chalk underdraw-ing can be seen only with the use of magnification. In terms of the identification of the medium of the drawings, van Miegroet 1989 cannot be relied on, as numerous mistakes

concerning this issue are made in the body of his text as well as in the catalogue entries.

16. Waagen 1867, p. 196; Conway 1908, p. 155;Winkler 1929, pp. 271–75; Friedländer 1967–76, vol.VIb (1971), p. 91; Mundy 1980a, pp. 55–71; Mundy 1980b, pp. 124–25; Hand et al. 1986, p. 131 n. 5; van Miegroet 1988d, pp. 131–33; van Miegroet 1989, p. 322; Ainsworth 1988, pp. 528–30.

17. On the possible identification of this head as Engelbert II, count of Nassau, see van Miegroet 1989, pp. 164, 169–70.

18. Brussels 1957–58, p. 94, no. 33.

19. See Mundy 1980b, pp. 122–25, and Ainsworth 1988, pp. 528–30.

20. Waagen 1867, p. 196; Meder 1908, no. 1407; Conway 1908, p. 155; Leprieur 1910, pp. 161–75;Winkler 1913, p. 271; Winkler 1929, pp. 271–75; Friedländer 1934, vol.VI, p. 98; ibid., vol. XIV (1937), pp. 106–7; Friedländer 1937, p. 14; Besancon 1951, p. 49; Benesch 1957, p. 13; Lugt 1968, p. 20, no. 57; Friedländer 1967–74, vol.VI (1971), p. 91; Mundy 1980a, pp. 62–63; Mundy 1980b, p. 125; Hand et al. 1986, p. 131 n. 5; van Miegroet 1989, pp. 134, 322.

21. Klinkosch sale (in note 7) as by Holbein;Waagen 1867, vol. II, p. 196; Conway 1908, p. 155;Winkler 1929, p. 275 n. 1; Lugt 1968, p. 20; Friedländer 1967–76, vol.VIb (1971), p. 91; Mundy 1980a, p. 58; Mundy 1980b, p. 125; Hand et al. 1986, p. 131 n. 7; van Miegroet 1989, pp. 134, 322–23; Ainsworth 1993a, p. 14.

22. See note 7 above; for Kraków literature not men-tioned in van Miegroet 1989, pp. 324–25, see M. Jarostawiecka, "Rysunki flamandzkie XVI wieku w Muzeum XX. Czartoryskich w Krakowie," *Przeglad historji Sztuki PAU 2* (1930–31), pp. 22 27.

23. For the most complete discussion of this painting and its dating, see Janssens de Bisthoven 1981, pp. 130–62.

24. The other is the *Portrait of a Goldsmith* in Vienna, Kunsthistorisches Museum.

25. Ainsworth 1989b, p. 24.

26. Waagen 1867, vol. II, p. 196; Conway 1908, p. 155; Winkler 1929, pp. 271–75; Paris 1959–60, pp. 49–51, no. 46; Friedländer 1967–76, vol.VIb (1971), p. 91; Mundy 1980a, p. 125; Hand et al. 1986, p. 131; van Miegroet 1989, pp. 133–34, 322–23; Ainsworth 1993, p. 16.

27. Paris 1878, no. 629; Leprieur 1910, p. 161; Popham 1926, p. 27;Winkler 1929, pp. 271–75; Adhémar 1954, no. 20.649; Lugt 1968, pp. 19–20, no 56; Friedländer 1967–76, vol.VIb (1971), p. 91; Mundy 1980a, p. 62; van Miegroet 1989, pp. 323–24; Ainsworth 1989b, pp. 9–10, and Ainsworth 1993, pp. 16–17.

28. Discussed in Ainsworth 1989a, pp. 123–30, and Ainsworth 1993, pp. 16–17.This darkening of the paint also has occurred in two other paintings by David, namely the *Virgin and Child with Saints and a Donor* (National Gallery, London) and the Saint Anne Altarpiece (National Gallery of Art,Washington), where a mixture of azurite and red lake turned almost black over time (see Wyld et al. 1979 and Metzger 1992).

29. Van Miegroet 1989, pp. 212, 217, and 227, nn. 88 and 90, for various opinions about a possible trip to Italy for

David. This matter will be discussed further in chaps. 2, 4, and 6.

30. See Sulzberger 1955b, pp. 105–11; Silver 1977, pp. 63–92, and Scailliérez 1991, pp. 53–61.

31. Pauli 1924, vol. I, no. 1; Winkler 1929, p. 274 n. 1; Lugt 1968, p. 20, no. 57; Mundy 1980a, pp. 60–61; van Miegroet 1989, pp. 137, 324; Ainsworth 1989b, pp. 22–23; and Ainsworth 1993, pp. 17–18.

32. Popham 1926, p. 27, no. 28; Lugt 1968, p. 21, no. 61; Friedländer 1967–76, vol. VIb (1971), p. 91; Mundy 1980a, pp. 61–62, 64; van Miegroet 1989, pp. 138, 325–26 (there rejected).

33. Bodenhausen and Valentiner 1911, p. 189; Philadelphia 1913, p. 11; Conway 1921, p. 288; Friedländer 1934, vol. VI, p. 151, no. 200; cat. Philadelphia 1941, p. 25, no. 330; Marlier 1957, p. 151, no. 24; Friedländer 1967–76, vol. VIb (1971), p. 105, no. 200; Philadelphia 1972, p. 29, no. 330; van Miegroet 1989, pp. 133, 283–84; Ainsworth 1989b, pp. 32–33.

34. See Lugt 1968, p. 21, no. 61, who mentions Italian attributions. Rejected by Friedländer 1967–76, vol. VIb (1971), p. 91, and van Miegroet 1989, pp. 325–26, but accepted by Popham 1926, p. 27, and Mundy 1980a, pp. 61–62.

35. Kwakkelstein 1994, pp. 117–18, n. 254; also Silver 1984, p. 46. See also further discussion in chaps. 2, 4, and 6.

36. Lees 1913, pp. 61, 63; Eisler 1963, pl. 14; Toronto 1965, pp. 87–88; Friedländer 1967–76, vol. VIb (1971), p. 91, pl. 230d; Mundy 1980a, p. 60; Hand et al. 1986, pp. 130–31, no. 44; van Miegroet 1989, p. 321.

37. Davies 1955, pp. 173–75.

38. Vandenbroeck 1985, pp. 174–78. See Friedländer 1967–76, vol. I (1967), p. 44. For an exact 15th-century copy, probably from Jan's workshop (Figure 190 and discussion in chap. 5), see Silver 1983, pp. 95–104; there, however, the copy is discussed as a later work, attributed to Dieric Bouts the Younger. The new attribution of the Berlin drawing to David was first presented by the author in Ainsworth 1985, p. 54.

39. Klein reports the earliest felling date to be 1494 and the wood from the same tree as that of MMA *Annunciation* panels, dated 1506 (see Appendix B). Sander 1993, pp. 233–43, where the painting and underdrawing are illustrated.

40. A similar type of minimal underdrawing can also be found in the central panel of the Saint Michael Altarpiece (Kunsthistorisches Museum, Vienna), also apparently modeled after another source, quite possibly the *Archangel Michael* (engraving; Bibliothèque Nationale de France, Paris) by the Master of the Gardens of Love (for other suggestions about the source, see van Miegroet 1989, p. 292). The Vienna painting was studied by the author in May 1984 with the assistance of Chiyo Ishikawa and with the kind permission of Karl Schütz.

41. See discussion in chaps. 3 and 4.

42. Unframed and studied by Maurice Sérullaz for the exhibition "Chefs-d'œuvres—dessins et gravures—du Cabinet Edmond de Rothschild," Paris 1959–60, pp. 49–51, no. 46.

43. Among the most important is the cathedral at Damme (in ruins since 1578), where Charles the Bold and Margaret of York were married in 1458. Damme also served as a major port entry to Bruges in the 15th century; it was

connected to the Atlantic port of Sluvis by the Zwijn River.

44. See C. Fischer, "Fra Bartolommeo's Landscape Drawings," *Mitteilungen des Kunsthistorischen Institutes in Florenz* 32 (1989), pp. 301–42.

45. Museum Boijmans Van Beuningen, Rotterdam, inv. no. N73. Lees 1913, p. 59; Friedländer 1924–37, vol. VIb (1928), p. 98; Winkler 1929, p. 275 n. 1; Baldass 1937, p. 19; Panofsky 1953, p. 438 n. 3; Rotterdam 1957, pp. 3–4; Friedländer 1967–76, vol. Vib (1971), p. 91; Mundy 1980a, pp. 67–68; van Miegroet 1989, p. 326.

46. Cabinet des dessins, Louvre, inv. no. 20.648; Paris 1878, no. 631; Lugt 1968, p. 21, no. 60; Friedländer 1967–76, vol. VIb (1971), p. 91; Mundy 1980a, pp. 63–64.

47. A. E. Popham, *Drawings of the Early Flemish School*, London, 1926, pp. 14, 15.

48. Cabinet des dessins, Louvre, inv. no. 20.652bis; Paris 1878, no. 633-1; Popham 1926, p. 27, no. 29; Lugt 1968, no. 58; Friedländer 1967–76, vol. VIb (1971), p. 91; Châtelet 1981, pp. 118, 221, no. 77.

49. E. Knab et al., *Graphische Sammlung Albertina, Europäische Meisterzeichnungen aus dem Zeitalter Albrecht Dürers*, exh. cat., May 25–Sept. 1971, Vienna, p. 18, no. 38, with pertinent literature; Châtelet 1981, pp. 118, 221-22, no. 79.

50. Cabinet des dessins, Louvre, inv. no. 20.652bis; Paris 1878, no. 633-2; Popham 1926, p. 27, no. 29; Besancon 1951, p. 43; Lugt 1968, p. 21, no. 59; Friedländer 1967–76, vol. VIb (1971), p. 91; Châtelet 1981, pp. 118, 221, no. 78; Mundy 1980a, p. 66.

51. Lugt 1968, no. 58.

52. Châtelet 1981, pp. 118, 221, no. 77, pls. 96, 97.

53. See the discussion by Van Bueren and Faries 1991, pp. 143–46.

54. Friedländer 1937, pp. 5–18. One of the paintings attributed by Friedländer to the Master of the Brandon Portraits came up at auction in 1983, there attributed to Joos van Cleve (Sotheby's, London, July 6, 1983, *Old Master Paintings,* lot no. 5). For other literature, see note 7 above concerning the recto of the study of *Four Girls' Heads and Two Hands*. The drawing is most recently discussed by Nathalie Toussaint and illustrated in "Le Maître des Portraits Brandon," in Patoul and Van Schoute 1994, pp. 514, 515.

55. This was pointed out by Lorne Campbell in his review of Hans van Miegroet's *David* (Campbell 1991, p. 624).

56. Toussaint, as in note 54 above, p. 515.

57. Lugt 1968, p. 20.

58. Evidence that a certain Antheunis Huyghe, with whom David shared his house, and whom van Miegroet would like to list as an assistant in David's shop, is not forthcoming. Although it may well be that this person was a painter and contributed to the production from David's atelier, no work can be definitively attributed to his hand. See van Miegroet 1989, pp. 22–26, 29, 30, 270.

59. Museum Boijmans Van Beuningen, Rotterdam, inv. no. N-137. Exhibited in Museum Boijmans Van Beuningen Dec. 17, 1948–Feb. 1, 1949, exh. cat. *Tekeningen van Jan van Eyck tot Rubens* (Rotterdam, 1949), p. 34, no. 35.

60. Friedländer 1967–76, vol. XI (1974), pl. 126, no. 154. Concerning authorship questions of the Isenbrant group, see Wilson 1995a.

61. The Christ figure in the painting, with his finely rendered, delicate facial features and particularly dark, round eyes, is especially close to the figure at the back right of the *Pentecost* painting in the Fogg Art Museum.

62. For an overview of this question, see the essay by Maurits Smeyers in M. Smeyers and J. Van der Stock, *Flemish Illuminated Manuscripts 1475–1550* (Ghent and New York, 1996), pp. 6–47, and suggested further readings, pp. 211–14.

63. W. H. J. Weale, "Documents inédits sur les enlumineurs de Bruges," *Le Beffroi 2* (1864–65), pp. 298–319; and IV (1872–73), pp. 111–19, 238–337; E. Baes, *La Peinture flamands et son enseignement sous la Régime des confrères de Saint Luc* (Brussels, 1882), *Mémoires couronnés et Mémoires des savants étrangers*, vol. 44, p. 103; C. Van den Haute, *La Corporation des Peintres à Bruges* (Bruges, 1913), pp. 88–89; Scillia 1975, pp. 195–96; A. Vanderwalle, "Het librariërsgilde te Brugge in ijn vroege periode," in *Vlaamse kunst op perkament,* exh. cat., Gruuthusemuseum (Bruges, 1981).

64. Museum Boijmans Van Beuningen, Rotterdam, Koenigs collection, inv. no. N-138; attributed by Otto Pächt to the Master of Mary of Burgundy (*The Master of Mary of Burgundy* [Oxford, 1948], pp. 70–71). For further discussion of the artists associated with this group, see also Patrick de Winter, "A Book of Hours of Queen Isabel la Católica," *The Bulletin of the Cleveland Museum of Art* 67, no. 10 (1981), pp. 342–427, esp. pp. 353–59.

65. Museum Boijmans Van Beuningen, Rotterdam, inv. no. N-124; Wescher 1946, pp. 194–95; Testa 1986, p. 176.

66. Van Miegroet 1989, pp. 73, 84, 287–88; Testa 1986.

67. See Testa 1992, pp. 7–84, esp. p. 16, fig. 3.

68. Possibly also related to manuscript illumination are two drawings, the recto and verso of a sheet in Copenhagen, representing a *Standing Female Figure* and a *Seated Man* (inv. no. 10090; F. Lees, *The Art of the Great Masters* [London, 1913], p. 59, fig. 74). But the pen work appears to be similar only in its basic drawing conventions and not in the specific features of the handling and execution of Gerard David.

69. Preliminary findings concerning David's drawings and underdrawings have been discussed in Ainsworth 1985, 1988, 1989a, 1989b, and 1993a.

70. Van Bueren and Faries 1991, pp. 141–50, and pls. 76–79b.

71. See Faries 1997a, pp. 243–59.

72. For a preliminary discussion of this issue, see T. H. Borchert, "Large- and Small-Scale Paintings and Their Underdrawings in the Menling-Group," in *Le dessin sous-jacent et technologie de la peinture. Perspectives, Colloque XI, 1995,* R. Van Schoute and H. Verougstraete, eds., with A. Dubois (Louvain-la-Neuve, 1997), pp. 211–22, and Ainsworth 1994b.

73. See Périer-d'Ieteren 1985, pp. 25–26 and 30–31; C. Thompson and L. Campbell, *Hugo van der Goes and the Trinity Panels in Edinburgh* (London, 1974), pp. 94–98.

74. Ainsworth 1994b, pp. 78–81.

75. Ibid.

76. For the iconography of this painting, see Ringbom 1962), pp. 326–30. The "Deipara Virgo" identification suggested by van Miegroet (1989, cat. no. 41, pp. 306–7) cannot be supported.

77. Illustrated in Sander 1993, figs. 149, 150.

78. Among these are: *Rest on the Flight into Egypt* (MMA and NGW); *Christ Nailed to the Cross;* the central panel and predella panels of the Saint Anne Altarpiece: the central panel and outside wings of the Sedano Triptych: the Philadelphia *Head of Christ:* the left wing of the Saint Michael Altarpiece: the National Gallery, London, *Adoration of the Magi;* the Frankfurt *Saint Jerome;* the Frankfurt *Annunciation* (figure of the Virgin only).

79. In this process a drawing on paper is pricked with a sharp pin or stylus around the main contours of the composition and even on lines of interior modeling. Then after the drawing is placed over a grounded panel, a pounce bag (usually made of a piece of loose-weave gauze) filled with charcoal or chalk dust is daubed over the drawing. The black particles from the bag sift through the pricked holes of the drawing and onto the panel, thus leaving a design in dots of the chief characteristics of the drawing (e.g., Figures 62, 63, and 268). Such pricked drawings or cartoons may be used repeatedly in order to produce a number of similar images. On copying methods, see Cennini 1960, chaps. 23–26; Taubert 1956, pp. 140–51; Taubert 1975, pp. 387–401; Sonkes 1969a, pp. 142–52; Comblen-Sonkes 1979, pp. 44–45; Comblen-Sonkes 1974–80, pp. 29–42; Périer-d'Ieteren 1982–83, pp. 79–94.

80. Taubert 1975, pp. 387–401; Arndt 1961, pp. 153–75; Périer-d'Ieteren 1982–83, p. 85.

81. See J. Jennings, "Infrared Visibility of Underdrawing Techniques and Media," in *Le dessin sous-jacent dans la peinture, Colloque IX, 1991,* R. Van Schoute and H. Verougstraete-Marcq, eds. (Louvain-la-Neuve, 1993), pp. 241–52.

82. For a listing, see van Miegroet 1989, pp. 286–87; Koch 1985, pp. 82–87.

83. On the basis of the infrared photographs alone, Comblen-Sonkes (1974–80), pp. 24–42, noted that certain of the compositions appeared to have been transferred by pouncing, while others had the distinct characteristics of a traced line (e.g., the Brussels version). Now that it has been possible to study all of these versions again with infrared reflectography, certain revisions of these preliminary statements can be made. In all four of the versions of this composition, a pricked cartoon was used. As was the case with the Munich *Adoration of the Magi,* the pounced pattern was subsequently gone over with brush and black pigment, apparently still on a slightly tacky ground, for the brush lines are broken up or have congealed because of the inability of oil and water media to mix.

84. For a fuller discussion, see Ainsworth 1997, pp. 103–8, and chap. 6 in this book.

85. Wilson 1998, pp. 87–160, and esp. chap. 6 in this book.

CHAPTER TWO

By His Own Hand:
Aspects of David's Working Methods in His Documented Paintings

Various theories from diverse points of view have been set forth about the career and oeuvre of Gerard David. Any discussion of his paintings is both enriched and complicated by the fact that he originated in the north and settled in the south Netherlands; he emulated and assimilated the differing styles of artists he encountered on his way to Bruges and after his arrival there in 1484, and probably traveled to Italy. David worked sometimes as an illuminator of manuscripts, but principally as a panel painter, and had an active workshop catering not only to local individuals but also to the thriving, open art markets of Bruges and Antwerp and the well-developed export trade in both cities. David's paintings range from the diminutive scale of manuscript illumination to monumental works on panel, not to mention more than a dozen drawings that reveal various stages of workshop practice.

The relative diversity of the production of Gerard David, though not particularly unusual for the period, has led to disputes about attributions, chronology, and the extent to which one can propose the participation of workshop assistants in various paintings.[1] The traditional method of reconstructing an artist's oeuvre is based upon documented works around which stylistically similar paintings are grouped. While this is generally a valid approach, documented paintings do not always afford the most complete or indeed characteristic index of style criteria by which the artist may be judged. A more fruitful approach to the understanding of an oeuvre attempts to relate the original conception, or the invention stage, to the other stages of realization of the work of art, thereby recovering indications of the painter's habitual

Detail of Figure 79

approach to the creation of a work. Here is where information can be gleaned from methods of technical investigation—that is, by taking into account evidence of the artist's underdrawing, brushwork, and painting procedures as it can be rediscovered through infrared reflectography and X-radiography. As with any research, the findings can be properly interpreted only when a large group of works by the artist is studied. This method represents an expansion of traditional connoisseurship practices—by more fully understanding the artist's working procedures, we can begin again with new information at hand to reconsider some very basic questions that lead to a fuller comprehension of the artist's contribution to the painting of his time.

A starting point for the reassessment of David's style and technique is his documented works:[2] the *Justice of Cambyses* panels, dated 1498 (Figures 65 and 66) and the *Virgin among Virgins* of 1509 (Figure 79). Oddly enough, however, though they are the linchpins of the artist's oeuvre, these paintings do not represent David's standard style and working technique, but rather exceptions to them, because of their large size and their particular requirements.

Perhaps not only because of the difficulties David had in coming to terms with the presentation of the Justice subjects, but also because of the revised requirements of the commission, these paintings were altered in various stages more than any other known examples by the artist. The *Virgin among Virgins* is notable not for changes made during the course of production but for the unique way in which David reformulated a standard theme in part to suit his own purpose, showing a working method of considerable innovation for a painting of 1509 and a new self-awareness. A study of both the *Justice of Cambyses* and the *Virgin*

65. Gerard David, *Justice of Cambyses: Arrest of Sisamnes*, 1498. Oil on oak, 182.3 × 159.2 cm. Groeningemuseum, Bruges

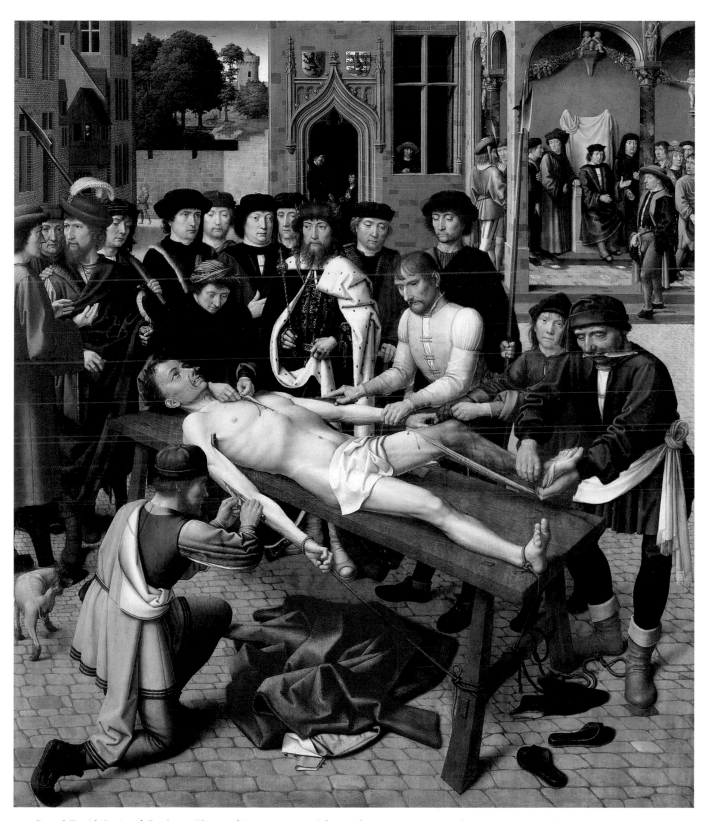

66. Gerard David, *Justice of Cambyses: Flaying of Sisamnes*, 1498. Oil on oak, 182.2 × 159.4 cm. Groeningemuseum, Bruges

among Virgins demonstrates a great deal about the artistic range evident in David's paintings and the marked evolution of his style in the decade between the completion of these works.

The Justice of Cambyses

Traditionally mentioned in connection with the *Justice of Cambyses* panels (Figures 65 and 66) are three archival documents found in the Stadsarchief in Bruges. The first, dating from September 1, 1487, to the end of February 1488, lists an advance payment of four pounds for a painting on wood of the "Jugement ende Vonnesse Ons Liefs Heeren" (usually interpreted as a Last Judgment and sometimes as Christ before Pilate*)*, destined to hang in the aldermen's chambers of the town hall. Subsequently added to the text, in different ink but in a contemporary hand, is the name of the payee, Gerard David.[3]

The second document, of January 1 to August 31, 1491, lists a payment to Gerard David of two pounds *groten* for certain painting by him for the aldermen's chambers.[4]

The third document in the accounts covers the period from September 2, 1498, to September 2, 1499, and pays out eight pounds ten shillings *groten* for the completion of a "large painting of portraiture" placed in the aldermen's chambers. It also mentions payment to various assistants or collaborators of David's. The payment is made to David by Jacob Spronc, Joos de Smet, Jan de Corte, and Jan de Trompes, treasurer.[5]

A number of theories have been proposed in the past concerning these frustratingly vague documents.[6] With new evidence in hand, we may now clarify certain issues and make a few basic assumptions. The first document refers to an advance payment for a work to be hung in the aldermen's chambers, and it is generally agreed that the subject was a Last Judgment, that is, a religious counterpart to the secular judgment scenes traditionally hung in these rooms.[7] In 1388–89 Bruges had paid its city painter, Jan Coene, 41 shillings and 4 pence for "eene barde daer 't jugement in staet bescreven"—a Last Judgment— for the aldermen's chambers of Bruges's town hall,

and in 1524–25 Jan Provost's *Last Judgment* hung in the same chambers.[8] It is Van der Velden's theory that the 1487–88 document refers to a commission made to replace Coene's one-hundred-year-old painting. The description of the subject in this document, however, varies from the wording for the payment to Coene. Here it is stipulated as a "Jugement ende Vonnesse Ons Liefs Heeren" (that is, a "Judgment and sentencing of our Lord"). Recently, Noël Geirnaert has returned to Siret's conclusion of 1869 and suggested that the subject was certainly not a Last Judgment, but a Christ before Pilate,[9] which, along with certain Old Testament scenes, such as the Judgment of Solomon or Susanna and Daniel, would have been an appropriate religious counterpart to a secular judgment scene.[10]

Although David received advance payment for this early commission, there is no further mention of the work, which apparently was never completed, a decision having been made along the way to carry out plans for a secular subject instead, namely, the *Justice of Cambyses* (to which the later payment of 1498–99 refers). No trace of the first commission has been thought to remain, but the recently rediscovered fragment of the *Mocking of Christ* (Figure 5) may well have been part of a larger depiction of Christ's judgment and sentencing that focused on the episode of Christ before Pilate and included various subsidiary scenes (such as this fragment) portraying the surrounding events from Christ's Passion.[11] Based on stylistic evidence as well as dendrochronological investigation, the *Mocking of Christ* dates from about 1488–90, the time of the prepayment document.[12] Its portrayal of a subject less often represented, except in large Passion cycles of multiple scenes, and its emphasis on the theme of the judgment and sentencing of Christ make it a suitable candidate for part of an ensemble for the aldermen's chambers. No other piece of this work appears to have survived, and it is possible that it was never completed, as the lack of any further documentation seems to suggest.

Concerning the second document, Van der Velden has recently pointed out that the word used to describe the work completed for payment, which is *schilderye*, in the late fifteenth century generally referred to painting in the broadest sense. To indicate a panel painting specifically, as the document previously has been interpreted, the phrase would have to have shown accompanying words such as *tafel* (meaning "panel") or *pointrature* (meaning "an individual painting"), or to be additionally clarified by the subject matter of the work. Moreover, the amount paid, the relatively small sum of two pounds *groten*, is more consistent with decorative painting in the aldermen's chambers rather than panel painting.[13] Such mundane assignments were routine for panel painters.

The third document, dated 1498–99, must concern a final payment for the *Justice of Cambyses*, which, according to the record, was already in position in the aldermen's chambers, installed at an unknown date. Records of previous payments made for this large panel, now in two parts but originally framed as one, are not extant.[14] Given the size and complexity of these panels, work must have begun a number of years earlier. A comparable example is perhaps Dieric Bouts's large-scale *Justice of Emperor Otto III,* one panel of which (Figure 68) took thirty months to complete.[15]

Secular judgment scenes were common and appropriate subjects for the council chambers of official city buildings.[16] Among the more noted ones of the period, of course, were paintings of the Justice of Trajan and Gregory and of Herkenbald made by Rogier van der Weyden for the town hall in Brussels (only tapestry versions of which remain, in the Kunsthistorisches Museum, Bern), and the *Justice of Emperor Otto III,* two of the four commissioned works of which were completed about 1475 by Dieric Bouts and his workshop for installation in the town hall of Leuven.

The Justice of Cambyses is a tale related with certain variations in Herodotus's *Historiae* and Valerius Maximus's *Facti et dicti memorabilia* (as well as in the *Gesta Romanorum*), but neither author mentions the scene of the Arrest of Sisamnes, which David features so prominently. It is more likely, as Van der Velden

points out, that David depended on a medieval tradition featuring the story of Cambyses as an exemplum of just judgment.[17] David related four main episodes of the story: the bribing of Judge Sisamnes in the background of the left panel; the judge's eventual arrest in the foreground (Figure 65); the grisly flaying of the corrupt Sisamnes, dominating the right scene; and the further reminder of the events in the depiction of Sisamnes' son obliged to sit in judgment on a seat covered with his father's skin (Figure 66)!

Various proposals have been set forth about the intrinsic meaning of the two paintings. The main question revolves around whether the paintings reflect specific contemporary events in Bruges, or whether they are indicative of a more general or universal meaning. Mary of Burgundy had died in 1482, and her husband, Maximilian I, thus lost his authority over the Netherlands. Undaunted by his diminished official standing, Maximilian nonetheless sought to retain his former position. The majority of the Burgundian states recognized Maximilian as regent, except for Flanders (that is, Ghent, Bruges, and Ypres), which sided with Louis XI and Charles VIII against Maximilian. In 1483 Maximilian and Mary's son, Philip the Handsome, was installed as count of Flanders with a four-man council of regency. But Maximilian would not submit to this council and planned to rule in his son's place, hoping to eventually conquer the duchy of Burgundy. Ongoing disagreements and battles between Maximilian and Flanders culminated in a meeting of the States General in 1487 in Bruges, where Maximilian hoped to finally resolve the matter. Supported by his own German troops, Maximilian entered the city with a show of force. Not intimidated by this, however, the Bruges corporations mounted their own counteroffensive and took Maximilian hostage, holding him in the house on the Markt called Craenenburgh.[18] In any event, Maximilian managed to penetrate the lines of the city limits to summon the supportive forces of Frederick III. Unable to equal the oncoming military might of the Germans, Bruges negotiated with Maximilian. Troubled times continued, but in 1491

Bruges had met her final defeat. In 1488 Philip became duke of the Netherlands and in 1494 regent of the Netherlands.

Early on, in an article of 1863, Weale suggested that the paintings were related to events in contemporary Bruges history, specifically to the revolt of Bruges against Maximilian and the condemnation of the aldermen convicted of corruption. Following the revolt against Maximilian in February 1488, the burgomasters Jan van Nieuwenhove and Jacob van Dudzele as well as the alderman Pieter Lanchals were condemned to death. Weale proposed that the new aldermen, designated under Philip the Handsome by the delegates of Ghent, decided to commission two paintings that would recall for the town councillors the impartiality and the integrity they must show.[19]

This theory has been supported more recently by van Miegroet, who suggested that the panels served to "remind city officials of their duty as judges, as well as to remind the populace of their civic duties to Duke Philip the [Handsome] and his councillors." In other words, the paintings served the purpose of "admonishing Bruges for its political misconduct," and its "lèse majesté and open revolt led by Philip of Cleves."[20] In further support of this thesis, van Miegroet cited the identification with Bruges in the depiction of the *poortersloge* (burgher's lodge) in the left background of the Arrest scene and in the view of the east facade of the town hall in the middle distance of the Flaying scene. He identified the young man at the left of Judge Sisamnes in the Arrest scene as Philip the Handsome, and an onlooker to the left of King Cambyses in the Flaying scene as Engelbert II, count of Nassau; neither suggestion has held up under closer scrutiny.[21]

Strubbe allowed for the parallel drawn by Weale between the corruption theme in local history and in the story of King Cambyses.[22] However, he urged careful consideration of the facts: while it is true that the aldermen dismissed from their responsibilities were accused of greed, the matter did not relate to corruption in the context of the administration of justice, as in the Cambyses story. In any event, Strubbe rejected the idea that paintings completed in 1498 would have deliberately perpetuated the memory of misconduct by certain aldermen dismissed in 1488. After all, the situation in Bruges in 1498 was substantially different from that in 1488. The aldermen were no longer in disgrace, and it is unlikely that this group would have allowed paintings recalling the rebellious behavior of their predecessors to hang in their own judgment chambers. Furthermore, as discussed below, a number of the portrait heads were changed at a late stage, probably to show the aldermen of the late 1490s, not those of the 1480s. If the paintings had been commissioned by Maximilian, the hypothesis of Weale and van Miegroet might be entertained, but this is not the case.

A more likely interpretation recognizes the *Justice of Cambyses* as part of a medieval tradition of exempla, depicting secular and religious judgment scenes that hung in the same town hall chambers together. The reference to contemporary matters in the *Justice* panels, like its precedent in Bouts's *Justice of Emperor Otto III*, is probably limited to portraiture of the aldermen and identifiable sites in Bruges, as well as to a statement of loyalty to Philip the Handsome, as is indicated by the coats of arms added in a late stage to the Arrest scene.

Complicating the interpretation of the paintings is the fact that they have undergone a number of substantial changes in composition and in the details of the figures themselves. These changes are evident through close observation of the painting (certain pentimenti are visible to the naked eye, and the obviously thick paint layers indicate reworking in areas) and through X-radiography and infrared reflectography, both of which help to identify the exact areas of modification.

Let us examine David's method in creating these complex panels in order to hypothesize about the evolution of the painting, as well as to clarify David's working methods in the last decade of the fifteenth century. His planning for this important commission doubtless led to a series of preparatory drawings, only a few of which survive. Nonetheless, the *Justice of Cambyses* panels offer a rare opportunity in David's oeuvre to evaluate the function of underdrawings in relation to preparatory drawings on paper.[23] On the verso and the recto of the same sheet (Figures 7 and 10) are, respectively, a study related to the standing King Cambyses in the Arrest scene and a head of one of the observers in the Flaying scene.[24]

The physical characteristics of the Frankfurt drawings provide clues to David's method. The medium of both sides of the drawing has not always been accurately described in the previous literature,[25] having been called "point of the brush, pen(?), and brown ink over metalpoint on prepared paper." In fact, there is a cursive notation in black chalk beneath a more exacting and meticulous rendering in pen and brown ink for the standing man, while the heads of the recto are in metalpoint over black chalk on prepared paper. As discussed in chapter 1, the function of the drawing of the standing King Cambyses was to work out the configuration of drapery folds and system of lighting on the figure—the face is only minimally suggested and the hands are missing entirely. One of the heads on the recto of the sheet was captured from life as a study for the man centrally placed among the bystanders observing the flaying of Sisamnes.

The technique and medium of the drawings have a direct relationship to David's underdrawings. David often made a preliminary sketch on the prepared panel in black chalk or sometimes charcoal, followed by a more detailed description of certain areas in brush or pen and black pigment. He used silverpoint on prepared paper for the delicate and very freely sketched studies of heads that constitute the majority of the artist's sketchbook subjects, as discussed in greater detail in chapter 1. The use of silverpoint for this purpose corresponds to David's use of black chalk for the underdrawings of painted heads. The sketches on paper, such as the one for the head of an onlooker in the Flaying scene, are studies not only of attitude but also of a particular system of lighting. The same lighting scheme found in the silverpoint drawing is carried over into the underdrawing of the man portrayed in the painting (compare Figures 7–9). However, whether the illumination of the head was studied with the painting already in mind is difficult to say.

Given the evidence of the Frankfurt drawings, specifically their direct relationship to details of the *Justice* panels, it can be presumed that there were a number of preparatory sketches for these rather complicated scenes. At a preliminary stage the juxtaposition of reds, blues, greens, and yellows were considered for balance within the composition. And David, like Bouts (see Figure 57), indicated the color scheme in the underdrawing with color notations on the figures (see Figure 73, where the man's coat at the left shows an "r" for "rot" or red). Not everything, however, was studied independently beforehand. The numerous alterations in the underdrawing and painted layers suggest a design that, to a large extent, evolved directly on the panels.

The *Arrest of Sisamnes,* which bears the date 1498 for the completion of the work, was the more substantially reworked of the two panels. X-radiographs of the paintings (first published by Marijnissen and Van de Voorde, Figures 67 and 72) indicate significantly revised areas in various figures, in the setting of the main scene, and in the background.[26] The background has been changed at least three times. As seen in the X-radiograph (Figure 67), the rough forms of an area left in reserve in the background appear to correspond to general shapes of landscape and small buildings from an earlier conception. The first plan, with a view of buildings to the right and left in the background and a vista into the landscape, is reminiscent of the settings commonly found in the paintings of the Master of the Tiburtine Sibyl, an artist from the circle of Geertgen tot Sint Jans in the Haarlem school, who, like David, apparently spent some time in the late 1470s in Leuven in the workshop of Dieric Bouts (see chapter 3).[27] David's *Arrest of Sisamnes,* in fact, appears to be inspired by the composition of his *Augustus and the Tiburtine Sibyl* in Frankfurt, though David adjusted that design to show a narrower space between the background buildings at the far right and far left.

A second idea for the background can be described only in an incomplete manner; it includes a pitched-roof building in the center distance and a figure (to the left of the porphyry column) looking onto the

67. X-radiograph of Figure 65 with indications of previous design (as in Marijnissen and Van de Voorde 1986)

68. Dieric Bouts (active by 1457–d. 1475), *Justice of Emperor Otto III: Ordeal by Fire*, 1475. Oil on oak, 323 × 182 cm. Musées Royaux des Beaux-Arts de Belgique, Bruxelles–Koninklijke Musea voor Schone Kunsten van België, Brussels

69. IRR detail of Sisamnes in Figure 65

70. IRR detail of three men at lower left in Figure 65

scene from a porch or loggia. Perhaps belonging to this same concept (or to the first one) is a change in the architectural forms and decoration of the building to the right in the background. It previously had a triangular-pitched roof instead of the present arched one, and the facade of the building showed a series of double-arched windows instead of the long rectangular ones featured in the final version. David apparently abandoned these more generalized settings, later incorporating at the back left a specific reference to known architecture in Bruges, namely the *poortersloge*, the meeting place of wealthy burghers.[28]

Marked alterations also took place in the throne of Sisamnes. Originally, Sisamnes sat beneath a canopy on a throne before a wall hung at mid-level with a curtain or tapestry (mostly visible in the X-radiograph, Figure 67). In keeping with these more Gothic-style forms, the throne also had arm rests decorated with lion finials, and Sisamnes put his left hand in his lap rather than on the armrest of the throne (Figure 69). The formerly double-stepped platform below perhaps extended considerably farther onto the tiled

floor (about halfway beneath the white dog), and the three men standing at the far right instead were two, much reduced in height (Figures 67 and 70). At this stage the Arrest scene would have looked quite similar to Dieric Bouts's Justice panel the *Ordeal by Fire* (Figure 68), which shows Emperor Otto with his left hand at his chest, sitting on a canopied throne, its double-stepped platform extended beneath a resting dog and two figures standing to the extreme right with their backs to the viewer while observing the scene; this is all placed on a floor of similar octagonal-, diamond-, and square-shaped tiles and likewise with a double-arched doorway opening to a city view beyond. The palette as well, favoring warm hues of red, yellow, blue, and green, is alike in both David's and Bouts's Justice scenes. All of this changed with David's substantial adjustments to the throne of Sisamnes: the garlands held by sculpted putti, the antique roundels to right and left on the back wall, and the escutcheons with the arms of Philip the Handsome at the left and those of the alliance between Philip and Joan of Castile (future heiress to the Spanish throne) at the right. These last changes, including the coat of arms, could not have been made before October 20, 1496, the date of the royal wedding, which serves as a terminus a quo. In terms of style, specific alterations that were made—especially the introduction of Italianate garlands and putti—show a shift in David's reference to models. He gravitated away from the influence of Dieric Bouts's work and embraced that of his esteemed predecessor in Bruges, Hans Memling.

Finally, and perhaps most significant, multiple changes were carried out in the figures represented. The costumes of some (at least nos. 2, 7, and 11 in Figure 71) were altered: the helmet and costume of the armored soldier (no. 4) to the left of King Cambyses were updated and the height of the figure was increased; the formerly brocade robes of figures nos. 7 and 11 were altered to match the official attire of the unjust judge (a long cloth robe with fur trim). Concerning the heads, certain differences in the density of lead white applications indicate those heads for which there was a reserve left and those that

were painted over a broad-based white tone. The application of lead white for the heads in areas left in reserve is restricted to the highlights of the faces—on the foreheads, noses, and chins (for example, nos. 1–3, 5, 9, 13, and 15 on the diagram); these appear to have been originally planned and not changed at a later stage. Certain heads, marked in the diagram as nos. 7, 8, 11, 12, and 14, appear to have been painted out and replaced by others, or to have been newly added over the darker background; this required a base tone of white to lighten the underpaint for the new faces. Head no. 14 shows ragged edges—a sign of having been scraped off before being repainted (see Figures 67 and 69). At the lower right, a third figure was added to the original two of the Arrest scene, and all were repositioned a head higher than their original placement (Figures 67 and 70). Whether the identity of all of these bystanders was changed at the same time is not possible to say with the evidence from the X-radiograph and infrared reflectography. However, the fact that these heads were actually painted out and not simply adjusted in the features of their faces, as were certain other heads, suggests a more substantial revision. The head farthest to the left at the edge of the crowd, often regarded as

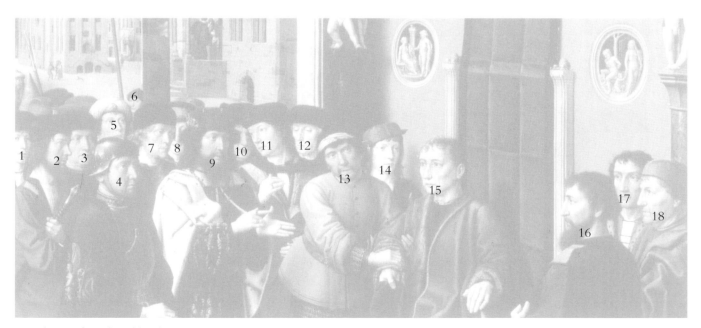

71. Scheme of numbered heads in Figure 65

David's self-portrait, was predictably planned from the beginning.

What is of particular interest for the issues at hand is that when David made these changes, he usually redrew the altered feature with his sketching tool—probably black chalk. The change in the three men at the far right (nos. 16–18 in Figure 71) from a lower to a higher position meant altering their heads and costumes (Figure 70). The drapery of the man to the far right in blue was redrawn on top of the previous drapery and then further adjusted in the final paint layers. The drawn demarcations for major folds were then gone over in brush. A rough, summary sketch of the features of the face of the man in the center sufficed to reintroduce the revised position of his head (Figure 78). This kind of sketching is also typical of the heads in the second row and the background positions of the figures in both paintings.

David substantially altered the attitude of Judge Sisamnes (Figures 67 and 69). He introduced a more animated expression by repositioning the judge's left hand as if ready to move rather than resting on his lap. As a result of these alterations, the drapery of Sisamnes had to be readjusted, and David again made a rough sketch in black-chalk lines to suggest the repositioning of folds in the red cloak of the judge. He replaced the Gothic lion finial on the armrest of the throne with cleaner lines, echoing the newly introduced Renaissance motifs of swags and putti, and the classical medallions in the upper part of the throne and on the back wall.

The *Flaying of Sisamnes* (Figure 66) does not appear to have undergone as many or as significant changes as its companion panel. The upper right background scene was adjusted to coordinate it with the alterations made in the Arrest scene (as it represents the same location at a later point in the narrative)—the newly introduced swags and putti, and the elimination of the canopy over the throne. Other adjustments were less total revisions than simply modifications of forms; the change in the angle of the flaying table at least three times, each time slightly increasing its angle in relationship to the baseline of the painting (Figures 72 and 73), necessitated the reworking of

the position of the kneeling man at the lower left (Figures 72 and 74). The rough sketch of this figure was carried out in a dry medium (probably black chalk), indicating a different pattern of folds for the tunic than was eventually painted and an adjusted position of his left leg, which was lower in the first stages of the painting. The details of the lighting system and volume of forms for this prominent figure were more fully worked out in a second stage in brush and black pigment.[29] These changes of the table angle and the position of the flaying figure also allowed for the enlargement of the discarded robe of Sisamnes, beautifully arranged like a still-life motif in the foreground (Figures 75 and 76).

As in the scene of the Arrest, a number of the heads in the Flaying were clearly part of the first stage of the composition, and were painted within a reserve area, with the application of lead white strokes restricted to the highlights on the faces (nos. 1–3, 9, 12–14, 16, and 17 on Figures 72 and 77; note that no. 13 is more broadly illuminated because of his foreground position). Others, nos. 4–8, 10, and 15 on the diagram, appear to have been painted as part of the second design campaign. While the underdrawing found in the first group of heads is in brush, used in part to describe the illumination of the heads in the preliminary stages, the heads of the second group are underdrawn in black chalk and are sketchlike and summary in nature, supplying only a rough indication of the placement of the heads and the features of the faces (Figure 78). Among these is the head of the man that is also found on the Frankfurt sheet (Figures 7–9), a drawing that, though relatively summary in form, apparently provided sufficient information for the detailed rendering of a portrait.

Presumably, many of the changes—the festoons and putti, classical medallions, and the coat of arms of Philip the Handsome and Joan of Castile (reflecting Philip's appointment as duke of the Burgundian

72. X-radiograph of Figure 66 with indications of previous design (as in Marijnissen and Van de Voorde 1986)

73. IRR detail of table edge and figures at left in Figure 66

74. IRR detail of flaying man at lower left in Figure 66

Netherlands in 1494, and his marriage to Joan in 1496)—were made before the triumphal entry of the ducal couple in March of 1497. However, David was not paid for the completion of the work until between September 2, 1498, and September 2, 1499, leaving open the possibility that final adjustments could have been made subsequent to the duke's

visit, especially in the many heads that were changed. Altogether the paintings contain possibly eighteen to twenty portrait heads, none of which are repeated from one panel to the next (the only repeated heads are those of the protagonists of the narrative, such as King Cambyses and Sisamnes).

It has been logically suggested that the portrait heads represent aldermen for whom this portrayal was meant as a warning to administer sentences impartially. Except for some irregularities in the troubled years of Bruges's revolt (1488–91), the town aldermen and councillors were elected annually on September 2.[30] A tabulation of the lists for the years 1488–98 shows that some served repeatedly in one or both capacities; for example, Adrian Basin (also listed as Adriaan Bazyn) served four times as alderman (in 1492, 1494, 1496, and 1497) and once as councillor

75. Detail of robe of Sisamnes in Figure 66

76. IRR detail of robe of Sisamnes in Figure 66

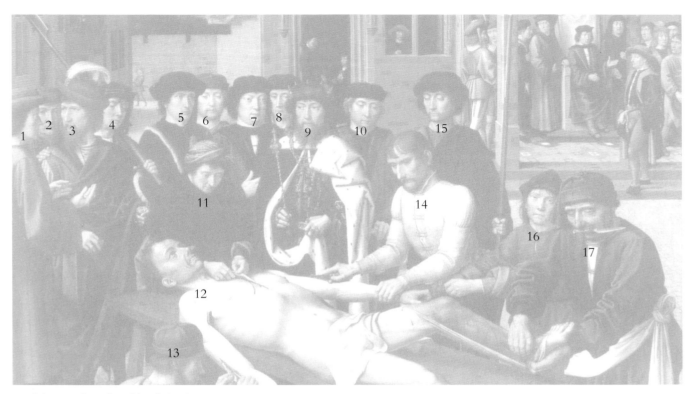

77. Scheme of numbered heads in Figure 66

(in 1498). Considering that David received final payment in 1498 (the date that appears on the Arrest), the election years closest to the complete form of the painting were 1496 and 1497.[31] Of the fifteen aldermen elected on September 2, 1497 (including the burgomaster and the two treasurers), seven were reelected from the 1496 group, while eight were new members.[32] Technical examination shows that approximately fifteen heads were replaced or added in the reworking of the paintings—eight in the Arrest and seven in the Flaying. It is tempting, therefore, to suggest that these represent the heads of the aldermen that served Bruges during the years 1496–97. However, no further proof of such a hypothesis can be offered at this time.

The various hypotheses about the reasons for the alterations in the two paintings are important to consider, since the Justice panels exhibit more changes than any other works by David. These theories must be evaluated with the new physical evidence available and with a critical appraisal of the historical facts. My own understanding is that the meaning of the *Justice of Cambyses* is consistent with the general theme of the administration of fair and unbiased judgments and is not particularly tied to events related to the revolt of Bruges against Maximilian in 1488, as Weale and van Miegroet have suggested. The changes introduced are in the nature of adjustments from the general to the more specific, from late Medieval to Renaissance style, from old-fashioned to au courant. Certain alterations may be seen as purely formal ones, which bring the painting up-to-date, such as the addition of swags and putti, and the classical medallions. In this regard the death of Memling (that city's leading painter until 1494) should be taken into account and David's likely interest in declaring himself the suitable successor. Other changes relate to the clients' wishes: that is, the possible official review of the painting by the town council, which may have necessitated the insertion of the portraits of newly elected aldermen and coats of arms, the latter in order to commemorate the marriage of Philip the Handsome to Joan of Castile and their triumphal entry into the city of

78. IRR detail of reworked portrait heads in Figures 66 and 65

Bruges in 1497, the occasion on which the citizens pledged their loyalty and Philip acknowledged their rights and privileges.

The Virgin among Virgins

The convent of the Carmelite order, called the Carmelites of Sion, was founded in 1488 on the Vlamijncdam (later Sint Jorisstraat) just inside the city walls of Bruges.[33] One of the most famous religious establishments there, it was especially noted for its art treasures.[34] As a result of the onslaught of Iconoclasm and other vicissitudes, however, the convent was extensively damaged, and between 1578 and 1584 it had to be abandoned by the sisters. Finally, in the period of suppression by Emperor Joseph II in 1783, the artworks belonging to the convent were confiscated and dispersed, after which time the buildings served as a military hospital.

Although nothing of the original buildings or of the church built between 1490 and 1499 remains today, an inventory of 1537 lists the treasures of the convent.[35] It confirms that Gerard David made and presented an oil painting in 1509 for the high altar of the church, depicting "Mary and her Child holding grapes, with two little angels and many holy virgins" (Figure 79). Furthermore, it states that the wood for the painting was paid for by the wife of a certain Lambijn, "called Packette at the court of our lord" (i.e., at the court of Philip the Handsome or Charles V),[36] who had also given alms to the hospital there and donated a holy-water basin for the front of the church, near the tomb of her husband. The wings of the altarpiece were unadorned inside and out, but at the time of the 1537 inventory they were to be taken down to be painted—a commission given to various persons at the direction of Sister Jacqmine Barnaerts.[37]

Completed eleven years after the *Justice of Cambyses,* this tightly cropped representation of the Virgin among Virgins is bold in every way, even unprecedented in northern art. The subject chosen for the altarpiece was especially appropriate for the convent, whose Carmelite nuns were devoted to the

79. Gerard David, *Virgin among Virgins*, 1509. Oil on oak, 118 × 212 cm. Musées des Beaux-Arts, Rouen (Photo Giraudon/Art Resource, NY)

Virgin Mary, their patroness.[38] Here she is celebrated as the Queen of Heaven, wearing a jeweled crown sparkling with twelve stars of the firmament, representing the attributes of the Virgin and the points of the Carmelite Rule: obedience, chastity, poverty, recollection, mental power, the Divine Office, the chapter, abstinence from meat, manual labor, silence, humility, and works of supererogation.[39] The Virgin is seated on a throne covered with a red cloth, indicating her regal stature as Queen of Heaven. Part of a long artistic tradition, she is flanked by music-making angels of the heavenly realm.[40]

The nearly frontal position of the Christ Child on the Virgin's lap and the central position of the bunch of grapes make an obvious and fitting reference to the Eucharist, particularly given the placement of the painting on the high altar at the site of the celebration of the Mass. Closer in meaning to this representation is the personification of Mary as the True Vine—signaled in a rather literal way by the Virgin's delicate hold on the stem of the bunch of grapes with her left hand—and of the Christ Child as the burgeoning fruit. Contemporary poetry and plays, and also the sermons of Nicholas of Cusa, described the Virgin and Child thus.[41] In Nicholas of Cusa's words: "From the nature of her flesh was the grape cluster brought forth, from which the wine was pressed, in which God and men rejoiced."[42] The Rule of Carmel invites all souls to come and eat of the "fruits of her vine and the best thereof, and clothes them as well in the garment of salvation and the livery of the Queen of Heaven."[43] The emphasis here is on the nourishment, both physical and spiritual, provided by the Virgin, through the intercession of the saints present, to the faithful and the donors of the altarpiece, Gerard David and his wife, Cornelia Cnoop.

The juxtaposition of the traditionally Greek saints—namely Catherine and Barbara—with Latin ones—Cecilia, Agnes, and Lucy—may well recall the Greek and Latin eras of the Carmelites, when the order spread throughout the East and the West; while Saints Fausta, Apollonia, Dorothy, and Godelieve and an unidentified saint with a rope at her neck may

indicate a local devotion to these saints in the Bruges house of the order.[44] Early on, the Carmelite order consolidated both hermit and mendicant factions, in essence reconciling the contemplative with the active apostolic life of its members,[45] a feature that is perhaps reflected in David's depiction, where certain saints are absorbed in their devotional readings while others direct their attention outward to the viewer's world. Two of the saints, Catherine and Barbara, anchor the composition left and right, epitomizing respectively the active and contemplative modes—Catherine as the most significant intercessor after the Virgin (because of her mystical marriage with Christ) and Barbara as the patroness of those in danger of sudden death without the benefit of last rites. Both female martyrs also embody the concepts of redemption and mediation, specifically serving as supplicants for the salvation of the souls of the deceased.[46] In other words, the iconography of the *Virgin among Virgins* may be understood to comprise both Eucharistic and memorial elements.

In this regard, it is perhaps significant that David's altarpiece was placed at the site where the remains of the first two wives and the son of Martin Reynhout had been moved from their initial location in front of the altar of Saint Anne upon the consecration of the choir of the church in 1499.[47] Reynhout's adopted daughter, Jeanette (later a sister of the convent), laid the first foundation stone for the church, and he himself laid the stone for the main altar and was the first founder and patron of the church, as well as its most important benefactor.[48] Furthermore, in the privileged position next to the high altar on the north wall, between the first two windows, was a triptych decorated with the portraits of Martin Reynhout (d. 1507) and his three wives along with their coat of arms.[49] Whether or not this man of considerable influence at the church of the Convent of Sion and his family are thus honored by the iconographic program of David's altarpiece, its inherent themes would have well suited such a memorial purpose.

Paintings depicting the *Virgo inter virgines* theme were popular in late-fifteenth- and early-sixteenth-

80. Master of the Legend of Saint Lucy, *Virgin and Child with Eleven Female Saints*, 1489. Oil on oak, 106 × 170 cm. Musées Royaux des Beaux-Arts de Belgique, Bruxelles–Koninklijke Musea voor Schone Kunsten van België, Brussels (Photo Copyright IRPA-KIK, Brussels)

century Flanders, and many appear to have been derived from a lost prototype by Hugo van der Goes, which, according to Winkler, was copied by Gerard David; the latter's work would have provided an intermediary version for most of the sixteenth-century replicas.[50] David's Rouen painting might refer to Hugo's composition, but one other precedent for the theme and the general arrangement of figures certainly known to David is the *Virgin and Child with Eleven Female Saints* by the Master of the Legend of Saint Lucy, which was donated in 1489 by the confraternity of *De Drie Sanctinnen* for the Onze-Lieve-Vrouwekerk in Bruges.[51] David's tightly cropped rendition of the theme and his bold presentation of the individualized female saints, however, dramatically depart from the examples of his predecessors. Moreover, the austere and somber manner, as well as the architectonic monumentality, of the centrally placed Virgin in David's painting may reflect certain

Byzantine icons of the *Hodegetria* type, and, for the Virgin alone, perhaps the influence of a remarkable sculpture by Michelangelo, the *Virgin and Child*, which had been acquired in Italy by a local cloth merchant, Alexander Mouscron, and was prominently installed in 1506, also in the Onze-Lieve-Vrouwekerk.[52] In his painting David compressed the space for a grouping of virgin saints and heightened the drama of the scene by introducing a strong illumination from the right instead of from the left as was his habit. These features may indicate that he planned the size, composition, and lighting scheme to suit the destined placement of the painting on the high altar of the church of the Convent of Sion. As the church no longer stands, such hypothetical intentions by David cannot be confirmed. However, the practice of creating a site-specific altarpiece, particularly by extending the lighting conditions of the actual environment into the illusionism of the painting, had already been

81. IRR detail of angel at left in Figure 79

introduced by the Van Eyck brothers in the Ghent Altarpiece. Here the painted shadows in the scene of the Annunciation on the exterior wings are coordinated with the direction of real daylight streaming in from the windows at the right in the chapel of the Vijd family, located on the south side of the apse in Sint Baaf's cathedral. On the other hand, David may have been following north Italian conventions, learned during the course of the production of the Cervara Altarpiece (to be discussed in chapter 4), according to which the painting on the high altar was illuminated from the right. Either way, as we shall see, the chosen lighting system very much suited David's personal agenda.

Perhaps in a further nod to realism, David individualized the physiognomy of each female saint, prompting Friedländer's suggestion that this is actually a group portrait of the convent sisters in the guise of saints.[53] Although only conjecture, such a notion is compatible with the intended realism of Netherlandish painting and the fact that this community comprised women from some of the most prominent families in Bruges, those for whom this kind of conceit would have been perhaps a clever form of flattery as well as an expression of these women's aspirations toward saintly behavior.[54]

Finally, infrequent in contemporary representations of this type is the depiction of David as both

82. IRR detail of angel at right in Figure 79

artist and donor. David (at the far left) and presumably his wife, Cornelia Cnoop (in the white headdress at the far right), appear prominently among the female saints as the donors of this lavish altarpiece destined for the most revered site in the convent church.[55] In addition to unabashedly announcing the authorship of the panel, this scheme underscores the relation of the artist and his wife with the Convent of Sion as patrons. What specific possible commemorative function this work may have served remains unknown, as does the exact relationship that existed between the donor pair and the convent. The altarpiece was not intended to adorn a family chapel, as was often the case in donor-

presented paintings. Neither David nor his wife was buried in the church of the Convent of Sion (David found his final resting place in the Onze-Lieve-Vrouwekerk, and his wife in an unknown location outside of Bruges). Furthermore, there is no reference to David's having been associated with the Carmelite order in any official capacity. On the contrary, in 1507, two years before the presentation of the *Virgin among Virgins,* David became affiliated with the Franciscan order by joining the Brotherhood of the Dry Tree. Given the prestige accorded the members of this confraternity, however, David's motivations may have been less religious than pragmatic in terms of garnering commissions from the elite group.

83. IRR detail of Saint Catherine in Figure 79

Sometime later, in 1521, David made a loan of ten *livres de gros* to the Convent of Sion, a sum he requested be returned two years later.[56] Coincidentally, Anne de Chantraines, a cousin of Cornelia Cnoop's, joined the convent that same year, a fact that raises the question of a link between David's loan and the cousin's entry.[57] At least one other instance of an artist's donating funds (as well as a painting, in this case) to a religious house is known, that of Rogier van der Weyden to the Carthusian's motherhouse at

Hérinnes, where Cornelis, his son, was a monk.[58] In David's case, however, as the money was clearly a loan and not a dowry paid to the convent on the occasion of the cousin's entering, as was customary at the time, no particular conclusion may be drawn in terms of cause and effect.

The presence of the portraits of David and his wife in the painting, therefore, may have less to do with any specific link to the convent than with more general themes of identity, that is, spiritual identity as devout followers of the Virgin and of the intercessory saints, social identity as having achieved an elevated status within the Bruges community, and corporate identity within the tradition of painter-donors in Netherlandish art.

Through association with this holy assemblage as the artist who created by his God-given skills such a masterly group portrait, David may have hoped to ensure his salvation, as well as that of his wife. Considered from a more practical point of view, this type of presentation might also be understood in terms of further self-promotion at a time when David was at the peak of his career: he had moved up through the ranks of the painters' guild, serving as second *vinder* in 1488 and subsequently as first *vinder* in 1495–96 and 1498–99, as well as dean of the guild in 1501. Having completed the *Justice of Cambyses* panels in 1498, David had gone on to receive his share of important commissions, including the large Italianate Cervara Altarpiece of 1506 (Figure 176) for Vincenzo Sauli, the sumptuous Baptism Triptych (Figure 213) for Jan de Trompes executed between 1502 and 1508, and important altarpieces for Richard de Visch van de Capelle and Canon Bernardinus de Salviatis, also produced in the first decade of the sixteenth century. The painting of this altarpiece and its donation by David to the church of the Convent of Sion might be seen, from the point of view of a savvy businessman, as helping to sustain the artist's position as Bruges's premier painter with close connections to wealthy local and foreign merchants and to the court (through the gift of the wood for the altarpiece by the wife of Lambijn, called "Packette" at court). After all, the

convent counted among its members the daughters of the leading families of Bruges and in addition enjoyed the patronage of its most affluent citizens, such as members of the Italian community, the Adornes and de la Costa families.[59] By his donation for the most revered place in the church, the high altar, David placed himself alongside the elite of society as an equal and, by the demonstration of his supreme abilities, advertised his skills as the painter of choice for future commissions.

David's ingenuous self-portraiture in the company of holy personages in the *Virgin among Virgins* draws upon two distinct but parallel traditions. In one, artists portray themselves as observers or participants at a sacred event.[60] A phenomenon that started with more subtle references to the artist, such as Jan van Eyck's barely visible bodily presence (though clear signatory evidence) in the painting of Giovanni Arnolfini and his wife as a witness to their double portrait in the National Gallery, London, or possibly along with his brother Hubert among the elect in the Adoration of the Lamb in the Ghent Altarpiece, accelerated with examples of Hans Memling in Bruges as a spectator within his religious scenes.[61] David apparently followed this pattern in his own paintings,[62] though never in the dual role of patron and painter until his *Virgin among Virgins.*

A parallel tradition more closely links the self-portrait of the artist with the maker of the work in question. Painters have long been associated with their patron saint, Saint Luke, particularly in representations of his drawing or painting the portrait of the Virgin.[63] At the core of this tradition are oral and written legends of paintings, such as one concerning the *Cambrai Madonna,* where the work was believed to be an actual likeness of the Virgin and Child painted by Saint Luke himself.[64] The distinctive, portraitlike physiognomies of the saint in works of the fifteenth and sixteenth centuries have perpetuated this legend to the extent that we readily accept the personage of Rogier van der Weyden as Saint Luke in his *Saint Luke Drawing the Virgin.*[65] The fact that Saint Luke was the patron saint of the guild of painters supports a hypothesis that his painted image

84. IRR detail of Saints Godelieve, Cecelia, and Barbara in Figure 79

would mirror that of a specific guild member or of the artist of the given painting, and the representation of other self-portraits within paintings of Saint Luke by Dieric Bouts, Hugo van der Goes, Dirk Baegert, and Jan Gossaert has also been suggested.[66] Certain artists further identified themselves as donors as well as painters of their works. Among these are possibly Rogier van der Weyden's *Saint Luke Drawing the Virgin,* probably given for the decoration of the painters' guild chapel of Saint Eloy in the Church of Saint Gudule (today the Cathedral of Saint Michael); Simon Marmion's painting, presumably a Saint Luke, for the high altar of Notre Dame de Valenciennes;[67] and Marten van Heemskerck's *Saint Luke* (where

the artist is depicted as Poetry inspiring Saint Luke) for the Haarlem painters' guild.[68]

In the *Virgin among Virgins* the artist is presented as donor, as observer, and as maker, declaring his privileged position like that of Saint Luke as the official portrait painter of the assembled Virgin, Child and female saints, and offering his product as his best work. But here David has deliberately used this painting as a replacement for the more standard self-conscious evaluation of his profession, as we see in *Saint Luke Drawing the Virgin.* Instead, as Cennini advocated, David shows himself able to pursue his profession as a gentleman, well dressed and comfortable among the elite of society.[69] As such, the artist presents us with a new phase of his self-awareness, where Jan van Eyck's famous motto *Als ich kan* is replaced by the featured portrait of the artist in a new, boldly self-confident demeanor.

David's intentions were quite deliberate and he emphasized his achievement—even singled himself out in a very dramatic way, as we shall see—by manipulating the lighting scheme of the composition to suit his purpose. The subtle means by which he guaranteed this intended outcome are made clear in the details of the painting's technique and execution.

First, it is important to review the state of the painting, which has altered considerably over time. Already in the 1950s open debates in the Rouen newspapers discussed a "suspect opacity" and the alarming condition of the blue and green draperies of the figures, which had previously undergone substantial restorations.[70] More recent study of the painting through infrared reflectography has revealed a further significant and irreversible change.[71] The background of the work has darkened, completely obscuring the original millefleurs tapestry hanging behind the figures (Figure 21),[72] a feature of local Bruges production that may have brightened the somber tone of the scene and suggested the traditional setting of a *hortus conclusus,* or enclosed garden, for the assembled virgins, denoting their purity. In visual effect it may have matched the millefleurs tapestries hanging behind figures in other paintings of David's design, the *Marriage at Cana* (Musée du Louvre, Paris) and the Virgin and Child and Saints Jerome and Benedict in the Cervara Altarpiece (Figure 176).[73] A hint of the plan for the millefleurs tapestry background is perhaps already evident in a preparatory study for a female figure, probably a saint, that I have suggested is linked to the *Virgin among Virgins* (Figure 22).[74] Though this half-length study was first sketched in black chalk and then gone over in a more finished manner with metalpoint, the flowers of the background are in metalpoint alone, added in the ultimate stage of the drawing process as David considered the specific use of the study.

After a series of preliminary drawings on paper, of which little remains (Figures 7, 19, and 22, as discussed

in chapter 1), David initiated the design directly on the prepared panel; this process included the placement of the figures and their draperies with his sketching tool, probably black chalk.[75] This is most clearly evident in the pale draperies of the angels (Figures 81 and 82), where the freedom and spontaneity of the drawing are readily apparent. David must have made use of certain patterns, for some of the figures are repeated from previous designs. The Saint Barbara bears a very close resemblance in facial type and pose to the Saint Barbara in the London *Virgin and Child with Saints and a Donor* of about 1506–8, for example. The figure of the Virgin, in particular, repeats a pattern that was used previously in the London painting—one that was developed even earlier for the 1506 Cervara Altarpiece. That a high degree of pattern duplication was already in use at this point in David's workshop has been demonstrated by Jean Wilson, who showed that this particular pattern for the Virgin or the Virgin and Child was an

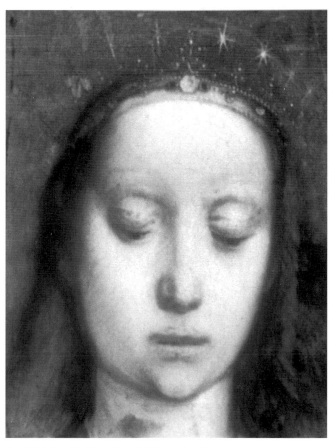

85. IRR detail of head of the Virgin in Figure 79

86. Detail of head of Gerard David in Figure 79

87. IRR detail of head of Gerard David in Figure 79

often repeated one among David's workshop assistants and close followers.[76]

This preliminary sketch on the panel was developed further with brush and a black pigment, employed for a different purpose than previously in his paintings. Whereas in the earlier *Justice of Cambyses* panels, as mentioned above, David used the brush in a second stage of the underdrawing to correct the initial sketch in black chalk and to add suggestions for the volume of forms, generally with a certain precision through fine lines (for example, Figures 74 and 76), here, in the *Virgin among Virgins* the strokes of the brush are much broader, similar to the application of a wash drawing. The purpose of those brush applications was specifically to describe areas of light and shade in the figures by a monochrome undermodeling in a carefully worked out scheme to be followed in the upper paint layers. In the draperies, particularly those of Saint Catherine (Figure 83), David used a wide brush to indicate the deepest areas of shadow with thick, dark strokes and narrower parallel hatching to mark the boundaries of shallower folds. Broader areas of halftone shadows toward the back of Catherine's draperies are sug-

gested by a wash underdrawing that clearly demonstrates a newly developed feature of David's technique. Some of this wash underdrawing appears to be located not directly on the ground preparation, but in the intermediate paint layers, providing for the system of volume and shade in what approximates an undermodeling.

The dramatic, seemingly theatrical effects in the *Virgin among Virgins* necessitated a careful plan for the fall of light on the faces of the saints from right to left across the painting. To achieve this, the underdrawing appears to have been carried out with a relatively dry brush, and very broadly worked in. Especially striking is the underdrawing in the faces of Saints Godelieve, Cecilia, and Barbara—its deliberately rough execution belying the subtle blending of the flesh tones on the surface of the painting (compare Figures 79 and 84). By contrast, the head of the Virgin is modeled in softer halftones along the left side of the face, preparing for a more broadly lit visage in the upper paint layers at the center of the composition (compare Figure 85).

Finally, in keeping with David's intention of asserting his presence, but in very subtle ways through lighting effects rather than through a prominent position within the composition, he produced his self-portrait in the most detailed manner of all the heads (compare Figures 86 and 87). The darkened background has significantly obscured the lighting scheme by which David planned to feature his own image. In rediscovering what visual effects he originally intended, we can partially reconstruct his method of achieving them through both traditional and rather revolutionary means. The careful brush underdrawing explicitly marks the details of the face and hair, and, through meticulous parallel hatching along the cheek as well as broader, more fully blended dry brushstrokes, works out the nuances of the volumes and shading of the head. In order to reinforce the spotlighted effect upon his likeness, David painted a deep shadow behind his self-portrait (just as one finds in contemporary independent portraits), which is now masked by the darkened paint in this area. Although he gave appropriate prominence to the Virgin and Child in a carefully balanced and symmetrical composition, and showed his uncompromising devotion by directing his gaze toward them, David guaranteed his position and self-reference in a subtle way through lighting effects. Only the natural occurrence of changes over time due to the artist's technique has considerably masked this bold plan.

David's use of underdrawing as undermodeling has until now been a technique thought to have been introduced in northern painting by later artists, such as Lucas van Leyden, particularly as revealed in his *Last Judgment* altarpiece of 1526–27.[77] David's *Virgin among Virgins* of almost twenty years earlier raises the question of the impetus for the appearance of this phenomenon in David's work, especially since it is not part of the standard working methods of his immediate predecessors, such as Hans Memling,[78] or even of his contemporaries, such as Joos van Cleve.[79] The evolution from creating shading by hatching to doing so by applied washes begins to occur in Netherlandish drawing practice certainly early in the sixteenth century. Jan Gossaert, Dirck Vellert, Bernaert van Orley, and Pieter Coeck van Aelst made pen and brush drawings with added wash for designs for stained glass, tapestries, and altarpieces.[80] But these are all from a period at the earliest about 1515 to the 1520s, nearly a decade or more after David's use of wash for his underdrawing of the *Virgin among Virgins.*

Of course, the practice of using broad washes for a monochrome undermodeling in paintings to define the volume and lighting of figures was already apparent earlier in Italy, and is particularly associated with Leonardo da Vinci and his followers in both Lombardy and Florence (for example, Fra Bartolomeo and Filippino Lippi, as well as the Milanese painters, among them Boltraffio, Giampietrino, Cesare da Sesto, and Luini).[81] Cennino Cennini, in fact, describes the procedure in his *Il libro dell'arte* in chapter 10: "And then shade the folds with washes of ink; that is, as much water as a nutshell would hold, with two drops of ink in it; and shade with a brush made of miniver tails, rather blunt, and almost dry."[82]

This raises the question of David's firsthand knowledge of Italian models. Although there is no specific record that David ever traveled to Italy, between 1503 and 1507 few documents mention David's presence in the North, and some have speculated that he may have ventured south at this time.[83] As will be discussed in subsequent chapters, David appears to have had advanced knowledge about the site for the altarpiece commissioned by Vincenzo Sauli for the Benedictine abbey at Cervara, near Genoa, and, furthermore, to have been well aware of certain models and compositions in Lombard painting, especially Milanese works, which he assimilated into his paintings.[84] If David did sojourn in Italy, specifically in Liguria (the eventual site of the Cervara Altarpiece) and neighboring Lombardy, he would have had the opportunity to acquaint himself with the working methods of north Italian artists even before taking on his Lombard assistant Ambrosius Benson, which could not have been until about 1518, when the Italian first registered as a citizen in Bruges, and which thus postdates the *Virgin among Virgins* by nearly a decade. In any event, recent investigations into the working methods of Benson have indicated that the Italian

88. Leonardo da Vinci, *Adoration of the Magi*, ca. 1481–82. Tempera and oil on wood, 243 × 246 cm. Uffizi, Florence (Photo Scala/Art Resource, NY)

learned and adopted the contemporary underdrawing practices of northern artists (black-chalk underdrawing with parallel and cross-hatching for the suggestion of modeling within figures)[85] rather than continuing in the methods of his earlier Italian apprenticeship.

The use of underdrawing as a tonal wash to map out areas of light and shade is evident in celebrated examples by Leonardo da Vinci, whose *Saint Jerome* (Pinacoteca Vaticana, Rome) and *Adoration of the Magi* (Figures 88 and 89) were left unfinished, the latter in the house of Leonardo's friend Amerigo Benci in Florence when he departed for Milan in 1482.[86] Even more intriguing in terms of what David may have seen in Lombardy is Leonardo's *Virgin of the Rocks*

begun for a chapel of the Confraternity of the Immaculate Conception in the Church of San Francesco in Milan in 1483, but left unfinished in 1490. Owing to various extenuating circumstances, it was not completed until 1506–8, when Leonardo returned to Milan, at which point a copy was also produced.[87] We know that Leonardo's technique of building up paint layers with monochrome washes was highly influential among his followers. Filippino Lippi, to name just one, appears to have been especially taken by Leonardo's technique, so much so that he adopted the use of monochrome washes in the underdrawings of his late paintings, as in the Altarpiece of Saint Sebastian, dated 1503, which he made for the Genoese church of San Teodoro.[88] As

89. Detail of Figure 88

other recent studies have shown, Leonardo's Milanese followers, namely Giampietrino and Boltraffio, also adopted his technique of dark underpainting for their works.[89]

Although it is conceivable that David traveled to Florence to see Leonardo's *Adoration of the Magi,* his acquaintance with wash underdrawing as a technical feature of paintings might better be explained from contact in Milan with Leonardo's art (in particular, perhaps the unfinished *Virgin of the Rocks*) and that of his followers, who were steeped in his style and technique from the periods that Leonardo spent there (1482–99 and again in 1506–13). Could David have visited Milan in the period 1506–8 (after the completion of the Cervara Altarpiece), when Leonardo was again in residence there, and learned of the Italian master's technique then?

As the discussion in chapter 4 concerning the details of technique of the Cervara Altarpiece of 1506 shows, David seems to have assimilated and incorporated the new feature of wash undermodeling subsequent to the work on his great Italian altarpiece, in which he used the brush only tentatively to implement a kind of undermodeling (see Figures 186 and 189). Furthermore, when David did incorporate this aspect of Italianate technique in his *Virgin among Virgins,* he did so without fully understanding it. While Leonardo and his pupils used a dark brown or brownish-gray application, "both as a relatively opaque, flat blocking-in of the composition and as a more elaborated undermodeling of form,"[90] David used a blackish wash solely for modeling purposes, proceeding to work up the paint layers in his usual manner (as far as it can be determined by the surface of the *Virgin among Virgins*).

David's most obvious use of the Italian style of wash underdrawing for mapping out the system of light and shade to be employed in a painting was short-lived and never again appears to the extent that it does in the *Virgin among Virgins.*[91] This suggests that the technique was more of a passing interest and not one that David fully mastered as an integral part of his working method.

Though there are consistencies to be found in David's approach to his two documented works, the marked variations in underdrawing function and style in the *Justice of Cambyses* panels and the *Virgin among Virgins* caution anyone who would claim to characterize the artist's technique by these paintings alone. Differences in size and purpose are only two of the factors that account for the considerable changes in David's working technique from one to the other project. These works may be considered as the poles of David's style and thus serve well as indicators of developments in the artist's working method over a decade in which he was open to a variety of new influences in the North and perhaps also in Italy. In this way, David expressed his progressive, even innovative tendencies in a period of transition.

1. For various approaches to the attribution of paintings by Gerard David, see Weale 1863c, 1886a, 1866b, 1866–70b, 1895; Bodenhausen 1905; Boon 1946; Friedländer 1967–76, vol.VIb (1971); Scillia 1975; Mundy 1980a; and van Miegroet 1989.

2. Folie 1963, pp. 183–88, 230–32.

3. Bruges, City Archives, Stadsrekeningen for Sept. 1, 1487–Feb. 1488, fols. 177r, 126v; published in Weale 1863c, p. 230; Bodenhausen 1905, pp. 127–31; Folie 1963, p. 231; Janssens de Bisthoven 1981, p. 123; and van Miegroet 1989, p. 332, doc. 2; on the question of the addition of David's name to this document, see Van der Velden 1995b, pp. 44–45.

4. Bruges, City Archives, Stadsrekeningen for Jan. 1, 1491–Aug. 31, 1491, fol. 161r; published in Weale 1863c, p. 230; Bodenhausen 1905, p. 129; Folie 1963, p. 231; Janssens de Bisthoven 1981, p. 123; van Miegroet 1989, p. 333, doc. 5; and Van der Velden 1995b, p. 46.

5. Bruges, City Archives, Stadsrekeningen for Sept. 2, 1498–Sept. 2, 1499, fols. 66r–67v. published in Weale 1863c, p. 230; Bodenhausen 1905, p. 129; Folie 1963, p. 231; Janssens de Bisthoven 1981, pp. 123–24; van Miegroet 1989, p. 334, doc. 9; and Van der Velden 1995b, pp. 48–49. Jan de Trompes, of course, is the same man who commissioned another important work from Gerard David, the Baptism Triptych (discussed in chap. 5).

6. Weale interpreted all three documents as pertaining to the Justice panels. He suggested that in the case of the first document, the clerk was probably not only uninformed about the payee (David's name was added later), but also misunderstood the subject of the painting (listed as a Last Judgment). Siret (1869) suggested that the subject was not a Last Judgment, but a Judgment and Condemnation of Christ. Friedländer (1903) noted the lack of clarity in the documents, but with the aid of the stylistic evidence and comparisons, supported the indisputable attribution of the Justice panels to David. Hulin de Loo (1902) and Bodenhausen (1905) reviewed the documents, the former declaring only the third one to be associated with the Justice panels. Friedländer concurred with this interpretation. Over the question of the reference in the documents to only one, instead of two, panels, Hulin de Loo suggested that the two panels originally hung as a diptych (i.e., as one unit), a fact that more recently has been confirmed by physical evidence (Janssens de Bisthoven 1981). He therefore maintained that the 1498 listing of one completed panel would mean the two paintings together, which were then dated only on the Arrest scene. Bodenhausen (1905, pp. 127–31) remained skeptical about the relationship of the documents with the panels. More recently, most scholars (including Van der Velden 1995b, pp. 40–48) concur with Folie (1963) and Strubbe (1956) in considering that only the third document may reasonably be linked with the Justice panels. Only van Miegroet (1989, pp. 145–46) has returned to the original arguments of Weale, that all three documents relate to the Justice panels.

7. Van der Velden 1995a, pp. 5–7, and Harbison 1976, pp. 51–64.

8. Van der Velden 1995b, p. 44, nn. 10, 12.

9. Siret 1869, pp. 51–53; and letter to the author of April 13, 1998, and further discussion forthcoming in an essay with Ludo Vandamme, "Cultuur en mentaliteit in het 16de-eeuwse Brugge," in Memling to Pourbus, exh. cat., Memling Museum (Bruges, 1998).

10. See Van der Velden 1995a, pp. 5–7.

11. Ainsworth 1997b.

12. See Appendix B.

13. Van der Velden, 1995b.

14. Ibid., pp. 48–49.

15. See F. Van Molle, "La Justice d'Othon de Thierry Bouts, Sources d'archives," Bulletin Institut Royal du Patrimoine Artistique I (1958), p. 9.

16. See Georg Troescher, "Weltgerichtsbilder in Rathausern und Gerichtsstatten," Wallraf-Richartz Jahrbuch 11 (1939), pp. 139–214; Van der Velden 1995a, pp. 5–39; Harbison 1976, pp. 56–62.

17. Van der Velden 1995a, pp. 5–34, esp. 8–9.

18. Weale cites the fact that David's first known commission in Bruges was to paint the shutters or guardrails on Jean de Gros's mansion, which served as Maximilian's house of detention (Weale 1895, p. 8).

19. Weale 1863c, pp. 223, 226.

20. Van Miegroet 1988, pp.116–33, and van Miegroet 1989, pp. 143–75.

21. Van der Velden 1995b, pp. 50–51.

22. Strubbe 1981, p. 122.

23. I am very grateful to Dirk De Vos for permission to study the Justice of Cambyses panels with infrared reflectography in March 1987. In this endeavor, I was assisted by Ronda Kasl and Molly Faries, who visited during the examination. I also thank Micheline Comblen-Sonkes and Liliane Maschelein-Kleiner, who allowed me to study the X-radiographs of the paintings in March of 1988 at the Institut Royal du Patrimoine Artistique, Brussels.

24. Mundy 1980b, pp. 122–25, and Ainsworth 1988, pp. 528–30.

25. Van Miegroet 1989, p. 322. Medium correctly identified in Ainsworth 1988, pp. 528–30, Sander 1995, p. 203, and Ainsworth, chap. 1 in this book.

26. Marijnissen and Van de Voorde 1986, 1, pp. 67–70.

27. Some examples are the Marriage of the Virgin (Philadelphia Art Museum), Augustus and the Tiburtine Sibyl (Städelsches Kunstinstitut, Frankfurt), and The Raising of Lazarus (Instituto Nacional de Bellas Artes, Mexico City). For the most recent bibliography on this master and a thorough discussion of the painting in Frankfurt from which he is named, see Sander 1993, pp. 66–86.

28. Duclos 1910, pp. 348–49; Weale 1862, p. 55; Janssens de Bisthoven 1981, p. 105; van Miegroet 1989, pp. 156–57.

29. There is no evidence that the design of this figure was transferred by pouncing, as has been published by Périer-d'Ieteren (1984, pp. 40–41, and 1985, p. 40, fig. 66, which is printed upside down). The specific area where pouncing is identified is simply the painting of the nap of

the fabric of the costume, which appears in the painting as raised black dots in the shadow areas and as raised white dots in the areas hit by direct light.

30. I am grateful to Noël Geirnaert, archivist of the Bruges City Archives, for information concerning the election of the aldermen and lists of the elected members from 1488 to 1498 (letter to the author, April 13, 1998).

31. I have excluded 1498 from consideration as that is the year inscribed on the *Arrest,* and the election would have taken place on Sept. 2 of that year, leaving relatively little time for the repainting of a presumably large number of heads.

32. Sept. 2, 1496 (*RW, 1468–1501,* fol. 232v.): Jan van Claehout, burgomaster; Jan van Nieuwenhove, alderman; Frans Ridsaert, alderman; Jan d'Hont, drapier; Lieven van Viven, alderman; Servaas vander Soaghe, alderman; Antoon Voet, alderman; Frans Parmentier, alderman; Joost van Doorle, alderman; Adriaan Basin, alderman; Antoon Janszuene, alderman; Jacob de Vos, alderman; Jan vander Haghe, alderman; Adriaan Drabbe, and Jacob Donckere, treasurers.

1497, Sept. 2 (*RW, 1468–1501.* f. 243 v.): Joost vander Zype, burgomaster; Joost de Deckere, alderman; Pieter van Riemslede, alderman; Mattheus de Brouckere, alderman; Adriaan Basin, alderman; Servaas vander Soaghe, alderman; Silvester Vanden Berghe, alderman; Anton Voet, alderman; Frans Parmentier, alderman; Karl Lopin, alderman; Joost van Doorle, alderman; Frans Wyts, alderman; Jan de Lannoy, alderman; Adriaan Drabbe and Jacob de Donckeere, treasurers.

33. Weale 1866–70a, pp. 46–53.

34. Duclos 1910, pp. 291, 396, 523.

35. On the inventory of the convent art objects see Weale 1866–70a, pp. 51–53, 76–93, 214–30; and Weale 1864–65, p. 289; also a 17th-century document in Weale 1864–65, p. 294; van Miegroet 1989, p. 350, doc. 70. Originally undecorated, the wings added to the painting apparently depicted the Birth of the Virgin and the Death of the Virgin (see Weale 1864–65, pp. 289–90).

36. Correction by Lorne Campbell in 1991, p. 624.

37. Van Miegroet 1989, p. 354, doc. 70. The suggestion that the wings were adorned after 1537 with depictions of the Birth of the Virgin and the Death of the Virgin is made by Weale (1864–65, pp. 289–90).

38. Emond 1961; Peter-Thomas Rohrbach, O.C.D., *Journey to Carith: The Story of the Carmelite Order* (Garden City, N.Y., 1966), pp. 46 ff.; van Miegroet 1989, p. 222; Scillia 1975, p. 33.

39. *Carmel* 1927, p. 188.

40. On the tradition of music-making angels flanking the Virgin, see Ainsworth 1996, pp. 149–58.

41. Mundy 1981–82, pp. 211–22, esp. p. 216.

42. Quoted in Smits 1933, p. 154 and n. 4; cited in Mundy 1981–82, p. 216, n. 24.

43. *Carmel* 1927, p. 217.

44. Kirschbaum and Braunfels 1968–76, vol. V, cols. 58–63, 217, 232–236, and 455–463; vol. VI, cols. 416–417; and vol. VII, cols. 415–420, van Miegroet 1989, p. 222.

45. Lawrence 1989, p. 216.

46. See Van Belle 1981, pp. 10–95, esp. p. 28; *Tussen heks en heilige,* exh. cat. (Nijmegen, 1985), pp. 94–95, esp. p. 99.

47. Van Belle 1981, p. 48.

48. Weale 1871, pp. 47, 49.

49. Ibid., p. 48.

50. For a thorough discussion of the variants see Lorne Campbell, *The Early Flemish Pictures in the Collection of Her Majesty the Queen* (Cambridge, 1985), no. 32, pp. 47–51.

51. Weale 1895, pp. 27–32.

52. On the influence of the *Bruges Madonna* on local art, see esp. Ewing 1978, pp. 77–105.

53. This speculation was made by Friedländer 1967–76, Vol. VIb (1971), pp. 79–80. It is not so far-fetched a notion when one considers the attempted effect of realism in portraiture and also the tradition of using contemporary figures as the models for saints or for the Virgin; for example, Jean Fouquet's Virgin in the Antwerp *Virgin and Child* is possibly taken from the likeness of the mistress of Charles VII, Agnès Sorel, and in Jan Gossaert's *Virgin and Child* (MMA). According to Van Mander's account, the Virgin is modeled after Anna van Bergen, lady of Veere. In David's Nativity Triptych (Figure 200) the donors are disguised as Saints Anthony and Catherine (see chap. 5 in this book).

54. Weale's archival work on the Convent of Sion, its members, families, and patronage, demonstrates an association with the upper classes of Bruges: the nuns were daughters of knights and of the elite members of the "conseil de Flandre à Grand" (1866–70a, p. 52, n. 15; p. 53, n. 21; p. 87, n. 55); van Miegroet 1989, p. 221.

55. Except for Bodenhausen (1905, p. 163), who suggested that the woman depicted is "the wife of Lambijn," who donated the wood for the altarpiece, and that David's wife instead appears in the guise of Saint Catherine, it is generally accepted that the female donor is David's wife, Cornelia Cnoop. See Ainsworth 1989a, p. 10; van Miegroet 1989, p. 354; and chap. 1 in this book. David's self-portrait is affirmed by the likeness identified as David in the *Arras Codex* (Arras, Bibliothèque Municipale, MS. 266, fol. 277), which itself is modeled on the Rouen likeness. There is not, however, a direct relationship between the two likenesses through the vehicle of a pounced cartoon, as was suggested by Périer-d'Ieteren (1982, p. 82).

56. Weale 1864–65, p. 293; van Miegroet 1989, p. 348, doc. 57.

57. Anne was the third daughter of Pierre de Chantraines and Louise van Stakenburg. See Walle de Ghelcke 1950, p. 159.

58. Elisabeth Dhanens, *Rogier van der Weyden, Revisie van de documenten: Verhandelingen van de koninklijke Academie voor wetenschappen, letteren en schone kunsten van België, klasse der schonen kunsten* 57, no. 59 (1995), pp. 80, 119, 121.

59. Weale 1871, pp. 52–53, nn. 15–21.

60. Contemporary with David's *Virgin among Virgins* are recognizable self-portraits of Dürer within his own works: the *Feast of the Rose-Garlands,* produced in Venice in 1508; the *Martyrdom of the Ten Thousand,* also of 1508; the 1509 *Assumption of the Virgin;* and the 1511 *Adoration of the Holy Trinity.* For these and other examples, see Ring 1913, pp. 101–23; Joseph Leo Koerner, *The Moment of Self-Portraiture in German Renaissance Art* (Chicago and London, 1993), pp. 106–14;

Günter Schweikhart, "Das Selbstbildnis im 15. Jahrhundert," in Poeschke 1993, pp. 11–39, esp. pp. 14–17; and Wilson 1995b, pp. 149–58. Precedent-setting earlier 15th-century Italian examples abound, such as the celebrated cases of Domenico Ghirlandaio's appearing in the *Expulsion of Joachim from the Temple* in his 1485–90 frescoes for the choir of Santa Maria Novella, and of Benozzo Gozzoli in his *Journey of the Magi* of 1459 in the chapel of the Palazzo Medici-Riccardi in Florence, and of the portraits of Luca Signorelli and his teacher Fra Angelico in the *Preaching of the Antichrist* fresco in Orvieto, among others.

61. The convincing identification of Giovanni di Nicolau Arnolfini and his wife rather than Giovanni di Arrigo Arnolfini and Giovanna Cenami in the National Gallery, London, painting was discussed by Lorne Campbell at the Van Eyck Symposium, National Gallery, London, March 13, 1998. For a list of the examples purportedly including Memling's portrait and comments on the reliability of this identification, see De Vos 1994a, pp. 352–54, and Lobelle-Caluwé 1997, pp. 43–53.

62. The most frequently cited identifications of David are the figure looking out at the viewer at the far left and the one to the right of the column in the *Adoration of the Magi* (Musées Royaux des Beaux-Arts, Brussels), and the one at the far left edge of the *Arrest of Sisamnes* (Groeningemuseum, Bruges), all of which bear a resemblance to each other and to the established portrait of David in the *Virgin among Virgins*. See Destrée 1913b, pp. 153–57; Sulzberger 1955a, pp. 176–78; Dirk De Vos, "Het Versamelaarsmerk van Peter Stevens (1590–1668) en diens aantekeningen over 15de-eeuwse Brugse Meesters," *Jaarboek 1982 Stad Brugge Stedelijke Musea* (1983), pp. 253–60.

63. See Dorothee Klein, *St. Lukas als Maler der Maria: Ikonographie der Lukas-Madonna* (Berlin, 1933); Colin T. Eisler, *New England Museums,* Les Primitifs flamands, I: *Corpus de la peinture des anciens Pays-Bas méridionaux au quinzième siècle,* 4 (Brussels, 1961), pp. 71–93; Gisela Kraut, *Lukas malt die Madonna: Zeugnisse zum künstlerischen Selbstverständnisse in der Malerei* (Worms, 1986); Jean Owens Schaefer, "St. Luke as Painter: From Saint to Artisan to Artist," in *Colloque international,* vol. I of *Artists, artisans, et production artistique au Moyen Âge,* Xavier Barral I Altet, ed. (Paris, 1986), pp. 413–27; J. Rivère, "Réflexions sur les *Saint Luc peignant la Vierge* flamands: De Campin à Van Heemskerck," *Jaarboek van het koninklijk Museum voor schone kunsten* (Antwerp, 1987), pp. 25–92; Belting and Kruse 1994, pp. 29–32, 161, cat. no. 61; and Purtle 1997.

64. C. Thelliez, *La Merveilleuse Image de Notre-Dame de Grâce de Cambrai: Cinq siècles d'histoire* (Cambrai, 1951); and A. Begne, *Histoire de Notre-Dame de Grâce, patronne du diocèse de Cambrai* (Cambrai, 1910); N. Veronee-Verhaegen, "*La Vierge embrassant l'Enfant Jésus* par Dieric Bouts," *Bulletin Musées royaux des beaux-arts de Belgique* 3–4 (1968), pp. 5–10; Ainsworth 1993b.

65. On the identification of Rogier van der Weyden as Saint Luke, see Erwin Panofsky, "Facies illa Rogeri maximi pictoris," in *Late Classical and Medieval Studies in Honor of Albert Mathias Friend, Jr.,* Kurt Weitzmann, ed. (Princeton, 1955), pp. 392–400, esp. pp. 397 ff.; and Borchert 1997,

pp. 61–87; Faries 1998, pp. 97–98; Kann 1997, pp. 15–22; MacBeth and Spronk 1997, pp. 110–11; and Marrow 1997, pp. 54–55.

66. For these identifications, see Borchert 1997, pp. 61–87; Faries 1998, pp. 97–98; Kann 1997, pp. 15–22; MacBeth and Spronk 1997, pp. 110–11; and Marrow 1997, pp. 54–55.

67. Albert Châtelet and Dominique Vanwynsberghe, "Simon Marmion," in *Valenciennes aux XIVe et XVe siècles: Art et Histoire* (Valenciennes, 1966), esp. pp. 155, 164. The apparent later change in function from altarpiece to Marmion's epitaph makes an interesting parallel with David's *Virgin among Virgins* altarpiece; see Faries 1998, p. 98, n. 55.

68. See Faries 1998, p. 98.

69. Cennini 1960, vol. 145, p. 91.

70. Van Miegroet 1989, p. 298.

71. This painting was studied in 1986 with the assistance of Katie Crawford Luber and permission of François Bergot. The preliminary results were first published in Ainsworth 1989b, pp. 25–27, 30; Ainsworth 1989a, pp. 127–30; 1993, p. 19.

72. Although in the case of the *Virgin among Virgins,* it is not yet known what pigments and material transformations are responsible for the darkening of the background, in other works by David an irreversible color and tonal change in a similar area has been caused by a darkened mixture of red lake and azurite. In the *Virgin and Child with Saints and a Donor* and the *Virgin and Child with Saint Anne,* portions of the multicolored brocade cloth of honor behind the Virgin in each work have changed to a flat, dark tone. See Metzger 1992, pp. 59–63, and Wyld, Roy, and Smith 1979, pp. 52, 60. No X-radiograph of the Rouen *Virgin among Virgins* has been made available to me for study.

73. For the local Bruges production of millefleurs tapestries, see Delmarcel and Duverger 1987, esp. pp. 107–11.

74. Ainsworth 1989b, pp. 9–10 and chap. 1.

75. The underdrawing in the *Virgin among Virgins* was first discussed by the author in Ainsworth 1989a, pp. 127–30, and in Ainsworth 1989b, pp. 25–30.

76. Wilson 1991, pp. 191–206; Wilson 1998, pp. 93–103.

77. Jan-Piet Filedt Kok, "Underdrawings and Other Technical Aspects in the Paintings of Lucas van Leyden," *Nederlands kunsthistorisch jaarboek* 29 (1978), pp. 1–184, esp. pp. 97–99.

78. Ainsworth 1994b, pp. 78–81, and Périer-d'Ieteren 1994, pp. 67–77.

79. Ainsworth 1983, pp. 161–67.

80. See *Jan Gossaert genaamd Mabuse,* exh. cat. (Rotterdam and Bruges, 1965), cat. nos. 63, 66, and 67; N. Beets, "Dirck Jacobsz. Vellert, IV," *Oude Kunst* 22 (1912), pp. 133–52; and Ellen Konowitz, "The Roundel Series of Dirick Vellert," in T. Husband, *The Luminous Image: Painted Glass Roundels in the Lowlands, 1480–1560,* exh. cat., MMA (New York, 1995), pp. 142–57 (including most pertinent bibliography); Ainsworth 1982; G. Marlier, *La Renaissance flamande: Pieter Coeck d'Alost* (Brussels, 1966), e.g., figs. 231–254, 314–319.

81. See chap. 6 regarding introduction of washes to Leonardo's drawings in the 1480s series of the *Virgin and Child with the Cat.* See Keith and Roy 1996 and M. C.

Galassi, "Gilippino Lippi's Underdrawing: The Contribution of Infrared Reflectography," in *Le dessin sous-jacent et technologie de la peinture: Perspectives, Colloque XI* (1995), R. Van Schoute and H. Verougstraete, eds. (Louvain-la-Neuve, 1997), pp. 153–59.

82. Cennini 1960, p. 7.

83. Castelnovi 1952, p. 22–27; Hoogewerff 1953, pp. 72–73; Röthel 1956, pp. 361–65; Koch 1965, pp. 278–79; Castelfranchi Vegas 1984, p. 270; van Miegroet 1987, pp. 37–38; and van Miegroet 1989, pp. 217.

84. See chaps. 4, 5, and 6 passim, where works by Foppa and Bernardino de'Conti are discussed.

85. M. C. Garrido and Van Schoute, "Panneaux attribués à Ambroise Benson en provenance de Segouie," at Colloque XII, "L'Étude du dessin sous-jacent et de la technologie dans la peinture" (Bruges, Sept. 11–13, 1997; publication forthcoming 1999). The underdrawing in the Benson paintings studied so far does not contribute to the generally dark tone of the figures and especially the flesh tones, which seems to be an effect achieved in the paint layers alone. This description is also true of the one painting attributed to Benson,

namely the *Lamentation* in the MMA, Linsky collection (acc. no. 1982.60.23).

86. The painting later entered the collection of Don Antonio de' Medici (1621 inventory). On the details of the *Adoration of the Magi,* including a good bibliography, see Becherucci 1985, pp. 39–44; for a discussion of the technique and good illustrations of details of the *Adoration,* see Baldini 1991, pp. 22–37.

87. The first version is presumably the one in the Musée du Louvre, Paris, and the copy is in the National Gallery, London. For a succinct history of the painting and its copy, see Dunkerton et al. 1991, pp. 382–85. A brief discussion of the technique of the *Virgin of the Rocks* in London is found in Keith and Roy 1996, p. 14.

88. Galassi (see note 81), pp. 153–59.

89. Keith and Roy 1996.

90. Ibid., p. 14.

91. It is interesting to note that Lucas van Leyden's most dramatic use of this same technique some twenty years later in the Last Judgment Altarpiece was also short-lived. See note 77 above.

CHAPTER THREE

The Progress of Early Achievements:
David's Origins and First Phase in Bruges

It is known from two seventeenth-century sources—the report of Sanderus in 1642 and a transcription of the epitaph on David's tomb in the Onze-Lieve-Vrouwekerk[1]—that he came from Oudewater, a Dutch town near Gouda, but there is no further documentation of his early training or whereabouts until he was received into the painters' guild in Bruges as a master in 1484. Not far north of Oudewater is Haarlem, the city that Karel van Mander praised in his *Het Schilderboek* as the artistic center of the north Netherlands, attributing its prominence to the painters Aelbert van Ouwater, Dieric Bouts, and Geertgen tot Sint Jans. Theories that place David under the tutelage of any of these masters, especially Geertgen tot Sint Jans,[2] or otherwise establish him in Utrecht working early on with miniaturists there have remained controversial because of the lack of any verifiable documentation.[3] The conflicts in the northern territories due to the Iconoclasm (1566) and the Spanish invasion (1572–73) caused significant destruction to the artistic legacy of the region and have thwarted attempts to reconstruct the development of early Dutch art and, in turn, its effect on the formative years of Gerard David.

Nonetheless, a small group of paintings shows a blending of characteristics of the renowned north and south Netherlandish artists of the day—both manuscript illuminators and panel painters—as well as specific traits that can be recognized in David's later, documented works (specifically the *Justice of Cambyses*), thus allowing us to attribute certain works to the young David. Among these is his earliest-known painting, the *Crucifixion* of about 1475 in the Thyssen-Bornemisza Collection (Figure 90). Closely connected to a *Crucifixion* miniature in the Utrecht-produced *Hours of Catherine of Cleves* of about 1440 (MS. 945, fol. 66v, Pierpont Morgan Library, New York), it assimilates the group of soldiers and Jews at the lower right of the cross in the miniature.[4] This group, in particular the figure in the exotic striped-yellow costume of the foreground, may ultimately be derived from a lost prototype of a *Crucifixion* by Robert Campin. At the left, the motif of the collapsing Virgin supported by Saint John and another Mary, though Rogierian in its sensibility, was made popular through an engraving of about 1480 of the *Crucifixion* by the Master IAM of Zwolle. David's figures, with their ovoid faces and sharp, triangular noses—rather similar to types found in the work of Aelbert van Ouwater—point to the artistic center of Haarlem. Moreover, the cityscape in the background belies north Netherlandish origins; it is a reprise from Eyckian-inspired manuscript illuminations, such as those by the Utrecht Master of Evert van Soudenbalch of about 1460, whose influence may also be seen in a very similar cityscape in the background of the Metropolitan Museum's *Christ Carrying the Cross* of about 1470.[5] In rather disparaging terms, critics have called this assemblage of motifs in David's *Crucifixion* an outright pastiche. Rather, it is the successful arrangement of popular north Netherlandish motifs, which were probably circulated as drawings in model books—just the type of production that is typical of the early works of a young master. Some have identified the figure looking out from the far right edge of the painting as a self-portrait of David himself, announcing the initial achievement of his career.[6]

Similar figure types, as well as evidence of David's isocephalic arrangement of male figures later found

Detail of Figure 102

90. Gerard David, *Crucifixion*, ca. 1475. Oil on oak, 88 × 56 cm. Thyssen-Bornemisza Collection, Madrid (Photo © Museo Thyssen-Bornemisza, Madrid)

in the *Justice of Cambyses* panels, are apparent in the unusual triptych *Christ Nailed to the Cross* (Figures 91–93), the wings of which depict Pilate and the Jews, and Mary with Saint John and female mourners.[7] Here the pathetic Christ with his achingly human expression, showing the anguished certainty of his imminent death, calls to mind the Christ in David's later works, especially in the *Mocking of Christ* (Figure 5) or in the Berlin *Crucifixion*.[8] Although certain subsidiary figures in the centerpiece of this triptych are badly damaged, the side wings are in a

better state of preservation and reveal the characteristics of David's early manner, which is above all influenced by the works of contemporary north Netherlandish artists.

Developing from the figure types David had introduced in the Thyssen *Crucifixion*, those here—especially of the Virgin, Saint John, and the female mourners—are conceived with a certain geometric simplicity: overly large, ovoid heads, sharply delineated, triangular-shaped noses, and thin doll-like bodies covered with massive and sculptural draperies with deep folds. The distinctive north Netherlandish palette favors orange-reds, lime-greens, yellows, and warmer brownish hues. The flesh tones of the male figures of the left wing are modeled with broad brown shadows, which strike a sharp contrast to the adjacent pale zones. Certain incidental details—such as the dog sniffing the skull in the immediate foreground of *Christ Nailed to the Cross*, taken over from the Thyssen *Crucifixion*—early on establish David's acute observation of daily life in an attempt to interject a sense of realism into his paintings. The composition, however, appears to be more indebted to David's new acquaintance with models he encountered in the south Netherlands, namely the Saint Hippolytus Altarpiece of about 1475 by Dieric Bouts (with a left donor wing by Hugo van der Goes; Groeningemuseum, Bruges), which finds a more tightly cropped echo in another Hippolytus Altarpiece, by an anonymous master influenced by Hugo van der Goes (Museum of Fine Arts, Boston).[9] David also quotes from Jan van Eyck's *Crucifixion* (The Metropolitan Museum of Art) or drawings after it, from which he copied the noblemen on horseback beneath the cross at the right for the group at the back left of his *Christ Nailed to the Cross*.[10] This combination of features indicates an early date for the triptych, perhaps about 1480, before David arrived in Bruges.[11]

The working methods evident in the artist's early phase are related to what little is known at this point about the painting practice of his predecessors and contemporaries from the north Netherlands, for example, Geertgen tot Sint Jans and Dieric Bouts. Owing to Van Mander's account, only one work, namely the *Raising of Lazarus* in Berlin, can be securely attributed to the other major Haarlem painter of the time, Aelbert van Ouwater. Although the *Lazarus* does show pen or brush underdrawing,[12] less can be inferred about Ouwater's standard working methods from this one example than about those of Geertgen and Bouts. The favored drawing implement of the latter two artists (as was true generally of painters up until the last quarter of the fifteenth century) was brush and ink or a black pigment (as yet undetermined), although Geertgen

also employed black chalk to correct and amend his compositions.[13]

The three panels of David's *Christ Nailed to the Cross* triptych (Figures 91–93) show brush underdrawing with some evidence of the use of pen in the right wing of the *Female Mourners* (Figures 58, 95–98). There is no sign of a rough preliminary sketch in a dry medium, a distinctive characteristic of David's later works. Presumably David relied upon a drawing for the initial layout of the design, perhaps one similar to a lost silverpoint sketch depicting Christ nailed to the cross (last seen at a Sotheby's auction in 1958, Figure 94)[14] that has direct parallels with David's composition and is attributed to an anonymous south Netherlandish artist. Because of the poor condition of the central panel and the dark pigments used in the left panel, little of the underdrawing is visible, but where it can be seen, its execution is relatively loose and free with a certain spontaneity in the handling of the brush. In the torso of Christ and in the figure of one of the soldiers (Figures 95 and 96) David attempted to model the bodies with short, curved strokes and dashes. But the parallel hatching at this early stage tends to flatten the forms rather than to create convincing three-dimensional volumes. Interestingly, color notations (otherwise only noticed in the *Flaying of Sisamnes* of the paintings studied by David) appear on a few figures.[15] Color indications have also been found in the underdrawings of paintings by Dieric Bouts (see Figure 57) and Geertgen tot Sint Jans,[16] but so far they have seldom been revealed in the underdrawings of contemporary south Netherlandish paintings. David's use of them here is perhaps due to practices he learned in the north Netherlands during his early training.

The left and right wings of the triptych indicate a variation in approach to the preliminary underdrawing. The figure to the far left of the left panel (Figures 91 and 97) reveals two layers of brush underdrawing possibly separated by a thin imprimatura, which had not dried completely before the second drawing was applied. This caused the strokes to bead up into tiny pools of dark paint or ink in a number of places.[17] It

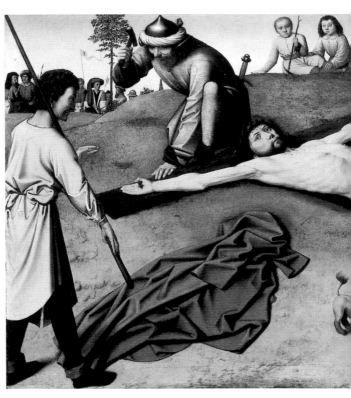

91. Gerard David, *Pilate and the Jews*, ca. 1480. Oil on wood, 45 × 42 cm. Koninklijk Museum voor Schone Kunsten, Antwerp

92. Gerard David, *Christ Nailed to the Cross*, ca. 1480. Oil on oak, 48.3 × 94 cm. National Gallery, London (Photo © National Gallery, London)

is a loose, free sketch providing only a rough layout of forms and a rudimentary indication of their modeling. In other words, it is a working drawing, not yet fully resolved.

In the *Female Mourners with Saint John* in the right wing, the underdrawing differs significantly from that in the other two panels (compare Figure 98 with Figures 95–97). It is a highly finished rendering with meticulous execution in brush working out the modeling of the figures in tightly controlled strokes of parallel hatching and crosshatching. This type of underdrawing is similar to that found in Dieric Bouts's *Justice of Emperor Otto III* panels, in which the brush is employed to broadly indicate the composition and in more precise strokes of parallel and crosshatching to suggest the modeling of individual forms (compare Figures 57 and 58).

An explanation for this striking contrast in the style of underdrawing between the left and center panels of the triptych and the right panel is that the latter probably copies preexisting workshop models.

As discussed in chapter 1 in regard to the *Virgin and Child with Four Saints* (Figures 37 and 59), this combination of a loose, free sketch and a meticulous, fixed underdrawing is a characteristic feature of David's working method. These workshop models are more likely to have existed for frequently depicted types (such as the Virgin, John, and the three Marys of the right wing) than for more unusual subjects, such as Pilate and the Jews on the left wing, which necessitated David's own spontaneous invention.

The model drawings of stock types used for the right wing of the London-Antwerp triptych were part of the standard paraphernalia of a workshop. Such examples are found in three extant sheets close in style to the figures in the *Mary and John with the Female Mourners*. These are drapery studies in pen and brown ink: two of a Mary Magdalene (one carrying an open book, and the other a closed book) on the same sheet in the British Museum (Figure 99) and a Mary Magdalene and a Saint Veronica in the Rijksprentenkabinet, Amsterdam, which Boon

93. Gerard David, *Mary and John with the Female Mourners*, ca. 1480. Oil on wood, 45 × 42.5 cm. Koninklijk Museum voor Schone Kunsten, Antwerp

recognized as originally belonging to the same sheet (Figures 100 and 101).[18]

The British Museum Magdalenes are precise studies of one female saint in two slightly varied poses and patterns of drapery. The figure types are closest to those found in the paintings of Hugo van der Goes and Dieric Bouts, although in terms of drapery style they are probably closer to Bouts than to Hugo. Yet the graphic mannerisms exhibited in the British Museum sheet are not near enough to Hugo's or Bouts's known handling to attribute these studies to either artist. Instead, the long, wispy strokes of parallel hatching for depressed areas of fabric, the short, staccato dashes, like stitching across the peaks of folds, and even the regular diamond-shaped crosshatching in the deepest fold areas recall the characteristics of the underdrawing in the *Female Mourners* (compare Figure 98 with Figures 99–101). Similar features of execution are also found in David's later *Virgin and Child at the Fountain* (Figure 35).

The two sheets in the Rijksprentenkabinet representing a Mary Magdalene and a Saint Veronica (Figures 100 and 101) also share the graphic mannerisms identified in the underdrawing of the *Female Mourners*. But the density of the working in pen and the tightness of the handling in the former are different from the latter, and the two are not indisputably by the same hand. If, in fact, these drawings can be associated with David, they would have to date quite early in his career, close to the time of his work on the altarpiece of *Christ Nailed to the Cross*, that is, about 1480. Although no definite attribution can be made here for the London and Amsterdam sheets, they show a type of drawing readily available as part of the workshop paraphernalia that David made reference to as he worked up the underdrawing, particularly for the right wing of his altarpiece. In this regard, an old inscription "Gerard van Bruges" on the upper left edge of the Saint Veronica sheet may be a fitting reference, after all, either to authorship or to ownership.

94. Anonymous, *Christ Nailed to the Cross*, ca. 1470? Silverpoint on prepared paper, 12.1 × 16 cm. Sale, Sotheby and Co., July 2, 1958, Lot 26

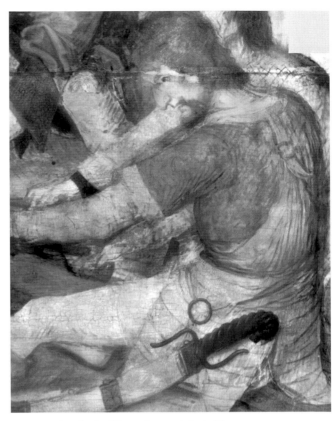

95. IRR detail of soldier at lower right in Figure 92

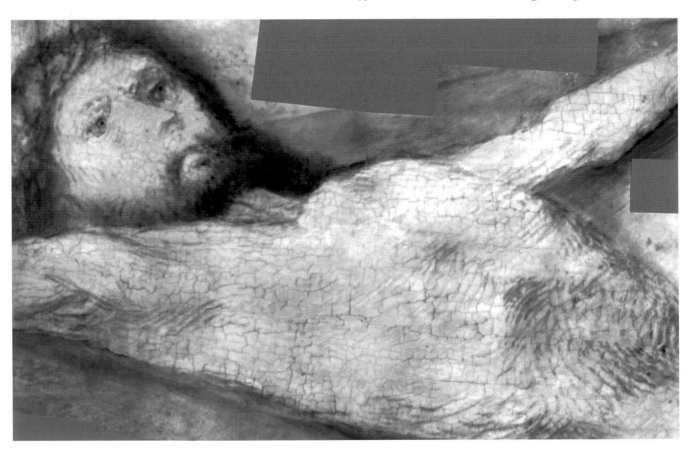

96. IRR detail of Christ in Figure 92

97. IRR detail of man at far left in Figure 91

98. IRR detail of Saint John and the Virgin Mary in Figure 93

99. Netherlandish, *Two Studies of Mary Magdalene*, late 15th century. Pen and brown ink on paper, 19.5 × 17.3 cm. The British Museum, London (Photo Copyright © The British Museum)

The figures in the *Female Mourners* show types that are related to those in the Thyssen *Crucifixion* (Figure 90) and, later on, to those of the Chicago *Lamentation* (Figure 141), especially in their sharply delineated and geometrically formulated facial features, which have little in common with the more

100. Netherlandish, *Mary Magdalene*, late 15th century. Pen and brown ink on paper, 18.3 × 8.4 cm. Prentenkabinet Rijksmuseum, Amsterdam

101. Netherlandish, *Saint Veronica*, late 15th century. Pen and brown ink on paper, 18.4 × 7.9 cm. Prentenkabinet, Rijksmuseum, Amsterdam

subtly modeled and expressive heads of the left and central panels of the triptych. The figures in the left wing, in their variety of pose, physiognomy, and age, reflect the rapid metalpoint studies David made of heads from life for just this purpose (Figures 1 and 2). The juxtaposition of conventional types from standard workshop models with heads that are studied from life is a characteristic feature of David's work

that continues throughout his career and may be recognized here in its incipient stages.

Following these earliest works, but still associated with David's formative years as a painter, are no fewer than ten paintings in New York (some of which belong to the same altarpiece), in The Metropolitan Museum of Art and the Frick Collection. None can be linked to a documented commission, and there are no indications of ownership or of the original destinations of these works. Except for the *Deposition* in the Frick Collection, these are relatively small-scale, portable works that probably served as private devotional paintings. In response to the requirements of religious practices of the time, they share a common theme—the life of Christ. Certain subjects, namely the Nativity and the Lamentation, were especially popular and provided David with an early business in workshop replicas. Pattern drawings for these compositions, as well as perhaps a finished example or two, would have been available in the atelier for the client's perusal. Such standardized output could then be customized according to the client's wishes with the addition of donor portraits, coats of arms, or other family identification of ownership. In the normal functioning of the workshop, plans were sometimes changed for any number of practical reasons. In the case of the Lehman Passion wings, as we shall see, the original concept perhaps for a sculpted centerpiece was abandoned, and a substitution of a painted one was made from the panels kept in stock.

During these years of changing economic climate in Bruges, a painter and his workshop achieved success by remaining flexible to the requirements of the available clients. In addition to carrying out routine projects—making replicas of especially popular compositions and collaborating with artists in other media—this may well have meant adopting different working methods. In what is likely to have been a commissioned work—although we do not know the name of the client or the destination of the painting—the large-scale *Deposition* was painted on canvas instead of wood. Guaranteeing easier portability for transport to a foreign destination and significantly reduced expense in terms of materials, tüchlein paintings (tempera on linen) were a large part of the production in Bruges at the time, although little has remained of these fragile products and only a few examples by David have survived.

What may at first appear to be a rather motley assortment of paintings from David's early years upon closer scrutiny yields important information about the daily business of a painter's workshop.

These indications of the standard output from the atelier help to provide a fuller picture of routine activities in David's shop at the same time that he was occupied with important commissions, namely the *Justice of Cambyses* for the town hall, the Sedano Triptych and the imposing *Adoration of the Magi* (Figures 65, 66, 149, 150, and 60).

Among David's earliest surviving works is a "triptych" of the *Nativity* (Figure 102).[19] Careful examination of the paintings that have formed the "wings," *Saint John the Baptist* and *Saint Francis Receiving the Stigmata* (Figures 118a,b), however, reveals that they were previously cut down at the bottom and painted out to the edges of the bare wood reserve at the tops and sides. Even in this altered state, together they do not exactly equal the size of the *Nativity,* which has a *barbe* on all edges, evidence that its original painted dimensions have remained intact. The wings were first joined with the *Nativity* in 1923, when the dealer Kleinberger sold the newly assembled triptych to the New York collector Michael Friedsam, who in turn gave the ensemble to the Metropolitan Museum in 1931.[20] Considering the *Nativity* separately from the wings allows for the rediscovery of David's aims in the *Nativity* and its related works without the added confusion of side panels that are doubtless of a somewhat later period, as will be discussed below.

There are two other associated Nativities from David's early career—one in Budapest and another in Cleveland (Figures 108 and 113)—which attest to the popularity of David's rendition of the theme. More than simply relating the subject of the Nativity, all of these versions include the Annunciation to the Shepherds (in tiny background scenes)[21] and their adoration of the Christ Child along with a pair of adoring angels and the ox and the ass. In addition to the biblical source for these events in Luke 2: 1–20, all three draw upon the fourteenth-century visions of Saint Bridget of Sweden found in her *Revelationes celestes,* in which the kneeling Virgin is described as

102. Gerard David, *Nativity*, early 1480s. Oil on oak, 47.6 × 34.3 cm. The Metropolitan Museum of Art, The Friedsam Collection, Bequest of Michael Friedsam, 1931 (32.100.40a)

103. Geertgen tot Sint Jans, *Night Nativity*, ca. 1475? Oil on wood, 34 × 25 cm. National Gallery, London (Photo © National Gallery, London)

having loose, flowing hair, the Christ Child as lying on the ground on her extended drapery, and the elderly Joseph as shielding his candle, whose flame was suddenly overpowered by the divine light of the newly born Son of God.[22]

The charming simplicity of the composition of the Metropolitan Museum painting as well as of the figures is derived from north Netherlandish prototypes. In particular, the works of the Master of the Brunswick Diptych (thought to be Jacob Jansz) and of Geertgen tot Sint Jans (see Figure 103) show similar

doll-like figures and a peasant-type Virgin with her long, flowing, reddish hair.[23] The composition, however, reflects the initial stages of David's intense interest in another north Netherlandish painter. It is not surprising to discover that the closest parallels in terms of the general composition are with Nativities from the workshop of Dieric Bouts, who himself had emigrated from Haarlem to Leuven by 1457.[24] He was named official city painter in 1468 and remained in Leuven until his death in 1475. Thereafter, Bouts's two sons, Dieric the Younger and Aelbert, who

104. Dieric Bouts, *Nativity* (fragment), ca. 1470? Oil on wood, 24.9 × 19.7 cm. Gemäldegalerie, SMPK, Berlin (Photo Jörg P. Anders, Berlin)

105. Dieric Bouts, *Nativity* (fragment), ca. 1470? Oil on wood, 21 × 18.5 cm. Louvre, Paris (Photo © RMN)

inherited their father's workshop drawings and cartoons,[25] continued the operation of the workshop, the latter until the middle of the sixteenth century.[26]

Versions of Nativities from Dieric Bouts's workshop now in the Los Angeles County Museum and two at the Wildenstein Gallery, New York (one of which was formerly in W. Müller collection, Berlin) appear to rely upon fragmentary remains of an original by Bouts (in Gemäldegalerie, Berlin, and Louvre, Paris; Figures 104 and 105).[27] They all show a composition (some in reverse) that is similar to the one of the Metropolitan painting: the adoring Virgin and the candle-carrying or candle-shielding Saint Joseph flanking the Christ Child, who lies on the ground; the foreground divided from the background by a masonry wall perforated by a double-arched window, through which two shepherds peer and which leads

beyond to a hilly landscape; and arched doorways to adjoining spaces at the far left or right of both, with the ox and ass stationed behind the Virgin.[28]

Depending on an earlier tradition established by Campin's Dijon *Nativity* and Rogier van der Weyden's Bladelin Altarpiece, the adoring angels or the precise pose of the kneeling Joseph, who shields the flame of his candle with a particular gesture of right over left hand, are also commonly found in paintings by Memling and his followers. It was a theme that was especially popular in Bruges from about 1470 on.[29] David's dependence upon the spatial constructions of Boutsian compositions and figure types of north Netherlandish, specifically Geertgenesque, paintings suggests that he painted this *Nativity* at the beginning of his career, perhaps in the early 1480s, when he was a newcomer to the southern Netherlands.[30]

In keeping with the characteristics of David's initial stage of production, the figures have rather squat proportions, and the faces are modeled with brownish tones (reminiscent of those of the left wing of the triptych of *Christ Nailed to the Cross*), which are more exaggerated in the shepherds than in the figures of

107. Gerard David, *Nativity* in the *Breviary of Isabella of Castile* (ADD MS 18851, fol. 29r). The British Library, London

Joseph, Mary, and the angels. The palette is relatively cool, with orange-reds predominating, slate-blue and deep blue shades for the Virgin's dress and cloak, and warm browns and purples for the costumes of the shepherds peering through the window. Little underdrawing is visible in the painting, and that is mainly in the two angels, who (as was the case with the underdrawing of the central panel of *Christ Nailed to the Cross*) are roughly worked in with swift, sure

106. X-radiograph of Figure 102

movements of the brush for their placement and a slight indication of the modeling of their forms.

The X-radiograph of the painting (Figure 106), aside from clarifying the extent of the paint losses in the picture, shows quite clearly that, even in these relatively early works, David had a keen sense of the role that the balance of light and dark would play for dramatic effect within the picture. The strongest concentrations of lead white mark the key features of the painting for illumination: the face of the Virgin, the Christ Child, the angels next to the Child, and

109. IRR detail of shepherds at lower left in Figure 108

the hands of Joseph, Mary, and the shepherd gesturing to the Child below—all features that surround the Christ Child and help to provide a sense of symmetry and balance within the composition.

The relationship of panel painting to manuscript illumination is a leitmotif throughout David's career. As was already noted in the case of the Thyssen *Crucifixion,* David's own work was inspired by manuscript illumination of the period, and the compositions and figure style of his own paintings were in turn assimilated by contemporary illuminators. Closely

108. Gerard David, *Nativity,* ca. 1485. Oil on wood, 76.7 × 56.5 cm. Szépmüvészeti Museum, Budapest

connected to the Museum's *Nativity* is an illumination made for a breviary produced in Bruges about 1496 (British Museum, London, Add. MS. 18851, fol. 29) and presented by the Spanish ambassador Francesco de Rojas to Queen Isabella of Castile (Figure 107). One of three illuminations in this book possibly made by David himself, it is almost a mirror image of the Metropolitan's *Nativity,* but it shows a more developed spatial conception and a Virgin type associated with David's later renditions of this theme.[31]

The evolution of David's early style, and indeed clues to the stops along his route to Bruges, can be followed through the investigation of the two other Nativity paintings, those in Budapest and Cleveland (Figures 108 and 113). Although they are generally very similar to each other, in the Cleveland painting the Nativity is brought closer to the viewer, and the composition it takes over from the Budapest version is simplified by eliminating two of the shepherds and reducing the extent of the architectural setting. In addition, the high key of the palette of the Budapest painting is replaced in the Cleveland example by more somber tones; the orange-reds and yellows of the costume of the shepherd at the left in the Budapest painting are considerably subdued in the attire of his counterpart in the Cleveland version.

Attention has been given to the chronological sequence of the works, which, particularly when the underdrawing is taken into account, is a rather straightforward affair.[32] In addition to helping to establish the sequence of the works, the underdrawing also confirms David's sustained interest in the art of Dieric Bouts. The bold brush underdrawing in the Budapest version (Figures 109–111) is similar to that found in other early works attributed to David, such as *Christ Nailed to the Cross* of about 1480 (compare Figure 109 with Figures 95 and 96) and the Brussels *Adoration of the Magi* of about 1490 (Figure 6).[33] It freely works out the composition in great detail, as well as the modeling of the figures.

The significant number of changes from the underdrawing to the final painted stage of this picture reveals that David continued to work out his ideas directly on the grounded panel, preoccupied

110. IRR detail of Joseph, Mary, the Christ Child, and angels in Figure 108

by the relationship of the figures to their space, in a landscape setting greatly expanded from that of the Metropolitan Museum *Nativity*. David deleted the shepherd doffing his hat at the far left and a companion dog below, changed the leg position of the shepherd in the yellow cloak from upright to bended knees, moved the young shepherd's head downward, adjusted the draperies of Joseph and Mary at their lower edges so that they would not overlap or interfere with other forms, shifted the placement of the ass and the ox, and reworked his plan for the landscape (Figures 109–111).

It is especially in the landscape in the upper-left corner that considerable differences are apparent between the underdrawing of the Budapest and Cleveland versions (compare Figures 111 and 114). Whereas in the Budapest painting David first conceived of a tower prominently placed in his cityscape and a large tree at the far left border of the composition, as well as numerous houses and rooftops throughout the intervening space—all with a large, fluttering angel and a star above—in the Cleveland painting he more or less proceeded in the underdrawing with the forms as they had been established

111. IRR detail of landscape at upper left in Figure 108

112. Dieric Bouts, Altarpiece of the Holy Sacrament, detail of *Abraham and Melchizedek* (upper left interior wing), 1468. Oil on canvas transferred from panel, 88.5 × 71.5 cm. Sint-Pieterskerk, Leuven (Photo Copyright IRPA-KIK, Brussels)

in the final painted version of the Budapest *Nativity,* that is, with the tree, a number of the town's houses, and the tower eliminated (the latter replaced by the Church of the Holy Sepulchre). Although there are some additional key differences between the two compositions (to be discussed below), the Cleveland version basically condenses the theme to the bare essentials and brings the figures and details of the landscape forward in a close-up view.

Perhaps even more telling than what David retained for the completed Budapest painting is what he chose to edit out, particularly the elements in the underdrawing that supply clues to early influences on David's career and indications of his whereabouts. When we consider the *Abraham and Melchizedek* (Figure 112) from Dieric Bouts's Holy Sacrament Altarpiece, installed in the Leuven Sint Pieterskerk by 1468,[34] David's source is immediately apparent. Following Bouts's model, in his underdrawing David planned a background landscape with a single tall tree at the far left, a densely composed village view with a prominent church or bell tower (initially

with a flat top, then with a peaked roof), and a series of overlapping hillocks culminating at the far right in a higher rocky mass (Figure 111). Between the grassy knolls and hillocks is a passageway leading from foreground to background, a pathway that in both the Bouts and the David paintings is slightly overgrown with scrub vegetation on the well-worn route (compare Figures 108 and 112). David has also followed Bouts's general arrangement of figures within the composition, adhering to his predecessor's sense of rhythm across the picture plane with carefully determined spatial intervals between figures and a lively variation in the position and height of their heads. In the underdrawing of the *Nativity,* David originally planned an arrangement of three figures at the far left—just as in Bouts's example—but modified the painted version to include just two (Figures 109, 112, and 108).

A lingering hint of the art of Geertgen tot Sint Jans is present in some of the figures of the Budapest

Nativity: the Christ Child mimics the figure in Geertgen's *Night Nativity* (compare Figures 108 and 103, itself perhaps modeled after a lost Hugo van der Goes painting) in the diminutive size, pose, and position of the Child within the composition; and the angels in the foreground recall those of Geertgen, one with its egg-shaped, profile-view head and similar robes tied at the waist.[35] A painting possibly of 1480–90 (that is, contemporaneous with David's own Nativities), Geertgen's *Nativity* might have been made in the south Netherlands on a sojourn there. A "Gheerkin de Hollandere" is referred to as an apprentice to a bookbinder in Bruges in 1475,[36] but there is no further mention to confirm that this person is, in fact, Geertgen tot Sint Jans, and Geertgen's whereabouts during his career, and indeed when and where he may have crossed paths with David, remain sketchy at best.

It is still the impact of Bouts that is most clearly present in the other figures of the Budapest *Nativity*—certainly in the mixture of male types, but above all in the Virgin, who is a reverse copy of Bouts's Virgin from a fragment of a *Nativity* in Berlin (Figure 104).[37]

Any discussion of the Cleveland Museum of Art *Nativity* must take into account its considerably damaged condition and the obvious replacement of the figure of Joseph by a hand other than David's. For these reasons, the attribution of the painting will doubtless remain highly problematic. Since key parts of the picture are nonetheless closely associated with David's art and development at this point in his career, it is instructive to discuss it as part of the David group.

The completed design of the Budapest *Nativity* was repeated for the underdrawing of the Cleveland version (Figures 108 and 114), but considerable changes between the drawing and the final painted stages were incorporated. In similar sketchy brush underdrawing, but with tighter parallel hatching for the modeling of the draperies, an artist who was most probably David worked out the entirety of the com-

position (Figure 114). The somewhat more measured handling of the brush and the more fixed state of the underdrawing suggest that David was following pre-established patterns, either the one from the completed Budapest *Nativity* or those provided by workshop drawings that are no longer extant.

The tightly cropped, close-up view of the Cleveland version necessitated further editing. The two figures originally planned at the far left (as in the Budapest painted version) were reduced to one, very similar to the shepherd in the yellow cloak and red stockings of the Budapest picture, but now quite subdued in brown cloak, orange undergarment, and green stockings (compare Figure 113 and 114). Otherwise, the features of the landscape at the upper left, the relationship of the announcing angel to the shepherds—one standing, one kneeling—at the upper right, the positions of ox and ass, all reappear in the Cleveland version as they are in the final Budapest painting. Although the grouping of the Holy Family with the adoring angels remains much the same in type and pose as in the Budapest version, the figures are larger and brought more closely together so that their forms and draperies overlap. In effect, by bringing the figures forward, David approximated even more the model of Bouts in the compositions of the Holy Sacrament Altarpiece, where a similar scheme is in play (see Figure 112).

The significant difference between the Budapest and Cleveland versions, of course, is in the two figures of Joseph. The underdrawing and the X-radiograph of the Cleveland *Nativity* (Figures 115–117) show that Joseph originally followed the pose of the Budapest figure, including the identical position of the hands shielding the flame of the candle. In a later repainting of this figure, however, significant changes were introduced: Joseph's head was enlarged and totally reworked into another, beardless type, the draperies were reconfigured to suit the changed position of Joseph kneeling on both knees rather than one knee, and the hands were joined in an attitude of prayer, with the candle eliminated (compare Figures 113 and 115). Although some have suggested that this significant alteration was David's own doing,[38] neither

113. Gerard David, *Nativity*, ca. 1485–90. Oil on wood, 85.2 × 59.7 cm. Cleveland Museum of Art, Leonard C. Hanna Jr. Fund 1958.320 (Photo © 1998 The Cleveland Museum of Art)

115. IRR detail of Joseph, Mary, and the Christ Child in Figure 113

the painting technique nor the execution of the over-size head and the reconstruction of the draperies, which fall on the right leg in unnatural folds, can be attributed to David. The consideration of the evolution of the figure of Joseph has not been facilitated by the restoration and reconstruction of the skinned figure. The paint is, however, quite old, and it is not inconceivable that the reworking took place very early in the history of the picture, perhaps when it

114. IRR of Figure 113

changed hands (as Bodenhausen suggested)[39] and the new owner was interested in superimposing another Joseph type at a time when the increased significance and resulting prominence of this figure responded to a growing cult of Saint Joseph.[40] Any identification of the head of Joseph as a portrait can be only conjecture but may follow the vogue of the sixteenth century by which actual personages were represented in the guise of saints or holy persons.[41]

The shift in palette from the Budapest to the Cleveland version of the Nativity already hints at a

116. X-radiograph detail of Joseph in Figure 113

117. IRR detail of Joseph in Figure 113

change in working venue. The brownish tones with the interjection in the shepherd of the unconventional combination of the bright yellow cloak and red stockings in the former give way to deeper, richer harmonies in more saturated colors in the latter, a palette that predominates as David established himself in Bruges.

The artistic environment in Bruges in 1484, when David acquired citizenship and joined the Guild of the Imagemakers and Saddlers, was still rich with the legacy of Jan van Eyck and more recently renowned with the eminent painter Hans Memling. David made notable shifts both in his style and in the details of his working methods as a result of the influence of these masters. In those panels in the Metropolitan Museum's collection that most likely may be situated within David's early years in Bruges—the triptych wings of *Saint John the Baptist* and *Saint Francis Receiving the Stigmata,* and the *Crucifixion* (Figures 118 and 125)—David changed his preferred underdrawing tool for the preliminary sketch on the grounded panel from brush to black chalk. This change in David's habitual practice may have had something to do with his growing awareness of the established working methods of Hans Memling, with whom he would have become acquainted but from whom he remained relatively aloof artistically.[42] Memling's earliest works, from the time when he was most likely associated with the workshop of Rogier van der Weyden, show brush underdrawing, but his Bruges-period production features very loose and free black-chalk underdrawings that are barely descriptive of the forms to be carried out in paint.[43]

As noted above, it has now been established with certainty that the two wings, *Saint John the Baptist* and *Saint Francis Receiving the Stigmata* (Figure 118), did not originally form a triptych with the Metropolitan Museum's *Nativity*.[44] Exactly what their original configuration was is now difficult to determine, because of the lack of remaining clues: both panels have been cut down at their lower edges to an unknown degree (probably only a centimeter or two); each was overpainted on the bare wood margins at the top and both sides and thinned slightly and cradled on the back, thus removing the evidence of any paintings that may have existed on the reverse sides; there are no other markings of ownership that might help to reconstruct the circumstances of the works' manufacture.

Aside from the famous example of the two *Saint Francis* panels attributed to Jan van Eyck[45] belonging to the well-known Genoese family in Bruges, the Adornes, representations of this saint in early Netherlandish painting are relatively rare. In a pairing with Saint John the Baptist, it is Saint John the Evangelist

or Saint Jerome, rather than Saint Francis, who appears far more frequently. Furthermore, instead of the traditional gray, Saint Francis wears the brown habit of the reformed branch of the Franciscans (the Recolleten, or Observant Friars), who had a cloister near the Ezelsport in Bruges. Perhaps one of the prominent Italian merchants associated with the Franciscans there ordered an altarpiece with the Metropolitan Museum wings, for the two panels apparently came from a collection in Genoa, where they may well have been exported rather early. On the other hand, such a triptych may have been commissioned by the Bruges monastery or a religious order, for both saints have strong links to monastic life. Saint John has always been highly regarded because of his exemplary solitary and austere life; Saint Francis was the founder of the Franciscan order. The rope girdle around the latter's brown habit shows three knots, signifying the saint's religious vows of poverty, chastity, and obedience.[46]

Both saints are also known for their experiences in the wilderness, a fact that is underscored by David's varied landscape depictions individualized to suit the details of each saint's life. Living an ascetic existence in the desert, Saint John is shown pointing to the lamb, thus representing John 1:29: "John saw Jesus coming toward him and said, 'Behold, the Lamb of God, who takes away the sin of the world!'" He then baptized Christ. The most significant event of Francis's life occurred on a night in 1224 when he was in the wild forests of Mount Alverna, praying on the Feast of the Exultation of the Cross. In the account of Thomas of Celano, a vision of a six-winged seraph on a cross appeared to Francis, miraculously transferring Christ's Crucifixion wounds, which remained until the saint's death a few years later. Oblivious to the event, Francis's companion, Brother Leo, sleeps nearby.[47]

A common theme that the representations of the two saints share is of the Crucifixion. Saint John alludes to it as he points to the lamb, signifying Christ's ultimate sacrifice for mankind. Saint Francis receives the stigmata, the symbolic markings of the Crucifixion. A far more likely subject than a Nativity

for the centerpiece of this triptych, therefore, would be a Crucifixion[48] (a Descent from the Cross or a Lamentation might also be possible).[49] Unfortunately, no likely candidates remain.

Although the art of Dieric Bouts and his workshop continued to be a source for David well into his early years of activity in Bruges, there is an intermittent but very distinct influence of the works of Jan van Eyck, whose rich legacy in that city could not be ignored by any newcomer. The *Saint John the Baptist* is clearly reminiscent of the Ghent Altarpiece (Figure 215) made for the church of Sint Baafs. In general, placing the saint in a clearing bordered by carefully described exotic types of trees—cypress and magnolia—and eliminating the route to the horizon, as in van Eyck's panels of the Hermit Saints, strikes a common chord.[50] In addition, the massive bulk and frontal stance of the figure of Saint John, with draperies of elaborately rhythmic and deeply cut folds, have direct associations with sculptural representations—specifically with the grisaille of Saint John on the exterior of the Ghent Altarpiece (Figure 119)—and with painted representations, such as the Cleveland *Saint John the Baptist* attributed to Petrus Christus, which probably derive from Eyckian workshop drawings that served for commissions of painting and sculpture alike (Figure 120).[51] In these prototypes Saint John also supports the lamb with a draped left arm forming a shelflike platform. In David's first light, rough sketch on the panel, as well as in the initial painting of the draperies, Saint John's cloak at the left side fell to the ground (Figure 121), just as in the Eyckian examples. For the most part David followed his preliminary sketch in the painted layers, making adjustments only to the length of the draperies at the base of the figure, as is characteristic

118a,b. Gerard David, *Saint John the Baptist* and *Saint Francis Receiving the Stigmata*, ca. 1485–90. Oil on oak, original painted surface, 44.8 × 14.9 cm and 44.8 × 14.6 cm. The Metropolitan Museum of Art, The Michael Friedsam Collection, Bequest of Michael Friedsam, 1931 (32.100.40bc)

119. Jan van Eyck, *Saint John the Baptist* (left exterior wing of the Ghent Altarpiece), 1432. Oil on oak, 146 × 51.8 cm. Sint Baafs, Ghent (Photo Copyright IRPA-KIK, Brussels)

of his working procedure throughout his career. The X-radiographs of *Saint John* and *Saint Francis* show that the whites for the flesh tones were broadly worked in, providing little advance preparation for the modeling of the faces, which took place mainly on the surface of the picture with the application of brownish scumbles (compare Figures 122 and 123).

The landscape of the *Saint Francis* panel also benefitted from the example of the van Eycks; it is organized similarly, but in reverse, to the *Saint Christopher with the Pilgrim Saints*, again from the Ghent Altarpiece (Figure 215). The figure of this saint is less rigid in form than the companion Saint John the Baptist. With his naturally arranged draperies (lightly sketched in

120. Circle of Jan van Eyck, *Saint John the Baptist*, 15th century. Silverpoint on prepared paper, 13.8 × 5.5 cm. Musée Bonnat, Bayonne

121. IRR detail of Saint John the Baptist in Figure 118a

122. X-radiograph detail of Saint John the Baptist in Figure 118a

123. Detail of upper torso of Saint John the Baptist in Figure 118a

black chalk, Figure 124) falling in soft folds and more refined facial type, Saint Francis looks toward David's depictions in somewhat later paintings, namely the *Crucifixion* (Figure 125), where the sympathetic treatment of the face of Mary Magdalene recalls the head of Saint Francis. This evolution in style toward a more elegant line of attenuated, less stocky figures implies the influence of David's Bruges contemporary Hans Memling, and a dating to David's early years in Bruges, about 1485–90.[52]

The designs of Rogier van der Weyden for various versions of the Crucifixion appear to have been widely known, probably through circulated drawings.[53] In Bruges, Hans Memling may well have been the conveyor of Rogierian designs, brought by him from his likely apprenticeship in Rogier's workshop.[54] Or they may have come through Louis Le Duc, Rogier's acclaimed nephew, who settled in Bruges in 1460–61.[55] David's muted response to Rogier can be found in the Metropolitan Museum *Crucifixion*

(Figure 125).[56] Here the swooning Virgin, collapsing in the arms of Saint John, who stares sorrowfully at the crucified Christ, derives from similar figures in paintings like Rogier's great Philadelphia diptych.[57] The prayerful Magdalene and the rather stiff, columnar body of Christ reflect works attributed to Robert Campin (or the Master of Flémalle) and followers of Rogier, especially Crucifixions in Dresden and Berlin, respectively,[58] which also present the scene in the immediate foreground within a landscape setting. David's *Crucifixion,* in turn, was the source for later adaptations by artists associated with his workshop, especially Adriaen Isenbrant and Ambrosius Benson.[59]

The theme is rendered here, however, not in Rogier's emotionally expressive mode, but instead in one of quiet reserve. Mary collapses, her arms crossed in silent resignation and in *compassio* with her dead son. In a gesture of blessing with his right hand, Christ acknowledges the new relationship between his Mother and the disciple John, who would henceforth take care of her: "Woman, behold your son!" and to John, "Behold your Mother!" (John 19:26–27). John and Mary Magdalene regard Christ in humble piety, sharing his agony and death, the Magdalene, a repentant sinner, in particular representing an exemplum for the viewer's own devotional appeal to Christ for salvation. Dressed as a cardinal, Saint Jerome, though present, is psychologically absent from the event at hand, experiencing it

124. IRR detail of Saint Francis in Figure 118b

instead through "the imaging of things given in a verbal description."[60] His is a spiritual vision found through his reading of the biblical text, whose translation from Hebrew and Greek into Latin in the fourth century was his great contribution to medieval Christendom.

The most likely original function of the *Crucifixion* was as a private devotional image within a monastery setting or as one for those devoted to Saint Jerome and eager for his particular intercessory powers.[61] In a fifteenth-century Office of Saint Jerome are prayers that the author presents as if they are spoken by Saint Jerome himself. Jerome prays to Jesus Christ crucified not only for himself, a miserable sinner, but also on behalf of his relatives and friends:

> Deign to free my soul from sin, turn my heart from wicked and depraved thoughts, free my body and soul from servitude to sin, drive concupiscence from me.

In addition, praying for mercy and eternal life, he entreats:

> Spare, O Lord, your people, whom you, Lord Jesus Christ, have redeemed with your blood; spare them and do not forget us in eternity.[62]

Although some scholars have considered this a late work because of the dark cloud formations,[63] the depiction of the sky is a descriptive feature of the subject matter, not a clue to chronology. As an indication of David's ongoing interest in the appropriate physical environment for the subject at hand, the sky is darkened as it was at Christ's death; a jawbone and a femur litter the foreground, indicating Golgotha, or the place of the skull; and the walled city of Jerusalem, with the Church of the Holy Sepulchre prominently placed at its center, can be seen in the distance. In keeping with David's characteristic naturalistic depiction, a lion wanders in the

125. Gerard David, *Crucifixion*, ca. 1495. Oil on oak, 53.3 × 38.1 cm. The Metropolitan Museum of Art, Rogers Fund, 1909 (09.157)

126. IRR detail of Mary Magdalene and Saint Jerome in Figure 125

middle distance as part of nature, not as an inanimate attribute of the saint.

A date for the *Crucifixion* of about 1495 can be reliably established through a consideration of David's landscape construction, palette, and figure types and a close look at aspects of his working technique. During this period David favored a series of overlapping planes for the construction of his landscapes, no doubt taking inspiration from Bouts's left wing of the Holy Sacrament Altarpiece, showing Abraham and Melchizedek (Figure 112), for the successive rocky mounds receding from foreground to mid-distance behind the cross. Here, as in the *Crucifixion,* are subtle tonal transitions from foreground browns to mid-distance greens to distant blue hues, which achieve a convincing progression of space to the far horizon. Although still favoring the palette of orange-reds, olive-greens, and gray-blues of his early works for draperies, David has abandoned the harsher brown tones for more subtle modulations in the flesh areas. Sweeter, softer facial types emerge, perhaps as a response to the prevailing influence of Hans Memling's art in Bruges.

With a dry medium, probably black chalk, David established a preliminary drawing for the composition and worked out the system of shading in the draperies of the figures. Some areas (such as the green dress of Mary Magdalene and the darkened blue of the Virgin's costume) remain opaque to infrared reflectography. Elsewhere, the spontaneity and assurance with which David worked out the design are self-evident. For the golden sleeves of Mary Magdalene's dress, he gave only a summary indication of the elaborate structure of the folds of fabric here rendered in the paint without specific underdrawn guide (Figure 126). In the Magdalene's cloak, however, David went over his preliminary sketch for the configuration of folds, making slight modifications and establishing the deepest ones with a second layer of drawing. The underdrawing in the figure of Saint Jerome, with its zigzag folds at the left side and rapidly worked parallel hatching for the shadows at the right side, is quite similar to the Frankfurt drawing of the standing King Cambyses (Figure 10),

127. After Robert Campin, *Deposition*, late 15th century. Brush and ink with white heightening on prepared paper, 27.5 × 25.9 cm. Fitzwilliam Museum, Cambridge

which supports a date contemporaneous with the *Justice of Cambyses* panels, certainly in progress by the mid-1490s and completed in 1498.[64]

Among the more influential works that were likely to have been in Bruges upon David's arrival there in 1484 was the famous Deposition Triptych by Robert Campin, of which only the fragment of the good thief remains, in the Städel Kunstinstitut, Frankfurt.[65] The suggestion of the Bruges location is based upon a number of early full or partial copies of the altarpiece, all by Bruges artists: one now in Liverpool with what Weale and Hulin de Loo identified as the Bruges coat of arms,[66] and on the wings the figures of Saints John the Baptist and Julian (the latter suggesting

that the original site of the copy was the Hospital of Saint Julian in Bruges),[67] and another of 1500, which was in Sint-Salvatorskerk (now in the Groeningemuseum) and is attributed to the Bruges Master of the Passion Scenes.[68] Campin's work also influenced manuscript illumination, namely by the Master of Catherine of Cleves,[69] the Master of the Llangattock Hours, and a miniature in the Turin-Milan Book of Hours,[70] as well as a free copy in the Prayer Book of the Prince of Arenberg and an engraving by the Master of the Banderoles.[71] The dissemination of Campin's model must have been facilitated by a number of drawings that copied individual figures or figural groupings, such as the one of the good

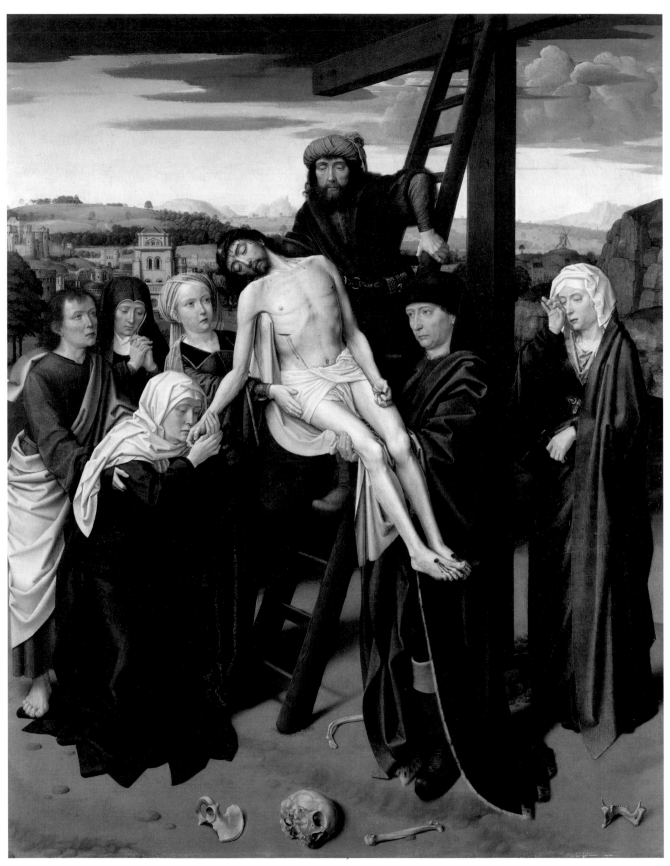

128. Gerard David, *Deposition*, late 1490s. Oil on canvas, 142.5 × 112.5 cm. The Frick Collection, New York (Photo Copyright The Frick Collection, New York)

129. Dieric Bouts, *Deposition* (center panel of a triptych), ca. 1455. Oil on wood, 191 × 155 cm. Capilla Réal, Granada

thief in the Fogg Art Museum, Cambridge, or of the main figures related to the *Deposition* in the Fitzwilliam Museum, Cambridge (Figure 127).[72] Campin's composition was still popular as late as the 1530s; a version of it was produced by another Bruges artist, Ambrosius Benson, for the Church of San Miguel of the Convent of San Antonio el Réal of Segovia.[73]

David's *Deposition* (Figure 128)[74] is certainly indebted to Campin's work, although only in part. The figures of Christ, Nicodemus, and Joseph of Arimathea are copied in reverse from Campin's figures,[75] and the weeping Mary at the far right of David's composition is taken from another Campin model, namely the weeping angel in the center panel of the Seilern Triptych (Courtauld Institute Gallery, London). Other portions, however, and the composition as a whole, have been considerably influenced by Dieric Bouts's art, particularly the center panel of Bouts's Deposition Altarpiece (Figure 129) in the Capilla Réal in Granada and an exact copy in Valencia.[76]

In general, the arrangement of the figures across the frontal plane of the picture and their relationship to the space around them, as well as to one another, are similar in the paintings of both Bouts and David. More specifically, David took over from Bouts the motif of John supporting the collapsing Virgin, who caresses the right hand of Christ. Bouts's color preference for red and green, expressed in two of the three Marys at the right, is repeated in David's painting, where the weeping Mary at the far right wears a red dress with a green cloak over it. Moreover, Joseph of Arimathea, on the top of the ladder, identified by the letters on his purse "DIAH" (Decurio Ioseph Arimathaeae Hebraeorum), wears a green shirt and red fur-trimmed jacket, and John and one of the Marys wear red and green, respectively.

As in David's other paintings of about this date, the landscape conception in the *Deposition* is also derived from the model of Bouts: David followed his scheme, similarly arranging his own landscape motifs by closing off the composition with a prominent rocky mass at the right and trees at the left; a cityscape nestled in the middle ground beyond the figures at the left, and a lone tower (in Bouts's painting) or a windmill (in David's painting) providing a spatial marker for the middle ground to the right of the cross. The foreground in both paintings is strewn with rocks and pebbles on the unevenly stepped, barren plateau; here David replaces the nails and pliers in Bouts's painting with a remarkable still life of various bones—skull, femur, pelvic bone, and jawbone.

Although the Frick *Deposition* has been variously dated to David's early, middle, and late career,[77] its style is closely related to paintings created in the last half of the 1490s. The careful attention to the body of Christ—the description of the way in which the flesh thinly covers the rounded protrusions of the rib cage, the sunken belly, the raised bluish veins in the arms, the agonized retraction of fingers in the wounded left hand—all readily call to mind the treatment of the same features in the likewise carefully modeled body of the flayed Sisamnes in the *Justice of Cambyses* (Figure 66), completed in 1498. The broad folds of the draperies, deeply cut in a sculptural approach, are also found in the *Justice* panels and slightly predate the softer, more flowing draperies of later works. In this regard a comparison between the closely related figures of John at the left in the *Deposition* and Saint John the Evangelist in the left wing of the Baptism Triptych is instructive (Figures 128 and 213): the former shows somewhat exaggerated and tightly bunched folds in drapery patterns almost identical to those of the latter, which more convincingly suggest the form of the body beneath. Both must be derived from a similar workshop pattern. The *Deposition,* therefore, most likely predates the *Baptism* panels, which were produced between 1502 and 1508, given the biographical evidence of the donors (see discussion in chapter 5).

Details about the working procedure evident in the *Deposition* also support a dating between about 1495 and 1500. Unusual among David's extant works, this painting was executed in oil on a fine linen of two pieces sewn together in a horizontal seam about eighteen inches from the bottom edge.[78] Only a fraction of the paintings from this period that were produced on linen instead of oak panel have survived,[79]

130. IRR detail of Joseph of Arimathea in Figure 128

and Bruges was a leading center for this specialized production. One other painting attributed to David of this type is known, namely the *Adoration of the Magi* in the Galleria degli Uffizi, which to judge by its proximity in figure style to the works of Geertgen tot Sint Jans, as well as to David's own early *Adoration* in the Musées Royaux des Beaux-Arts de Belgique, Brussels, is also an early work.[80]

The marked difference between the Uffizi *Adoration* and the *Deposition* is David's introduction of oil paint to the latter, whereas the former was painted in traditional tüchlein technique. Often designated as the

first known painting in oil on linen (or very fine-weave canvas), the *Deposition* probably did not originally hold that distinction but has gained it because so few in this technique remain. Other examples of about the same date, such as the series of the Legend of Saint Ursula by a Cologne master and the Legend of Saint Lawrence of about 1510 by a member of this master's workshop, are also conventional oil paintings made on chalk grounds in an animal-glue medium.[81]

As he did with his contemporary paintings in oil on panel, David proceeded with an underdrawing in a dry medium (probably black chalk) on the ground preparation (Figures 130–132).[82] Similar to the under-drawing of the *Crucifixion,* this is a relatively loose compositional sketch for the figures and their draperies, which is augmented only here and there with brush underdrawing working out some of the details of the modeling of the forms in parallel hatching (Figures 131 and 132). There are few adjustments from the underdrawing to the completed painted forms; in David's typical manner, he reworked the length and breadth of the draperies at the bottom of the figures of the Virgin and Nicodemus, retracting a far larger area left in reserve for the Virgin's drapery (Figure 133), presumably to provide additional space for the exquisitely painted skull and bones, which were executed without a preliminary under-drawing in the paint layers alone at a more advanced stage of the painting process.[83]

A by-now-familiar feature visible in the X-radiograph is David's plan for the system of lighting to be employed in the painting (Figures 133 and 134). Reserve areas were maintained for the general forms of the landscape and darkest portions of the sky. Over this David painted in the prominent church tower at the left and mountains at the right and left on the horizon, and he lightly touched in strokes of white for the clouds over the dark streaks of the sky.

The heads of the figures show David's interest in establishing the light effects in the preliminary stages—the strokes of lead white are mostly restricted to noses, foreheads, and chins, already providing an indication for the modeling of the faces. The head of Nicodemus is a notable exception here (Figure 134). This head is broadly brushed in a flat tone, as was David's practice in portrait heads in the *Justice of Cambyses* panels (Figures 67 and 72).[84] Its portrait aspect is further evident in the individualized features of the face, the man's detached expression, his prominent placement in the forefront of the composition, and his larger size in relation to the other figures in the painting. The representation of Nicodemus as a portrait is in keeping with a tradition whereby this figure is singled out as an exemplum of decorum and behavior with which the viewer is meant to identify.

The *Gospel of Nicodemus* (*Evangelicum Nicodemi*) reached the height of its popularity in the late fifteenth century, when it was incorporated into the Middle Dutch Passion narrative, *Dat Lyden ende die Passie Ons Heren Jhesu Christi.* Nicodemus's account of the last days of Christ's life was considered to be especially authentic and based on historical fact, as Nicodemus, unlike the disciples who fled after Christ's arrest, was present as an eyewitness.[85] Other texts, such as contemporary Passion plays, under-score the piety and humility of Nicodemus, who says to Joseph of Arimathea, "Take thou the head, I [am worthy only to] take the feet [of Christ]."[86] The Nicodemus of the Frick painting may well be a disguised portrait of the patron or a known individual whose presence here in this capacity forges a link between the depiction of the Deposition and the viewer.

David's decision to paint the *Deposition* on linen rather than on oak panel may have had something to do with the painting's size and destination or with considerations of cost. As it is a very large painting (142.5 × 112.5 cm), it would have been practical to produce it on the far less weighty linen rather than a heavy wooden support. This would have been a consideration, particularly if the painting were to travel a considerable distance. Horizontal stress cracks are evident in several places in the painting, indicating that it was rolled at one time, perhaps for transportation. An old tradition names Genoa as its ultimate destination, but any slight verification of this theory comes only from meager circumstantial evidence. Now barely visible halos, an uncommon feature of Netherlandish paintings that remained in the north, encircle the heads of Christ and all of the figures at the left. Although Mary Magdalene (identified by her red hanging purse and rich costume), John, and the Virgin would customarily receive this adornment, the other "Mary" (here in a nun's black habit) would not normally be included with the beatified group. If the woman is not one of the Marys but instead represents Saint Scholastica, the sister of Saint Benedict, however, this might well explain her halo, her Benedictine habit, and the linking of the painting with

131. IRR detail of Nicodemus in Figure 128

132. IRR detail of figure in Figure 128

the region around Genoa in Italy, where she was particularly venerated.

Like that of Campin, David's *Deposition* was especially popular: a very careful copy is attributed to Isenbrant, and there were a number of replicas that reproduced the composition, cropping it to the central grouping of five or six figures.[87] Increased market demand encouraged streamlined methods of manufacture, and it was possibly for this reason that a drawing in the British Museum that Popham described as "in brush and Indian ink on vellum, heightened with white" was incorporated for workshop use (Figure 135).[88] Its closest painted parallel is a panel attributed to David's workshop that was last known in the P. T. Grange collection in London (Figure 136).[89]

Although my suggestions here for the type and use of the British Museum drawing are preliminary and must be the subject of further physical study of

the material aspects of the sheet, the present state of research suggests that it is not at all a freehand drawing, but a counterproof. Of little or no aesthetic merit, this drawing of the Deposition (which also shows part of a male head in the upper right corner) is concerned mainly with the composition and outlines of forms, which it shows in reverse of David's designs. There is no searching quality to the drawing, and there are few trial strokes, except for those added in brush to describe the chest of Christ. In addition, there is no evidence of the use of either a quill or a reed pen—the former generally showing a more liquid and pliant stroke, and the latter often revealing a telling split in the middle of the line. This is a contour-conscious drawing with long, jagged lines of unevenly deposited pigment. There is a sudden increase and decrease in the width of the strokes, as well as irregular interruptions at random points,

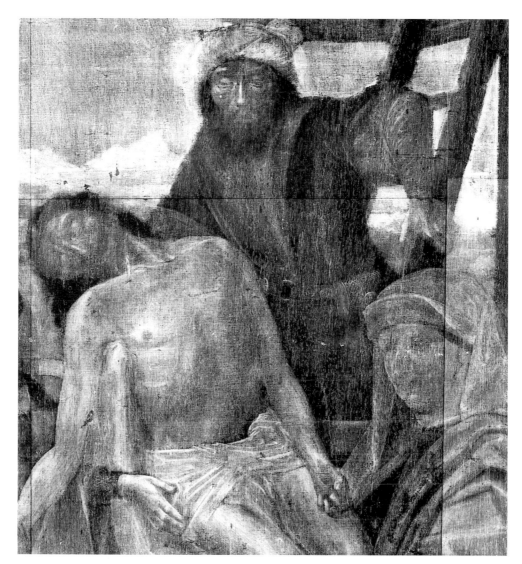

134. X-radiograph detail of Christ, Joseph of Arimathea, and Nicodemus in Figure 128

as if the medium of the application had been lifted up—all features characteristic of a counterproof.

It is most likely that this sheet served to quickly transfer the basic outline of David's composition to a grounded panel to be worked up or that it was made as an experiment to test the suitability of the composition in reverse, as was carried out in the Grange collection version. The vellum, which may have been prepared with an oily substance, was subsequently moistened in order to facilitate the lifting of the design lines from an inked prototype. This is evident from the sponge mark at the upper right of the sheet and the vertical streaks of material that appear to

133. X-radiograph of Figure 128

have reticulated or coagulated with the nonmixture of a water-and-oil-based application. The prototype from which the counterproof was pulled may have been a painting, an intermediary drawing, or a tracing. Such meager evidence of workshop practice in this instance gives only a small indication of the patterns of various types and sizes that were incorporated to supply the demand for this very popular subject, of special interest in Bruges.[90]

A further sign of David's accommodation of changing market demands is suggested by the puzzle of the Passion wings in the Lehman Collection. The exterior panels of the Annunciation were split before 1903 from their reverse sides, which depict Christ Carrying the Cross and the Resurrection (Figures

135. Workshop of Gerard David, *Deposition*, ca. 1500. Brush and ink with white heightening on vellum, 26.2 × 18.7 cm. British Museum, London (Photo Copyright © The British Museum)

137 and 138)[91]—the latter two especially show designs that are manifestly old-fashioned for David, but in working technique and execution these paintings represent David's full maturity as a master in Bruges and are strikingly innovative in some details. These wings are unique in David's oeuvre in two particular ways. One is that the *Annunciation* panels represent the artist's only surviving semi-grisaille images on the exterior of an altarpiece. All other exterior wings painted by David show various holy figures and donors presented in full color as living beings. In his characteristic interest in naturalism, however, David portrayed the Annunciation (Figure 137) not as painted statues on socles, but (as Memling was, perhaps, the first to do in the *Annunciation* wings in Groeningemuseum, Bruges) as "demi-grisailles."[92]

136. Workshop of Gerard David, *Deposition*, ca. 1500. Oil on wood, 37 × 27 cm. P. T. Grange collection, London (Photo © IRPA-KIK, Brussels)

The heads and hands of Gabriel and the Virgin are rendered in full color as "living sculptures," even though their static poses and the solid stone-gray of their draperies and Gabriel's wings suggest their inanimate state. In further allusions to reality, the dove descends without a connecting wall strut, draperies naturally spill out over the edge of the niche, and nicks in its stone ledge indicate the acci-

dents of time and wear. The attention given to the execution of the feathers of Gabriel's wings gives them an uncommonly tactile quality for simulated sculptures.

A second way in which David's representation here is atypical is that the interior panels display the only known instance where the artist depicted episodes of a sequential narrative on lateral wings of

137. Gerard David, *Annunciation*, ca. 1505. Oil on oak, 86.4 × 27.9 cm. The Metropolitan Museum of Art, Robert Lehman Collection, 1975 (1975.1.120)

138a,b. Gerard David, *Christ Carrying the Cross* and the *Resurrection*, ca. 1505. Oil on oak, each 86.4 × 27.9 cm. The Metropolitan Museum of Art, Robert Lehman Collection, 1975 (1975.1.119)

139. Passion Altarpiece from the parish church of Pruszcz, ca. 1500–1510. Warsaw Muzeum Narodowe, Warsaw (Photo © IRPA-KIK, Brussels)

an altarpiece. In part in order to accommodate the desired scenes in such a tall and narrow format— the *Crucifixion* above *Christ Carrying the Cross,* and the *Road to Emmaus* and the *Supper at Emmaus* over the *Resurrection*—David had to temporarily abandon the advances he had made toward naturalistic landscape depiction in the *Crucifixion* (Figure 125) and the *Deposition* (Figure 128). Here the scenes are artificially linked by the structure of the landscape, with no real sense of depth. This is in stark contrast to the far more naturally arranged additional episodes found in the background of the Baptism Triptych (Figure 213), which is of about the same date.[93]

But David may have had a quite deliberate reason for introducing a presentation so antithetical to his own more progressive inclinations. The arrangement of episodes stacked one on top of another with a very high horizon line is characteristic of painted wings that are made to go with sculpted altarpieces where individually carved elements are often mounted one on top of another (for example Figure 139).[94] It seems entirely plausible that the missing central portion of the altarpiece was originally planned as a multi-episodic sculpted, rather than painted, scene.[95] If so, this may also account for David's singular choice within his oeuvre of simulated sculpture for the exterior *Annunciation,* perhaps a deliberate reference to the medium of the triptych's featured center piece.

As Lynn Jacobs notes in her recently published study of early Netherlandish carved altarpieces, "painted wings . . . were a very standard accompaniment to the polychromed *caisse* of South Netherlandish carved altarpieces."[96] However, there do not seem to have been any standardized workshop procedures that governed collaboration between wing painters, sculptors, and those who carried out the polychromy of the sculptures. Noted panel painters—among them Hieronymus Bosch and Jan van Coninxloo— are documented as having participated in these collaborative ventures with sculptors, who often would have been in a different workshop in a different guild (as in the case of Brussels manufacture) or even in a different town.[97] Although subcontracting of one artisan group by another did occur, this was not always the case, and in certain situations collaborative ventures between sculptors and painters were under the client's control instead.[98] In Bruges, an ordinance of 1431 of the carpenters' guild stipulated that carvers could not subcontract work to painters, or vice versa, thus leaving it to the buyer to arrange for the completion of individually purchased parts of an altarpiece.[99]

If David originally conceived of the Passion scenes as the painted wings of a sculpted and polychromed *caisse,* nothing but his portion of this project remains. It may have been that the initial plans changed, and

140. Hypothetical reconstruction of the Passion Altarpiece (including wings in Figure 138 and *Lamentation*, Philadelphia Museum of Art)

the work was never carried out, leaving two beautifully executed wings—painted on both sides—that could be used instead for another purpose. The work most often accepted as the central panel belonging to the hypothetical reconstruction of a painted triptych was first suggested by Valentiner in 1913.[100] This is the Johnson collection *Lamentation*.[101] The compatible dimensions of the Philadelphia and the Lehman panels would make a suitable match.[102] But Robert Lehman raised a dissenting voice concerning the inharmonious nature of the landscapes,[103] an objection to which other observations may be added (see the hypothetical reconstruction in Figure 140). The joining of the three panels does not provide one continuous landscape, but a disjointed one in which the wings show a vertically built landscape with no view into the distance, while the *Lamentation* continues as far as the eye can see. Although the brownish rock formation added on top of the tree at the left

edge of the *Lamentation* might be imagined to fit with similar features at the right side of *Christ Carrying the Cross,* or the grayish rocks at the right edge of the *Lamentation* to match those at the left edge of the *Resurrection,* the rocky hills of the wings (especially of the *Resurrection*) are in the foreground and those in the *Lamentation* are in the middle distance. Two tomb openings—an arched one in the *Lamentation* and a rectangular one behind Christ in the *Resurrection*—are an unnecessary and unlikely duplication. In addition, the change from brownish hills to greenish ones is an abrupt color shift, a jarring misfit at a time in David's development when he was particularly concerned with the representation of naturally conceived space and theme-appropriate settings.

Certain other formal considerations also argue against the proposed match of the Lehman wings with the Philadelphia panel. The figures of the wings and the *Lamentation* are not of the same scale, those of the latter being larger than the former. This is the reverse of what is occasionally a scale difference between figures of altarpiece wings and the central panel. In two of David's other altarpieces, the Baptism Triptych and the Nativity Triptych (Figures 213 and 200), the donor figures are slightly larger than their patron saints and the figures of the central panel, because they are physically closer to the viewer's space when the wings are open at a slight angle. Furthermore, the close-up view of the *Lamentation* figures, along with those in the tightly cropped side panels, makes for an especially crowded ensemble across the foreground plane. In other examples from David's workshop where the Lamentation is the theme of the central panel, single saints adorn the wings, thereby focusing greater attention on the central *Andachtsbild*.[104] If wings were intended for the Philadelphia *Lamentation,* which does not appear to have been the case for the most closely associated versions of this composition, in Winterthur and Burgos (as well as an earlier arched-top panel in Chicago; Figure 141),[105] they would probably have shown saints with or without donor figures.

This group of paintings of the Lamentation instead appears to have been an independent production of a popular theme that already at this stage indicates a well-developed practice of pattern reuse. The earliest version is the Chicago painting of about 1485 (Figure 141), which slightly postdates the Antwerp and London Christ Nailed to the Cross Altarpiece (Figures 91–93), showing similar patterns of drapery folds and geometrically formed heads with sharp angular facial features.[106] In the late 1490s, David re-employed the same model of the figure of Mary Magdalene and an adjusted version of Saint John the Baptist and added them to a new motif of the Virgin and Christ, where she embraces him, which more closely approximates a design that had originated in the workshop of Rogier van der Weyden (of which the original is probably the one in Musées Royaux des Beaux-Arts de Belgique, Brussels).[107] David's paintings in the Church of San Gil, Burgos (formerly attributed to Isenbrant, but certainly by David, Figure 142)[108] and in Philadelphia (see center of reconstruction, Figure 140) appear to take advantage of a working method employed for the late versions of Rogier's design, that is, the rearrangement of separate patterns of simple or grouped figures according to the requirements of the client.[109] Although the underdrawing of the figures in the San Gil panel (Figure 143) is coherent and stylistically consistent with David's work, it is clear from the somewhat awkward juncture and overlapping draperies of Mary Magdalene with the grouping of Saint John, Christ, and the Virgin that separate patterns existed that could be rearranged to fit the space available.[110]

Close technical examination indicates that certain alterations were made to the Philadelphia *Lamentation* at an unknown but early date in order to fit it with the Lehman wings:[111] it was cut down at the lower edge, thereby eliminating most of a skull at the bottom, which was afterward overpainted with the brown ground and the plants; a new skull was less adeptly rendered near the base of the cross, just as a misunderstood and poorly executed pelvic bone was added to the lower edge of the painting; the brown rock mass at the left and the gray one (now mostly removed) at the right were painted on top of the completed landscape and tomb opening, respectively; and dark streaks were worked in over the existing clouds (the reverse of David's execution in the Lehman wings and in the Frick *Deposition*) to match those of the lateral panels. Furthermore, the draperies of Saint John and Mary Magdalene were substantially repainted.[112] Although what is known of the provenance of the Lehman paintings does not match the little information available about the Philadelphia *Lamentation,* it seems clear that at one time they were joined and adjusted to fit together as an ensemble.

In their style and technique, the Lehman wings again reflect a knowledge of works from the atelier of Dieric Bouts. The wings are taller and narrower in format, but the compositional arrangement, figure types, and palette relate to Boutsian workshop paintings, especially to two panels by the so-called Master of the Munich Arrest of Christ, named for the *Arrest of Christ* and the *Resurrection* wings of an altarpiece now in the Alte Pinakothek (Figures 144 and 145).[113]

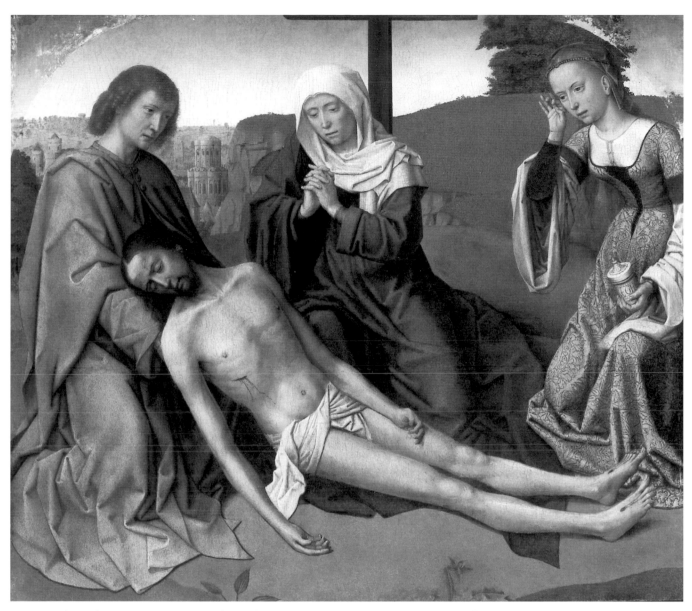

141. Gerard David, *Lamentation*, ca. 1490. Oil on oak, 56 × 63 cm. Art Institute, Chicago (Photo © 1997, The Art Institute of Chicago. All rights reserved)

These two panels are of uncertain authorship; the estimated felling date of the wood used for them is 1476, as determined by Peter Klein—that is, in the period of Bouts's successors in his workshop, which continued after his death in 1475.[114] In each panel large-scale figures crowd the foreground space, portions of them cut off by the close cropping of the composition, while subsidiary scenes are found in the background above. The Lehman wings are more restricted in their far-distance view, but they share the same general construction of a vertically built landscape: coulisse elements that give way to prominent hillocks and a middle distance populated by pathways leading to background vignettes. If the Munich wings were to be further compressed in width, an even closer link with the Lehman wings can be imagined. The figures are crowded, but within a strict schematic order; the soldiers of each *Resurrection* are evenly arranged on three sides of Christ in contrasting poses and states of slumber, wakefulness, or surprise. Unexpected color combinations, and in particular a dependency upon Bouts's red-green juxtaposition, animate David's composition, as does the variety of contrasting gestures—hands that are open and closed,

142. Gerard David, *Lamentation*, ca. 1500. Oil on wood, 91 × 79.7 cm. Church of San Gil, Burgos

relaxed and poised to strike. A passion for recording details of costume, reflections in armor, and differences in attitude and physiognomy of the deliberately varied figure types is shared by both artists. These effects are consistently found in the Bouts workshop, and the specific pose of the Lehman resurrected Christ appears in Resurrections by Aelbert Bouts (for example, in the Mauritshuis, The Hague) and the Master of the Retable of Enghien.[115]

For certain details of composition and figure motifs, David also once again relied upon his close connections with manuscript illumination, specifically with the designs of the Master of the Older Prayer Book of Maximilian I, probably Alexander Bening. A nearly identical grouping of figures as in David's *Christ Carrying the Cross,* is found in this master's *Way to Calvary* in at least two Books of Hours from the last years of the fifteenth century—the *Book of Hours* of Queen Isabella the Catholic (Cleveland Museum of Art, 63.256, fol. 69) and the Munich *Book of Hours* (cod. lat. 28345, fol. 112v). Figure motifs in the Lehman *Resurrection*—namely the reclining figure

143. IRR detail of Figure 142 (IRR documentation by A. Balis and N. Van Hout)

in the foreground and the seated, sleeping solider—likewise appear in somewhat later illuminations, such as the *Grimany Breviary* of about 1515.[116]

As unusual as these wings may be in format, they are entirely consistent with David's working technique. The Lehman wings are among the earliest in David's oeuvre to show underdrawing in a dry and a liquid medium where the latter approaches the use of an undermodeling. Although in the *Justice of Cambyses* David produced the underdrawing on the panels in both media, he used the brush to correct and finalize

the preliminary plan sketched out in a dry medium, probably black chalk (Figures 74 and 76). This corrective function of the brush underdrawing is also employed in portions of the Passion wings, but a new use is evolving here.

In *Christ Carrying the Cross* (compare Figures 138a and 146a), David made the rough sketch of the entire composition, including the subsidiary scenes in the background, with a dry medium, probably black chalk. Here and there, for example in the drapery folds of the underside of Christ's right arm or in

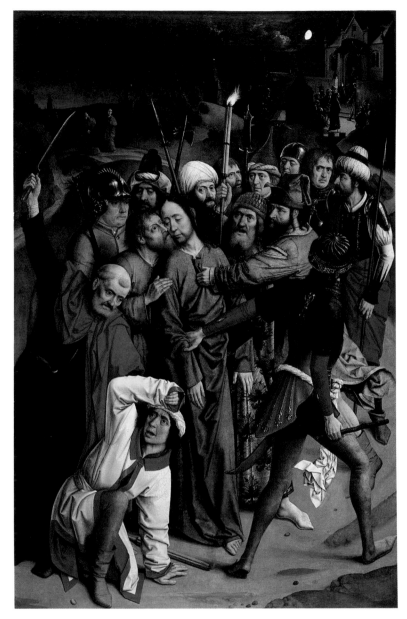

144. Master of the Munich Arrest of Christ, *Arrest of Christ*, ca. 1480. Oil on oak, 105 × 68 cm. Alte Pinakothek, Munich (Photo Artothek, Munich)

the gatherings just below his rope belt, he worked out the modeling of the forms and the system of lighting by parallel hatching and crosshatching. The changes that David introduced to the preliminary layout of the composition he did mostly at a mid-stage in the painting process, after having blocked in the background color around the forms of the first drawn design: he moved the right leg of Christ farther forward, and increased the size of the running dog's head. Other decisions, namely, shortening the trailing draperies of Christ's robe and adjusting the

vertical and horizontal dimensions of the cross, he also carried out at the stage of painting, as the pentimenti of both changes are now easily visible. The use of brush and a black pigment for the purposes of modeling forms was restricted here to a few brief strokes in the face of the soldier at the far right with the whip and minimal parallel hatching running perpendicular to the deepest folds of his green cloak.

Although David initiated the design of the *Resurrection* in a dry medium, he proceeded differently and

145. Master of the Munich Arrest of Christ, *Resurrection*, ca. 1480. Oil on oak,
105 × 68 cm. Alte Pinakothek, Munich (Photo Artothek, Munich)

in a manner that is very telling for the development
of painting technique in early Netherlandish art, as
well as for David's important transitional role (Figures
138b and 146b). Over his preliminary layout, probably in black chalk, David further worked up the details
of his composition in brush underdrawing. This is
clearly visible in the soldier sprawled across the foreground of the scene, who shields his eyes from the
brilliant and sudden appearance of Christ. The folds
of his cloak, first lightly sketched in with black chalk,
are rearranged in bold brush drawing; then they are

further changed in the painted layers to modify the
specific configuration of the folds. This is similar to
the way David used the brush in the underdrawing
of the *Justice of Cambyses* or the outside left wing of
the Baptism Triptych (Figure 148), that is, for the correction of forms.

For the figure of Christ, David continued in a
slightly different manner. After sketching in the rough
layout of the figure (including the contours of the
right leg beneath the drapery), David secured his
design with brush, but here he made only minor

146a,b. IRR of Figures 138a and 138b

147a,b. X-radiograph of Figures 138a and 138b

148. IRR detail of Virgin and Child in Figure 213

through for a longer period of time during the painting process, providing a toned area without the necessity of building up the shadows with multiple glazes in the final applications of paint on the surface. It is telling that he did this in the red draperies and not in the deep blue-gray of the reclining soldier's cloak, for in the latter, the dark color would prevent the undermodeling from showing through and serving the same purpose as in the red.[117] This use of underdrawing as undermodeling in the Passion wings is an advance in David's working method and provides a link with the Cervara Altarpiece (1506) and the *Virgin among Virgins* (1509), in which this technique further evolves (see chapters 2 and 4).

The X-radiograph (Figure 147) shows the same developing sense of confidence in the placement of motifs within the composition and in the preliminary modeling of the flesh areas of the figures in touches of white for the highlights. Reserve areas were left for the general layout of the landscape and the buildings at the upper right of the *Resurrection*. In his typical manner of continuing to work out the details directly in the painted layers, David added the crosses of the *Crucifixion* directly over the sky and modified the form and size of the trees and architecture on the horizon of the *Resurrection*. In working technique and execution, the Lehman wings demonstrate both a confidence and spontaneity in approach that signal David's mature phase of production. In quickly and assuredly building up the preliminary paint layers of his work, he reserved time for the finishing touches on which he lavished attention, in order to produce the convincing modeling of lifelike forms in some of David's most exquisitely executed passages anywhere— for example, the *Resurrection* soldier sleeping with crossed hands.

In David's ongoing endeavors to communicate successfully the theme of his paintings to the viewer, he assimilated the lessons learned from the art of Jan van Eyck and Dieric Bouts, which profoundly influenced him. David's early works benefitted from the elements of style that defined the achievements of his two predecessors: their concepts of space, light, color, and volume of form. In particular, David

changes in the fall of the draperies or the direction of folds. Instead, and perhaps for the first time, he saw the advantage of using the brush underdrawing as a kind of undermodeling to reinforce the darkest areas of the folds of his red cloak to the right. In considering shortcut methods and with the assurance of his approach and technique, David realized that the dark brush drawing below the thin red paint layers of the draperies would slightly show

emulated the compositional schemes of Bouts, which easily accommodated volumetrically conceived figures in a setting of carefully studied nature, all bathed in a warm, unifying light. David followed the precision of van Eyck and Bouts in the treatment of various textures in costumes, foliage, and flowers and, above all, the attention given to detailed description of heads and hands, which he developed to a heightened degree in order to successfully convey the meaning of the theme at hand. His increasingly acute observation of natural phenomena, along with a deeper understanding of the devotional tenor of the times, led to his most inspired production in the first decades of the sixteenth century, in which he achieved a highly successful blending of form and function.

NOTES

1. Sanderus 1641–44, p. 154; Bruges, Episcopal Archives, Verzameling Grafschriften van de Onze-Lieve-Vrouwekerk, fol. 41v; see also Weale 1863c, p. 225, no. 10, and Weale 1895, p. 14. David's tomb is now beneath the tower of the church.

2. The basis of this is stylistic associations between David's early works and those attributed to Geertgen tot Sint Jans. See Panofsky 1953, vol. I, p. 351; Snyder 1985, p. 187; Friedländer 1967–76, vol. VIb (1971), p. 93. On a suggested apprenticeship of David with Geertgen, see Baldass 1936, pp. 91–93. On Geertgen in Ghent, see Winkler 1964, p. 282; and in Bruges, see Koch 1951, p. 259. Châtelet believes that Geertgen's active life extended ca. 1465–75 (Châtelet 1981, pp. 93–120, 218–22), and Snyder (believing that David was older than Geertgen), from 1475 to 1495 (1971, p. 458, and 1996, p. 230), an opinion followed by Scillia (1975, pp. 114–16).

3. On Gerard David and manuscript illumination, see Weale 1863c, pp. 223–34; Weale 1866b, p. 500; Weale 1895, pp. 47–70; Winkler 1913, pp. 271–80; Schöne 1937, pp. 170–74; Parmentier 1942, p. 9; Boon [1946], pp. 11–12 n. 1; Van de Walle de Ghelcke 1952, pp. 399–422; Scillia 1975; Kren 1983, pp. 40–48; Brinkmann 1997, pp. 135–40, 143–49.

4. Boon [1946], pp. 4–5, 8; Ebbinge-Wubben 1969, pp. 95–96; James Snyder observed this (1985, p. 187); J. H. Marrow, "Dutch Manuscript Painting in Context: Encounters with the Art of France, the Southern Netherlands, and Germany," in *Masters and Miniatures, Proceedings of the Congress on Medieval Manuscript Illumination in the Northern Netherlands (Utrecht, 10–13 December, 1989),* vol. III, *Studies and Facsimiles of Netherlandish Illuminated Manuscripts,* K. van der Horst and J-C. Klamt, eds. (Doornspijk, 1991), p. 60; a review of David's possible sources and the pertinent literature may be found in Eisler 1989, pp. 134–37. Van Miegroet (1989, cat. no. 63, p. 318) rejects the attribution to David. For dendrochronology, see Appendix B.

5. For the above discussion of influences, see Scillia 1975, pp. 78–95. For the *Christ Carrying the Cross,* see entry by Ainsworth in Ainsworth and Christiansen, eds. 1998, cat. no. 8.

6. A. L. Mayer, "Die Austellung der Schloss Rohoncz, München," *Pantheon* 6 (1930), pp. 297–302; H. van Hall, *Portretten van Nederlandse beeldende kunstenaars* (Amsterdam, 1963), p. 75.

7. Van Miegroet 1989, cat. no. 4, pp. 47–48 and 277–78.

8. See Ainsworth 1997b and van Miegroet 1989, ill. p. 72, cat. no. 16, pp. 285–86.

9. Scillia 1975, pp. 162–63; van Miegroet 1989, no. 4, pp. 277–78; ill. in Friedländer 1967–76, vol. III (1968), pl. 43, and vol. IV (1967), pl. 117. For other formal influences on David's central panel, see the discussion in Mundy 1980a, pp. 161–99.

10. See Davies 1955, pp. 173–75. For a color ill. and up-to-date discussion with bibliography, see Ainsworth and Christiansen, eds. 1998, cat. no. 2.

11. For dendrochronology, see Appendix B.

12. I am grateful to Stephanie Buck, Kupferstichkabinett, Berlin, for this information (letter of April 17, 1998).

13. On the working technique of Bouts in his two documented works, the Last Supper Altarpiece and the *Justice of Emperor Otto II,* see respectively Comblen-Sonkes 1996 and Philippot 1957, pp. 55–80, and F. Van Molle et al. 1958, pp. 7–69; for Geertgen, see van Bueren and Faries 1991, pp. 141–50.

14. Sotheby's and Co., July 2, 1958, Lot 26; *Christ Nailed to the Cross,* on prepared ground, 4¾ × 6⅝ in. Douwes photo in Getty Center Photo Archives.

15. I am grateful to the Paintings Conservation staff and to Alistair Smith, then curator of Netherlandish paintings at the National Gallery, London, for permission to study the *Nailing to the Cross* in Sept. 1984 with the assistance of Chiyo Ishikawa. Further thanks are due to Lorne Campbell (letter of June 26, 1997) for pointing out additional color notations on figures in the painting. Campbell notes three that are all different on the robes of the men in yellow, red, and purple surrounding Christ's upper torso; *bs* (probably for *blauw,* "blue") were found in the blue trousers of the man digging and in the blue shirt of the soldier in the lower right-hand corner. I am further grateful to Dr. E. Van Damme at the Royal Museum in Antwerp for the opportunity to study the wings of the altarpiece in the spring of 1986 with the

assistance of Katherine Crawford Luber. Although X-radio-graphs of the London painting are available for study, they do not exist for the Antwerp panels at this time.

16. Van Bueren and Faries 1991, pp. 142–43.

17. This phenomenon has also been observed in later works from David's atelier, namely the *Adoration of the Magi* (Alte Pinakothek, Munich), the outside left wing of the Baptism Triptych (Groeningemuseum, Bruges) and the *Rest on the Flight into Egypt,* as well as the central panel of the Saint Anne Altarpiece (both in the National Gallery of Art, Washington).

18. Boon (1978, p. 9, nos. 16 and 17) first noticed a stylistic link between these drawings and those in the British Museum and places them within the circle of Hugo van der Goes.

19. For a review of the literature, see van Miegroet 1989, cat. no. 1, pp. 273–74.

20. The early provenance of the central panel and the wings indicates that they only came together in the early 20th century. For the central panel: Count de Galliera, Paris, by 1874; Mr. Gore, London; Steinmeyer, Lucerne, 1923; F. Kleinberger & Co., New York, 1923; Michael Friedsam collection, New York, 1923–31. For the wings: private collection, Genoa; Richard von Kaufmann collection, Berlin, 1898–1917; sale Cassirer and Helbig, Berlin, Dec. 7, 1917 (lot 76–77); Omnes van Nijenrode, Breukelen; sale Muller, Amsterdam, July 10, 1923 (lot 7); Paul Bottenweiser, Berlin, 1923; F. Kleinberger & Co., New York, 1923; Michael Friedsam collection, New York, 1923–31.

21. The angel in the MMA *Nativity* has been severely abraded and can only be recognized as a darker patch of blue in the form of an angel at the top center of the painting. For a review of the literature on the Budapest and Cleveland versions, see van Miegroet 1989, cat. nos. 2 and 3, pp. 274–76.

22. For a full discussion of the iconography of the Nativity, see Lievens–de Waegh 1991, pp. 33–38.

23. Van Miegroet 1989, p. 36. For a parallel with the Master of the Brunswick Diptych, see Friendländer 1967–76, vol. V (1969), pl. 18. David's Joseph type here is also perhaps derived from Geertgen tot Sint Jans, for it is first found among works attributed to David at his most Geertgenesque stage, such as the *Adoration of the Magi,* a tüchlein painting in the Uffizi (for a good color ill., see L. Berti, A. M. P. Tofani, C. Caneva, *The Uffizi* [London, 1993], p. 207).

24. The development of this theory of David's connection with the workshop of Dieric Bouts contradicts the notion of Hans van Miegroet (1989, ch. 2, "The Early Style I [ca. 1480–98]: The Ghent Connection," pp. 35–93) that David was above all influenced by Hugo van der Goes.

25. On evidence of this standard practice, see Campbell 1981a, pp. 52–53.

26. Friedländer 1967–76, vol. III (1968), p. 38.

27. For these versions, see Friedländer 1967–76, vol. III (1968), pls. 41 (25a) and 90 (nos. 80 and 80a). A version attributed to Aelbert Bouts in the Gallerie Robert Finck in 1965 (formerly Convent of the Assumption, Kensington) attests to the continued popularity of this composition.

28. Some of these same features are also found in Dieric Bouts's Prado Infancy of Christ Triptych, in the Nativity scene, where the angels appear in adoration of the Christ Child (see Friedländer 1967–76, vol. III [1968]), pl. 1).

29. For the Memling versions of this theme, see De Vos 1994, cat. nos. 13, 15, 32, a tiny scene in 38, A14, B1, and B4.

30. The significantly abraded state of parts of the MMA *Nativity* (even an angel above and two shepherds on the background hills have been almost completely effaced) and an overgenerous previous restoration of the Virgin's head had obscured the delicacy of execution of this painting. Now, with the painting newly restored, its light touch can again be appreciated, as well as the details in relatively fine state, including the wide-eyed, intelligent-looking child, the angel at the right, and the figure of Joseph. Peter Klein's dendrochronology report (Aug. 14, 1997) notes that the earliest felling date for the panel of the *Nativity* is 1477. With a minimum of two years' storage and seasoning time for the wood, the earliest creation time for the painting would be 1479. See Appendix B.

31. See Scillia 1975, pp. 182–84, 190–94, 212–13, 282, 288–89, 293; de Winter 1981, pp. 344–47; Kren 1983, pp. 40–48; van Miegroet 1989, pp. 327–28, no. 85; Brinkmann 1997, p. 135.

32. S. Urbach 1987b, pp. 83–94, and Périer–d'Ieteren 1987, pp. 95–106. Dendrochronology has not been carried out on the Budapest or Cleveland Nativity paintings.

33. Very similar broad-brush underdrawing is evident in the figures and architecture of the Brussels painting. Reflectogram assemblies are housed in the Sherman Fairchild Paintings Conservation Department, MMA.

34. For a full discussion of this altarpiece see Comblen-Sonkes 1996, pp. 1–84.

35. Following J. Destrée (*Hugo van der Goes* [Brussels and Paris, 1914], pp. 115–16), van Miegroet (1989, p. 42) sees these angels as an homage, in reverse, to those in the foreground of Hugo van der Goes's Portinari Altarpiece; they are, however, much closer to the quiet, naive types of Geertgen than to Hugo's more adult and actively engaged angels.

36. Koch 1951, pp. 259–60.

37. This juxtaposition is made visually in van Miegroet 1989, pp. 42–43, but in the text (p. 42) he states oddly that David's Virgin is borrowed from Hugo's Virgin in the Portinari Altarpiece.

38. Following William Suhr's condition report of Feb. 1963 (J. Paul Getty Center Archives), Will Reel suggested that David made these changes himself (Reel 1985, pp. 399–401). Van Miegroet (1989, pp. 42–43) states that David intentionally covered over his first figure of Joseph to match in reverse Hugo van der Goes's Joseph in the Berlin *Nativity* (see juxtaposition of illustrations on p. 44). As early as 1905, Bodenhausen (p. 93) had noted correctly that the head of Joseph had been overpainted by a different artist, possibly to make the features conform to those of a 16th-century owner of the painting. The Joseph figure as we see it now was further changed by the 1957–58 restoration of William Suhr. See further discussion of this in the 1960 Detroit exh. cat. (pp. 186–89) and in Urbach (1987b, p. 89) and Périer-d'Ieteren (1987, p. 102).

39. Bodenhausen 1905, p. 93.

40. See especially J. Dusserre, "Les Origines de la dévotion à Saint Joseph," extract from *Cahiers de Joséphologie* (Montreal, 1954).

41. See discussion in chaps. 2 and 5 concerning the Nativity Altarpiece and the representation of the donor figures as saints or the suggestion that the convent sisters are shown as the female saints in David's *Virgin among Virgins*.

42. As De Vos notes (1994, p. 396), Memling's art may have been responsible for a certain "stateliness and purity of color" that entered into David's paintings when he established himself in Bruges. But aside from limited influence in terms of certain compositions (the Sedano Triptych, for example), David learned far more from the specific lessons of Jan van Eyck and Dieric Bouts, whose essential artistic character was closer to his own.

43. On Memling's underdrawings and technique, see Ainsworth 1994b, pp. 78–87; Périer-d'Ieteren 1994, pp. 67–77; De Vos 1994, pp. 377–85; Campbell 1997, pp. 71–80; Borchert 1997, pp. 133–46; Faries 1997a, pp. 243–59.

44. For the early provenance of these paintings, see note 20 above. For further references, see van Miegroet 1989, cat. no. 1, pp. 273–74.

45. See van Asperen de Boer 1997.

46. Hall 1979, p. 131.

47. Ibid., pp. 131–33.

48. A single panel in the Chrysler Museum attributed to David, but most likely by a follower, shows a Crucifixion with Saints John the Baptist and Francis in attendance (see J. C. Harrison, *The Chrysler Museum: Handbook of the European and American Collections, Selected Paintings, Sculpture, and Drawings* [Norfolk, 1991], p. 7).

49. A triptych in the Escorial that has been attributed to David has a Lamentation in the center and wings representing Saint John the Baptist and Saint Francis, and a rare instance of these two saints with a Virgin and Child is in Zurich (private collection, illustrated in Friedländer 1967–76, vol. VIb [1971], pl. 174, and pl. 269, no. Add. 299 respectively).

50. Both the *Saint John the Baptist* and *Saint Francis Receiving the Stigmata* have suffered heat damage in the past, altering a previous greater tonal range and differentiation among the trees that must have once existed.

51. Ainsworth 1994b, cat. no. 3, pp. 78–85. Although a painting attributed to Aelbert van Ouwater in Granada, Capilla Réal, has been related to David's Saint John, the associations are probably more in terms of setting (see chap. 5) than formal traits. It is interesting to note that David specifically avoided reproducing the Saint John type of Memling, which existed in numerous examples, thanks to the local popularity of the saint in Bruges.

52. For dendrochronology, see Appendix B.

53. Sonkes 1969b, cat. nos. B12, B13, B14, C18, C24, D19.

54. On the question of Memling's apprenticeship with Rogier van der Weyden, see Ainsworth 1994c, pp. 78–81, and De Vos 1994, pp. 361–64.

55. Campbell 1995, p. 5.

56. Little of the provenance of the MMA's painting is known: Matteo Sarasqueta (by 1892); Robert Dell, London (until 1909). For further references, see van Miegroet 1989, cat. no. 7, pp. 279–80.

57. Illustrated in Friedländer 1967–76, vol. II (1967), pls. 32–33, no. 15.

58. Illustrated in ibid., pl. 95, no. 68, and pl. 108, no. 91.

59. For versions attributed to Isenbrant now in the collection of Her Majesty the Queen, see Lorne Campbell, *The Early Flemish Pictures in the Collection of Her Majesty the Queen* (Cambridge, 1985), no. 78, pl. 95; for those in Worcester, Mass., and the Cathedral in Cuenca, Spain, see Friedländer 1967–76, vol. XI (1974), nos. 159, 159b, and for one in Brussels associated with Benson, pl. 167, no. 248. It is notable that the Cuenca and Brussels versions are also closely connected to David's workshop through the replication of the specific drapery patterns found in the Magdalene's cloak as it spreads out below her left leg.

60. S. Ringbom, "Devotional Images and Imaginative Devotions: Notes on the Place of Art in Late Medieval Private Piety," *Gazette des Beaux-Arts*, ser. 6, 73 (1969), p. 162.

61. This panel may not always have stood alone, for the left edge of what is probably the original frame has remnants of two hinges that suggest a link with another panel, and hence that it formed part of a diptych. Although it is an iron plate, the uniform metal sheet of the upper hinge appears to be of modern fabrication rather than handcrafted; the cut sections for the metal are extremely neat and shallow for an early hinge; the use of five nails is unusual for a small plate; and the nails themselves have not rusted like iron of the late 15th century—all suggesting that the hinges were added at a later point for the attachment of another panel that was not originally part of the format. The right vertical element of the frame has been replaced. I am grateful to George Bisacca for studying the details of the frame with me.

62. Rice 1985, p. 80.

63. Bodenhausen and Valentiner 1911, p. 186.

64. This concurs with the dendrochronological date determined by Peter Klein, who established the earliest possible felling date of the tree from which the panel comes as 1489, and the creation time of the painting about a decade later, given the period of time necessary for the drying and seasoning of the wood panel. See Appendix B.

65. For the most recent discussions of this altarpiece and full bibliographies, see Sander 1993, pp. 129–53; Kemperdick 1996, pp. 56–87; Châtelet 1996, pp. 78–91, 289–91. For a discussion of another possible Deposition in Bruges, by Hugo van der Goes, see Kemperdick 1996, pp. 77–82.

66. For a discussion of the coat of arms and disagreements about its association with Bruges, see Kemperdick 1996, p. 69; Liverpool 1977, p. 40.

67. First suggested by Georges Hulin de Loo, *Catalogue critique: Exposition de tableaux flamands des XIVe, XVe, et XVIe siècles* (Bruges/Ghent, 1902), pp. xl, 6, no. 22, p. 31, no. 120; in agreement are Friedländer 1903, p. 7, no. 15; 1903b, p. 73; Weale 1903, p. 205; Floerke 1905, p. 148; Voll 1906, p. 94; Frinta 1966, p. 100. The suggestion of Saint Julian's Hospital

was made by Weale, *Exposition des primitifs flamands et d'art ancien*, exh. cat. (Bruges 1902), p. 10 f., no. 22; also Weale 1903, p. 205; and Pächt 1960, p. 416; for all, see Sander 1992, pp. 138–39 and notes.

68. The most recent discussion of this artist and painting with a bibliography is in Patoul and Van Schoute 1994, pp. 511–14, 642.

69. Book of Hours of Catherine of Cleves, New York, Pierpont Morgan Library, MS. 948, fol. 69v.

70. See Kemperdick 1996, pp. 70–71.

71. Friedländer 1967–76, vol. II (1967), p. 71 and pp. 13, 16, 60, no. 3, pl. 6; Conway 1882, p. 213, and Conway 1884, p. 27.

72. Alain Arnoud and Jean Michel Massing, *Splendors of Flanders* (Cambridge, 1993), pp. 64–65.

73. Held 1949, pp. 197–202.

74. Provenance: Rumored to have come from Spain (?); Nieuwenhuys collection, Amsterdam; collection of William II of Orange, King of the Netherlands; sold on Aug. 12, 1850 (lot 35); acquired by De Vries by Dingwall, Surrey; J. Dingwall, Tittenhurst, Sunninghill, Berkshire; Mary Ann Driver (Lady Martin-Holloway); bought in 1912 from Miss Driver's estate by Colnaghi and Orbach; Knoedler, New York; acquired by Frick in 1915. For various opinions and literature, see van Miegroet 1989, cat. no. 15, pp. 284–85.

75. Kemperdick (1996, p. 72) also notes the skull in the foreground and the motif of Saint John stepping on the drapery of the Virgin (although in the Liverpool copy, he steps on his own drapery, which Kemperdick suggests must be a mistake of the copyist).

76. For a full discussion of this altarpiece, see R. Van Schoute, *La Chapelle royale de Grenade*, Les Primitifs flamands, I: Corpus de la peinture des anciens Pays-Bas méridionaux au quinzième siècle 6 (Brussels 1963), pp. 36–53.

77. For a summary of the opinions, see van Miegroet 1989, cat. no. 15, pp. 284–85.

78. The oil medium and linen support of this painting were first suggested by William Suhr during the course of his examination and treatment of the painting in 1955 and confirmed more recently by Christopher McGlinchey (report of May 7, 1997). I am grateful to both Christopher McGlinchey and Hubert von Sonnenburg for help in carrying out this investigation and to Bernice Davidson and Edgar Munhall of the Frick Collection for permission to study the painting.

79. See Wolfthal 1989, cat. no. 505, pp. 50–51.

80. Pertinent literature is found in van Miegroet 1989, p. 312, where it is erroneously considered to be by a follower of David's.

81. L. Campbell, S. Foister, and A. Roy, eds., "Early Northern Painting," *National Gallery Technical Bulletin* 18 (1997), p. 24.

82. I am grateful to Bernice Davidson, curator of the Frick Collection, for the opportunity to study the Frick painting with infrared reflectography in Feb. 1990, with the assistance of Jeffrey Jennings.

83. This was also true of the bones in the foreground of the MMA *Crucifixion*.

84. See discussion in chap. 2.

85. See Werner J. Hoffmann, "The *Gospel of Nicodemus* in Dutch and Low German Literatures of the Middle Ages," pp. 337–60 in *The Medieval Gospel of Nicodemus Texts, Intertexts, and Contexts in Western Europe*, Z. Trydorczyk, ed., (Arizona, 1997).

86. Réau 1955–59, vol. 2, p. 515.

87. For these various replicas, see Friedländer 1967–76, vol. XI (1976), pl. 128–129, no. 165, 165a, 165c; pl. 167, no. 251; vol. IVb (1971), pl. 200, no. 192a, 192b.

88. Popham 1932, p. 15.

89. Friedländer 1967–76, vol. IVb (1971), pl. 200, no. 192b.

90. I am particularly grateful to Carmen Bambach for discussing with me the details of this drawing. The type of pattern reverse discussed here also occurs in many other examples, one of which is the Virgin and Child in the Sedano Triptych (Figure 150) and in the Philadelphia *Virgin and Child Enthroned with Two Angels* (Figure 280).

91. Weale (1903, col. 276) reports that they were already separated and cradled by the time they were in the Willett collection (an old photograph in the Friedländer archives of the Rijksbureau voor Kunsthistorische Documentatie, The Hague, is inscribed "Willett/XII.97/MJF"). The paintings belonged to the 4th earl of Ashburnum, Ashburnum Place; Henry Willett, Brighton (by 1897); Rudolph Kann, Paris; sold by the estate (1905) of Rudolph Kann to Duveen Bros., New York (by 1908); Philip Lehman (by 1913). For further references, see van Miegroet 1989, cat. no. 6, pp. 278–79.

92. Philippot 1966, pp. 225–42.

93. For further discussion on this painting, see chap. 5. Compare the heads of Christ in the *Baptism* and in the *Resurrection*, for example, which indicate a particularly close type and execution very close in date.

94. On contemporary south Netherlandish sculpted retables with painted wings see Philippot 1979, pp. 29–40; Jacobs 1986, esp. pp. 48–82; Nieuwdorp 1993 for numerous examples; and Périer-d'Ieteren 1996, pp. 91–117; and Jacobs 1998, esp. pp. 1–145.

95. Other examples of similar painted wings now missing their centers, which may well have been sculpted, are a *Christ Carrying the Cross* and *Resurrection*; a *Deposition and Entombment of Christ* attributed to Jacob Jansz (all in Musées Royaux des Beaux-Arts, Brussels, nos. 8737, 8738, and 92); and the *Arrest of Christ* and the *Resurrection* attributed to the Munich Master of the Taking of Christ (Munich, Alte Pinakothek, 806 and 809; Figures 144 and 145). These all share a common theme of Passion scenes.

96. Jacobs 1998, pp. 96–114, esp. p. 99.

97. Ibid., pp. 100–101.

98. For example, in the famous Crucifixion Altarpiece of Jacques de Baerze with painted wings by Melchior Broederlam. See Jacobs's discussion in ibid., p. 101 and n. 143.

99. Ibid., pp. 218–19.

100. Valentiner 1913, p. 10.

101. Friedländer 1967–76, vol. VIb (1971), p. 89; Sterling 1957, nos. 14 and 15; Szabo 1975, pp. 88–89; De Vos 1987, cols. 208–220; van Miegroet 1989, cat. no. 6, pp. 278–79; Wolff 1998, cat. no. 20.

102. The Philadelphia panel measures 85.4 × 64.8 cm, and the Lehman wings are 86.4 × 28 cm each.

103. Lehman 1928.

104. For example, the Escorial *Lamentation* with Saints John the Baptist and Francis attributed to Gerard David (Friedländer 1967–76, vol. VIb (1971), pl. 174).

105. For illustrations see Friedländer 1967–76, vol. VIb (1971), pl. 173, no. 163a and b, and pl. 202, no. 195.

106. See van Miegroet 1989, no. 5, p. 278.

107. Stroo and Sypher-d'Olne 1996, pp. 100–113 and n. 27.

108. Reconsidered by the author at the 1995 exhibition in Antwerp Cathedral; see *Vlaanderen en Castile y León,* exh. cat. (Antwerp,), pp. 202–3. My sincere thanks to Arnout Balis and Nico Van Hout for documentation of the underdrawing that helped to prove the attribution to David.

109. See Stroo and Sypher-d'Olne 1996, n. 27.

110. Verougstraete and Van Schoute 1997, pp. 21–27 and plates, describe a similar situation with the Pietàs of Rogier van der Weyden, which were, they convincingly show, created from separate cartoons of individual and grouped figures for a serial production accommodating the requirements and wishes of each client.

111. I am very grateful to Mark Tucker, paintings conservator at the Philadelphia Museum of Art, for a very fruitful collaboration in the ongoing study of this painting. In a preliminary investigation, the pigments of the reworked areas of the *Lamentation* prove to be consistent with David's time.

112. The multiple layers and thickness of these painted draperies explain why no underdrawing could be made visible here. Summary black-chalk underdrawing is found in the landscape.

113. For references, see Châtelet 1981, pp. 80–84 and 213, cat. no. 55a and b.

114. Klein 1991, pp. 36–37.

115. See Friedländer 1967–76, vol. III (1968), pl. 69, no. 56.

116. For illustrations of the mentioned illuminations, see de Winter 1981, esp. p. 373, figs. 49 and 51, and Ferrari, et al. 1973, pl. 35; also noted by Wolff (1998, cat. no. 20).

117. For a similar effect in the Uffizi *Lamentation* of Rogier van der Weyden, see Asperen de Boer et al. 1992, p. 31.

CHAPTER FOUR

Art for Export:
Commissioned Paintings for a Foreign Clientele

Bruges was renowned in the late Middle Ages and early Renaissance as the most prominent commercial center of northwestern Europe. The Hanseatic League established one of its main headquarters there, importing grain, charcoal, fur, and oak planks for panel paintings, while the English merchants, known as the Merchant Adventurers, developed a thriving trade with the city in wool. An especially strong economic link between Bruges and both the Iberian Peninsula and Italy was developed at the beginning of the thirteenth century. Vital for the cloth industry of Flanders was the wool imported by Castilian merchants, who acquired business privileges just after the Catalans in 1348. They officially set up their own colony in Bruges with consuls and governors appointed by the king of Castile as early as 1428 and a consulate before 1483. The Spanish community established itself on the Beursplein, and later, in 1494, the Castilian merchants set up their house on the Lange Winkel (later renamed Spanjaardstraat), creating a Spanish quarter. The first appearance of the Italians in Bruges came by way of the galleys of the Genoese using established sea routes between southern and northwestern Europe. Although the Venetians soon followed, it was the relationship forged between Bruges and Genoa that endured. The Genoese brought alum for the dyes essential for Flemish cloth manufacture, and they were well situated to control the shipping routes from the Mediterranean to the North Sea, passing through Flanders and England on the way. Colonies of Genoese, as well as Venetians, Luccans, and Florentines, settled in Bruges on the Vlamingstraat. In addition, the Italians were the primary controlling force in the

world of finance and monetary exchange, and established in Bruges the most important branch of the Florentine Medici bank between 1439 and 1490.

During these times, both Italians and Spaniards joined the wealthy upper classes, participating in the political life of Bruges, marrying into prominent families, and establishing themselves as an integral part of society. Among the Italians were the Arnolfini, Portinari, Lomellini, and Adornes—names that have endured not only because of their prominence in the political and economic arenas of Bruges life, but also because of the lasting legacy of their commissions for paintings.[1]

These wealthy foreigners were both short- and long term residents, who requested paintings for their private devotional use, for the chapels associated with their foreign community and businesses, and for memorials at their burial sites either locally or abroad. Orders for altarpieces also constituted a sophisticated expression of status in such a diverse community as Bruges was at the time, and a particular interest of the growing merchant class to "vivre noblement," as Wilson expressed it.[2] Paintings that were personalized through the addition of donor portraits or heraldry enhanced the image of the patron as possessing a certain level of power and wealth and sometimes a close connection to the ducal court.

Commissions from foreigners made for local display as well as for export accounted for a significant part of the production of art in Bruges. Although a number of these paintings were among the most highly refined and indeed largest works produced in the Netherlands at the time—Hans Memling's Last Judgment Altarpiece made for Angelo Tani, for example—there was also a thriving trade in smaller works, many of which were of considerably more

Detail of Figure 175

average, even mediocre, quality.[3] Often the latter were bought in bulk at art fairs in Bruges and Antwerp and at the highly important Medina del Campo fair, which by mid-century was the leading center in Spain for economic exchange between Bruges and Castile.[4]

Among David's patrons was a group of foreigners who, having become fully assimilated into the economic, political, and religious institutions of that city, commissioned works for public installation, for private devotion, and for shipment abroad. There are, for example, the diptych ordered by Canon Bernardinus de Salviatis, the illegitimate son of a Florentine merchant, for Sint Donaaskerk;[5] a lost *Adoration of the Magi* mentioned in the will of Gaspare Bonciani, another Florentine merchant, for the high altar of a church outside Bruges;[6] or the triptych with the Virgin and Child (Figures 149 and 150) and possibly a panel of the *Marriage at Cana* made for Jan de Sedano, a Spanish merchant.[7] Those works that remained in Bruges tend to conform to relatively traditional standards in terms of style and iconography, while certain paintings that were commissioned for export, such as the Saint Anne Altarpiece, the Cervara Altarpiece, and probably the Sedano Triptych, more obviously reflect concessions made by David to Spanish or Italian taste and the specific requirements of works destined for foreign locations.

The diversity in formal treatment and quality that these foreign commissions present has stimulated discussion about attribution. Occasional outright dismissals of authorship, however, have not taken into consideration the patron's requirements, nor David's endeavors to suit them by varying his habitual style on the one hand or, for practical purposes, by enlisting the participation of workshop assistants on the other.

Among David's masterpieces, and clearly a work that represents the extent of the artist's efforts and abilities to accommodate a patron for a particular foreign commission, is the Cervara Altarpiece, of which the Metropolitan Museum *Annunciation* panels are a key part (Figures 174 and 175 and reconstruction, Figure 176). In order to recognize the remarkable achievement of this work, it is important to reconsider it in the context of two other commissions that David received from foreign clients, the Sedano Triptych and the Saint Anne Altarpiece, both works with manifestly different requirements and resulting solutions to them.

First, however, let us take a brief look at the development of the taste for paintings from Bruges among Italian and Spanish clients. This helps to explain the phenomenon of the accommodation of artists to their patrons' demands as an emerging pattern in Bruges even preceding Gerard David's activity there.

Foreign interest in Bruges painting had been established as early as the 1430s. The works of Jan van Eyck and Petrus Christus were especially admired in the courts of Ferrara and Naples, as well as by the noble families of Genoa.[8] Avid collecting of northern painting by foreign rulers was a result not only of its remarkable qualities of verisimilitude, but also of its technical and coloristic virtuosity and heightened expressive mode as described by, among others, Bartolomeo Fazio in his *De viris illustribus* of 1456. Netherlandish paintings also held a certain prestige as art specifically connected with the lavish court life of the dukes of Burgundy.

Early on the art of Bruges had reached collections in Italy.[9] Michele Vianello, the Venetian collector, owned two paintings, a self-portrait and another of a rather curious subject, a drowning of the pharaoh in the Red Sea, by the hand of "Janes da Brugia" (most likely Jan van Eyck). Both were acquired by Isabella d'Este upon Vianello's death in 1506. Marcantonio Michiel noted various Bruges paintings in Italian collections—a diptych of 1470 by Hans Memling in the collection of Pietro Bembo, thought to have comprised the *Saint John the Evangelist* and *Saint Veronica* (now divided between the Alte Pinakothek, Munich, and the National Gallery of Art, Washington); a half-length image of money changers of 1440 probably by Jan van Eyck in the Casa Lampugnano in Milan; and a painting of an otter hunt on canvas by "Gianes de Brugia" in Padua, in the collection of Leonico Tomeo. Various portraits by Hans Memling found their way to Florence, as did additional works by Jan van Eyck, possibly including the two versions of his *Stigmatization of Saint Francis* that had been bequeathed to the daughters of Anselm Adornes in 1470. The Medici owned a *Saint Jerome* (perhaps the one in the Detroit Institute of Arts) by Van Eyck and a *Portrait of a Woman* by Petrus Christus, often thought to be the celebrated panel now in the Gemäldegalerie, Berlin. The close economic links between Bruges and Genoa provided ample opportunities for the acquisition of Netherlandish paintings by wealthy Genoese merchants. Battista Lomellino commissioned an Annunciation Triptych from Jan van Eyck, which he passed on to Alfonso V of Aragon, king of Naples, while his family ordered a triptych from Jan's successor Petrus Christus (the wings are in the National Gallery of Art, Washington). Van Eyck's famous Dresden Triptych was acquired by Michele Giustiniani.

By Gerard David's time, there was a thriving trade in northern paintings, which were regularly exported to Italy, particularly to Genoa. Paintings from Bruges had acquired a special prestige, such that the inscription on the Triptych of Saint Andrew commissioned by Andrea della Costa for his family church near Santa Margherita Ligure was inscribed "This [I] had made in Bruges in 1499." On the coast between Santa Margherita Ligure and Portofino was the Benedictine monastery of San Gerolamo della Cervara, for which David made his large-scale altarpiece for Vincenzo Sauli. Other works—a triptych of the life of Saint John for the Church of Santa Annunziata del Vestito, an *Adoration of the Magi* by the Master of the Turin Adoration, and Provost's Annunciation Triptych for San Colombano—all ended up in Genoa. The presence of Bruges art in Liguria was keenly felt.

The Spanish—particularly the ruling dynasties—were also drawn to Netherlandish painting. Under the rule of the Catholic monarchs in Spain, Ferdinand and Isabella (reigning from 1474 to 1516), the influence of Netherlandish art in Castile was widespread. Jan van Eyck had visited the Iberian Peninsula in the late 1420s as an envoy for his patron Duke Philip the Good and thereby established a presence and following of "Eyckian" Iberian artists such as the Portuguese Nuno Gonçalves and the Spaniard Luis Dalmau. The latter's famous *Virgin of the Councillors* of 1445 is a free combination of Eyckian motifs, while the many copies in Spain after the *Fountain of Life* reflect a well-known painting by Van Eyck that had particular resonance for the Spanish.

Queen Isabella regularly bought Netherlandish paintings in quantity—in 1503 she paid for twelve large devotional works and fifty-two smaller ones on linen to be brought to her from the Medina del Campo fair. Painters, sculptors, and architects from the north were hired to carry out some of her most prestigious projects.[10] This group included two probably trained in Bruges, Michael Sittow and Juan de Flandes, who were contemporaries of Gerard David's. Both painters were in the employ of Isabella at the turn of the century—Sittow from 1492 to 1504, and de Flandes from 1496 to 1504. Attracted by such possibilities of earning a livelihood in Spain, several other Bruges artists emigrated there: Lodewijk Allyncbrood to Valencia (from 1439 to 1463); his son, Joris, also to Valencia after becoming a master in Bruges in 1460; Cornelis Brommin to Bilbao after achieving free master status in 1489; and Petrus Christus II, who moved to Granada to paint wings for sculpted altarpieces in 1507, remaining there until his death in 1530.

A thriving export of art from the Netherlands to Spain continued, and the churches were filled with examples of painting and sculpture. By the mid-sixteenth century there were six Spanish merchants who specialized in shipping large altarpieces. In one year, thirty-six shipments of at least one altarpiece each were sent.[11]

Through these already well developed connections between the Netherlands and southern markets, Spanish and Italian merchants, bankers, and diplomats arrived in Bruges in the latter part of the fifteenth century favorably predisposed to commission works from the resident artists. Moreover, at a time when merchants and bankers rivaled the dukes in wealth —even, on occasion, lending money to them for various military campaigns—they were in a position to use their wealth to garner favor at court. A

149. Gerard David, Sedano Triptych, exterior wings: *Adam* and *Eve*, ca. 1490. Oil on panel, 91.1 × 30.1 cm and 91.1 × 30.4 cm. Musée du Louvre, Paris (Photo © RMN)

clear sign of this newfound status was the acquisition of luxury objects, including works of art. In due course, this class of wealthy merchants and bankers became a force in the art world, establishing themselves as favored clients of the resident Bruges artists.

Painters not appointed at the court, that is, those with no particular guarantee of a livelihood, found some of their most lucrative individual commissions and steady business from the merchants and bankers. The fact that a significant number of them were for-

eigners influenced the manner in which art developed in Bruges. There are cases where this influence seems to have been the catalyst for temporary or long-term modifications in the habitual style of certain artists.

An early example of this phenomenon is found in the art of Petrus Christus, a painter from Baerle in Brabant, who settled in Bruges as a free master in 1444. An assessment of his relatively small surviving oeuvre indicates that approximately one-half of his

150. Gerard David, Sedano Triptych, interior, ca. 1490. Oil on panel, 91.1 × 71.5 cm. Musée du Louvre, Paris (Photo © RMN)

paintings were commissioned by Italians, have an Italian or Spanish provenance, or were copied early on by Italian artists—the last documenting their early availability in southern locations as influential models.[12] This statistic offers powerful economic evidence of foreign patronage of Christus's work, and it comes as no surprise that he apparently made adjustments in his style to accommodate the taste of his clientele. Christus's adoption of certain Italian modes of expression, such as the *sacra conversazione* for his *Virgin and Child with Saints Francis and Jerome* (Städelsches Kunstinstitut, Frankfurt), the assimilation of Italian portraiture style as in his *Portrait of a Man* (Los Angeles County Museum of Art), and his exploration of one-point perspective, particularly in

the paintings destined for southern European sites, all indicate a deliberate effort to attract and sustain a certain business by catering to pre-established aesthetic sensibilities.[13]

The oeuvre of Hans Memling (active in Bruges from about 1464 until his death in 1494) reflects the patronage of the Italian merchant community, especially Florentine bankers, which accounted for about 20 percent of his total known business.[14] Among the most ambitious works produced by Memling is the Last Judgment Triptych, ordered by the Bruges branch manager of the Medici bank, Angelo Tani, for his chapel in the church of the Badia Fiesolana (but which was captured en route to Florence by pirates and ended up in Gdansk instead). On a smaller scale is the *Panorama with Scenes of the Passion of Christ,* produced for Tomasso Portinari, perhaps initially displayed in the parish church of Sint Jakobs in Bruges,[15] but ultimately destined for the Portinari chapel in Santa Maria Nuova in Florence.[16] Alternatively, one of Memling's few Spanish commissions, the monumental panels *Christ as Salvator Mundi with Musical Angels,* a reflection of Van Eyck's Ghent Altarpiece, originally formed part of the high altar of the church of the Benedictine monastery of Santa María la Réal, in Nájera, Spain.[17] In these examples Memling did not adjust his style to suit conventions of Italian or Spanish art, but demonstrably celebrated his native Flemish manner, which, in fact, may accord with the wishes of his clients. Modest concessions to Italianate artistic taste are found on some of Memling's Virgin and Child paintings, to which decorative embellishments of swags and putti have been added (Figure 152).

The case of portraiture, however, is different. The majority of Memling's commissions from foreigners was due to his unrivaled abilities in this genre. His conception of portraiture—a combination of unstinting verisimilitude and a certain idealizing mode—apparently matched the image these wealthy businessmen wished to project of themselves and their elevated status within the community,[18] and such portraits account for about one-third of those surviving by Memling. Recently Dirk De Vos has suggested that Memling responded positively to these clients by adjusting his style to suit them. It is "likely that Memling, possibly influenced by the Italian colony in Bruges, adopted the idea of the open-air portrait, which was originally an Italian custom, and then developed it in the Netherlandish landscape tradition . . . , and in so doing created a new type."[19] This synthesis of form may have especially appealed to Italian patrons, both suiting conventions familiar to them and offering novel additions. Another instance of Memling's nod to Italian types might be found in his *Virgin and Child* (National Gallery, London), the exceptional sculptural quality of which may reflect Memling's attempts at Italianizing his northern Virgin type.[20]

By the time that Gerard David arrived in Bruges in 1484, the lucrative business of making and marketing art for foreign nationals was well established, and, in particular, a pattern of adjusting style to suit the client's taste had begun to emerge. One of David's most ambitious early commissions, doubtless following the specifications of his client, but also perhaps shrewdly aimed at identifying himself as the successor of the rich legacy of two of Bruges's painters, Jan van Eyck and Hans Memling, was the Sedano Triptych (Figures 149 and 150). Along with his son (who, holding a cross in his hands, was most likely deceased), the donor, Jan de Sedano, is identified by the coat of arms at the base of the interior left wing; the paternal arms on the shield (on the lower right wing) of Sedano's wife, known from other documents to be a woman named Marie, have not yet been identified.[21] Originally of Spanish origin (Sedano is a village near Burgos in the province of Castile), Jan de Sedano was part of the merchant community living in Bruges. From 1501 until his death in 1518, he was a member of the prestigious Confraternity of the Holy Blood and with his wife, Marie, made a donation in 1517 to the convent of the Hermits of Saint Augustine in Bruges, which was located in the middle of the trade quarter and housed the chapels of many of the foreign nations.[22]

On the exterior wings of the altarpiece are Adam and Eve (Figure 149), symbolizing the Fall of Man, redeemed through the Incarnation of Christ, the theme revealed on the centerpiece of the interior when the triptych is opened (Figure 150). Here the Virgin and Child are enthroned beneath a cloth of honor and garlands held by putti and accompanied by musical angels in an open-air loggia. In their

151. Hans Memling, Saint John Altarpiece, exterior wings: *Adam and Eve,* ca. 1485. Oil on panel, each 69.3 × 17.3 cm. Kunsthistorisches Museum, Vienna

152. Hans Memling, Saint John Altarpiece, interior, center panel: *Virgin and Child with an Angel and a Donor;* wings: *Saint John the Baptist* and *Saint John the Evangelist,* ca. 1485. Oil on panel, center panel 69 × 47 cm, wings each 69.3 × 17.3 cm. Kunsthistorisches Museum, Vienna

154. Jan van Eyck, *Virgin and Child with Saints and Canon van der Paele*, ca. 1434–36. Oil on panel, 122.1 × 157.8 cm. Groeningemuseum, Bruges

role as patron saints, but also among the most revered saints of Bruges, John the Baptist and John the Evangelist present the donors to the Virgin and Child. The general design followed by David was formulated by Memling, notably in a triptych in Vienna (Kunsthistorisches Museum, Figures 151 and 152).[23] It was adapted in various ways for other clients of Memling—in more elaborate versions, the triptychs for Sir John Donne of Kidwilly and

153. Hubert and Jan van Eyck, Ghent Altarpiece, interior wings: *Adam* and *Eve*, 1432. Oil on panel, 204.3 × 33.2 cm and 204.3 × 32.3 cm. Sint Baafs Cathedral, Ghent (Photo © IRPA-KIK, Brussels)

Benedetto Pagagnotti,[24] as well as more routine production restricted to the design of the central panel and made available for sale as single paintings.[25]

Although David was unquestionably inspired by Memling's design, the initial impression of the Sedano Triptych must have been distinctly Eyckian. Abandoning Memling's conventional figures in type and pose for the outside wings, David returned to Van Eyck's *Adam and Eve* from the Ghent Altarpiece (compare Figures 149 and 153), even further accentuating their lifelike corporeality with theatrical lighting and impromptu pose, their bodies barely fitting into the shallow niche and their feet jutting out beyond its edge.

When the triptych was opened, a Bruges resident could not have mistaken a reference to another of Jan van Eyck's masterpieces, the resplendent *Virgin and Child with Saints and Canon van der Paele* (Figure 154), an altarpiece that was probably installed in the chapel of Saints Peter and Paul in the Sint Donaaskerk as a memorial for van der Paele.[26] Sint Donaaskerk, it should perhaps be noted, was across the square from the Basiliek van het Heilig Bloed, where Sedano would have attended regular meetings as a member of the confraternity. He certainly knew Van Eyck's altarpiece and may well have stipulated that it be copied in part in the work he commissioned from David.

In overall effect, the triptych refers to Jan van Eyck's Canon van der Paele altarpiece, with its relatively compressed space barely able to contain its expansive architectural setting and oversized saints. David copied his Virgin and Child from Jan's altarpiece but reversed the position of the Christ Child on the Virgin's lap from left to right, and replaced the parrot and flower bouquet with a book. He maintained the introspective mood and the pose of the Virgin, however, with her head angled downward to the right, and paid particular attention to reproducing the details of Jan's Virgin type—an elaborate crown in the underdrawing (Figure 156) was changed into Van Eyck's simple jeweled diadem over abundant, loose, flowing hair, framing a face with a broad, square forehead, widely spaced eyes, and thin eyebrows. This Virgin type is distinctly different from the sweeter and more delicate one that David introduced in his Nativity paintings or the *Adoration of the Magi* of nearly contemporary date (Figures 60, 108, and 113) and indicates the artist's accommodation of his client's demand for a "Van Eyck."

The evidence of David's working method shows that in a deliberate attempt to approximate the essential features of his model, he treated the motifs adapted from Van Eyck's painting differently from the other figures in the triptych. The underdrawing for Adam and Eve and for the Virgin and Child (Figures 155, 156, and 279) is carried out in brush in a fixed design for the modeling of the nude figures and for the draperies, indicating that the designs had been worked

out in advance and copied over from preliminary drawings on paper. As he did for the heads of the popes and bishops drawn after the Ghent Altarpiece (Figure 33), David most likely recorded the figures of Adam and Eve and the Virgin and Child from Van Eyck's works and then adapted these patterns to suit the concept of his overall design. The other figures in the triptych, namely the donors and their patron saints, show summary underdrawing probably in black chalk for the general placement of forms but no further indication of their details.

David underpainted the heads of the Virgin and Child with a broadly brushed-in layer of white rather than a selective application of the paint for the highlights on their faces as he did for the angels (compare the X-radiographs in Figures 157 and 158). This particular detail of execution in the heads of the Virgin and Child may reflect David's attempts to approximate the densely painted and porcelain-like quality of the prototype; or, on the other hand, it might indicate that David reworked these areas, not at first satisfied with his initial efforts to render faces close in style to Van Eyck's model.

The Sedano Triptych could have been installed in Bruges for a period of time before being sent to Spain, where it ultimately came into the possession of the Benito Garriga family, its earliest traceable provenance.[27] In the absence of any surviving contract, it is impossible to establish whether Jan de Sedano specifically requested an altarpiece in the style of Jan van Eyck, although the visual and technical evidence would seem to support this hypothesis. As Dijkstra has shown,[28] late-fifteenth- and early-sixteenth-century clients often ordered copies of another work that had a particular spiritual or auctorial value. Furthermore, such a request would be in line with the enthusiasm of Spanish clients for works by or after Jan van Eyck, a taste stemming from the fame of the artist, who had visited there, the multiple copies of his works that existed in Spain from early on, and the great admiration for Jan's works by the royal households.[29]

In stipulating that the new work should reflect principally the art of Van Eyck and not of Memling,

Sedano would have been following a pattern already developed by his compatriots. Earlier, the Ghent Altarpiece and the *Virgin and Child with Canon van der Paele* had been sources of inspiration for Luis Dalmau's *Virgin of the Councillors*. Petrus Christus had produced his version of Jan van Eyck's *Last Judgment,* as well as an *Annunciation* dependent upon Rogier van der Weyden and the Master of Flémalle, and a Master of Flémalle-style *Nativity* in his altarpiece wings for a Spanish destination (initially the cathedral of Burgos and eventually a convent in Segovia).[30] Some have suggested that Christus was also responsible for a *Fountain of Life* modeled after a lost work by Jan van Eyck. This example came from the monastery of Nuestra Señora del Parral in Segovia and was copied many times.[31] And Hans Memling excerpted the musical angels and God the Father from Jan van Eyck's Ghent Altarpiece for part of an ensemble adorning the high altar of the church of the Benedictine monastery of Santa María la Réal, Nájera.[32]

Furthermore, the Sedano Triptych is contemporary with some of the most concentrated activity in the copying of Netherlandish works for Spanish royalty. Among the famous examples are the replica requested by Isabella of Castile of Rogier van der Weyden's Miraflores Altarpiece.[33] The trend of commissioning copies of famous Netherlandish paintings for the royal households of Spain continued into the sixteenth century, when Michiel Coxie was hired by Mary of Hungary to produce a copy of Rogier's *Deposition* to replace the original in the Crossbowman's Guild in Leuven that Philip II had so admired.[34] In 1557 Philip himself commissioned from Coxie a copy of the Ghent Altarpiece, which he placed in the chapel of the Royal Palace in Madrid. It was perhaps in emulation of this ongoing pattern of collecting and the prestige accompanying it that those of the wealthy merchant class, such as Jan de Sedano, followed suit, hoping thereby to establish an elevated status by association.

What would better illustrate the epitome of Netherlandish painting at the time than an Eyckian work, à la Memling, painted by the new premier artist of Bruges, Gerard David—and all presented in the most up-to-date ogee-arch framing?[35] Considered in this way, David's altarpiece for Jan de Sedano may be viewed more appropriately in terms of its image-enhancing intentions. Such deliberate intentions on the part of the patron would not have contradicted David's own aims in the 1490s—that is, to appropriate the clients abandoned by Memling at his death in 1494 and to establish himself as his successor. It can hardly be coincidental that David moved in 1494 to a house "across the Flemingbridge" (now Sint-Jorisstraat) to open his atelier on the same street where Memling had long enjoyed a thriving business.[36] Rather than solely a sign of artistic dependency, then, David's deliberate quotations from Jan van Eyck's works within a Memlingesque setting may well have been a matter of self-reference and self-identification with Bruges's famed artistic tradition.

It is not known at what point the Sedano Triptych left Bruges for Spain. In the case of certain other foreign commissions, however, their size, content, and provenance indicate export upon completion for a predestined site. As such, they raise a different set of questions. To what extent were these altarpieces produced from standardized patterns and motifs for a burgeoning market abroad[37] or custom made and specifically individualized for a particular patron and location? Or is the product a combination of the two? Within David's oeuvre, the Saint Anne Altarpiece and the Cervara Altarpiece represent varied approaches to commissioned art for export.

A significant number of Netherlandish altarpieces sent to Spain and Italy during the latter half of the fifteenth century and first part of the sixteenth century were large in scale, created for churches and chapels. Although some of the most celebrated examples—Hugo van der Goes's Portinari Altarpiece or Hans Memling's Last Judgment Altarpiece for the Tani family—appear to have been produced by the master painter himself with little or no workshop collaboration, many altarpieces necessitated the participation of assistants in completing within strict time limits what was literally a monumental task.

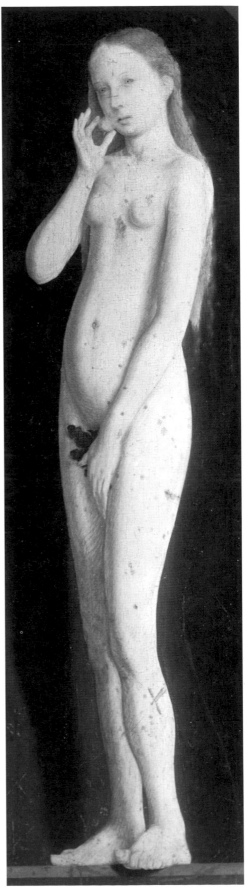

156. IRR of head of Virgin in Figure 150

157. X-radiograph detail of Virgin and Child in Figure 150

158. X-radiograph detail of angel in Figure 150

155. IR photograph of Figure 149

The specific nature of collaboration between artists on altarpieces is not always easy to establish, particularly in most cases where an intention of stylistic uniformity prevails. In these instances the identification of individual hands sometimes seems to be a rather subjective and even futile endeavor. Categorical decisions based on too little physical evidence, however, have occasionally led to precipitate conclusions about the authorship of a given work—often that it must be wholly rejected.

Such has been the case with the Saint Anne Altarpiece (Figure 159) comprising the enthroned Saint Anne, Virgin, and Child, flanked by Saints

Nicholas and Anthony of Padua—three separate panels united by the perspective indicated in the platform for the throne. Below, six predella panels (now dispersed) illustrate episodes from the lives of the two featured saints.[38] It has been suggested that a *Lamentation* (Figure 141) originally from the Despuig collection, as are the other panels, may have been part of the predella, placed in the center between three panels each for Saints Nicholas and Anthony, but given its demonstrably earlier date, this is unlikely.[39]

Although we do not know who commissioned one of the largest altarpieces to come from Gerard David's atelier, its nineteenth-century provenance in the collection of Cardinal Antonio Despuig y Dameto of Raxa, Palma de Mallorca, implies that it was exported either to this island off the eastern coast of Spain, to mainland Spain, or possibly to Italy, where the cardinal spent time and could have acquired it. If the altarpiece was originally sent to Palma de Mallorca, then it might have been placed in the Church of Saint Nicholas there, though there is at present no compelling physical evidence to support this suggestion.[40]

The cult of Saint Anne had already been formed in the eighth century, but it became widespread in the late thirteenth and fourteenth centuries, as is evident from numerous representations in paintings and sculpture.[41] Signifying her role as the mother of Mary, who was widely believed to have been conceived without the taint of original sin, Saint Anne here provides the actual support for, and, indeed,

the genealogical reference to, the maternal side of Christ's forebears. Such an arrangement is known by the commonly used German term that readily expresses the unity of the three figures, the *Anna Selbdritt.*

The miraculous deeds of Saint Nicholas, bishop of Myra (at the left), whose relics remained in Bari, in Italy, and Saint Anthony of Padua (at the right) are depicted in the narrative episodes of the predella panels. The chosen saints as well as the *Anna Selbdritt* represent the popularity of these holy figures individually in this period, although their appearance together is unusual and doubtless relates to the liturgical function and destined site for the altarpiece, which may well have been Italy, given the most common geographical associations of the two saints. Unfortunately, other than the Italianate or Spanish format of the altarpiece, with its predella and fixed rather than folding lateral panels, there are no internal clues about the work's ultimate destination. Despite its large size, the production in terms of handling and execution is not exceptional. Details of setting, lighting, costume, palette, and figure types are not individualized in any particular manner but instead represent the routine, even standardized, output of an early-sixteenth-century workshop.

In the case of the Saint Anne Altarpiece, the question of authorship has been complicated by the fact that the portion automatically assumed to be the most reliably autograph, that is, the centerpiece, is the weakest in handling and execution.[42] The distinctly wooden quality of the Virgin, Child, and Saint Anne has provided ample reason for some to disattribute the entire work,[43] particularly by comparison with the approximately contemporary Cervara Altarpiece of 1506 (Figure 176, to be discussed in greater detail below).[44]

An investigation of the working technique evident in the altarpiece, and the recent restoration of the three large panels in the National Gallery, have allowed us to reassess the question of attribution, to evaluate workshop practice in David's atelier, and by inference to draw certain conclusions about the nature of export art. The underdrawing, which can

159. Gerard David and Workshop, Saint Anne Altarpiece, ca. 1500–1506. Oil on panel, center: *Saint Anne with the Virgin and Child*, 236.1 × 97.5 cm; left wing: *Saint Nicholas*, 236.1 × 75.9 cm; right wing: *Saint Anthony of Padua*, 235.4 × 75.9 cm. National Gallery of Art, Washington, Widener Collection (Photo © 1998 Board of Trustees, National Gallery of Art, Washington). Predella panels, all oil on panel: *Three Miracles of Saint Nicholas: Saint Nicholas Gives Thanks to God on the Day of His Birth, Saint Nicholas Slips a Purse Through the Window of an Impoverished Nobleman, Saint Nicholas Restores Three Dismembered Children to Life*, each 55.9 × 33.7 cm. National Galleries of Scotland, Edinburgh; *Three Miracles of Saint Anthony of Padua: The Mule Kneeling before the Host*, 57.3 × 34 cm; *The Drowned Child Restored to Life*, 55.1 × 32.7 cm; *Saint Anthony Preaching to the Fishes*, 55.6 × 32.6 cm. Toledo Museum of Art, Gift of Edward Drummond Libbey

160. IRR detail of Saint Anne's face in Figure 159

161. IRR detail of Virgin's face in Figure 159

162. IRR detail of Saint Anne and the Virgin and Child in Figure 159

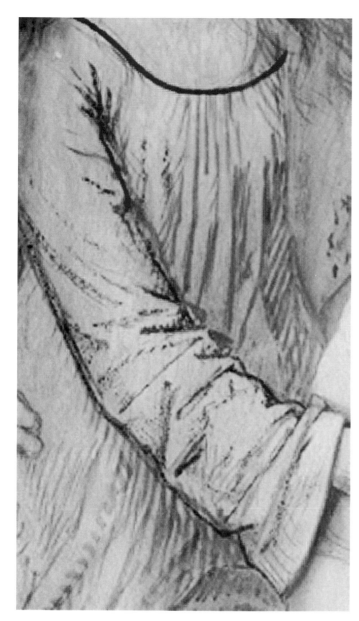

163. IRR detail of Virgin's sleeve in Figure 159

164. IRR detail of putto on throne in Figure 159

group and predella panels (Figures 160–163 and 167); a far more meticulously rendered definition of the draperies of Saint Anne in thick, bold brush lines in a liquid medium (Figure 162); and finally, an irregular charcoal drawing found in the upper paint layers of the Virgin's sleeve that corrects the folds of the sleeve, making adjustments that are subsequently followed in the final paint layers (Figure 163).

The rough sketch for the saints and subsidiary portions of the central panel, particularly the putti on the throne (Figures 164–166), exhibits the spontaneous nature and authority of handling of similar preliminary underdrawings in David's autograph paintings (for example, Figure 281). In contrast, the finicky, overly elaborate, and relatively dry execution in brush of the draperies of the Virgin and Saint Anne (Figure 162) is not immediately identifiable as David's handling and more likely indicates that of an assistant

be helpful in sorting out questions of workshop participation in all of the related panels, is of four types: a rough compositional sketch in a dry medium, probably black chalk, which constitutes the preliminary layout in the three main panels and the predella of Saint Nicholas, as well as minimal underdrawing in one of the Saint Anthony predella panels (Figures 165–167); a liquid underdrawing (going over the preliminary sketch) in brush or pen that establishes the composition more precisely in the central figural

165. IRR detail of Saint Nicholas in Figure 159

assiduously copying a workshop model. Furthermore, there are corrections, particularly in the Virgin's right sleeve (Figure 163), made in a greasy-looking medium, which are followed in the upper paint layers. This seems to indicate the intervention of a more skilled hand, perhaps that of the master correcting his assistant's work at a relatively advanced stage.

In a recent investigation of the painting technique of the three large panels of the Saint Anne Altarpiece, the central panel showed a more labored method of working than the rest of the altarpiece, one harking back to established procedures of the earlier part of the fifteenth century, in which paint was applied in multiple layers to achieve the desired effect. These elaborate steps included "sealing the

166. IRR detail of Saint Anthony in Figure 159

167. IRR details of predella panels in Figure 159: *The Mule Kneeling Before the Host, The Drowned Child Restored to Life*

underdrawing, laying in the light tones, followed by modeling layers and glazes, with the addition of new drawing as guidelines."[45] In this exacting process, except for the slightly changed position of the Virgin's head (Figure 161), the underdrawing is closely followed in the painting. A far more spontaneous execution, however, is evidenced in the lateral panels of Saints Anthony and Nicholas (Figures 159, 165, and 166), with modifications and corrections from the underdrawing and an abbreviated layering structure in paint, achieving remarkable effects and refinement with an economy of means. This indicates the self-assurance and authority in handling of a master.

As a result, technical evidence supports the attribution of the lateral panels to David himself and the main portions of the central panel to a workshop assistant, contrary to what one might normally have assumed. These findings directly contradict the auctorial hierarchy normally given to large altarpieces, that

is, that the master carries out the work on the central, or presumably most important, part of the altarpiece, and the workshop assists with the side panels.

This conclusion requires further explanations, at least some of which can be made on the basis of a greater understanding of workshop procedures—specifically those in David's own atelier. Centerpieces of triptychs or retables often represent the standardized portions, those of traditional themes for devotional practice. As has been discussed in chapter 1, stock patterns of repeated motifs were kept in multiple examples in the artist's workshop readily available for a variety of different uses. The side panels, or the wings of an altarpiece, are the portions that respond to the more personal requirements of the patron—representing his patron saints or scenes that relate to the life or habitual devotions of the client.

168. Gerard David, Saint Michael Altarpiece, ca. 1505–10. Oil on panel, center panel: 66 × 53 cm; side panels each: 66 × 22.5 cm. Kunsthistorisches Museum, Vienna

Thus, in the case of the Saint Anne Altarpiece, the motif of Saint Anne with the Virgin and Child was perhaps available as a workshop pattern that could be copied in detail and executed in paint by an accomplished assistant.[46] Except for the addition of the figure of the Virgin Mary, this motif is not remarkably different from the Virgin and Child with the book in the Philadelphia *Virgin and Child Enthroned with Two Angels* (Figure 280), which (as we have seen in chapter 1 and is further discussed in chapter 6) is a flipped version of the pattern for the Sedano Triptych's Virgin and Child (Figure 150). The Philadelphia and Washington paintings also share the same orientalizing carpet on the platform of the throne.

The figures of the lateral panels, like the putti on the throne of Saint Anne, exhibit a higher quality of

execution than the figures of Saint Anne, the Virgin, and the Child of the central portion. Here greater attention has been paid to the effects of light on the shimmering brocade chasuble of Saint Nicholas, for example, and the faces of the saints are more lifelike as a result of the adept handling of the modeling of the flesh tones. These figures also present an assured approach to the rough layout sketch of the black chalk underdrawing that is characteristic of David. Perhaps it was these customized portions of the altarpiece that could be more easily and efficiently produced by David himself. Even here, however, workshop patterns were employed. A nearly identical

169. Gerard David, *Adoration of the Magi*, ca. 1510–15. Oil on panel, 59.5 × 58.5 cm. National Gallery, London (Photo © National Gallery, London)

170. IRR detail of Virgin and Child and kneeling king in Figure 169

figure of Saint Anthony is found in another work of considerably smaller scale, the right interior wing of the Saint Michael Altarpiece (Kunsthistorisches Museum, Vienna; Figure 168); here pose, costume, drapery-fold patterns, the Christ Child on the open book (albeit in a different pose) are all similar and must be derived from the same workshop pattern.[47] The figure of Saint Nicholas, of course, is different in fundamental ways from the Saint Jerome on the left interior wing of the Vienna altarpiece; nonetheless, it is interesting to note how the artist relies upon standardized conventions in figure poses, or the way light strikes a staff held in the proper left hand, or the manner in which the draperies of both

ecclesiastical costumes fall in similar deep V-shaped folds down the center front of the figures.

The predella panels (Figures 159 and 167) vary in their quality of execution, which further suggests the collaboration of workshop assistants. Here, too, certain standard patterns for the scenes of Saints Nicholas and Anthony were employed. The *Mule Kneeling Before the Host,* for example, is derived from the composition that is found in at least five earlier and contemporary illuminations for breviaries produced in Bruges.[48]

These details of manufacture all suggest that the work on the Saint Anne Altarpiece was the type of routine, rather uninspired production that resulted from well-developed collaborative efforts within the same shop and a high degree of reliance on both standard patterns and shortcut methods. In the case of this commission, perhaps it was only the subjects to be depicted and the size of the ensemble that were stipulated in the contract, for there are no particular details of manufacture—beyond the polyptych format for the altarpiece with its predella—that further indicate a customized treatment of any kind. Since we do not know the destination of this large-scale altarpiece, we cannot evaluate its suitability to the site; it seems unlikely that David himself had much additional information at hand at the time it was created in his workshop. Further evidence of collaborative efforts on the same altarpiece may be found in other paintings from David's mature phase, which were not made for export so far as we know. The *Adoration of the Magi* and the *Deposition* (Figures 169 and 172), both in the National Gallery, London, most probably belonged to the same altarpiece that included other, now lost scenes from the life of Christ.[49] While the *Adoration of the Magi* brings new life, particularly in its representation of space, to a composition faintly reminiscent of Hugo van der Goes's Monteforte Altarpiece in Berlin,[50] the *Deposition* repeats patterns already available and previously used for other paintings from David's workshop.[51] It is perhaps not surprising, therefore, that the underdrawing for the *Adoration* is in David's typical style, finely rendered in brush, that includes the modeling of the figures (Figures 170 and 171), while the *Deposition* shows the rigid contour lines of a transfer from a workshop cartoon (Figure 173). The execution in paint also follows the same division of labor—the *Adoration* is most certainly by David, while the *Deposition* displays weaknesses in form (especially in the vapid expressions of the figures) as well as in handling that are attributable to a workshop assistant (possibly the same artist responsible for the Lehman *Virgin and Child,* Figure 259).

By comparison with the generalized, rather average production of the Saint Anne Altarpiece by David and his workshop, the individualized, custom-designed treatment of the altarpiece for the abbey church of San Gerolamo della Cervara near Genoa is striking (Figure 176). Specific elements of its style and execution reveal David's personal attention to every detail of this altarpiece, suggesting that he had specific information about the site, either from firsthand experience or through an intermediary source.

As noted above, the connections between the cities of Bruges and Genoa were especially close, and during the late fifteenth and early sixteenth centuries, a number of monumental altarpieces were exported from the former to the latter. The development of a

171. IRR detail of standing king in Figure 169

172. Workshop of Gerard David, *Deposition*, ca. 1510–15. Oil on panel, 92.9 × 61.5 cm. National Gallery, London (Photo © National Gallery, London)

kind of Bruges painters' colony in Genoa at the time has been suggested but cannot be documented.[52] Among this group may have been the Master of Saint John the Evangelist, the Master of the Turin Adoration, and Jan Provost, all of whom produced major works for the region of Genoa. Less than a decade before David's commission from Vincenzo Sauli to paint a large-scale altarpiece for the abbey

173. IRR detail of Mary Magdalene in Figure 172

of San Gerolamo della Cervara, a Genoese merchant in Bruges, Andrea della Costa, had ordered a triptych depicting the martyrdom of Saint Andrew, the Marriage at Cana, and the raising of Lazarus for his family's parish church of San Lorenzo in nearby Santa Margherita Ligure.[53] The inscription on the altarpiece reads: "HOC OPUS FIERI FECIT ANDREAS DE COSTE Aᴼ 1499 BRUGIS," proudly stating that the work was made in Bruges, the adopted home of della Costa, who served as the receiver general of Maximilian of Austria and orator of the city's deanery. The anonymous master of this altarpiece may have been associated with David's workshop, for the *Marriage at Cana* (Musée du Louvre, Paris) appears to show

evidence of the same hand alongside that of David.[54]

The Cervara Altarpiece (reconstruction, Figure 176), which originally included the Metropolitan Museum's *Annunciation* panels (Figures 174 and 175), is the result of a considerably different type of commission than that for the Sedano Triptych or the Saint Anne Altarpiece, for in it David has taken into account the destined site and function of the work in specific ways.[55]

Gian Vittorio Castelnovi first published a now lost inscription on the original frame of the altarpiece, which read: "Hoc opus fecit fieri d'nus Vincentius Saulus MCCCCCVI. die VII Septembris [Vincenzo

174. Gerard David, *Annunciation* (part of the Cervara Altarpiece): *Gabriel*, 1506. Oil on panel, overall 79.1 × 63.5 cm. The Metropolitan Museum of Art, Bequest of Mary Stillman Harkness, 1950 (50.145.9a)

Sauli had this work made on September 7, 1506]."[56] The frame as described by Spinola was a heavy wooden gilt one of the type found in Ligurian altarpieces (see Figures 178 and 179). In his 1759 inventory of the objects in the church, Spinola attributed a *Crucifixion* to "Luca d'Olanda" (Lucas van Leyden)[57] and the six panels of the Cervara Altarpiece to Albrecht Dürer[58] (both artists' names were often used out of convenience by Italian com-

mentators for northern Renaissance paintings of uncertain authorship). In the mid-nineteenth century several different artists—among them Hugo van der Goes, Bernaert van Orley, and Gossaert—were considered responsible for various parts of the altarpiece.[59] By 1895 Weale had recognized the similarity of the Virgin and Child to the same figures in David's documented *Virgin among Virgins* of 1509, after which other critics followed in nearly unani-

175. Gerard David, *Annunciation* (part of the Cervara Altarpiece): *Virgin*, 1506. Oil on panel, overall 79.1 × 64.1 cm. The Metropolitan Museum of Art, Bequest of Mary Stillman Harkness, 1950 (50.145.9b)

mously attributing the panels of the Cervara Altarpiece to David.[60]

Details of the life of Vincenzo Sauli are now better known, thanks to the recent archival research of Mary Howard and Helen Hyde.[61] He was probably born about 1467 and lived to about 1555, when he dictated his will to a notary.[62] Sauli held important government positions, was a successful banker (even general depositor of the Apostolic Chamber

in Rome between 1507 and 1515), and served as ambassador to Pope Julius III in 1550.[63]

Founded as early as 1361, the monastery of San Gerolamo della Cervara was built by 1364, and a church dedicated to the Virgin and Saint Jerome completed in 1366.[64] Situated on the coast between Santa Margherita Ligure and Portofino, by 1460 it had become a member of the Congregation of Santa Giustina of Padua. The congregation was known for

176. Gerard David, Cervara Altarpiece, reconstruction: *God the Father*, Musée du Louvre, Paris (Photo © RMN);
Crucifixion, *Virgin and Child*, *Saint Jerome*, *Saint Benedict*, Palazzo Bianco, Genoa; *Annunciation*, The Metropolitan Museum
of Art, New York

177. Perspectival alignment in the Cervara Altarpiece reconstruction

its piety and erudition, a reputation that further fostered its growth and prominence, to the extent that the motherhouse of the Benedictine order, Montecassino, became a member in 1505. The Sicilian Benedictines joined in 1506, and the French island monastery of Lérins in 1515—thereby allowing the order to establish a number of houses in Provence.[65] Given the importance of the monastery of San Gerolamo for the Benedictine order, the commission of the work for the high altar of the church was of great significance.

Although the motivations for Vincenzo Sauli's patronage must have included his spiritual salvation, he could not have been unaware of the status and prestige associated with such a gift. After all, the site of the church was near the country houses of prominent noble families, the Spinola among them, who frequented the church and thus would be acquainted with the wealth and social prominence that Sauli's benevolence signified. In making such an extravagant donation, Sauli joined the ranks of other noted patrons, such as the Lomellini and the Pesano families.[66] In addition, members of some of the same families—the Spinola and Lomellini—were foremost among the Genoese community in Bruges and would have been well aware of the status associated with such a commission from the city's leading painter of the day.[67]

There appears to be no indication that the main altar of the church was decorated with an altarpiece before Sauli's commission. This may have been because of various building campaigns; the damage to and restoration of the church and monastery in 1413 and 1435, respectively; or simply the fact that no suitable patron had come forward.[68] In any event, it was not until 1498 that plans got under way for an altarpiece, as well as accompanying silk curtains and tapestries, a gift provided for by the sale of two holdings (or *luoghi,* valued at about two hundred lire) given upon the entry of Giovanni Pallavicini into the monastery. Complications arose over the sale of the *luoghi,* however, and the sum for the commission was not secured. This made it necessary to seek the approval of new plans in a papal brief

of 1500, in which Pope Alexander VI gave permission for the transfer of the commission to a new patron.[69]

At this point Vincenzo Sauli apparently was in a favorable financial position to honor the original plans for the altar. The sum necessary was substantial, the equivalent of two hundred lire, which, as Hyde points out, was roughly twice the normal sum allotted for this purpose.[70] Although the available funds were meant to cover not only the altarpiece but also associated curtain hangings and tapestries, the handsome sum and prestige of the commission no doubt insured David's personal attention to every detail.

The surviving documentation unfortunately yields no specific information about Gerard David's relationship with his Italian clients. Some have speculated that David traveled to Italy between 1503 and 1507, because of the assumed lack of records of any transactions or payments during this time.[71] Lorne Campbell, however, has called attention to a will of Gaspar Bonciani, dated April 8, 1506, in which the Florentine merchant in Bruges notes:

Io voglio e lascio la mia tavola delli tre Re che al presente si fa per le mani di M.o Gherardo qui in Bruggia dipintore che sia donata alla chiesa dell'Osservanza al Grande altare qui fuori di Bruggia dove morendo io sarò sepelito sopra il Coro dove si canta la Santa Epistola[72]

thus placing David in Bruges at that time. The years 1503–7 were also a period of intense activity on large-scale commissions for Bruges patrons, such as the Baptism Triptych (of 1502–8), the altarpiece for Canon Bernardinus de Salviatis (beginning in 1501–2), and the *Virgin and Child with Saints and a Donor* (painted about 1506–11).

In any event, if David received the commission for the Cervara Altarpiece in 1506 on a trip to Italy rather than delivering the finished work, then it is unlikely that he encountered Vincenzo Sauli himself, who in that year was often traveling in France, Asti, and Rome on official business.[73] Alternatively, van Miegroet suggests that members of the Genoese community in Bruges, namely the Adornes family, may have served as mediators for such a commission between the abbey of Cervara and David.[74] One needn't go beyond the Sauli family itself, however, to find a list of possible intermediaries, among them Paolo Sauli, a banker and cousin of Vincenzo, and Francesco and Gaspare Sauli, who were in Bruges as bankers in 1506; the family had a presence in the city extending into the 1520s.[75] Furthermore, as previously noted, there were already a number of Bruges altarpieces in the area around Genoa and well-established communication between artists and clients for commissions.

As there are no existing documents that establish the details of the commission or stipulations of the contract, we must look at the works themselves for further clues. In his chronicle of 1790, Spinola described the altarpiece installed in the apse of the abbey church of San Gerolamo della Cervara as an ensemble of six panels.[76] Based on Spinola's description, Castelnovi attempted a reconstruction that included the following: on the lowermost tier are the *Virgin and Child,* flanked by *Saint Jerome* (to whom the church was dedicated along with the Virgin) and *Saint Benedict* (founder of the order of monks inhabiting the monastery);[77] on the second tier are the *Angel Gabriel,* the *Virgin Annunciate;* and on the third tier, a lunette of God the Father.

In addition to these panels, the *Crucifixion* in Figure 176 can be traced back to the abbey of Cervara and probably formed a part of the second tier of the altarpiece before the restoration of the main chapel in 1628–31 and the subsequent relocation of the *Crucifixion* by 1658 to the abbot's bedroom as a single unframed panel.[78] Castelnovi at first included the *Crucifixion* in the reconstruction of the Cervara Altarpiece, but later eliminated it because Spinola had not mentioned the painting as part of his eighteenth-century description of the altarpiece.[79] It is clear, however, as is demonstrable from the forthcoming discussion of the details of its style and iconography, that the *Crucifixion* originally formed part of the Cervara Altarpiece in David's carefully planned program.[80]

Portions of the panel of the Virgin are missing at the upper and lower edges (probably about 19 cm below, if the millefleurs tapestry running through the three lower tier panels is properly aligned).[81] The lower section originally may have included the inscription of the commission, perhaps at the base of the Virgin's throne, or it could have been placed on the frame or within a predella that was mentioned by Spinola.[82] The panels are thus presented in typical Italian altarpiece format in a fixed architectonic framework, probably in a heavy wooden frame, gilded and decorated as was common for Ligurian altarpieces of the late fifteenth and early sixteenth centuries (for example, Figures 178 and 179).[83] The frame no longer survives, having been destroyed when the altarpiece was dismembered, perhaps during the suppression of the monastery in 1799.[84]

The commission for an altarpiece for the high altar of the abbey church of San Gerolamo della Cervara dictated its subject matter and presentation. The lower tier represents the foundation of and justification for the abbey church and monastery: devotion to the Virgin Mary and veneration of Saints Jerome and Benedict. The enthroned Virgin Mary holding the Christ Child is the focal point, as the church is dedicated to her. Saint Jerome, for whom the monastery is named, stands at the left dressed as a cardinal,[85] and with his attributes—a precious opened volume, undoubtedly his renowned translation from Hebrew into Latin of the canonical books of the Old Testament, the lion representing his famous miracle, and an elaborate processional staff decorated with a cross above a tiny church in which stands a figure of Charlemagne. Jerome, one of the four great doctors of the Western Church, was devoted to the Virgin Mary and wrote the book that became the foundation of Western Mariology, above all affirming her perpetual virginity. He is thus often represented among the saints surrounding the Virgin Mary in altarpieces.

Saint Benedict stands at the right in his capacity as abbot and founder of the Benedictine order, whose *Rule,* in his left hand, was written in its final version at Montecassino, the motherhouse of the

178. Carlo Braccesco, *Virgin and Child with Saints*, 1478. Oil on canvas, 286 × 146 cm. Santuario di Montegrazie, Imperia

179. Giacomo Serfoglio, *Annunciation Altarpiece*, 1496. Oil on canvas, 262 × 235 cm. Santuario di N. S. del Monte, Genoa

order near Naples. Since Montecassino joined the congregation of which Cervara was a member in 1505, this altarpiece and Saint Benedict's representation in it have particular meaning. The abbot's crozier in Benedict's right hand is decorated at the base of the crook with a hexagonal component in intricate goldsmith work showing the figures of the Virgin and Child and a female saint with an open book (probably Saint Scholastica, Benedict's sister and the head of the community of Benedictine nuns) in tiny niches; at the uppermost tip is a figure kneeling before the Virgin and Child, suggesting the donor of the altarpiece or Saint Benedict himself. Saints Jerome and Benedict share the same space with the Virgin and Child (a millefleurs tapestry hanging continues at the back of all three panels), serving as intercessors for the monks to the Virgin Mary as well as exempla of monastic life.

In addition to appearing as rich decorative effects, the processional staff, crozier, and millefleurs tapestry also reveal details connoting the teachings of Saint Jerome, which were held in common with the fundamental tenets of the Benedictine Rule. Although the flora and fauna of the tapestry may initially suggest the paradisal state in which the saints exist and toward which they shepherd the faithful, there are menacing and lascivious animals within—a monkey, rabbits (one attacking a cockerel), an owl—that warn of evil, darkness, and the temptations of life and a state of uncontrolled nature.[86] Saints Jerome and Benedict stand with their backs to these temptations, living the virtuous life. Jerome was an advocate of the importance of celibacy, believing that a "perfect Christian life is impossible without abstinence and ascetic practices."[87] The miracle of the taming of the lion (seen here at Jerome's feet) and the removal of the thorn in his paw, as Rice notes, was also a "metaphor for taming the bestial in man, the triumph of law over unregimented nature, of morality over passion and instinct, of civilization over savagery." He goes on to explain that "in a Christian perspective, it [the miracle] represents the victory of love, holiness, and grace over the sinfulness of unredeemed and fallen nature."[88]

Additional themes of Resurrection, the sacrifice of Christ, and the Eucharist are expressed by the decoration of Saint Jerome's processional staff, whose cross has at its center a pelican pricking its breast in order to restore its young to life by its own blood.[89] The cross sits atop a tiny church with Charlemagne (identified by his crown, scepter, and orb and wearing a cloak over armor; the fleurs-de-lis denote his dominion over the French territories) at its entrance. Charlemagne here reflects the themes of both sexual temptation and redemption through the celebration of the Mass: at a miraculous communion offered by Saint Giles, he was pardoned by an angel for having committed incest with his sister Gisela.[90]

It is this first tier of the altarpiece that prepares the viewer for the mystery revealed in the upper two tiers. "The blood of Christ nourishes the mystical body of the church. The Christian receives it through the sacraments and by imitating Christ, by conforming himself to Christ crucified"[91] and by emulating the lives of virtuous saints—here Jerome and Benedict. The model of contemplative life includes "psalmody or the Divine Office, the celebration of the cycle of the mysteries of salvation, reading accompanied by meditation, private prayer, and—most important of all—the celebration of the Eucharist."[92] It is the vertical axis of the altarpiece that is devoted to the mysteries of the Incarnation and Transubstantiation, themes entirely appropriate for the high altar, the site of the Mass.

Owing to the suppression of the monasteries during the Napoleonic Era, many book and manuscript collections, particularly those of the north Italian houses, were destroyed or dispersed.[93] It is difficult, therefore, to confirm the regular liturgical practices of the Benedictine monks of this abbey or to establish the specific request of the patron in regard to the theme. We can only say that in general terms this altarpiece reflects the themes of the congregation's early piety, which, as Collett notes, was ascetic, liturgical, and Christocentric.[94] In the late fifteenth century the ascetic way of life of the *Devotio Moderna* was absorbed into the practice because of its view of salvation achieved through ardent inward devotion and moral purity. Seemingly reflected in the Cervara Altarpiece, the tenets of the *Devotio Moderna* began with "man's emptiness and ignorance which man may surmount with the help of grace, until by following the ascetic example of Christ, the soul was liberated from the flesh, and ascended to God. It was a pattern in which the Cross was seen as the supreme example rather than the unique instrument of man's salvation."[95]

High above, the all-seeing and all-knowing God raises his hand in blessing, as does the crucified Christ, on all that is below: the Annunciation, which led to the Incarnation and ultimately the Crucifixion, where Christ shed his blood for the salvation of mankind; and the Virgin and Child, who, holding the bunch of grapes, symbolizes the Eucharist and represents the Real Presence of the Body and Blood of Christ.

The physical setting for the Virgin and Christ Child, the throne and canopy above with curtains, refers to Mary as the living receptacle of Christ and may be associated with the tabernacle that holds the host, or with early *Vierge ouvrante* figures. This is also evident in the Virgin and Child panel of Carlo Braccesco's polytych (Figure 178). The opened curtains allude to those hanging on either side of the altar, which hid the mystery of the Transubstantiation until they were opened at the moment of the elevation of the host to show the transformed host.[96] Because the panel of the Virgin and Child is cut at the top, it is not possible to see exactly how the large dark curtain pulled to either side of the throne was affixed above it, although it is clear from the way that it hangs that when closed, it would have hidden the Virgin and Child from view.[97] Originating as a motif in models of Asiatic monarchs of antiquity, as well as in late antique and Byzantine examples, the curtain was the "formal expression of ceremonial concealment" of the monarchs from their subjects.[98] Later on, in Western art, it became an attribute associated with high-level church officials and saints,[99] and about the eleventh century, with the developing cult of the Virgin Mary, it became her particular attribute.[100]

The medieval liturgist Durandus's *Rationale divinorum officiorum* provides the liturgical explanation for the parted curtains.

> The veil symbolized the piece of precious cloth that was hung between the columns—represented here by the variegated marble columns flanking the seated Virgin—of Solomon's temple to separate the sanctuary where the Ark of the Covenant was kept from the rest of the sacred enclosure. The veil alluded to the darkness that overshadowed the human mind before Christ's Passion; before his sacrifice, the significance of holy scripture was veiled, hidden and obscure. However, just as the veil of Jerusalem's temple was torn asunder at the moment Jesus died, so were the altar hangings lowered and reopened on Holy Saturday to manifest God's Word. When the *"Gloria in excelsis"* was intoned during the Mass of Holy Saturday, the veils covering the altars were removed and hangings moved aside so that through Christ's sacrifice the truth of the Law stood revealed to human sight.[101]

Part of the original commission for the altarpiece at Cervara also included curtains, tapestries, and an altar frontal for the main altar. As Hyde explains, the silk curtains that were to be provided, and would indeed echo the curtains on either side of the Virgin's throne in the central panel, are more difficult to trace—if they were used to cover the altarpiece, this would explain their absence from the inventories, as only the paintings and goods of the sacristy and the rooms of the monastery are listed. Spinola notes how in the mid-eighteenth century the abbot, D. Vittorino Maria Federici, removed the old "apparati di damasco rosso del Santuario e fatto di essi altro uso."[102] If these were the original curtains (there is no mention of expenditure on such an item in the documents detailing the restoration

of the chapel), they would have echoed in their red color the tones of the three lower-tier panels and the painted tapestry in them.[103] Covering the painting on the high altar with curtains was customary and widespread in Italy in the Renaissance, and equally common in Liguria and in Lombardy.[104]

On the second level of the altarpiece is the *Annunciation,* which, divided into two parts (as is common for Italian altarpieces; see Figures 178 and 179), flanks the *Crucifixion.* This represents the Incarnation of Christ and his ultimate sacrifice for the salvation of humankind. The words ALPHA ET OM[EGA] and [VIRTUS AL]TISSIMI OBOMBRABIT T[IBI] adorn the border of Gabriel's cope: from Revelation 1:8 are the Lord's words "I am Alpha and Omega, the beginning and the ending," and from Luke 1:35, "the power of the highest shall overshadow thee," that is, Gabriel's words at the Annunciation to the Virgin. On the hem of Mary's dress, beginning in Flemish, are the words MOEDER ONS HER[N] (Mother of our Lord), AVE MARIA MATER GRACI[A]E M[ATER] MISERICORDI[A]E TU NOS ABHOS[TE] [PROTEGE] . . . Translated as "Hail Mary, Mother of Grace, Mother of Mercy, protect us from the enemy, [and at the hour of death take us]," this is part of a hymn sung at vespers and lauds in the Office of the Virgin and the Commendation of the Soul.[105] On the hem of the Virgin's cloak, below on the first level, are further liturgical references in the Salve Regina: SALVE REGINA. MATER MISERICORDIAE, VITA, DULCEDO ET SPES NOSTRA, SALVE . . . (Hail, Queen, Mother of mercy, Our life, our sweetness and our hope, hail!). This is followed by a response added by the seventh century to the Salve Regina: O CLEMENS! O PIA! O DULCIS VIRGO MARIA! (O merciful [clement]! O pious [loving]! O sweet Virgin Mary).

Throughout the altarpiece the disparate parts are united by lighting scheme, scale, perspective, the form of haloes, all in accordance with the iconographic program. Unusual for David is the illumination of his paintings from the right instead of the left, a change in direction that in northern examples might be taken as a sign that the artist attempted to unite an actual exterior light source with the depicted light within his painting. Jan van Eyck is thought to have been among the first artists to have achieved this by taking into account the window to the right of the Ghent Altarpiece in the chapel where it first was placed.

A look at the conventional treatment of light within contemporary Italian altarpieces, however, suggests a different motivation for David's lighting scheme. Although altarpieces in Italian churches would have been illuminated principally by artificial sources—that is, by candlelight and hanging lamps—the treatment of pictorial light in Italian altarpieces (principally those in Venetian churches) was meant to suggest a real or natural source.[106] Natural light within a church could conceivably come from a variety of sources that would shift over the course of a day, but it became important for Italian artists to portray a single light source within their paintings, and during the fifteenth century certain conventions were established. According to this practice, altarpieces placed at right angles to the nave, the high altars or altars in the apse chapels at the east end were lit from the south, that is to say, the right. If David adhered to these ruling conventions of light in contemporary Italian altarpieces, as seems quite likely in the carefully planned Cervara Altarpiece, he may well have incorporated the practice in other altarpieces in this same period of intense production. The *Virgin among Virgins* of 1509, for example, adopts a lighting scheme from the right for a painting that was meant to be installed on the main altar of the convent of Sion.

Just as Jan van Eyck had done in the Ghent Altarpiece, David considered the position of the viewer below the baseline of the altarpiece, looking upward, and his distance from the scenes depicted. The scale of the figures in each of the three tiers of the altarpiece (see reconstruction, Figure 176) is adjusted accordingly. The lower-tier figures, closest to the observer, are the largest. Those of the second tier of the *Annunciation* and *Crucifixion* are equivalent to one another, but they are smaller in scale and their proportions are elongated in order to take into account the fact that they are seen from below. Coordinated with this scheme, the horizon line of the

Crucifixion is lowered more than in any other of David's paintings. Finally, God the Father looms over all, suggesting his omnipotence and his freedom from nature's laws. Although by contrast to the smaller figures of the *Crucifixion* and *Annunciation,* he appears largest in scale, God the Father corresponds in size to the Virgin and saints, while the red, feathered seraphim accompanying him match the scale of the figures on the second level.

In the majestic symmetrical arrangement of the altarpiece, flanking figures accompany the key iconographic components—the Virgin and Child, the Crucifixion scene, the crucified Christ himself, and finally God the Father—mounting to a climax at the apex. Within this schema, beginning at the tip of God the Father's miter, the central axis of the altarpiece passes through the heart-shaped jewel of the morse on his cope, the center of the figure of Christ, and then bisects the Virgin through the jewel in her diadem, her heart, and the area where the hand of the Christ Child and Virgin meet at the bunch of grapes. The main figures along this axis are further unified by the cruciform halos adorning God the Father, the crucified Christ, and the Christ Child, while circular aureoles surround the heads of the three depictions of the Virgin Mary, as well as those of Saints Jerome and Benedict.

An internal system of sight lines (see Figure 177) continually directs the viewer's eye up through the figures to God the Father or to the crucified Christ by way of carefully positioned motifs: Saint Jerome's processional staff is slightly angled to direct the viewer's eye up to Gabriel's staff, which in turn leads toward God the Father, or up to Gabriel's right hand, which points toward the head of Christ; Benedict's crozier is positioned to indicate the descending dove that is in a sight line that includes the heads of the Annunciate Virgin and God the Father; the scepter of God the Father once again leads down to the head of the crucified Christ and to the central axis of the painting.

The first and second tiers of the altarpiece each have a unified one-point perspective scheme that is intentionally off-center. The orthogonals of the floor

180. Hubert and Jan van Eyck, Ghent Altarpiece, detail of *Gabriel* and the *Virgin* of the Annunciation (Photo Copyright IRPA-KIK, Brussels)

tiles in the paintings of Saints Jerome and Benedict meet at a point (or very close to one point) slightly to the left of the Christ Child's eye level. Just as in the placement of the Virgin's head against the red stone back of the throne, the slightly off-center perspective achieves a kind of informality and relief from the rigid symmetry of the altarpiece. It allows for a softer, more naturalistic approach to the Christ Child, who looks out toward the viewer communicating the mystery of Transubstantiation. Above, the orthogonals of the floor tiles in the two panels of the

Annunciation meet at a point within the figure of the Virgin, near the horizon line of the *Crucifixion,* and on the same vertical axis that intersects the focal point of the lower level. In accordance with the viewer's position below, David accelerated the recession of space most evident in the floor tiles of the *Annunciation* and presented the *Crucifixion* with a lowered horizon line. There can be no mistaking the Italianate organization of the altarpiece, which was modeled after Ligurian altarpieces of the late fifteenth and early sixteenth centuries.[107] In its style, however, it is a synthesis

181. Vincenzo Foppa, *Angel Gabriel*, ca. 1468, from frescoes in the Portinari Chapel in Sant' Eustorgio, Milan

of northern and Italian modes that reflects the Sauli family's personal and professional ties to both regions.

In the solemnity and reduction of form, and in the solid pyramidal shape of the motif of the Virgin and Child seated on a monumental throne, the focal point of the altarpiece is imbued with Italian Renaissance spirit. The Virgin's brooding expression, a poignant synthesis of sorrowful prescience and stoic acceptance, is appropriate to the theme. David's intent here and his accommodation of Italianate style in this regard are at once apparent when the Cervara Virgin is compared with the Virgin from the *Virgin among Virgins* (compare Figures 276 and 274), which in pose (including the

184. Detail of vase in Figure 175

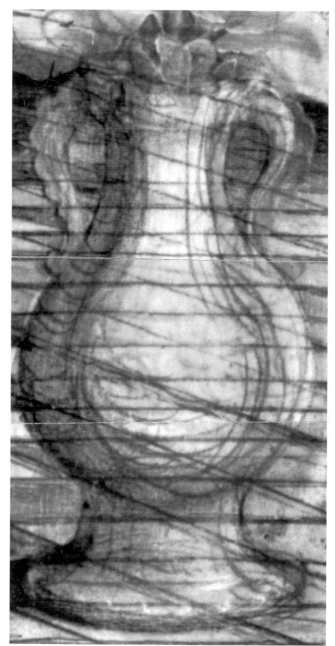

185. IRR detail of vase in Figure 175

Virgins of 1509) as a result of a more profound contact with the working techniques of Italian artists, are not yet manifest here, as we shall see.

How did David achieve the remarkable effects in what is his most ambitious surviving altarpiece? Where was it made and how was it produced? The complexity of this altarpiece and the evident care with which it was planned suggest a series of preliminary drawings in which David worked out the relationship of the individual components to each

other as well as the overall concept. Although there may have been discussions with the patron or intermediaries about the plans, the original contract would not necessarily have specified anything other than the subjects to be included, their exact location within the altarpiece, and the overall measurement of the space where the polyptych would be installed.

186. IRR of Gabriel in Figure 174

187. IRR detail of head of the Virgin in Figure 276

With present information it is not possible to determine where the commission took place, but we can draw certain conclusions about the location of manufacture of the panels themselves. A key detail is the fact that the paintings are on oak, the indigenous support of northern European paintings, and not poplar, the habitual wood for paintings made in Italy. Wood panels, of course, can be transported from one location to another, and there are certain cases where we know of paintings produced in southern Europe that were made on oak;[111] but seldom are they of the monumental size of the *Virgin, Saint Jerome,* and *Saint Benedict.* Furthermore, the ground preparation of the Cervara Altarpiece panels is chalk, or calcium carbonate, a material typical of northern paintings, instead of gypsum, or calcium sulfate, commonly found in southern European painting.[112] As

this preliminary paint layer is not an important aesthetic consideration for the painting and is simply composed of indigenous materials, it is thus an unequivocal indicator of the place of manufacture, that is, in northern Europe, not in Italy.

The panels were not painted in an engaged frame, as was usual for Netherlandish works of this period.[113] The edges of the oak boards (here of the *Annunciation,* Figure 183) show the various paint layers brushed out onto the bare wood edge. Taking into account the size of the altarpiece, the painting of the panels outside of their frame was a practical consideration. The evidence suggests that the paintings were executed in Bruges and transported to the abbey of Cervara, where an elaborate frame was awaiting their arrival for fitting.

The underdrawing for each of the seven paintings is relatively detailed, working out directly on the panel elements of the composition, the figures, and the modeling of forms. In his typical fashion David first made a rough draft of the forms with his sketching tool, in this case charcoal,[114] and then went over these lines with brush and a black pigment here and there to adjust the forms and fix the design. Although the thickness of the paint and the pigments used to some extent obscure David's initial steps toward the perspective design, in some places ruled lines are visible, especially in the vase of lilies, which is painted over the preliminary floor design (Figures 184 and 185). Elsewhere this drawing goes partially underneath the draperies of the figures, for example in Gabriel (Figure 186). This allowed David to place the figures within the organized space before he returned to the perspective scheme to fix the final plan for its horizontal and orthogonal lines with a second layer of underdrawing. Tiny tack holes at regular intervals along the unpainted border of the panels of Gabriel and the Virgin Annunciate probably indicate the placement of a cartoon for each figure on the panel in order to check its size in relationship to

its setting. The accommodation of figures to the spatial concept required only minor readjustments, a circumstance that indicates that the general scheme was already worked out in advance, in preliminary drawings on paper. For example, in the panel of Gabriel, David adjusted the height of the banquette to the right of his fluttering drapery. Only in a few instances did the perspective scheme (which may have been as intuitive as it was measured) need further correction in the painted layers (notably at the left edge of the dais of the Virgin's throne).

The initial concept for the figures, likewise, was clearly worked out in advance, for there are no major changes from the underdrawing to the final painted stage in any of the panels. Furthermore, the bold manner and assurance with which the underdrawings of figures and their draperies are executed suggests the redrawing of forms already far along in their stage of creation. Compare the underdrawing of the Virgin and Child or of Gabriel with their final painted state (compare Figures 275 with 276 and 186 with 174). New workshop drawings must have

188 Detail of head of Saint Benedict in Figure 176

189. IRR. detail of head of Saint Benedict in Figure 176

been established at this time for this commission, since the exact drapery patterns for certain of the figures, namely the Virgin, were reused for other, later paintings, in this case for the Virgins in the *Virgin and Child with Saints and a Donor* and in the *Virgin among Virgins* (Figures 273 and 274).[115]

Of particular concern for David, however, was establishing the lighting system within the paintings, perhaps a new preoccupation for one who wished to emulate the chiaroscuro effects of Italian artists. He worked out the details of an overall plan at every stage of the painting process. David gave particular attention to the head and neck of the Virgin (Figure 187), indicating the zone of deep shadow at the left with even parallel hatching. In the draperies of figures, David redrew the lines of folds he wished to emphasize and boldly indicated areas of shadow with broad parallel hatching. This prepared the exact areas to be modeled with glazes in the final paint layers (compare Figures 186 and 174, of Gabriel).

David's special interest in the lighting effects coincided at this point with initial attempts to simplify his painting technique. An example of this is found in the underdrawing for the heads of the saints, which approaches a kind of undermodeling. The features of Saint Benedict's face are accentuated by swift, broad brushstrokes of wash that at once indicate both the form and the modeling (Figures 188 and 189). A comparison with the painted surface shows that this bold effect of the underdrawing is significantly muted in its final form, where the lighting effects are less dramatic.[116]

On the upper levels of the altarpiece, a method of indicating the areas of darker emphasis through accents with the brush, thus creating a shortcut execution of a modeled form, is more readily apparent. In the heads of both the Virgin and Gabriel, as well as in their hands, David precisely placed dark brushstrokes for shadowed forms and lightly scumbled over them (Figures 190 and 191; Figures 192 and 193). Here and there where the scumbled layer has been abraded away, the dark brush undermodeling shows very clearly (as in Gabriel's left hand, Figure 194). In the faces, in addition to the

190. Detail of head of Gabriel in Figure 174

191. IRR detail of head of Gabriel in Figure 174

192. Detail of Gabriel's right hand in Figure 174

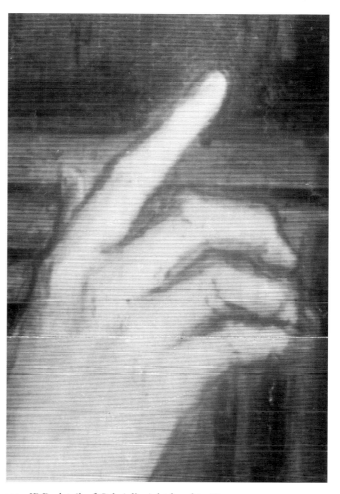

193. IRR detail of Gabriel's right hand in Figure 174

194. Detail of Gabriel's left hand in Figure 174

bold brushstrokes, he also indicated areas of half-shadow by lightly touching in an interrupted line with the tip of his brush as in the area beneath the Virgin's eyes (Figures 195 and 196).[117]

David appropriately took into account the fact that these figures would be seen from below and from a distance, for some of his brushwork is very bold indeed, not carefully blended as he did in his smaller-scale paintings, which were intended to be studied closely. Although there is certainly a thin integrating glaze missing from the upper layer of Gabriel's cope (Figure 174), the effect of the red and green brushstrokes, which is quite strident when viewed at close range, would have appeared considerably muted when seen at a distance, creating a vibrant *couleur changeante* effect. This technique of disengaged strokes used in the upper paint layers and the striking execution of the darks, particularly in

195. IRR detail of Virgin's head in Figure 175

196. IRR detail of Virgin's head in Figure 175

draperies, is the beginning of a trend that finds its fullest treatment in the *Virgin among Virgins* of 1509 (see chapter 2).

In his extraordinary achievement in the Cervara Altarpiece, David brought to bear all of his creative abilities. In no other work by him are the varied and complicated elements presented by the conditions of the commission so beautifully integrated into the overall conception. Particularly impressive is David's merging of Italian and Netherlandish sensibilities, a feature of this altarpiece deliberately intended to accommodate his client, Vincenzo Sauli.

The success of this integration is not likely to have been achieved simply through the inspiration of Italian drawings or prints transported to the north, but from firsthand knowledge of art that David saw in Italy. Exactly when David might have traveled

there is difficult to say, but if we take into account the evidence presented by the paintings themselves, a reasonable hypothesis might be developed. Clearly the impact of certain elements of Italian painting are already evident in the Cervara Altarpiece, at least in its incipient stages—the Foppa-like Gabriel, the monumentality and solemnity of the Virgin, the use of a perspective scheme, and above all the adherence to Ligurian altarpiece form. But what makes an appearance only after about 1506 is David's more profound understanding of particular features of Italian painting technique, especially the use of washes for the undermodeling of forms, as found in his 1509 *Virgin among Virgins* (see Figures 83 and 84). A comparison of the heads of the Virgins in the Cervara Altarpiece, the *Virgin and Child with Saints and a Donor,* and the *Virgin among Virgins* (compare

197. IRR detail of Virgin's head in the *Virgin and Child with Saints and a Donor* in Figure 23

198. IRR detail of Virgin's head in the *Virgin among Virgins* in Figure 79

Figure 187 with Figures 197 and 198) shows the evolution in technique: the Cervara Virgin's head is modeled with parallel hatching in chalk or charcoal, while the latter two examples show the use of the brush and the application of broader strokes in a new, more fluid and integrated undermodeling of the forms. Since the Cervara Altarpiece already suggests an acquaintance with Italian art, and as we know from the details of its manufacture (the oak panels, the material of the ground preparation, and the fact that they were painted out of their frames) that it was made in the north and not in Italy, it is reasonable to assume that David made an initial, brief trip to Italy between about 1503 and 1506, perhaps to visit the site of his prestigious commission at the Benedictine abbey and to acquaint himself with Ligurian altarpiece style. After 1506, a second wave of Italian influence seems to have been assimilated in David's paintings, and it is possible that he experienced a more profound understanding of Italian painting—especially its technique—through a second trip, made perhaps to deliver his altarpiece in 1506. The Cervara Altarpiece, then, marks David's firsthand experience with Italian art at the beginning of his subtle assimilation of its lessons into his own idiom. This new focus on the art of Italy places David, not as a follower, but rather as a pioneer of its embrace by sixteenth-century painters, above all those in Antwerp, such as Joos van Cleve and Quentin Massys, at the beginning of a new age.

1. On the communities of merchants and bankers, particularly the Italians and the Spanish, see esp. Balbi 1996 (regarding the Genoese in the Netherlands); A. Vandewalle 1992, pp. 158–81; A. Vandewalle and N. Geirnaert 1992, pp. 224–51 (with extensive bibliographies); Montias 1996, pp. 25–54; Walsh 1982, pp. 369–96; Van Houtte 1966, pp. 29–47.

2. Blockmans 1995, p. 17; De Vos 1992, pp. 328–38; Wilson 1998, pp. 41–84.

3. This was true not only of Bruges but of other locations as well and in both earlier and later times. Lorne Campbell (1994, pp. 1–24) discusses this in regard to export pictures from the Rogier van der Weyden group. In his "Commentarios de la pintura . . ." (ca. 1560) Felipe de Guevara disparages the fact that countless forgeries of works by Bosch were being produced and exported (see F. J. Sánchez Cantón, ed., *Fuentes literarias para la historia del arte español,* 5 vols. [Madrid, 1923–41], vol. I, pp. 159–60). See also Jacobs 1998, pp. 209–37.

4. Campbell 1976, pp. 188–98; Ewing 1990, pp. 558–84; Wilson 1983, pp. 474–79; Wilson 1986, pp. 1759–66; and Wilson 1990b, pp. 621–27; Fuchs 1977, pp. 2–7; González in *Vlaanderen en Castilla y León,* exh. cat. (Antwerp, 1995), pp. 106–10.

5. Now split between the National Gallery, London, and the Gemäldegalerie, Berlin. Lorne Campbell has suggested that the Berlin *Crucifixion* by David is part of the same altarpiece (in his forthcoming catalogue of the early Netherlandish paintings at the National Gallery, London).

6. Cited in Campbell 1991, p. 614.

7. See van Miegroet 1989, ill. 198, cat. no. 42.

8. For a review of these issues, see M. Baxandall, "Bartholomaeus Facius on Painting: A Fifteenth-Century Manuscript of the 'De viris illustribus,'" *Journal of the Warburg and Courtauld Institutes* 27 (1964), pp. 90–107; Canfield 1995, pp. 35–39; and D. Thiébaut, *Le Christ à la colonne d'Antonello de Messine,* Les Dossiers du musée du Louvre (1993), pp. 28–38; Nuttall 1989 and Nuttall 1992, pp. 70–77.

9. For a general review of this issue, see De Vos 1992, pp. 328–50, and Keith Christiansen's "The View from Italy," in Ainsworth and Christiansen 1998, pp. 39–61; see also Boccardo and Di Fabio 1997.

10. See Brans 1959 and Fuchs 1977. One example is the site of the royal tomb of Ferdinand and Isabella at the Cartuja of Miraflores, on which German and Netherlandish artists were gainfully employed. See the forthcoming dissertation of Ronda Kasl, "The Cartuja of Miraflores" (Institute of Fine Arts, New York).

11. Jacobs 1989, pp. 214 and n. 46.

12. Ainsworth 1994c, pp. 60–62.

13. Ibid., pp. 46–49, 136–41; 146–53; 154–57. Given the already well established link of Petrus Christus with foreign markets, it comes as no surprise that his son, Petrus Christus II, established himself as a painter in Spain.

14. M. P. J. Martens 1997, pp. 35–41.

15. De Vos 1994b, pp. 105–9.

16. Ibid., p. 109.

17. Ibid., pp. 289–93.

18. On Memling's portraiture, see ibid., pp. 365–70.

19. Ibid., p. 368.

20. Suggested by the author at the Leventritt Lectures (Fogg Art Museum, Cambridge, Mass., fall 1996, publication forthcoming). See also De Vos 1994b, pp. 98–99.

21. Adhémar 1962, pp. 106, 109–10.

22. Ibid., p. 109.

23. De Vos 1994b, pp. 212–16.

24. Ibid., pp. 180–83, 210–11, with 276–77, as reconstructed by Michael Rohlman, "Memling's *Pagagnotti triptych,"* *Burlington Magazine* 137, no. 1108 (July 1995), pp. 438–45.

25. De Vos 1994b, pp. 276–77; see also D. Martens 1993, pp. 129–74.

26. M. P. J. Martens 1992, pp. 179–84. Winifried Wilhelmy (1993, p. 95) places the panel on the northeast side of the church, on one of the pillars of the nave. According to Craig Harbison (1991, pp. 48, 57), it is not specifically recorded as on public view until the mid-16th century at Sint Donaaskerk.

27. Van Miegroet 1989, pp. 281–82.

28. Dijkstra 1990, pp. 7–28.

29. Fuchs 1977, pp. 8–38.

30. For a review of this issue, see S. Buck, "Petrus Christus's Berlin Wings and the Metropolitan Museum's Eyckian Diptych," in Ainsworth, ed., 1995, pp. 65–83.

31. De Vos 1992, p. 347.

32. De Vos 1994, pp. 289–93.

33. Dijkstra 1990, pp. 78–109; Ainsworth 1992, pp. 59–68.

34. C. G. Perez, "L'Étude d'une copie de la *Descente de Croix* des Abalétriers de Louvain de Rogier van der Weyden conservée au Musée du Prado, Madrid (cat. no. 1894)," in *Le dessin sous-jacent dans la peinture, Colloque VIII (1989),* H. Verougstraete-Marcq and R. Van Schoute, eds. (Louvain-la-Neuve, 1991), pp. 109–21.

35. The panels have not been cut to fit this frame but were originally made in this shape. See Adhémar 1962, pls. 126 and 141. Although less directly connected, the *Virgin and Child in an Apse* (known as the Virgin of Salamanca), produced in multiple copies after a design by Robert Campin, may have been the source for the musical angels. See Ainsworth 1996, pp. 149–58.

36. Suggested also by De Vos 1988, p. 142.

37. By way of comparison, on standardization, patronage, and quality issues in carved altarpieces see Jacobs 1989, pp. 207–29, and Jacobs 1998, pp. 149–237.

38. Van Miegroet 1989, pp. 314–16, where this altarpiece is considered a workshop product; and Hand and Wolff 1986, pp. 68–74, and Hand 1992, ill., pp. 4–5, figs. 2–3.

39. See Appendix B.

40. On questions of provenance, see Hand 1992, pp. 11–14.

41. Brandenbarg 1995, pp. 31–65.

42. Hand 1992, pp. 7–8; van Miegroet 1989, pp. 314–16; and Bodenhausen 1905, p. 171.

43. For opinions on attribution, see van Miegroet 1989, cat. no. 52, pp. 314–16.

44. See Appendix B. Dendrochronology of the Saint Anne Altarpiece by Peter Klein indicates that the earliest felling date for the panels making up the altarpiece is 1490, with a likely creation time (assuming the addition of fifteen sapwood wings and a storage period of ten years) of about 1506. One possible explanation for the character of the figures of Saint Anne, the Virgin, and the Child is that they are actually meant to represent polychromed wooden sculpture (a suggestion made at a symposium on the Saint Anne Altarpiece at the National Gallery of Art, Washington, May 20–22, 1991). However, to my knowledge attempts at trompe l'oeil sculpture in early Netherlandish painting are limited to grisailles on the exterior wings of altarpieces and to representations of carved altarpieces within paintings (the latter, for example, as seen in the illustrations for the article by Kim Woods, "The Netherlandish Carved Altarpiece c. 1500: Type and Function," in *The Altarpiece and the Renaissance*, Peter Humfrey and Martin Kemp, eds., [Cambridge, 1990], pp. 76–89).

45. See Metzger 1992, pp. 59–63; and Metzger and B. H. Berrie, "Gerard David's Saint Anne Altarpiece: Evidence for Workshop Participation," in *Historical Painting Techniques, Materials and Studio Practice*, A. Wallert, E. Hermens, and M. Peek, eds. (preprints of a symposium, University of Leyden, the Netherlands, June 26–29, 1995), pp. 127–34, esp. pp. 132–33.

46. Other works that may possibly be attributed to the workshop assistant who painted the figures of the Virgin and Child and Saint Anne are a *Virgin and Child* in the Lazaro-Galdiano Museum, Madrid (there attributed to Gerard David) and the Darmstadt *Virgin and Child Enthroned* (Figure 282).

47. The gray robe of Saint Anthony remained opaque to infrared reflectography and therefore the underdrawing could not be observed.

48. See de Winter 1981, p. 418, figs. 124–126, and pl. IV.

49. See discussions in van Miegroet 1989, pp. 234–37, cat. nos. 31 and 44, pp. 299, 309–10.

50. A further development of this composition in the style of David is found in the *Adoration of the Magi* in the Linsky collection, MMA (see Ainsworth and Christiansen 1998, cat. no. 84).

51. Among them Lamentations or Depositions attributed to David or to Isenbrant. See ills. in van Miegroet 1989, cat. nos. 6, 6a, 6b, 43, and pp. 238–39.

52. Hoogewerff 1961, pp. 185–91.

53. A. Morassi, *Trittico fiammingo a San Lorenzo della Costa* (Florence, 1947); M. J. Friedländer, "Trois Peintres des Pays-Bas à Gênes," *Zeitschrift für bildende Kunst* 61 (1927), pp. 274–75; R. dos Santos, "O mestre triptico Costa é Francisco Henriques," *Bellas Artes* 4 (1952), pp. 15–17.

54. A comparison of the female types and especially the details of the physiognomy in the two paintings shows distinct similarities. (See ill. in van Miegroet 1989, p. 207.)

55. For the most recent published discussions of this altarpiece, see Hyde 1997, pp. 245–54, and Di Fabio 1997, pp. 59–81.

56. Castelnovi 1952, p. 23, quotes Don Giuseppe Spinola from the manuscript held in the University Library in Genoa; see also ibid., p. 25. For confusion about the correct identity of Vincenzo Sauli, see Hyde 1994, vol. I, p. 23.

57. Hyde 1994, vol. II, p. 48, in appendix, doc. 3.86, after A. R. Scarsella, *Annali di Santa Margherita Ligure dai suoi primordi sino all'anno 1914 soritti per uso ei Sammargheritesi colti* (Rapallo, 1914; repr. Bologna, 1969), vol. II, pp. 38–39.

58. As in Hyde 1994, vol. II, p. 255; G. Spinola, *Le Memorie Storiche del Ministero, e Badia di S. Girolamo della Cervara del Ordine Benedettino–Cassinese dall'anno di sua fondazione 1360 al 1790, Raccolte da Don Giuseppe Sponola Professo, Decano, e Cellerario dello Stesso Ministero, tra Pastori Arcadi della Conolia Sabauda Lamindo Tiricio, ms. of 1790* (Biblioteca Universitaria di Genova), pp. 597–98.

59. See van Miegroet 1989, pp. 294–95, for a summary of the attributions.

60. Except for Scillia 1975, pp. 54–55.

61. I am very grateful to both Mary Howard and Helen Hyde for sharing the results of their investigations into the identity of the correct Sauli: Howard, personal communication (March 22, 1989), and Hyde 1994, vol. I, esp. pp. 234–38, and Hyde 1997, p. 246.

62. Hyde 1994, vol. I, p. 234.

63. Hyde 1994, vol. II, pp. 11–14, 17–18, and Hyde 1997, p. 246, nn. 33–35.

64. Hyde 1994, vol. I, p. 239.

65. Collett 1985, p. 9.

66. Hyde 1994, vol. I, p. 240.

67. On the Genoese families in the Bruges community see Balbi 1996, p. 84.

68. Hyde 1994, vol. I, p. 242.

69. Ibid., p. 243, and Hyde 1997, p. 247.

70. Hyde 1994, vol. I, p. 243, and Alizeri, p. 244; see also for comparison Peter Humfrey's account (1993, pp. 151–57) of costs and payments for contemporary Venetian altarpieces.

71. Regarding an Italian journey, see Castelnovi 1952, pp. 22–27; Hoogewerff 1953, pp. 72–73; Röthel 1956, pp. 361–65; Castelfranchi Vegas 1984, p. 270; Koch 1965, pp. 278–79; and van Miegroet 1989, p. 217.

72. Campbell 1991, pp. 624–25; E. Viviani della Robbia, "Un mercante a Bruges nel sec. XV," *Illustrazione toscana e dell'Etruria* 9 (1941), pp. 8–15.

73. Vito Vitale, "Diplomatici e consoli della Republica di Genova," *Atti della società ligure di storia patria* 63 (1934), pp. 4, 48, 134–35; and Emilio Pandiani, "Un anno di storia genovese (giugno 1506–1507)," *Atti della società ligure di storia patria* 37 (1905), pp. 13, 18–23, 65–66. I am very grateful to Mary Howard for calling my attention to these notices.

74. Van Miegroet 1989, p. 212.

75. Hyde 1994, vol. I, pp. 264–65. For the Genoese in Bruges, see R. Janssens de Bisthoven, "La Loge des Genois à Bruges," *A.S.L.S.P.* 66, pt. 2 (1915), pp. 143–71, esp. p. 152; see also J. A. Goris, *Étude sur les colonies marchandes meridionales à Anvers de 1488 à 1567* (Louvain, 1925); and Balbi 1996.

76. Spinola (see note 58 above), pp. 597–98; see Hyde 1994, vol. II, Appendix, p. 44, doc. 3.76, published in Castelnovi 1952, p. 23.

77. There has been some confusion over the identity of this saint: Crowe and Cavalcaselle (1872, p. 353) thought he was Anthony of Padua; he is unidentified by Bodenhausen (1905, p. 164); and Castelnovi called him Saint Maurus (1870, pp. 146–48), founder of the Benedictine order in France. Di Fabio (1997, p. 67) also called the saint Maurus (noting the fleur-de-lis on his crozier as an attribute). See also I. Tagliaferro and C. Di Fabio, *La gallieria di Palazzo bianco Genova* (Milan, 1992), p. 40. However, as the figure carries a crozier, the sign of a bishop or abbot, neither of which Saint Maurus was, and the French presence was not strongly felt in the congregation of Santa Giustina of Padua until 1515 (Collett 1985, p. 9), he is certainly Saint Benedict.

78. Hyde 1994, vol. I, pp. 254–56, and Hyde 1997, pp. 249–51.

79. Castelnovi 1952, p. 23, and Hyde 1994, vol. I, p. 256.

80. Hyde (1994 and 1997) and Di Fabio (1992, pp. 38–43) also agree with this suggestion.

81. Castelnovi suggested this (1952, p. 24).

82. Spinola, p. 599 (see note 58 above); Castelnovi 1952, p. 25; and Adhémar 1961, pp. 142–43.

83. For other examples, see Morassi 1946, figs. 7, 10–13. All of these show a Crucifixion in the middle of the second level, just as is proposed here for the Cervara Altarpiece.

84. According to Remondini (A. and M. Remondini, *Parrochie dell'Archidiocesi di Genova,* [Genoa, 1887], vol. II, p. 158), the monks left on March 21, 1799. Subsequently the church and monastery were taken over by the Trappists; today the church and monastery are being restored privately and there is no access to the site. There is no surviving early 16th-century description of the church; a 1650 report relates a structure of three naves and seven altars (see T. Leccisotti, "I monasteri cassinesi di Genova alla metà del '600," *Benedictina* 14 [1967], pp. 77–108, esp. pp. 99–105).

85. For an explanation of how Saint Jerome came to be known as a cardinal although this is not historically accurate, see Rice 1985, pp. 33–37.

86. See Heinrich Schwarz and Volker Plagemann, s.v. "Eule," *Reallexikon zur deutschen Kunstgeschichte* (Stuttgart and Munich, 1937–81), vol. VI, cols. 267–322, esp. cols. 272–278, 284–292. For the ape and rabbits, see Hall 1979, pp. 22 and 257.

87. Rice 1985, p. 19.

88. Ibid., pp. 39–40.

89. M. Rubin 1991, pp. 310–12.

90. Hall 1979, pp. 64–65.

91. Rice 1985, p. 80.

92. See Jean Leclercq, O.S.B., "*Otium monasticum* as a Context for Artistic Creativity," in *Monasticism and the Arts,* Timothy Gregory Verdon, ed. (Syracuse, 1964), pp. 63–80, esp. p. 67.

93. Collett 1985, p. 12; the dispersed material ended up in various Italian libraries in Padua, Mantua, Rome, the Vatican, and esp. the Biblioteca Laurenziana at Florence, and in Paris.

94. Ibid., p. 7.

95. Ibid., p. 17.

96. The function of the curtains is explained by Lane 1984, p. 53; in the notes to the sources of W. Durandus, *The Symbolism of Churches and Church Ornaments,* trans. of book 1 of *Rationale divinorum officiorum* (Leeds, 1843); in ch. 3, p. 35, in Barthélemy 1854, pp. 57 ff., and Neale and Webb 1893, pp. 62 ff.; for opening of curtains, see Pugin 1868, pp. 107 ff., 237 ff.; Jungmann 1951, vol. II, p. 140 and n. 11.

97. A similar arrangement is shown in the exterior left wing of David's Baptism Triptych (See Figure 214).

98. J. K. Eberlein, "The Curtain in Raphael's Sistine Madonna," *Art Bulletin* 65 (1983), pp. 61–66, as in Allesandro Nova, "Hangings, Curtains, and Shutters of Sixteenth-Century Lombard Altarpieces," in *Italian Altarpieces, 1250–1550: Function and Design,* Eve Borsook and Fiorella Superbi Gioffredi, eds. (Oxford, 1994), p. 180.

99. Eberlein 1983, p. 66 (as in note 98 above).

100. Ibid., pp. 66–68.

101. Durandus 1843 (as in note 96 above), pp. 72–75, and in Nova 1994 (as in note 98 above), pp. 177–89, esp. p. 180 for quotation.

102. Hyde 1994, vol. I, p. 287, n. 148.

103. Ibid., p. 252.

104. Nova 1994, p. 181–82 (see note 98 above).

105. G. M. Dreves and C. Blume, *Analecta hymnica medii aevi* (Leipzig, 1978), vol. II, p. 42 and nn. 60 and 61.

106. Gould 1981, pp. 21–25, and P. Humfrey (*The Altarpiece in Renaissance Venice* [New Haven and London, 1993], p. 55), who observes, "Altarpieces placed in chapels or on the wall in the nave (i.e., those aligned with an east-west axis of the church) were usually illumined as if from the west door, so that those on the south wall were lit from the right, and those on the north wall were lit from the left." Those works placed near the east end of the church in the transept were lit from the east.

107. See note 83 above.

108. This has been noted often: Bodenhausen 1905, p. 157; Panofsky 1953, pp. 351–52; and Blacksberg 1991, pp. 57–66.

109. See Appendix B, where Peter Klein notes that the Museum's *Annunciation* panels and the panels used for the Frankfurt *Annunciation* come from the same tree.

110. Delmarcel and Duverger 1987, pp. 107–9.

111. One example is the MMA's *Christ Appearing to His Mother* by a follower of Rogier van der Weyden, which was painted on oak, but has a calcium sulfate ground preparation typical of southern European manufacture. See Ainsworth 1992, pp. 59–68.

112. I am grateful to Marycolette Hruskocy for carrying out the microchemical test for the analysis of the ground preparations in the two *Annunciation* panels by David; this test showed the positive reaction for calcium carbonate (communication of May 20, 1991).

113. A *barbe*, signifying a juncture of the paint layers with a framing element, brace, or holding piece for the application of the ground and pigmented layers, occurs only at the bottom edge of these panels. For panel and frame

construction in northern Renaissance paintings, see H. Verougstraete-Marcq and R. Van Schoute, *Cadres et supports dans la peinture flamands aux 15e et 16e siècles* (Heure-le-Romain, 1989).

114. The identification of the underdrawing material as charcoal was made by Laura Juszczak (formerly of the Sherman Fairchild Paintings Conservation Department, MMA) in the spring of 1984. The identification of carbonized plant material was made by studying with polarized light microscopy a small sample of the underdrawing material taken from the edges of the two paintings. The findings were discussed by Ainsworth at the Sept. 10, 1984, I.C.O.M. meeting in Copenhagen.

115. Wilson 1990a, pp. 523–27, and chap. 6 here.

116. Similar effects are found in *Saint Bernardinus de Salviatis and Three Saints* and in the *Virgin and Child with Saints and a Donor* (both in the National Gallery, London) and ultimately lead the way to the more developed under-modeling in the *Virgin among Virgins* (see chap. 2).

117. Although this effect looks like pouncing, it should not be mistaken for this method of transfer, which is not found elsewhere in the painting and which would have been illogical to use only for this fine detail of the Virgin's face. The documentation of the underdrawing in the other panels of the Cervara Altarpiece took place in Paris in 1986, with the assistance of Katherine Crawford Luber and permission of Jacques Foucart, and in Genoa in 1987, with the assistance of Ronda Kasl and permission of Laura Tagliaferro.

CHAPTER FIVE

Landscapes for Meditation

Such a pastoral introduction to an altarpiece as is found on the outside landscape wings of the Nativity Triptych (Figures 199 and 200) was unprecedented in Netherlandish painting of the early sixteenth century. Even judged by criteria of the twentieth century, the panels were considered so innovative and modern that they were assumed to have been a later addition to the altarpiece— an assumption that apparently provided justification for separating the outside wings from the rest of the altarpiece after it entered the Bache collection in 1928.[1] The outside wings were subsequently sold to the Rijksmuseum in Amsterdam and today reside on long-term loan at the Mauritshuis in The Hague.[2]

David's portrayal of serene, meditative woods— what we still prize today as the bucolic setting for spiritual renewal—was soon eclipsed by the popularity of the world-view landscapes that Joachim Patinir produced in the nearby busy economic port of Antwerp. But it was precisely the sense of "rustic simplicity and shadowed seclusion" in David's landscapes that endured as seventeenth-century Dutch and Flemish artists considered the form most appropriate for evoking a sylvan retreat.[3]

The Nativity Triptych with Saints Jerome and Leonard and Donors and the detached Mauritshuis wings have attracted considerable attention over the decades, principally because of the remarkable and seemingly sudden appearance of the presumed first pure landscapes in Flemish painting.[4] Although this claim is overstated—these scenes on the outer wings are not independent but are an integral part of the intended meaning and visual experience of the triptych as a whole—the work certainly merits our

Detail of Figure 234

consideration for a number of reasons. Primary among these is the novelty of a naturalistic forest view constituting the sole image of the closed triptych, as well as the innovative way in which this scene introduced the interior theme of the Nativity to contemporary viewers. Even more significant for the history of landscape painting is David's break from the stylized, formulaic depictions used for the backdrops of subjects in paintings to the introduction of landscape studied from nature in its individual parts and as a complex whole. In both theme and representation, the Mauritshuis panels signal the peak of the development of David's landscape art and provide an important precedent for landscape as an independent genre in sixteenth- and seventeenth-century Dutch and Flemish painting.[5]

The closed altarpiece shows an isolated clearing in a forest, unpopulated except for an ass resting in the foreground of the left wing, along with a tit perched on some vines and an ass and an ox grazing near the pond on the right wing.[6] At the left, in a poor state of preservation and extensively restored, is a house with an adjoining tower.[7] These elements are comfortably settled in a lush environment of locally identifiable character—oak, walnut, and beech trees, as well as plantain, yellow iris, and the grasses that grow on the moist banks of a pond or stream.

The outside wings of Netherlandish triptychs traditionally represent a precursor or introduction to the theme to be presented on the interior when the doors are opened.[8] For a Nativity, the Annunciation or Adam and Eve in Paradise are the two scenes most commonly depicted, as they both prefigure the coming of Christ. There is no trace of any figures here, however, not even of Adam and Eve (thought by Friedländer to have existed previously and to have been overpainted)[9]—a circumstance that refutes the

assumption that these exterior wings were meant to represent Paradise or the Garden of Eden.[10]

Alternative theories have been suggested, the most convincing of these recently by Ursula Härting and by Edwin Buijsen, who believe that the panels relate to passages in the Book of Job or the Book of Isaiah, respectively. Job 39:5–9 describes wild asses and a wild ox roaming freely and unfettered in nature, as depicted on the exterior wings, while they kneel, obediently attentive to the Christ Child as their master, on the interior of the altarpiece.[11] Probably more closely connected, the Book of Isaiah, traditionally a source of passages prefiguring the coming of Christ, in chapter 32, verses 9–20, not only mentions the ox and the ass but, as Buijsen notes, also the forest, "thorns and briars," "the waters," and the now deserted "joyous houses" and closes with a passage seemingly descriptive of our scene: "Happy are ye that sow beside all waters, who let the feet of the ox and the ass range free."[12] The text may thus be interpreted as a prophecy of the coming of Christ and as an introduction to the Nativity revealed on the interior of the altarpiece.

Although Isaiah may have provided a specific textual source for the elements of the landscape scene, the manner in which the viewer encounters the closed and then opened triptych is related more generally to the concept of naturalism, already developed in medieval thought, and to contemporary devotional treatises, in particular the very popular *Vita Christi* literature.

In David Summers's succinct discussion of the rise of naturalism in *The Judgment of Sense,* he notes that in the later Middle Ages the dialogues about art very much depended on the treatise known as the seventh book of Hugh of Saint Victor's *Didascalicon* and on its assertion that beauty inspires wonder.[13] "God himself is the true artist, and it is the harmony and continuity of the order of the world that testifies to God's wisdom." The *Didascalicon,* furthermore, embraced a concept of the world that, above all, considered heightened sensitivity to the forms, colors, and sounds of nature. These notions "gave the deepest possible justification for an art appealing first of all to sense, because on such a view it is possible to ascend from the pleasing qualities of objects to the real presence of divine grace; they also meant that sensation, and the pleasures of sensation, could be justified as a new means for edification."[14]

Summers goes on to explain,

Our natural desire to know, Aristotle wrote, is evident in the value we place upon our senses; and if we must learn through sense, then we must be taught through sense. . . . [T]his most general principle had very concrete consequences. . . . [it] placed the traditional doctrine of images in a rather different light. Images had always been justified as educational, but now it was recommended that they be accommodated to the conditions of finite human knowledge: not that they be simply visible, as an icon might also be, but that they be *like* the visible; not that they be encountered, but that they be *as if* encountered, set in a world that, because it was like the present, could carry the imagination and therefore the soul to the past and future events. In this crucial transformation images became like phantasms, inward images of visible outward things and events, standing at the beginnings of human knowledge and immediate to the spiritual mainsprings of will and desire. . . . This laborious endeavor of inventing both vision and painting was the long and splendid development of optical naturalism in the late Middle Ages and early Renaissance. . . . It was in these terms that naturalism came to be regarded as a simple and powerful teaching device and means to meditation. Naturalism was essential to the devotional imagery widespread in the late Middle Ages and Renaissance.[15]

In the evolution of artistic representation, as Sixten Ringbom has noted, iconic images were

199. Gerard David, *Forest Scene* (outer wings of Figure 200), ca. 1510–15. Oil on oak, each panel 89.9 × 30.7 cm. Mauritshuis, The Hague

200. Gerard David, *Nativity with Saints Jerome and Leonard and Donors*, ca. 1510–15. Oil on canvas transferred from panel, central panel 86.6 × 71.1 cm; wings each 89.6 × 31.4 cm. The Metropolitan Museum of Art, The Jules Bache Collection, 1949 (49.20a–c)

increasingly expressed as part of a narrative filled with anecdotal detail and a new sense of naturalism in order to enhance the empathic response of the viewer to the sacred image.[16] Reindert Falkenburg has further elaborated on this idea, noting that late-fifteenth- and early-sixteenth-century paintings "can be regarded as visual aids for meditation on the pilgrimage of life," referring to parallels between this imagery and contemporary devotional literature used to stimulate and guide meditation.[17] The *Vita Christi* literature of Ludolph of Saxony and the *Meditationes* of

Pseudo-Bonaventure, as well as certain texts devoted to the Seven Sorrows of the Virgin Mary, describe the sufferings of the Holy Family in considerable detail as a succession of incidents, accompanied by exhortations inviting the reader's identification with these holy figures and imitation of their actions. Contemporary paintings show striking visual parallels with the *Vita Christi* literature, depicting subsidiary scenes that take up the same themes. The inference that the viewer is meant to follow Christ on a pious pilgrimage through life is further supported

with the "pilgrimage of life"—significantly influenced David's paintings of the first quarter of the sixteenth century in which landscape played a featured role. He established the meditative mood of the Nativity Triptych through the setting in tranquil, secluded woods, which with their stately oaks, walnuts, and beech trees, offered a locally familiar sense of nature. Sixteenth-century viewers, no doubt, would have recognized the ox and the ass on the outside wings as allusions to the story of the birth of Christ,[20] and the contemporary house within the forest perhaps as the inn where Joseph and Mary were refused lodging, which forced them to find alternative shelter on the very night of the birth of Christ. This episode of the narrative was communicated more directly by David in his earlier *Nativity* in Budapest (Figure 108), where the refusal at the inn is shown as a subsidiary scene at the far left in the background.

Here, however, in the spirit of the *Vita Christi* literature, the viewer, as participant in the narrative, experiences the rejection, exhaustion, and disappointment of the couple in their quandary and the overwhelming sense of jubilation when the wings of the triptych are opened to reveal the sacred event within. It is the essence of Isaiah 9:2–7 that is expressed: "The people that walked in darkness have seen a great light; they that dwelt in a land of the shadow of death, upon them hath the light shined," and, continuing in the familiar text associated with Christ's birth, "For unto us a child is born, unto us a son is given; . . . and his name shall be called 'Wonderful, Counselor, the Mighty God, the Everlasting Father, the Prince of Peace.'"

The makeshift dwelling of the triptych's interior has been reached by traversing the broad, open plain from the densely forested area of the outside wings, now seen at the upper right on the inside. A similar-looking, but not identical, house at the edge of the forest recalls the inn on the exterior wings. Along with the donors, their saints, and the shepherds in the mid-distance, the viewer encounters the splendid event of the Nativity: Mary, Joseph, the ox, and the ass, as well as a host of angels, all in adoration of the Christ Child.

by the frequent references to travel in the compositions as a whole and in particular motifs, such as the walking stick, traveling basket, and pilgrim's costume, in the paintings themselves.[18] Pilgrimages, a prevalent form of religious expression during this time, entered into the visual arts, especially in panel painting and manuscript illumination, as a reference to both real and imagined experience; and images were enlivened by written accounts of pilgrim travel.[19]

These trends—that is, interest both in a new found naturalism and in personal experience associated

In contrast to the unconventional nature of the exterior wings, the interior of the altarpiece presents a comparatively orthodox treatment of a popular theme, but in a magnificently conceived space. Taking his inspiration from paintings by Hugo van der Goes, in particular the Portinari and the Monteforte Altarpieces,[21] David set his scene in the ruins of a mansion or palace with an open view into the distance, where the Annunciation to the Shepherds takes place. Such a dilapidated palace is often referred to as the former residence of the Old Testament King David, a progenitor of Christ. As in Hugo's constructions, the architectural foil sets off the foreground devotional scene.

The centermost part of Hugo's Berlin *Nativity* may have provided a general model for David's version, in which the angels, ox and ass, Virgin and youthful Joseph all crowd around the Christ Child in a manger.[22] Spilling out from David's painting into the viewer's space is the skillfully arranged and exquisitely painted wicker basket with swaddling cloth, the sheaf of wheat (individual pieces of which are loosely strewn about the foreground),[23] and Joseph's walking stick (Figure 201). In its prominent placement and remarkable detail of execution, this grouping of objects signals the nascent interest in still-life painting, which was developing as an independent genre in the early sixteenth century.

In meaning, the basket and sheaf of wheat draw attention to the ultimate purpose of Christ's birth, that is, his sacrifice for and redemption of humankind. In particular, there is a Eucharistic emphasis provided by the wheat, indicating the source for the "bread of life," or Body of Christ, and the carefully rolled cloth in the basket, suggesting (beyond its immediate function as a swaddling cloth) the wrapping used to prepare Christ's body for burial after the Crucifixion. Directly above, lying on a cloth in a manger, is the Christ Child as the *corpus verum,* or the venerated object of the first Mass, here attended by Mary, Joseph, the host of angels, and the ox and the ass. Along the same vertical axis, growing out of cracks in the architecture, is a dandelion, which blooms at Easter, the time of Christ's sacrificial death and Resurrection.[24]

In a dramatic shift from David's earlier Nativities, in which an old man is depicted in long robes (see chapter 3, Figures 102, 108, and 113), Joseph here takes on a youthful appearance in accordance with the writings of Jean Gerson (the Parisian scholar and chancellor of the University of Paris who became dean of Sint Donaaskerk in Bruges after 1397).[25] Gerson believed that Joseph was a young man, not older than thirty-six at the time of Christ's birth, for otherwise he would not have been able to fool the devil or to muster the strength to safeguard his

201. Detail of basket, sheaf of wheat, and walking stick in Figure 200.

young wife, Mary, and the Child on the long trip to Egypt.[26] It is not only Joseph's youthful appearance but also his costume that sets him apart from the norm: he wears traveler's garb—a short robe, long hose, soft shoes, and a cloak—and he has laid down his walking stick prominently on the sheaf of wheat in the front of the picture. This cannot have been overlooked by contemporary viewers as a reference to the travel of the Holy Family and, by extension, to humans as travelers or pilgrims following the path of Christ. As such, Joseph serves as an exemplum for the attitude of the beholder as he crosses his arms on his chest in humility, "in order to express the prayer and the desire to acquire grace by the virtue and by the merits of the passion of Christ and of the cross."[27]

Kneeling in prayerful attitudes and in slightly larger scale than Mary and Joseph, as they are depicted in a space closer to the viewer, are the donors presented by Saints Jerome and Leonard.[28] These donors themselves are shown in the guise of saints—the man as Saint Anthony with his attribute of a pig and the woman as Saint Catherine, sumptuously dressed, with her crown, sword, and wheel. Although it was previously thought that these attributes had been added later to convert donors into saints,[29] recent technical examination through X-radiography shows that a reserve area was left for the wheel (including a broken spoke, now overpainted), which was therefore a feature conceived from the outset of the painting process. Close microscopic examination of the woman's crown, the sword, and the man's pig reveals that they also were originally planned as part of the composition (despite the fact that they have been considerably worn and restored).

The donors thus may be an Anthony and a Catherine who were devoted to Saints Jerome and Leonard, but nothing further can be deduced at this point about their identity. Nor is anything certain about the commission of the altarpiece. The suggestion that the patrons were Spaniards,[30] perhaps working or temporarily living in Bruges in the large Spanish mercantile community there, might be supported by the Spanish provenance of the altarpiece, which goes back to the Urrutia family of Navarre.[31]

The highly decorative costume of the female donor[32] and the gold edging of the Virgin's dress add a rich effect to this sumptuous altarpiece, doubtless created for important, but unfortunately still unknown, donors. The halo of the Virgin, who in Netherlandish painting is seldom shown with this manifest attribute of divinity, is also of a distinctly Spanish sixteenth-century type (in its flat, planar form it ignores David's adherence to naturalism) and may either have been painted by David in accordance with Spanish conventions or have been added once the painting reached Spain.[33]

Before discussing David's means of creating the landscapes in the Nativity Triptych,[34] which represent the peak of his achievement in this genre, it is important to consider how he arrived at this point. His highly unusual depiction of a forest devoid of human presence did not suddenly appear without precedent, as is often the claim of the critical literature. Nor is it precisely true that these wings show the "first pure landscapes in Flemish painting."[35] David, however, had made significant advances in the genre beyond his predecessors, Rogier van der Weyden, Hugo van der Goes, and Hans Memling. For these painters, landscape was never realized beyond its function as a backdrop for the subject at hand. Memling simply followed the model of his probable teacher Rogier van der Weyden, the formula he adopted consisting of "round, garland-shaped dotted little trees . . . , [and] greenery in the foreground, which covers the earth in a rather schematic and stylized manner, like a pattern printed on a green background."[36] How paradoxical that these formulaic landscape depictions of Memling's were mimicked by the great masters of Italian painting—among them Ghirlandaio, Filippino Lippi, and Fra Bartolomeo[37]—in an age when their compatriot Leonardo da Vinci was so brilliantly codifying the multifarious forms in nature from direct observation! That these two divergent routes existed simultaneously—model-book formulas for landscapes as well as depictions that took natural observation into account—is indicative that this was a period of transition and the dawning of the age of scientific discovery.

Take, for example, Geertgen's *Lamentation* and the *Burning of the Bones of Saint John the Baptist* in Vienna, where the episodes of the narrative effectively take place in an appropriate setting, not simply against a generic backdrop to the scene (Figures 202 and 203). There is also the remarkable and precedent-setting landscape of *Saint John the Baptist in the Wilderness* (Figure 204) of about 1490, where the enclosed forest scene with its accompanying wildlife serves as a metaphor for the isolation and seemingly perplexed contemplation of the saint. In artistic sensibility Geertgen shuns the conventions of formulaic repetition in this painting,[43] instead seeking to particularize the species of trees and other plants and to arrange them according to the rules of nature rather than those of medieval pattern books.

Lessons learned from Geertgen, such as the depiction of theme-appropriate flora and landscape

204. Geertgen tot Sint Jans, *Saint John the Baptist in the Wilderness*, ca. 1490. Oil on panel, 41.9 × 27.9 cm. Gemäldegalerie, SMPK, Berlin (Photo Jörg P. Anders, Berlin)

205. Aelbert van Ouwater?, *Saint John the Baptist*, ca. 1460. Oil on panel, 70 × 31 cm. Capilla Réal, Granada (Photo Copyright IRPA-KIK, Brussels)

206. Simon Marmion, *Saint Jerome*, from the *Huth Hours* (ADD. 38126, fol. 227v).
Tempera on vellum, 14.8 × 11.6 cm. British Library, London

type are practiced early on by David in his wings
for a triptych, the *Saint John the Baptist* and *Saint
Francis Receiving the Stigmata* (Figure 118). Perhaps
recalling a *Saint John* (Granada, Figure 205) attributed
to Ouwater or Geertgen's example, David's *Saint
John* is truly within his wilderness environment, any
hints of a horizon or far-distant space closed off by
a thick forest that includes cypress and magnolia
trees (the late-fifteenth-century perception of a
Middle Eastern habitat). Saint Francis, on the other
hand, receives the stigmata in the clearing of the

woods, beyond the walls of the monastery at Assisi,
where he founded his order. Thus David intentionally varied the landscape settings for these two saints
in accordance with stories of their lives, a concept
foreign to the work of his predecessors in the south
Netherlands, Rogier van der Weyden and Hans
Memling, whose landscape type and form remain
monotonously consistent regardless of the subject
represented.

Not to be discounted is Guicciardini's own testimony in 1567 about another painter of the Haarlem

207. Master of the Embroidered Foliage, *Virgin and Child*, ca. 1500. Oil on panel, 83.8 ×
60.4 cm. John G. Johnson Collection, Philadelphia Museum of Art

school, "Dirick d'Harlem," or Dieric Bouts, and his
contribution to landscape painting. Petrus Montanus,
the editor of the French (1609) and Dutch (1612)
editions of Guicciardini, provided a detailed description of an early Haarlem landscape purportedly
painted by Bouts:

> The excellent altarpiece, made with all
> patience, which formerly stood in the

monastery of the Regulars, and which depicted
the history of the Saint Bavon, who was the
patron saint of Ghent and Haarlem, with moreover the fine countryside around the town of
Haarlem; and the likeness of that he made from
life, with the Regulars' monastery, the Huis ter
Kleef, Aerden-Hout, and the hollow tree that
was famous then, as well as the north side of
the great churchyard of Haarlem. It is today

208. Master of the Morrison Triptych, *Virgin and Child with Saints and Angels in a Garden*, ca. 1500. Oil on panel, central panel 67 × 43.5 cm; left wing 67 × 17.5 cm; right wing 67.9 × 17.8 cm. National Gallery, London (Photo © National Gallery, London)

still in the possession of an art lover who treasures it dearly.[44] [The French edition of 1609 identifies the owner as "Maistre T. Blin".]

If we can take Guicciardini at his word, here is a topographically accurate landscape view that sets a precedent for the artists, David among them, who early on featured identifiable sites in their paintings.[45]

Running parallel to developments of landscape in panel painting was the art of manuscript illuminators, particularly those from the Ghent-Bruges school, with whom David was in close contact and who specialized in landscape depiction.[46] In addition to Jan van Eyck's remarkable bas-de-page scenes in the Turin–Milan Hours (which we cannot be certain that David actually knew firsthand, but perhaps only by reputation),[47] there are the achievements of the

Master of Mary of Burgundy, the Master of James IV of Scotland, and certainly Simon Bening, all of whom excelled in the treatment of landscape in their illuminated books, the Master of Mary of Burgundy being credited with the introduction of the first aerial perspective in northern art.[48]

The representation of pure landscapes occurs initially in manuscript illumination about 1470–80 in works such as folio 345v of the *Trésor des histoires,* which illustrates a topographical text produced in Bruges and is attributed to Simon Marmion.[49] Originally from Valenciennes, Marmion may have been in Ghent about 1475–78[50] and, in addition, had other connections en passant to David. Before 1491 his widow married Jan Provost, a Bruges painter by 1494 and a follower of David. Marmion's development of dense forest views completely enveloping the figure of Saint Jerome within them in the Huth Hours (Figure 206) or the Houghton Hours of the late 1480s sets a precedent for David's own expansion of the idea in panel painting.[51]

At the same time, late editions of the thirteenth-century *De proprietatibus rerum* by Bartholomeus Angelicus united the encyclopedic study of the physical world and properties of things with a new interest in landscape depiction.[52] As Walter Cahn notes:

> The extraordinary painting in a copy of the work made in the southern Netherlands and perhaps attributable to . . . Simon Marmion is attached to Bartholomeus's explanation of the four basic elements constitutive of man (Book 4), normally depicted in schematic or allegorical form, and not easily imaginable as the subject of a landscape. The painter's attempt to treat the interplay of fire, air, water and earth as a purely sensory spectacle is *Landschaftsgefühl* in an almost excessive sense, and can hardly be said to have been provoked in a literal fashion by the sober science of the text. A painting in a manuscript perhaps made at Bruges around 1470–80 fuses the author's methodical enumeration of trees into a convincing forest.[53]

Simultaneously, in about 1485 in Haarlem, Jacob Bellaert published a Dutch version, *Van de proprieteyten der dinghen . . .,* with eleven full-page woodcuts. Among the earliest representations of landscapes in prints, one woodcut shows various indigenous plants alongside a brook in the foreground and a group of trees in the background hills. In a celebration of pure landscape, these images include no human presence.[54]

In 1500 Simon Bening, the illuminator from Ghent who was to become the most acclaimed landscape miniaturist of his day, came to Bruges to register his illuminator's mark at the Painters' Hall. In 1508 he officially joined the illuminators' Guild of Saint John and Saint Luke. From the evidence of the workshop drawings discussed in chapter 1, we already know of the likely association of Simon Bening with David, a connection that must have been very close indeed

in the first two decades of the sixteenth century to judge by the remaining visual evidence.[55] As Thomas Kren has recognized, Bening was the most innovative illuminator of his day in terms of portraying landscape—in both its topographic and its climatic variety.[56] These achievements did not escape David's notice, as the two artists shared a common interest and sensibility in this relatively new genre of Netherlandish painting.

Also contemporary with David's essays into naturalistic renderings of forest views are the accomplishments of the Master of James IV of Scotland, who, as Kren describes, in the November illumination of the Grimany Breviary of about 1515 (a book that certainly has connections with the art of Gerard David)[57] "presents a landscape that suggests a continuity with the viewer's space that is not apparent in his [written] source. He moves the trees into the foreground and uses them as a device to draw the viewer into a continuous landscape of rolling hills, with the finest details—the blades of grass, the leaves on the boughs of the trees, the contours of a church on the distant horizon—beautifully observed."[58] The device of pushing the trees into the foreground and then using tree trunks as markers throughout the space of the landscape also was employed by David, as is clearly evident in the Mauritshuis wings (Figure 199).

The precedent set by manuscript illuminators in landscape depiction influenced David not only specifically in respect to composition, but also generally in the type of landscape pictured and the resulting experience derived from viewing it. The naturalistic image enlivened the theme presented but also provided an intimate and meditative mood for reading a devotional text. The meditative aspect is the overriding characteristic of David's landscapes and the one that simultaneously most closely ties his work to illuminated books and separates it from the world-view landscapes being produced in Antwerp from about 1515 on, whose main proponent was Joachim Patinir.

Taking his inspiration from the precedents set by north Netherlandish panel painting and Ghent-Bruges manuscript illumination, David attempted to advance the representation of nature beyond the contemporary pattern-book mentality so prevalent among south Netherlandish panel painters. The formulaic nature of Memling's landscapes became even more exaggerated in late-fifteenth- and early-sixteenth-century Bruges and Brussels among artists such as the Master of the Embroidered Foliage (Figure 207), whose wooded scenes appear much like the two-dimensional patterning of a splendid brocade or tapestry weaving, for which these two cities were renowned. Or, there is the Master of the Morrison Triptych (Figure 208), whose trees are arranged according to a rigid, gridlike plan that has nothing whatsoever to do with natural observation.[59] Although from the little that remains, we cannot know the extent of David's initial attempts at the depiction of nature, they seem to have begun in earnest during the first decade of the sixteenth century.

Contemporaneously with similar investigations of landscape and its details by Leonardo da Vinci and Albrecht Dürer, David proceeded to make studies from nature for use in his paintings.[60] In the delicate metalpoint study of a tree (ca. 1505–10) that shares the same side of a sheet with the study of the head of a man (Figure 38), David recorded the manner in which branches grow from the trunk and how the fall of light and the movement of gentle breezes affect the clarity or blurring of branches and their leaves. About 1498–1500, Leonardo had produced a study (Figure 209) recording his scientific observations on the same sheet:[61]

The part of the tree which has shadow for background is all of one tone, and wherever the trees or branches are thickest they will be darkest, because there is no little interval of air. But where the boughs lie against a background of other boughs, the brightest parts are seen lightest and the leaves lustrous from the sunlight falling on them.

The sense of liveliness and spontaneity in David's rendering was maintained when he re-created his observation from nature in the underdrawing for a tree in the *Resurrection* (compare Figures 38 and 39 with Figure 138). At the painted stage, however, the tree was made to conform to the overall balance of the composition—an issue that took precedence over the more naturalistic effect of David's first creative impulse. The tree thus was diminished in size and lost its sense of light and atmosphere in order to comply in this particular case with the prevailing and more conventional view of landscape as a background setting for the foreground scene.[62]

Still tied in a certain way to the model-book mentality of the age, the individual tree in David's paintings is emblematic of nature itself.[63] It populates many of his paintings and is featured in a prominent position in some. In the underdrawing of the tree in his *Saint Jerome* of about 1510 (compare Figures 210 and 211),[64] the lesson David learned of the particular way in which branches grow from the trunk and the irregularity of fuller and more sparsely foliated branches is taken into the painted stage. Likewise, large rock formations secure a new prominence in David's paintings in the first two decades of the sixteenth century. Varied from the *Saint Jerome* to the Saint Michael Altarpiece[65] to the Baptism Triptych (Figures 210, 168, and 213), these rocky masses convey a solidity of form without losing their descriptive nature in David's detailed rendering. They are more coherent and convincing, doubtless as a result of studies from nature of the type that Leonardo carried out in Milan for the *Virgin of the Rocks* in various versions from 1483 until 1508.

In a development that looks forward to his more mature landscape depictions, David began to standardize his working methods. X-radiography and infrared reflectography provide clues to his step-by-step procedure. David's spontaneous drawing for the tree on the ground preparation for the *Saint Jerome* was followed by an intermediate stage in which he very rapidly brushed in a light tone for the sky (compare Figures 210–212), leaving reserve spaces for the tree branches suggested by his underdrawing. He then covered the reserve areas with a darker application, that is, the base tone for the densest areas of

209. Leonardo da Vinci, *Study of a Tree*, ca. 1508. Red chalk, 19.1 × 15.3 cm. Windsor Castle, The Royal Collection (Photo © 1998 Her Majesty Queen Elizabeth II)

210. Gerard David, *Saint Jerome*, ca. 1500. Oil on oak, 31 × 21 cm. Städelsches Kunstinstitut, Frankfurt

the tree. In a final stage David worked back over the tree, adding the details of branches and individual leaves with staccato applications of green paint and touching in the highlights.

Although Saint Jerome and his lion are prominently placed in the foreground, the landscape has become more than a simple backdrop; rather, in its variety of trees, reflecting pool of water, and realistically painted rocky embankment, it is a naturally arranged environment in which the two appropriately and comfortably reside.

A major development in David's ability to integrate the figures of his scene more successfully into the landscape setting came with the triptych of the *Baptism of Christ* of 1502–8 (Figure 213), completed in several stages for Jan des Trompes, who appears with his first wife (Elisabeth van der Meersch) and family on the interior wings of the altarpiece, while his second wife (Magdalena Cordier) and a daughter are featured on the outside right wing (Figure 214).[66]

It is not only the more successful integration of figures into space that signals David's stylistic maturity in the *Baptism of Christ*—it is the width, breadth, and variety of scenery across the three interior panels that offer an astonishing display of carefully studied forms from nature. In its unified composition across multiple panels and in the particular emphasis on details depicted with botanical accuracy, David's triptych recalls Van Eyck's model in the Ghent Altarpiece (Figure 215). Both show the adoring figures arranged along the horizontal axis, while the Lamb of God (literally in the Van Eyck, and metaphorically in the David), the Holy Spirit (dove), and God the Father are placed along the central vertical axis with a keyhole view of the distance, allowing for the full visual stretch of the landscape. But David has lowered the horizon, brought the figures forward, and changed

211. IRR of Figure 210

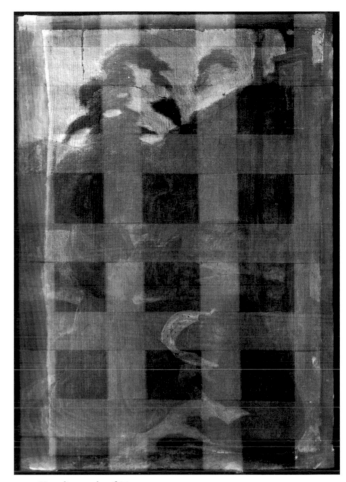

212. X-radiograph of Figure 210

the viewpoint of the picture in order to suggest a continuous space between the painting and the observer. When the triptych is installed approximately three feet above the floor and viewed from a distance of about eight feet (as is the case in the Groeningemuseum in Bruges, where the triptych resides), the standing viewer is at the eye level of Christ, and the plant life of the foreground is seen from above, so that the viewer is allowed to "step" directly into the landscape. This very successful merging of pictorial and viewer space is new in early Netherlandish painting of the time, and David is among the first to achieve it.

In the Baptism Triptych David has observed in close detail and re created the species found on the banks of streams and in local forests. He has considered the various effects of light in wooded areas, the individual characteristics of different species of trees, as well as the particular features of bough and leaf formation. Likewise he has not neglected the study of cloud formations and has made remarkable advances in the depiction of water, not only in the transparencies of and reflections on water but also in the very nature of the movement of waves. As the viewer comes upon this scene, Jesus has just waded into the river Jordan (Figure 216), creating concentric circles of water around his legs that intersect with the waves produced by the natural current of the river.

In the integration of the particular into the whole, David also must have recalled the lessons of Dieric Bouts, whom the Leuven professor Johannis Molanus referred to in 1572 as mastering the "inventory of representations of the countryside."[67] Bouts's passionate

213. Gerard David, Baptism
Triptych, interior, 1502–8.
Oil on panel, central panel
132 × 96.6 cm; each wing
132.2 × 42.2 cm.
Groeningemuseum, Bruges

response to nature in his paintings is evident, both in the loving depiction of details of plant life and in their arrangement within a logically constructed whole. Such works as *Jesus with Saint John the Baptist and a Donor,* or particularly the wings of the Adoration of the Kings Altarpiece (both in Alte Pinakothek, Munich; the latter now attributed to a follower of Bouts, the Master of the Pearl of Brabant), corroborate the chronicler Molanus's claim that Bouts was the quintessential landscape painter.[68] In his *Jesus with Saint John the Baptist and a Donor,* Bouts's scheme of framing his figures with landscape on all sides (employing rocky cliffs as a foil), and thereby creating an enclosed natural setting and facilitating the integration of the figures into their environment, was assimilated by David in the interior wings of the Baptism Triptych. For his central panel David used the construction found in the *Saint John* and the *Saint Christopher* wings of the Pearl of Brabant Altarpiece. Building up the forms of nature at the edges of the composition, he placed an exquisite vista into the distance at the center, drawing the observer's eye to the pivotal figure before it. David must have noted the success of Bouts's means—and, indeed, those of Jan van Eyck before him—of establishing the illusion of spatial continuity through meandering roads and rivers extending from the foreground to the far distant horizon, and of creating a further sense of the expanse of nature through the placement of trees that tower over the horizon and stand out against the broad area of the sky, for he used some of the same methods himself. In his construction of the landscape David inherited the symmetry and heightened sensibility to nature of both Jan van Eyck and Dieric Bouts.

David's development beyond Bouts's achievement follows a detailed analysis of nature itself. In the central panel of the Baptism Triptych, for example, he explored and exploited the middle distance, comfortably nestling subsidiary scenes in the more densely wooded area, thereby extending the sense of humanity within nature. He achieved continuity among all three panels by bridging the frame with two small figures pointing from the left wing toward the center and an arrangement of trees at the right that extends into the central panel. The separation of the wings from the central panel appears to be only an artificial one; David has created a truly unified space.

David's own studies in natural observation prompted him to attempt the painted equivalent of the gradual disappearance of Christ's legs in the river's depth and to take note of the rippling effect of water—an effect that to my knowledge has no equal in painting in Italy or the north before this time. There are only Leonardo's written observations about this phenomenon, which David could not have known until after 1519 (when they were assembled by Melzi), too late for the text to have been influential on any of his works discussed here, though similar investigations appear to have been the focus of both artists. David's depiction of Christ in the river Jordan (Figure 216) seems to be described by Leonardo: "the natural color of something submerged will be the more transformed into the green color of the water to the extent that the thing submerged has a greater quantity of water above it."[69] Leonardo further notes: "The waves that in concentric circles flee the point of impact are carried by their impetus across the path of other circular waves moving out of step with them, and after the moment of percussion leap up into the air without breaking formation."[70] In addition to these, David has captured the quickening pace of waves as they lap onto the shore or rocks.

There is also a hint of weather conditions as the sunny sky with cumulus clouds of the left wing of the Baptism Triptych becomes progressively more overcast toward the right wing, spilling full sunlight and dark shadows, respectively, over the trees beneath. Such a phenomenon is thus described by Leonardo: "When the sun illuminates the forest, the trees in the wood will be displayed with defined shadows and lights, and for this reason appear to be closer to you, because they are rendered clearer in shape. And that part of them which is not exposed to the sun appears uniformly dark, except for the thin parts which are interposed between the sun and yourself."[71]

214. Gerard David, Baptism Triptych: exterior wings, 1502–8. Oil on panel, each 132 × 42.2 cm. Groeningemuseum, Bruges

215. Hubert and Jan van Eyck, Ghent
Altarpiece, interior, completed in 1432.
Oil on panel, 375 × 520 cm. Cathedral of
Sint Baafs, Ghent (Photo © IRPA–KIK,
Brussels)

Van Eyck 1432

216. Detail of Christ in central panel in Figure 213

in front of the lightest background trees, thereby extending the recession of space in this lush wooded area that blocks the view to the horizon. Light and color are judiciously used to provide a full sense of the illusion of nature and natural phenomena. Leonardo described it thus: "The countryside which is illuminated by the light of the sun will have shadow of great darkness on any object, and to someone who sees the object from the opposite side to that which is exposed to the sun it will appear darkest, and things far away will appear close."[72]

Like the intention of contemporary manuscript illuminators of the Ghent-Bruges school mentioned above, David's aim, by composing a verdant landscape with a naturalistically portrayed river Jordan, was to draw the viewer into closer communication with the event at hand, the Baptism of Christ. Individual features within the landscape are immediately recognizable, such as the Jerusalem Church in Bruges (featured directly above Christ's head in the background), and lend the triptych a sense of realism, even though the triptych as a whole is a carefully arranged ideal landscape replete with detailed descriptions of forest plant life rendered in their most perfect form. David achieved a resolution between the particular and the general through a method that joins botanical accuracy with natural observation and a technique that combines effects of light and color in brushwork that he varied according to the object depicted. This work represents a new phase in which the plants, intended to convey symbolic meaning, are depicted as they might be found in their natural environment. Although the landscape may still be understood part by part, it is meant to be enjoyed as a whole, encompassing experience.

The study of individual species from nature must already have been a part of the painter's workshop activity by the mid-fifteenth century, as is evidenced in the remarkable sense of realism found in the details of the van Eycks Ghent Altarpiece and in the foreground details of plants in Rogier van der Weyden's Frankfurt *Madonna* or Hugo van der Goes's Monteforte Altarpiece. The recent discovery of a drawing

The right wing, showing Elisabeth van der Meersch, her daughters, and Saint Elizabeth, in particular reverses the conventional organization of Netherlandish landscapes by placing the darkest trees

of peonies (J. Paul Getty Museum)[73] by Martin Schongauer illustrates that parallel developments were also under way in Germany even before the advent of Dürer's notable achievements in this genre.[74]

In keeping with the developing age of scientific discovery in the early sixteenth century, and a further key to David's sense of accuracy in his representations of plant life, is the new availability of printed herbals, particularly three important ones that appeared before 1500: the *Herbarius,* a book in Latin from 1484; the *Gart der Gesundheit* of 1485; and the *Hortus sanitatis* of 1491.[75] The herbal, which was the principal source of medical knowledge from antiquity to the Middle Ages, evolved relatively little over the centuries. Its use by artists as more of a field guide to flora than simply a medical reference began when artists became involved with the recording of specimens from life to be included in the herbals. This evolution may be seen, as Peter Parshall has pointed out, by comparing images in the *Herbarius* of 1484 and those in the *Gart der Gesundheit* of just a year later. The former shows plants rendered in a highly stylized fashion, while the latter represents them in a more natural arrangement of leaves and blossoms, sometimes even picturing them as growing in the ground instead of pruned and plucked from it.[76] This new depiction of plants in the *Gart der Gesundheit* was consistent with a principal aim of the book as it is described in the introduction, that is, as a work composed "in admiration of God's creation."[77]

Most of the flora in the *Baptism* can be identified[78] and some linked with the type of plants found in the *Gart der Gesundheit* (Figures 217a,b). The clarity of the depiction of individual plants ensured their identification and the understanding of their symbolic function for the overall meaning of the painting, but David has arranged them to suggest their proper place within an actual landscape.

Let us take a closer look so that we may recognize David's manner of achieving unity within his representation. He has filled his humid river forest with plant life characteristic of this setting: garden sorrel (*Rumex acetosa*), spring snowflower (*Leucojum vernum*), greater celandine (*Chelidonium majus*), and

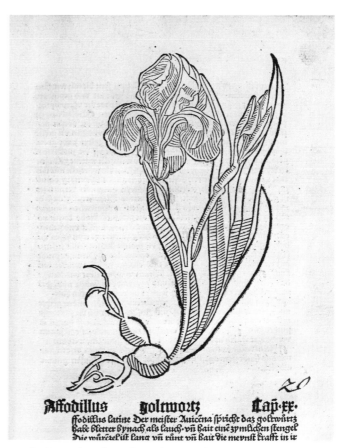

217a,b. Examples of a violet and an iris (here wrongly identified as a daffodil) from *Gart der Gesundheit.* Mainz, 1485

yellow iris (*Iris pseudacorus*); the trees common to this environment are also here—forest beech (*Fagus silvatica*) and chestnut (*Castanea sativa*). The beech tree dominates, typical as it is of a transitional woodland. Realistically painted as all of these varieties are, they are not consistently placed by David within their normal plant groupings. Furthermore, all plants are shown in their flowering stage (as they are in the *Gart der Gesundheit*), regardless of the fact that they actually bloom at different times from early spring to summer. Thus, as is true generally of much of early Netherlandish painting, the reality of the depiction exists in parts but not as a whole.

David's source for the precise rendering of the plants in the painting may have been the *Gart der Gesundheit,* for all species are individually recognizable in the way that they appear there, except for the alpine marsh violet (*Viola palustris*), a white-to-lilac, slightly veined pansy often found in late medieval sources. The medicinal properties, specifically the cleansing or purgative value, of all of the plants

represented were well known. Only the poppy (*Papaver somniferum*) stands apart from this group; it was a sedative that when taken in excess would result in poisoning and death. The associations of the first group of plants with the purification and cleansing of Christ's body through baptism and of the poppy with his death perhaps would have been clear to a viewer aware of the medicinal value of plants, and their prominent placement within the painting is intentional for the communication of this reference. The dandelion appearing at the center front is represented both flowering and in the seeded state. It is symbolic of Christ and the Resurrection, for it blooms at Easter time, its petals soon afterward changing into whitish tendrils carrying the seeds away

218. Detail of foreground plants in central panel in Figure 213. Reading left to right: lily of the valley, pansy (above), poppy, and greater celandine

219. IRR detail of underdrawing in central panel in Figure 213

with the wind to germinate elsewhere. Behling also drew attention to the wild pansy (*Viola tricolor*)—a symbol of the Trinity—that David painted in the grassy bank directly in front of Christ. It is thus on the same vertical axis as the Trinity—God the Father, the dove, or Holy Ghost, and Christ.[79]

The other plants are more or less naturally arranged and represent a certain kind of forest environment that may have been familiar to a general audience. To create this effect, as well as a more realistic depiction of the chosen plants than can be found in herbals, David must have made drawings after nature. Taken together, what David achieved here was not an accurate portrayal of nature, but an "apparently natural reflection of nature; . . . [that is], natural because the form, the structure of the plant is in accordance with reality, but 'apparently natural' because the plant in relation to its environment either does not belong in the place painted or lacks many plant species that should be there as well."[80]

How did David achieve the unity of color, light, and space in a natural environment? After compiling his source materials—drawings from nature and perhaps specimen illustrations from the *Gart der*

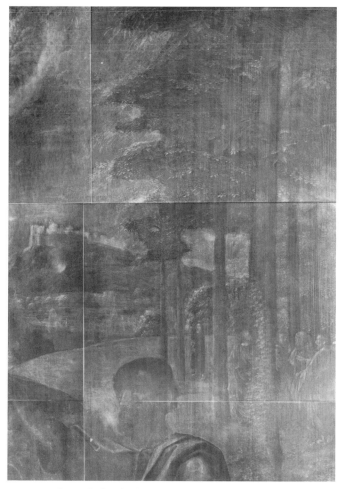

220. X-radiograph detail of trees in central panel at right in Figure 213

222. Simon Bening, *Saint John the Baptist Preaching* and *Baptism of Christ*, ca. 1510. Tempera on parchment mounted on wood, 15.5 × 3.4 cm; 15.5 × 3.5 cm. Groeningemuseum, Bruges

223. Simon Bening, *Baptism of Christ* from the *Prayer Book of Cardinal Albrecht of Brandenburg*, ca. 1525–30. Tempera, gold paint, and gold leaf on vellum, 16.8 × 11.5 cm. J. Paul Getty Museum, Los Angeles

224. Simon Bening, *Baptism of Christ* from the *Chester Beatty Rosarium* (Cod. Ms Western 99, fol. 25r), ca. 1540. Tempera on vellum, 12.4 × 8.4 cm. Chester Beatty Library, Dublin

However, the mounting cumulative evidence seems to indicate that David indeed was in Lombardy and Liguria for a period of time, perhaps both prior to and after the completion of the Cervara Altarpiece. That he recalled Foppa's forest scene when he began to design his own is an intriguing suggestion.

Although David may have begun the Mauritshuis landscape wings (Figure 199) with a preliminary draft of the composition in black chalk on the prepared ground of the panels, this is no longer evident because of the multiple and opaque paint layers applied over it. For this more complicated representation than any he had previously attempted, David made a rough sketch for the trees and branches with brush, visible as the lightest-appearing applications

in the infrared reflectogram assembly (see Figure 226 and the detail of the right wing in Figure 227). An indication of how this may have looked before the next layers of paint were applied is revealed in the detail of the view out the window in the *Virgin and Child with the Milk Soup* (Figure 228). The infrared reflectogram assembly shows a brush underdrawing for the tree at the left of the landscape view, its lower branches underdrawn in brush but not painted in the final version. The Mauritshuis panels have a first-draft brush underdrawing that appears very much like the lightly brushed-in branches with their mere suggestion of leaves in the *Milk Soup* vignette.

Following the procedure of his earlier landscapes, David used the mid-stage of painting, that is, the

225. Vincenzo Foppa, *Martyrdom of a Saint*, in the Portinari Chapel of Sant'Eustorgio, 1468. Fresco. Sant'Eustorgio, Milan

blocking-out stage, to firm up his design for the composition, deciding upon the exact placement of the trunks of trees and the fullness of the branches. At this point he broadly painted in sections of the sky, leaving spaces in reserve (as can be seen in the X-radiograph, Figure 229) where he would return to paint in the foliage in greater detail. This mid-stage must have appeared very much like a chiaroscuro

drawing, with the light and dark values describing in general terms the emerging forms of the forest. David may well have worked out the lighting contrasts of the woods initially in chiaroscuro drawings on paper. Although such studies from David's workshop have not survived (except the drawing of the

226. IRR detail of trees in outside wings in Figure 199

228. IRR detail of tree in landscape view in Figure 284

kneeling Christ for a night scene of *Gethsemane;* see chapter 3, Figure 48), chiaroscuro drawings of trees of a somewhat later date in the *Errara Sketchbook* (Figure 230) represent the type of study that may have served this purpose.

Evidence that such drawings existed in David's studio as workshop models is provided by the relationship between the Mauritshuis wings and a copy of the painting attributed to Ambrosius Benson, a

227. IRR detail of trees in right outside wing in Figure 199

Rest on the Flight into Egypt (Figure 231), in a private collection in Genoa.[86] This painting, which is one continuous forest scene not divided into two parts as is David's, shows a large tree in the center of the composition, which exhibits the stiffness of a copy, with the branches and leaves not as naturally arranged, with less variation in the angle in which the leaves are shown and less attention to naturalistic effects of light and shade. The same central tree (as well as the groupings of trees at the far left and right) in Benson's composition may be recognized in parts on

229. X-radiograph of outside landscape wings in Figure 199

the right and left inside edges of David's two wings. As the X-radiographs of the two wings indicate (Figure 229), David originally intended to follow the general plan of the configuration of trees seen in the Benson version, with more of the divided center tree featured in part on the left and on the right wing. At a mid-stage in the painting process, however, David revised his plan and extended the large tree at the top left of the left wing farther across the top of the painting, over the area he had already brushed in for the sky.

David continued to revise his plan as he went along, eliminating some tree trunks to make the forest more readable; the trunks of the trees chosen for the final version, he painted solidly in darker paint. In considering the balance of light and dark in the forest, he used color relationships as well. Leonardo da Vinci describes this phenomenon best as he examines "why the same trees appear brighter close to than far away":

Trees of the same species show themselves as being brighter nearby than far away, for these reasons:

1. shadows show themselves to be darker nearby and on account of such darkness the illuminated branches which border on them look brighter than they are;

2. on taking the eye further away, the air which is interposed between this shadow and the eye, having a greater thickness than it used to possess, brightens this shadiness and gives it a color which takes on a blue hue, on which account the illuminated branches are not

230. Anonymous Netherlandish, *Landscape Study* from the *Errara Sketchbook* (fol. 29), ca. 1530–40. Pen and brush with gray and brown ink, black chalk, white heightening on blue prepared paper, 13.5 × 21 cm. Musées Royaux de Beaux-Arts de Belgique, Brussels

231. Attributed to Ambrosius Benson, *Rest on the Flight into Egypt*, ca. 1525. Oil on panel, 61 × 53 cm. Private collection, Genoa

shown with as definite a contrast as previously, and they come to seem darker;

3. the images of lightness and darkness which such branchings send to the eye have their boundaries mingled together and become confounded. Because the shadowy parts are always of greater quantity than the luminous parts, these shadows are more readily recognizable at a long distance than the lesser amounts of brightness.

And for these three reasons trees show themselves as darker at a distance than nearby.[87]

Using a very dark green for the background foliage, David quickly brushed in the leafy branches. A mixed green was used for the boughs closer to the viewer, and finally a lead-tin yellow for the leaves on the branches closest to the viewer and in full light. David employed broad strokes for the background foliage, considerably varying his brushstroke from longer, engaged strokes to short dabs of impasto paint, and making allowances for the angle of the leaves as they are observed in nature (Figure 232).

The relation between David's Mauritshuis wings (which open onto the scene of the Nativity) and Benson's *Rest on the Flight into Egypt* is not limited to formal concerns but is also suggestive of greater thematic issues. Considered from more than simply the practical point of view of the use of patterns within David's workshop, the fact that depictions of both the Nativity and the Rest on the Flight into Egypt used the same forest view implies another relationship, that is, that this forest provides continuity of environment or setting in which an extended narrative takes place over a series of paintings. If we then look at the paintings by David and his workshop of the Rest on the Flight into Egypt, in the Metropolitan Museum and in the Prado,[88] the possibility of an intentional extension of the narrative not just from scene to scene within one work, but from painting to painting becomes apparent.

In the *Rest on the Flight into Egypt* (Figure 234), David introduced a dense forest view behind the Virgin and Child, calling to mind the setting for the Nativity Triptych. The Holy Family is seen en route at the upper right of the painting as they emerge from the woods through which they have been traveling. This suggests that the landscape is as continuous as the narrative of Christ's life and the viewer's pilgrimage through it.

The use of the landscape as a vehicle through which the pilgrim travels is all the more convincingly suggested by the artist's increasingly successful integration of figures into their space. Although traditionally thought all to date from the same period, the version in the National Gallery of Art, Washington (Figure 233), exhibits a different emphasis in theme from that of the others in New York and Madrid, for example (Figures 234 and 235), as well as an earlier execution from the point of view of painting technique and of sophistication in mastering three-dimensional bodies in space. But it is the particular way in which David focused on the subject in his depiction of landscape that is our concern here.

All of the versions of the *Rest* place the Virgin and Child front and center in an *Andachtsbild*.[89] Appealing to the viewer's association of these pictures with the manner in which the Rest on the Flight into Egypt was treated in the widely popular devotional literature of the day, principally that of Ludolph of Saxony, the *Meditationes* of Pseudo-Bonaventure, and the texts relating the Seven Sorrows of the Virgin Mary, the theme is presented as a series of events, all of which are meant to be experienced and imitated in devotional practice.

Thus, in the background of the Washington version (Figure 233), more or less following the myriad stories of the Rest, we find Joseph tapping the chestnut tree to gather sustenance for his family; the Virgin rests in the foreground with a traveling basket at her feet, holding the Christ Child, who plucks a bunch of grapes. Taken from contemporary exegeses of Isaiah, Genesis, and the Song of Songs, Mary is the vine and Christ the bunch of grapes.[90] Analogous

232. Details of leaves from outside wings in Figure 199

233. Gerard David, *Rest on the Flight into Egypt*, 1500–1505. Oil on oak (painted surface), 41.9 × 42.2 cm. Andrew W. Mellon Collection, National Gallery of Art, Washington (Photo © Board of Trustees, National Gallery of Art, Washington)

234. Gerard David, *Rest on the Flight into Egypt*, ca. 1510–15. Oil on oak, 50.8 × 43.2 cm. The Metropolitan Museum of Art, The Jules Bache Collection, 1949 (49.7.21)

with the flowing of the Virgin's milk, the grapes may signify the nourishment of the faithful by the church, but they also carry Eucharistic meaning.[91] Multivalent is the symbolism that is also attached to the individually featured plants arranged across the foreground strip of landscape: plantain, mint, strawberry, fern, and violet, associated with the iconography of the Garden of Paradise and conveying the themes of Christ's Incarnation, Passion, and Resurrection, as well as the Virgin's humility.[92]

Apart from the chestnut tree tapped by Joseph, the other trees are generalized in type and deliberately arranged to close off the composition at right and left, emphasizing a finite point in time rather than a momentary stop in a continuous narrative as is the case with the Metropolitan Museum *Rest.* Furthermore, the plants of symbolic meaning are evenly placed in a row across the immediate foreground like a series of individually studied specimens; there is no attempt at a more natural arrangement within an indigenous environment. The Virgin sits on a rocky ledge before the landscape rather than fully in it, a result of her frontal placement with her draperies arranged in a lateral configuration across the foreground plane. Spatial recession is achieved through a series of parallel, overlapping planes of different wedges of color in alternating dark and light tones, similar to the arrangement of the landscape in the Metropolitan Museum's *Crucifixion* by David (Figure 125), suggesting a related dating for the Washington *Rest on the Flight into Egypt* of about 1500–1505, rather than about 1510, as is more commonly assumed.

The composition and thematic emphasis of the subject are considerably altered in the New York and Madrid versions (Figures 234 and 235). Instead of representing an individual scene excerpted from the Rest narrative as the Washington panel does, these versions underscore the continuous travel of the Flight in a series of scenes. In the middle distance at the right, the Virgin Mary with the Child proceeds on the donkey out of the forest into a clearing, followed by Joseph dressed as a traveler, with a straw hat and basket mounted on his walking stick, which is flung over his shoulder. At the left in the distance is their ultimate destination, symbolizing Egypt, mentioned in the *Golden Legend* and Pseudo-Bonaventure's *Meditations on the Life of Christ* as Helyopolis or Hermopolis and in an associated fifteenth-century Christmas song as being "a very fine city."[93]

In close proximity to the viewer, the Virgin pauses on this arduous journey and nurses the Child, giving him sustenance. The accounts of female mystics in the Low Countries are possibly alluded to here, wherein holy food—or the Eucharist—is equated with ordinary eating.[94] Just as the Virgin suckles her child with her milk, so too Christ nourishes the faithful with his own sacrificed Body and Blood. This message is indicated in the New York painting (Figure 234) as the Christ Child turns toward the viewer in invitation to this nourishment, and is emphasized directly below by the glimpse of the Virgin's underdress in red (the color of Christ's Passion) and the broad-leaf plantain, popularly known for its medicinal value as the stancher of blood. That Christ's act is redemptive of humanity's transgressions is clear from the bough with apples to the right of the Virgin, a reminder of the original sin of Adam and Eve, and the ivy at the left indicative of the Resurrection.

This landscape of the *Rest on the Flight into Egypt* shows an integrated knowledge of light, color, and volume of forms and a cohesive character to the composition, which is hardly imaginable without the lessons of Italian art. A symphony of greens and blues is handled with striking clarity in the foreground, in the deeply saturated hues of the Virgin's dress and cloak, and in the rich green, nichelike foil of the trees behind her. The remarkably subtle modulations of color in the background left achieve a sense of light and atmosphere and a unity of the heavens and the earth that David realized only in his most mature works.

The successful integration of three-dimensional figures within a landscape is due to David's understanding of Italian lessons of geometric form and the importance of shadow in creating perspective. He had somehow learned, as Leonardo had expressed it, that:

[s]hadows and lights are the most certain means by which the shape of any body comes to be known, because a color of equal lightness and darkness will not display any relief but give the effect of a flat surface which, with all its parts at equal distance, will seem equally distant from the brightness that illuminates it.[95]

Thus the Virgin and Child sit like a great pyramid on the rocky ledge; their faces are modeled with subtle sfumato effects and the Virgin's draperies in a chiaroscuro treatment à la Leonardo. Behind the Virgin and Child, the foil of trees, varied in type as in the contemporary Nativity Triptych (Figure 200), enfolds them like a niche. These developments in composition and in the impressive balance of color and light are characteristic of David's paintings of about 1510–15.

A weaker version of the *Rest* in Madrid (Prado; Figure 235) fails to show these nuances of light, color, and form and must have been produced by a workshop assistant in close collaboration with David. In this Prado version the lush foliage of the Metropolitan painting is abbreviated, becoming more formulaic and patternlike. The travel theme, however, is further emphasized: both the traveling basket and Joseph's walking stick are placed in the foreground next to the Virgin. This theme is played out in a version in Antwerp (Figure 236), where Joseph, in traveling attire of straw hat, snoozes by the basket, water gourd, and walking stick.

The emphasis in these later versions of the Rest on the Flight into Egypt specifically on travel and progress from one location to another necessitated a different type of setting, one that would more effectively express change of venue than the static scene of a singular time and place of the Washington painting (Figure 233). To accommodate his revised version of the theme, David changed the square format of the Washington painting to a vertical rectangle for the later versions; in so doing he provided the necessary space for the tall trees of the wooded glen from which the Holy Family emerges. The lush forest, which curves around behind the Virgin, recalls the closed, intimate, and meditative environment David had achieved in the Baptism and Nativity Triptychs.

Any preliminary studies David made for the forest view of the *Rest on the Flight into Egypt* have not survived. That David probably made such studies is clear from the repeated use of the pattern for the placement of trees in the various versions, with slight variations provided by the modified placement of branches on those trees.

David took advantage of the studies he had already made for his other landscapes, but for this theme he needed to consider the locale for an "Egypt." This he did with another study from nature, but one made with its eventual use already in mind (Figure 40). Like Fra Bartolomeo, whose drawings of landscapes with hill towns and farmhouses are well known,[96] David appears to have made his study from nature with the eventual use of the drawing in mind. On the small sketchbook sheet he has recorded a church and scattered houses within a wooded area. What is particularly interesting, however, is the placement of this sketch on the page. David has rendered the wooded village scene as a distant view, placed at the top of the page, while small plants on a grassy knoll are viewed close-up in the left foreground. While not copied exactly from the drawing to the painting, this general formula of distant village view within a wooded area and close-up view of plants on a hillock is followed in the series of the Rest on the Flight into Egypt paintings. Again, as with the lone tree study, David made his sketch from nature in order to study the far view of the landscape setting, expressed by Leonardo thus:

The gaps made by air within the bodies of trees and the gaps made by trees within the air will not be shown to the eye over a long distance, because where the whole is perceived with effort, the parts are distinguished with difficulty. Rather, a confused mixture is made, which mostly takes on [the appearance of] the part having the greater bulk. . . . there is made a mixture of air and darkness within the shadowy tree, which run together into the eye which sees them.[97]

236. Workshop of Gerard David, *Rest on the Flight into Egypt*, ca. 1515. Oil on panel, 81 × 58 cm. Koninklijk Museum voor Schone Kunsten, Antwerp

In a radical departure from his predecessors, but following key innovations already evident in manuscript illumination and attuned to a developing market demand in Antwerp, David made landscape a central theme in his paintings. He may be duly credited with introducing the forest landscape to panel painting, replete with local, recognizable features, in order to draw his viewer into a role as pilgrim and sojourner within the religious scene. The lush naturalism of the flourishing forest served as a metaphor

235. Workshop of Gerard David, *Rest on the Flight into Egypt*, ca. 1510–15. Oil on panel, 60 × 39 cm. Prado, Madrid

for the dominion of God over all living things, a subject often treated in contemporary literature.[98]

David's landscape vision, often described as "poetic,"[99] is one of meditation, of retreat from the hectic world, an intimate, enclosed place for private devotion. It is diametrically opposed to the world-view landscape simultaneously in development by Joachim Patinir not far away from Bruges in Antwerp. Although David and Patinir were both admitted into the Antwerp painters' guild in 1515, their landscape sensibilities could not be more different, perhaps a result of the environments in which they each found their inspiration.

It is undoubtedly no mere coincidence that, at the time both David and Patinir were developing landscape as a more specialized art form than it had heretofore been, the characters of Bruges and of Antwerp were becoming increasingly different. Having already suffered the expulsion of its foreign merchants by Maximilian as a result of the 1488 revolt, and with its major link to maritime trade, the Zwin River, silting up, Bruges found itself being superseded by Antwerp, and it became more and more an isolated community. Antwerp had become an all-powerful economic force and major center of international trade in Europe. This, as Dan Ewing has aptly pointed out, was reflected in the city's art:

> Certain recurrent features of Patinir's land-scapes are consistent with merchant culture. These include the emphasis on travel, in the many ships and overland travelers who popu-late his pictures; the map-like conventions behind his panoramic views; and the promi-nence of ports and harbors. The livelihood of the Renaissance merchant depended upon these very elements: travel, map-reading and shipping, and ports. Patinir's landscapes, thus, are not just a "mirror of the earth," as Gibson

suggested. They are also, and more precisely, a "mirror of merchants' experience."[100]

Ewing states further: "Patinir's idiosyncratic style would have made his pictures highly marketable," their elements creating "a high degree of product identity." He adds: "The creation of product identity is a classic method for individuating, and stimulating demand for, a market good."[101] This is an example of what De Marchi and van Miegroet call "creative differentia-tion": the process by which, in a competitive market, "competitors . . . alter the basis on which they com-pete . . . [in order to gain] some particular advantage."[102]

David's individualized form of landscape—the enclosed forest view—may be understood as part of this same development of product identity within an increasingly competitive market environment. Just as Patinir's world-view landscapes with their craggy rock formations immediately advertised a "Patinir," so too may David's forest scenes and lone-standing trees studied from nature have signaled a "David."[103] Each landscape type, in its own way, was representa-tive of what the buyer wanted, whether as an impetus to devotional practice in a quiet place of meditation, or as a reflection of the confluence of sacred and secular worlds and their broader horizons.

NOTES

1. The earliest known provenance for the triptych is the Urrutia family, Navarre, whence it came to the collection of Ramón F. Urrutia in Madrid, by 1920, when the triptych was still intact. By 1928 it had been acquired by Duveen Bros., Paris and New York, which sold it to Jules S. Bache, New York, in 1928. Bache in turn placed it on loan to the Museum from 1943 and bequeathed it six years later. Negative comments about the attribution of the landscape to David from Mayer (1920, p. 97; and Antwerp 1930, p. 36), as well as other extenuating circumstances, may have prompted the removal of the outside wings from the triptych between 1930 and 1932, when they were sold to the Rijksmuseum, Amsterdam. (Later, Scillia [1975, pp. 239–40] suggested that the two panels are of a different style than the interior of the Nativity Triptych and probably were originally one inde-pendent painting cut into two parts.) While the landscapes remained on the panels (though thinned down and mount-

ed on another wood support), the New York paintings were transferred to canvas. This altered the surface characteristics of the paintings (the upper glaze layers were considerably worn and portions of the modeling of the faces—particu-larly of the donors and saints—were lost) and has contribut-ed to the loss of portions of the ground and underdrawing layers. For references, see van Miegroet 1989, cat. no. 30, p. 298.

2. For the history of the purchase of the outside wings by the Rijksmuseum, see Bruijnen 1997, p. 13 and n. 22. A certain picturesque restoration of the house and tower in the left wing may also have caused doubts about the attribu-tion to David; this was corrected in later restorations (see ibid., pp. 13, 17).

3. Stechow 1966, p. 64.

4. Van Puyvelde 1947, no. 3; Haverkamp-Begemann and Chong 1985, p. 58; van Miegroet 1989, pp. 232, 298.

5. Such naturalistic forest views, depending on locally identifiable sites, are not presented again until nearly two decades later, in Bernaert van Orley's famous Hunts of Maximilian tapestry series. See Ainsworth 1982, esp. pp. 79–144, and Balis et al. 1993, pp. 10–37, 54–123.

6. The number and identification of the animals on the wings have been misread in previous publications and were not clarified until the 1987 restoration of the painting. See discussion in Bruijin 1997, pp. 17 and 21 and nn. 27 and 28.

7. On the earlier confused state of this building and its subsequent restoration, see ibid. p. 17, and figs. 5–9.

8. On the opening and closing of altarpieces and the relationship of outside to inside themes, see Teasdale Smith 1959; Butzkamm 1990, pp. 142–43; Belting and Kruse 1994, pp. 60–62; Buijsen 1997, p. 31, and discussion in Jacobs 1998, pp. 12–18.

9. Friedländer 1924–37, vol. VI (1928), p. 143, no. 160.

10. See Baldass 1936, p. 95, and Boon [1946] p. 51 n. 1, where Friedländer's claim is rejected.

11. Härting 1995 and Buijsen's critique of this interpretation in 1997, pp. 27–28, 33.

12. Buijsen 1997, pp. 32–34. For other interesting references to the ox and the ass, see Lievens–De Waegh 1991, pp. 35–36.

13. Summers 1987, pp. 311–35, esp. p. 311.

14. Ibid., p. 312.

15. Ibid., p. 313.

16. See Ringbom 1984.

17. Falkenburg 1988, p. 9.

18. See ibid.; Harbison 1993, pp. 157–66; and Botvinick 1992, pp. 1–18.

19. See, for example: J. J. Jusserand, *English Wayfaring Life in the Middle Ages,* trans. L. Toumlin Smith (New York, 1961); D. R. Howard, *Writers and Pilgrims: Medieval Pilgrimage Narratives and Their Posterity* (Berkeley, 1980); and J. Sumption, *Pilgrimage: An Image of Medieval Religion* (Totowa, N.J., 1975).

20. Haverkamp-Begemann and Chong 1985, pp. 57–58, and van Miegroet 1989, p. 298.

21. Mayer 1920, p. 97; Baldass 1936, p. 94; Winkler 1964, p. 152 n. 4.

22. Friedländer 1967–76, vol. IV (1967) pl. 25.

23. Although a number of these pieces of wheat are repainted, remnants of the original lie beneath these restorations.

24. See Behling 1967, pp. 33–36, 79–80; and Levi d'Ancona 1977, p. 126.

25. See Maegawa 1959, pp. 181–94; Maegawa 1960, pp. 9–39, 251–92.

26. See Maegawa 1960, p. 35. This view is also stated by Jan van Denemarken of Utrecht in his *Die historie, die ghetiden ende die exempelen van der Heyligher Vrouwen Sint Annen* (written in 1486), as in Brandenbarg 1995, p. 51.

27. As discussed by Denis the Carthusian in his treatise on the Mass, *Exposito Missae.* See Hedeman 1995, p. 194.

28. Saint Leonard was identified in earlier literature as Saint Vincent (see Mayer 1920, p. 97) and thereafter as such in the literature and as Saint Lawrence (in archival material housed at the Getty Research Institute for the History of Art and the Humanities concerning the sale of the triptych by Duveen to Bache, kindly reported to me by Jocelyn Gibbs, processing archivist, in a letter of Sept. 25, 1996). However, the object that he carries in his left hand is broken fetters, the attribute of Saint Leonard. For an example, see ill. no. 141 in John Plummer, *Die Miniaturen aus dem Stundenbuch der Katharina von Kleve* (Berlin 1966). See Kirschbaum and Braunfels 1968–76, vol. VII (1974), pp. 394–98; Réau 1955–59, vol. III (1958), pp. 799–802.

29. L. Campbell, unpublished manuscript of 1981 in the European Paintings Department files, MMA, and Bauman 1986, p. 29.

30. Originally stated by Mayer (1920, p. 97), who identified Saint Leonard as Saint Vincent, a saint more commonly venerated in southern Europe (L. Campbell, unpublished manuscript 1981, as above in note 29).

31. See note 1, above.

32. Bruijnen 1997, p. 22 n. 2, citing M. Madou in the identification of the headdress, jewelry, and neckline style of the dress as Flemish, but the wide sleeves and the elaborate brocade pattern as unusual. However, the wide sleeves and sumptuous dress may also be found in the *Virgin among Virgins,* esp. the figures of Saints Barbara and Catherine (Margaret Scott, letter of April 3, 1998, to the author). See Figure 79 in chap. 2.

33. For a similar alteration of the Petrus Christus *Nativity* in the National Gallery, Washington, see Metzger 1995, pp. 169–71. The center panel inspired two Nativities attributed to Ambrosius Benson (the Hermitage and Yale University Art Gallery), as well as one attributed to William Benson (in the Queen's Collection) and several in the group ascribed to Isenbrant (Mayer van den Bergh Museum, Antwerp, and Öffentliche Kunstsammlung, Basel).

34. The details of David's working procedure in the interior of the Nativity Triptych are somewhat difficult to reconstruct owing to the transfer of the paintings to a canvas support, which caused some loss of the ground preparation and the preparatory underdrawing on it. It can be ascertained, however, that the figures of the wings were mostly laid out in a summary black-chalk sketch, and the figures of the central panel were further worked up over a summary black-chalk sketch in brush and a dark pigment that described the modeling of the draperies of the Virgin and Joseph.

35. Nieburg 1946; Van Puyvelde 1947, no. 30; Stechow 1966, p. 64; Snyder 1985, pp. 191–92; Haverkamp-Begemann and Chong 1985, pp. 57–58; Devisscher 1992, p. 191; Ridderbos 1995, pp. 123–24.

36. De Vos 1994b, p. 363. On a greater appreciation of Memling as a landscape artist, see Reynolds 1997, pp. 163–70.

37. Rohlmann 1993, pp. 235–58.

38. On David and landscape painting, see W. Conway, *Early Flemish Artists and Their Predecessors on the Lower Rhine* (London, 1887), pp. 269–302; Baldass 1918, pp. 111–57; Baldass 1936, pp. 89–96; Van der Wetering 1938; Friedländer 1947, pp. 38–45; Koch 1968; Franz 1969; Gombrich 1978; Genaille 1986; Falkenburg 1988; Gibson 1989.

39. Leeflang 1998, pp. 82–83.
40. Van Mander 1994, p. 81, fol. 205v.
41. See chap. 3, pp. 93 and 149, n. 2.
42. See van Miegroet 1989, pp. 35, 89 nn. 3 and 4.
43. Châtelet 1981, p. 116.
44. Guicciardini 1567, pp. 98 ff.; L. Guicciardini, *Beschrijvinghe van alle de Neder-landen (. . .)* (Amsterdam, 1612), p. 80a; Van Mander 1994, vol II, pp. 270–71 and n. 6.
45. On this issue and the accuracy of these topographical views, see Harbison 1995b, pp. 21–34.
46. For an introduction to this issue and a selected bibliography on the subject, see Smeyers and Vander Stock 1996, pp. 6–47 and 211–14.
47. For the most recent discussion of the Turin-Milan Hours and its history, see Van Buren, Marrow, and Pettinati 1996; regarding Van Eyck and landscape, see K. C. Luber, "Recognizing Van Eyck," *Bulletin of the Philadelphia Museum of Art* 91, nos. 386–87 (spring 1998), esp. pp. 7–23.
48. Pächt 1948, pp. 25–26.
49. Pächt 1978, p. 5, and Kren 1983, p. 6.
50. Kren 1992, pp. 111–255, and Châtelet and Vanwynsberghe 1996, pp. 151–79.
51. See Kren 1983, pp. 31–39, esp. p. 34.
52. Cahn 1991, pp. 11–24.
53. Ibid., pp. 22–23.
54. M. J. Schrethen, *Dutch and Flemish Woodcuts of the Fifteenth Century* (London, 1925), pp. 22–29, and Leeflang 1998, p. 83.
55. This issue has been recently discussed by the author at Colloque XII of "Le dessin sous-jacent dans la peinture" in Bruges, Sept. 10–12, 1997 (publication forthcoming).
56. For a thorough discussion of Bening's contribution to the art of landscape illumination, see Kren and Rathofer 1987–88, esp. pp. 203–73.
57. See Ferrari et al. 1973.
58. Kren 1983, p. 6.
59. Delmarcel and Duverger 1987, pp. 106–11 and passim, for Bruges millefleurs tapestry production. Lorne Campbell kindly conveyed information about the technical investigation of the National Gallery, London, *Virgin and Child with Angels and Saints John the Baptist and John the Evangelist* (no. 1085), which shows no particular underdrawn perspective scheme for this arrangement of trees (personal communication).
60. Koreny 1985 and Kemp 1989, pp. 159–89.
61. Windsor, RL 1243iv; Popham 262A; Clayton 1996, p. 64.
62. See discussion, chap. 3.
63. See Esther Cleven's discussion (1990, esp. p. 11) of David's landscapes and identifiable hallmarks of his works that create product identity.
64. Sander 1993, pp. 222–32.
65. Van Miegroet 1989, cat. no. 21, p. 291.
66. For a thorough discussion of the altarpiece, see Janssens de Bisthoven 1981, pp. 130–62; see also van Miegroet (1989, cat. no. 23, pp. 292–93) for various attributions and references.

67. Snyder 1960a, p. 45.
68. Panofsky 1953, vol. I, pp. 318–19.
69. Kemp 1989, pp. 170–71 (Urb 160r; McM 525).
70. Kemp 1989, pp. 234–35.
71. Ibid., p. 189 (Urb 258v; McM 975)
72. Ibid., p. 161.
73. Fritz Koreny, "A Coloured Flower Study by Martin Schongauer and the Development of the Depiction of Nature from van der Weyden to Dürer," *Burlington Magazine* 133 (1991), pp. 588–97.
74. For these, see Koreny 1985.
75. Oldenburger-Ebbers 1974, pp. 59–73.
76. Landau and Parshall 1994, pp. 245–52.
77. Oldenburger-Ebbers, 1974, p. 61.
78. See Janssens de Bisthoven 1981, pp. 135–36.
79. L. Behling, "Viola Tricolor," in *Festschrift für Heinz Ladendorf,* P. Bloch and G. Zick, eds. (Cologne and Vienna, 1970), pp. 137–43.
80. Oldenburger-Ebbers 1974, p. 73.
81. Inv. no. 211 in the Groeningemuseum, Bruges. This perhaps could have been a triptych of the type discussed by Cecile Scailliérez (1992, pp. 16–31, esp. fig. 3), for the vellum has been attached to a panel. It is labeled in a 16th-century hand on the reverse of the *Baptism* "Nr 70 Meestr Geeraert van Brugghe L. 1–10–0." The most complete bibliography concerning these miniatures is found in *Le siècle des primitifs flamands,* exh. cat., Musée Communal des Beaux-Arts (Bruges, 1960), pp. 158–59, no. 63.
82. A. W. Biermann, "Die Miniaturenhandschriften des Kardinals A. von Brandenburg," *Aachner Kunstblätter,* 46 (1975), pp. 15–310; and J. Testa, *The Beatty Rosarium,* Studies and Facsimiles of Netherlandish Illuminated Manuscripts (Doornspijk, 1986).
83. On this issue, see Benjamin 1973, esp. pp. 160–201, and L. Benjamin, "Disguised Symbolism Exposed and the History of Early Netherlandish Painting," *Studies in Iconography* 2 (1976), p. 16.
84. G. A. Malfatti, "Hans Memling à Milan: Une hypothèse," in Verougstraete, Van Schoute, and Smeyers 1997, pp. 105–13.
85. Walsh 1982, pp. 369–94.
86. See Bruijnen 1997, p. 21. Benson also later used various parts of the pattern for the trees of the forest in at least two other paintings, namely the *Triptych with the Virgin and Child and Prayer Texts* and the *Rest on the Flight into Egypt* (both in the Groeningemuseum, Bruges).
87. Kemp 1989, p. 185 (Urb 254r; McM 952).
88. Another *Rest on the Flight into Egypt,* attributed to Benson (Groeningemuseum, Bruges; 0.223) shows not an exact but a similar arrangement of forest trees on the right side of the panel (illustrated in De Vos 1982, p. 78).
89. Falkenburg 1988, pp. 24–33.
90. From passages of Isaiah (63:1–6), Genesis (49:11), and the Song of Songs (1:13). Thomas 1974, pp. 185–95; Mundy 1981–82, pp. 211–22.
91. Mundy 1981–82, pp. 211–22.

92. For various interpretations of the plant symbolism in the foreground, see Hand and Wolff 1986, p. 64.

93. Van Miegroet 1989, p. 246.

94. Bynum 1987, pp. 117, 270–71.

95. Kemp 1989, p. 88 (E17r/ R153; Urb 149r/ McM 448).

96. See Chris Fischer, "Fra Bartolommeo's Landscape Drawings," *Mitteilungen des kunsthistorischen Institutes in Florenz* 33, nos. 2–3 (1989), pp. 301–6. It is interesting to note that Fra Bartolomeo was in Venice in 1508, and one wonders whether David could have had any contact with the artist or his landscape drawings. Contemporary with Fra Bartolomeo's exercises, of course, were the landscape drawings of Albrecht Dürer. The growing interest in recording natural observations of the visible world pervaded northern and southern Europe at the same time, making attempts to track the influence of such endeavors futile.

97. Kemp 1989, pp. 186, 188 (G25v; R450; Urb 265v; McM 963).

98. Glacken 1967, pp. 151–253, and Summers 1987.

99. Genaille 1986, pp. 59–82.

100. Ewing 1994, p. 12.

101. Ibid., p. 11.

102. N. De Marchi and H. J. van Miegroet, "Art, Value, and Market Practices in the Netherlands in the Seventeenth Century," *Art Bulletin* 76 (1994), p. 452.

103. Cleven 1990, pp. 2–14.

CHAPTER SIX

Hallmarks of Bruges
and the Beginning of Mass Production

The modern-day prejudice against copies is due to our preoccupation with concepts of creativity, invention, and originality in works of art. In the field of early Netherlandish painting, this bias was fostered to a certain extent by one of the preeminent scholars in the field. Max J. Friedländer made an enormous contribution through his systematic categorization of groups of paintings that he attributed to known and eponymous masters. He concentrated his efforts on questions of attribution, authenticity, and originality—issues of primary consideration for art historians of the 1940s. In his introduction to the initial volume of *Die altniederländische Malerei* in 1924, Friedländer seized upon "the growth of individual expression" in the Renaissance as the fundamental key to defining the masters of the age.[1] By emphasizing the specific characteristics of each artist, he focused on originality in order to differentiate the works of one artist from those of another.

Any serious consideration of the production of copies in the Netherlands in the fifteenth and early sixteenth centuries might well be regarded as the antithesis of Friedländer's approach. As Jean Wilson has noted, ". . . he essentially dismissed these works because they did not reproduce his own conception of the creative process which he believed guaranteed the identification of authenticity."[2] Copies are mentioned by Friedländer in the volumes of *Die altniederländische Malerei* only as verification of the characteristic traits of certain artists, or as testimony to the individual and original production of previous Netherlandish painters on whose works they depend. For Friedländer the sight recognition of a copy as part of a general group sufficed. He understood copies to be "equivocal in what they revealed of [a

painter's] nature,"[3] and, therefore, he left unstudied the various groupings he had compiled.

The recent reconsideration of the phenomenon of copies at the turn of the sixteenth century has been prompted by three separate but equally rapidly developing branches of art historical inquiry: the renewed study of documents concerning commissions for paintings, the effect of socioeconomic factors (mainly art markets) on artistic production, and the technical investigation of original works of art.[4] Jelly Dijkstra has discovered that, in contracts for commissioned works of art, one-third of those from the late fifteenth century and one-half of those from the early sixteenth specifically request a copy of an existing work.[5] New research has looked into art-market sales and questioned how the widespread production of copies at this time directly reflected prevailing tastes of the buying public, as well as identified the specific themes that were in favor. Finally, though technical investigation of paintings is not new, increased emphasis on it has provided a significant amount of previously unknown information about how copies were made and when they were made, thus leading to a better understanding of why they were made.

As far as the works of Gerard David are concerned, the close study of copies produced by him and his workshop reveals shifts in the manner in which paintings were produced that resulted from changing client demand and the way in which art was marketed at the time. As it will become clear in the following discussion, some copies were produced on commission to the specifications of the client. These can be distinguished from copies that were created for the open art market. The latter group shows developments in subject matter from a distinctly religious to a more secular content, in addition to early indications

237. Jan van Eyck and Workshop, *Virgin and Child with Saints Barbara and Elizabeth and Jan Vos*, ca. 1441–43. Oil on panel, transferred to Masonite press wood with oak veneer and cradled, original painted surface: 43 × 58.2 cm. The Frick Collection, New York (Photo Copyright the Frick Collection, New York)

of streamlined methods of manufacture introduced in order to meet increased market demand. Herein lies the physical evidence of David's progressive tendencies and efforts to retain a competitive edge in a period of artistic and economic transition.

Hallmarks of Bruges

In Flanders "La piété mariale domine toutes les autres, tant par son itensité que par la multiplicité des traces qu'elle laisse ou des faits qu'elle suscite."[6] The evidence of a cult following and particular veneration of the Virgin Mary was ubiquitous in the south Netherlands in the late fifteenth and early sixteenth

centuries. In Bruges statues of the Virgin graced the facades of Les Halles, the Hôtel de Ville, the Belfry, the city gates, and the plâce de la Bourse, for example, as well as important town residences of the Italian and Spanish community of merchants and bankers. Nearly every street corner had a niche filled with a small statue of Mary, illuminated at night by lanterns.[7] Just as today, the Onze-Lieve-Vrouwekerk dominated the cityscape, and a number of smaller churches and religious confraternities were devoted to particular events of the Virgin's life or her nature—for example, Sint Salvatorskerk to her Assumption and Seven Sorrows, and the Minorites and the Confraternity of the Dry Tree to the Virgin's Immaculate Conception.[8]

This thriving devotion was fostered by the tangible evidence of the Virgin, such as relics of her hair and her milk, housed in Bruges at the Sint Donaaskerk,[9] and by the outcome of contemporary theological debates over Christian beliefs. Attempting to resolve differences between the Roman Catholic and Eastern Orthodox churches, the Council of Ferrara-Florence of 1438–45 found common ground in their devotion to the Virgin Mary. These years of conflict with the Eastern Church fostered an interest in, and the introduction of, certain Byzantine icons to the West.[10] Among them, and perhaps the most famous of all, was a painting brought by Canon Fursy de Bruille (who had attended the Council of Ferrara-Florence) from Rome to Cambrai in 1440 to be installed in the cathedral there. Although actually of Sienese origin from the second quarter of the fourteenth century, the so-called *Cambrai Madonna* (Figure 254) was modeled on a Byzantine prototype. At the time, it was believed by those who worshiped before it

to be an actual portrait of the Virgin and Child painted by Saint Luke himself. Presented thus, the painting assumed a cult status upon its arrival in Cambrai as the source of miraculous events.[11] In an effort to perpetuate the spiritual value of the *Cambrai Madonna,* Jean de Bourgogne, the comte d'Étampe, nephew of the duke of Burgundy, ordered three exact copies of the painting to be made by Petrus Christus in 1454. About the same time the chapter of the cathedral commissioned another twelve from Hayne de Bruxelles, one of which may be identified as a panel in the Nelson-Atkins Museum in Kansas City.[12]

In discussing this phenomenon of copies, Hans Belting observed that ". . . the replica was a witness of the original and aroused the same hopes as the latter. It was known from cult legends that images had multiplied miraculously and had worked miracles through their copies. The copy was therefore expected to share in the privileges enjoyed by the authentic original, in this case through the will of the Virgin. . . . By the duplicate one honored the unique original. This is why the duplicate makes sure that the original is being easily recognized as [a] type."[13]

The power of the *Cambrai Madonna* was such that its influence extended from the religious into the political sphere. The commission of copies followed shortly after the fall of Constantinople to the Ottoman Turks in 1453, an event that prompted Philip the Good's plans for a crusade against the "infidels." It was possibly in an effort to solicit support for this campaign, as Jean Wilson argues, that the comte d'Étampe ordered copies, perhaps for the purpose of distributing them to noblemen wavering in their backing or to churches where funds might be raised for the crusade.[14]

Except for the *Cambrai Madonna,* the influence and assimilation of Greek icons, often by way of Italian versions, into the mainstream of early Netherlandish painting have been little studied up to this point and were far more pervasive than has been recognized. Certain Virgin and Child types thought to have originated in the oeuvre of early Netherlandish painters

238. Greek icon of the *Hodegetria* type, State Museum of Russia, Saint Petersburg, Russia (Photo Scala/Art Resource, NY)

239. Petrus Christus, *Virgin and Child in an Archway*, ca. 1450–55. Oil on panel, 55.5 × 31.5 cm. Szépmüvészeti Múzeum, Budapest

240. Master of the André Madonna, *Virgin and Child in a Porch*, ca. 1500. Oil on panel, 62 × 32 cm. Thyssen-Bornemisza Collection, Madrid (Photo © Museo Thyssen-Bornemisza, Madrid)

undoubtedly find their source in Greek or pseudo-Greek icons. One example is the Virgin and Child found in the Eyckian *Virgin and Child with Saints Barbara and Elizabeth and Jan Vos* (Figure 237).[15] Although the Virgin and Child are placed in the contemporary context of a Flemish landscape and architectural setting and accompanied by the appropriate saints and the donor, Jan Vos, their poses, especially that of the Child, who holds an orb with a cross and blesses the devout with his right hand, originate in the *Hodegetria* type of Greek icon

(Figure 238) and are found in numerous versions in Italian art preceding their introduction into the north.[16]

The efflorescence of this image in Bruges was the result of its status, enhanced by the actions of Bishop Martinus of Mayo, who consecrated and attached indulgences to the Eyckian painting on September 3, 1443, along with two others given to the Carthusian monastery at Genadedal by its prior, Jan Vos.[17] The same prior commissioned Petrus Christus to make an additional small devotional panel for his own private use, wherein he is depicted kneeling before this particular Virgin and Child (Gemäldegalerie, Berlin).[18] Thereafter, in the context of a different setting, which affects the meaning of the image, the identical Virgin and Child are found in another painting by Petrus Christus, of about 1450–55 (Figure 239), which provided the model for at least two other copies (one formerly in The Hague, now on loan to the Museum Boymans-van Beuningen; and a lost one formerly in the Stroganoff collection, Saint Petersburg).[19] A connection of this image specifically with Bruges, and probably again with the Carthusian monastery at Genadedal, can be made with the version by a follower of Gerard David's, the Master of the André Madonna (Figure 240);[20] here a Carthusian monk is seen strolling in the garden in the background before the cityscape of Bruges.[21]

In a parallel development, and often wrongly confused with the Virgin and Child type of the previous discussion, is the one found in the Metropolitan Museum *Virgin and Child with Four Angels* (Figure 241).[22] In this painting the Child—his back to the viewer—is closely held by the Virgin's embrace. This type is often connected to its earliest known Netherlandish manifestation, Jan van Eyck's *Virgin and Child at the Fountain* of 1439 (Figure 242). The tender embrace of Mary and Christ, and particularly the awkward-looking position of the Child's arms— one around the neck of the Virgin and the other turned outward and extended across her proper right shoulder—are its identifying features. In light of the evolution of the Virgin and Child discussed above, it is not surprising to find that this type too originates in earlier icons, as a variant of the *Eleousa* type (Figure 243).[23]

Widely known as the Pelagonitisa Virgin, the earliest example of this Virgin with the squirming Christ Child is found in a thirteenth-century miniature from a Serbian Gospel. Lasareff noted that this type, with its "strongly accented genre element, makes a definite break in the tradition of the hieratic austerity characteristic of Byzantine art" and appears to have been the "logical outcome of a revitalization affecting all the art of the thirteenth century." From the Christian East the so-called Virgin with the Playing Child was assimilated into dugento and trecento painting in Italy, all the time assuming increasingly naturalistic postures.[24] It is perhaps again through Italian examples—as in the case of the *Cambrai Madonna*—that this charming type became known in the north.

Neither the specific icon nor the impetus for Van Eyck's assimilation of this type for his *Virgin and Child at the Fountain* is known.[25] The deliberately shallow space and the decorative cloth of honor, however, suggest the planar designs and gold backgrounds of traditional icons,[26] while the tightly cropped composition, its individual features enfolding the Virgin in a nichelike space, also evokes the setting for sculpture. Craig Harbison, in fact, has suggested that the inspiration for this representation may have been a statue initially referred to as *Our Lady of the Fountain,* which was reputedly discovered in 1403 by Philip the Bold (grandfather of Philip the Good) near a fountain of water during a military campaign to fortify the coast at Dunkerque.[27] Later known as *Our Lady of the Dunes,* the statue inspired great devotion. Given the apparent stylistic association of the motif of the Virgin and Child with Eastern icons, however, it is perhaps more likely that Philip the Good, Van Eyck's great patron, shared with him his small collection of Greek icons, listed in his inventories as paintings *de la façon de Grèce,*[28] one of which may have been a forerunner of the type depicted by Jan. The fountain in his painting probably relates to the contemporary association of such Virgin and Child images with the text of the Song of Solomon (4:12 and 15).[29]

The number of paintings depicting this motif of the Virgin and Child attest to its celebrated status as an image for veneration. These include an exact copy probably from Van Eyck's workshop;[30] an illuminated page from a book of hours of about 1450;[31] a later version in Berlin (perhaps intended for export to

242. Jan van Eyck, *Virgin and Child at the Fountain*, 1439. Oil on panel, ca. 19 × 13 cm (without frame), shown with original frame. Koninklijk Museum voor Schone Kunsten, Antwerp

Italy, for it shows an enclosed garden of southern flora);[32] a variant with the Virgin and Child in a porch, of about 1500; David's own version in the Metropolitan Museum, along with an exact copy from the late sixteenth (?) century;[33] and one

241. Gerard David, *Virgin and Child with Four Angels*, ca. 1510–15. Oil on panel, 63.2 × 39.1 cm. The Metropolitan Museum of Art, Gift of Mr. and Mrs. Charles Wrightsman, 1977 (1977.1.1)

attributed to Isenbrant that reflects the popularity in the early sixteenth century of roadside-shrine Madonnas (Figures 244–248).[34]

The setting of the Metropolitan Museum painting (Figure 241), identical to that of the painting of the Master of the André Madonna discussed above (wherein a different Virgin and Child icon is depicted, Figure 240),[35] again suggests a link with the

243. Unknown Bohemian painter, *Virgin and Child Facing the Man of Sorrows*, ca. 1350. Tempera on panel, 18.5 × 25 cm. Staatliche Kunsthalle, Karlsruhe

Carthusian monastery of Genadedal. This raises the questions of whether Philip the Good, who with the other dukes of Burgundy was a generous benefactor of the Carthusian order,[36] gave an icon of this type to the monks there, or whether the prototype was another of the three paintings given by Prior Jan Vos and consecrated and granted indulgences by Bishop Martinus of Mayo on his 1443 visit to Genadedal. The two other paintings receiving this elevated status, aside from the Frick panel, were also images of the Virgin.[37] One is described as a Virgin nursing the Child (left) along with a Resurrection (right)— possibly a diptych; a third is listed as a Virgin carrying the Child. But the entry is brief and cannot be linked definitively with the model for our painting.

The *Virgin and Child with Four Angels* (Figure 241) by Gerard David has sometimes been referred to as archaistic, as a painting that harks back to Jan van

Eyck's *Virgin and Child at the Fountain* of some seventy years earlier.[38] Considering the painting thus as a derivative knockoff of an earlier famous work ignores its primary importance as a devotional object for the veneration of an esteemed icon. Moreover, to maintain the label of archaism, one must necessarily establish that there was no replication of the image in the intervening years, which, as has been demonstrated here, is patently not the case. Rather than archaistic, David's interpretation may be seen as part of the natural evolution of the representation of this particular icon of the Virgin and Child in late-fifteenth- and early-sixteenth-century Netherlandish art—presented in a fashion that, contrary to being in any sense *retardataire,* is decidedly modern.

This repeated use of Jan van Eyck's motif of the Virgin and Child in a chronological continuum over a period of about eighty years is not due to a lack of

244. Workshop copy after Jan van Eyck, *Virgin and Child at the Fountain*, ca. 1440. Oil on panel, 18.4 × 11.7 cm. Private collection, Antwerp

modernized it in order to engage the empathy of the contemporary viewer. The Virgin stands at the *Porta Coeli,* which here is not simply a door or gate to heaven, but a porch with an up-to-date, grand Renaissance arch and columns with Italianate capitals.[39] To the accompaniment of sweet melodies from the lute and the harp, she is poised to be crowned as Queen of Heaven by the two angels above. David included the musical angels from another well-known pictorial tradition—that originating in the art of Robert Campin and his popular composition of the *Virgin and Child in an Apse* (Figure 249)[40]—along with the golden tiled floor and the gold strings on the instruments of the angels to reinforce the notion that the porch where the Virgin stands is the heavenly realm. Although various copies of Campin's design must have been known to David (indeed, one in the Phoenix Art Museum is even attributed to his

245. Anonymous French painter, *Virgin and Child with Two Angels* (from HM 1100, fol. 182), ca. 1450. Detail. Tempera on vellum. Huntington Library, San Marino, California

imagination on the part of Bruges school painters, or an impoverished reserve of motifs from which to draw. Rather, it points to the sustained popularity of a certain image—perhaps one with indulgences attached to it or one that had gained particular spiritual value or worth because of miracles believed to have been performed through the icon—and the desire on the part of patrons and clients to share in the power and privileges of the authentic original through its copies.

The setting for the icon, however, could be changed from painting to painting in order to reflect different devotional emphases at the time. David's presentation is conventional in many ways, but he

246. Anonymous Netherlandish painter? after Jan van Eyck, *Virgin and Child at the Fountain*, ca. 1480–1500. Oil on panel, 57 × 41 cm. Gemäldegalerie, SMPK, Berlin (Photo Jörg P. Anders, Berlin)

247. Anonymous Netherlandish painter, *Virgin and Child*, ca. 1500. Oil on panel, 58.4 × 30.8 cm. The Metropolitan Museum of Art, Marquand Collection, Gift of Henry G. Marquand, 1889 (89.15.24)

workshop), his immediate association of musical angels with the Virgin and Child was likely inspired by the example of Hans Memling, his predecessor in Bruges, who employed them in several compositions throughout his career.[41] Memling's paintings include the arch over the Virgin (though she is invariably sitting, not standing) and the enclosed garden behind her. Far from representing an archaistic trend with the *Virgin and Child with Four Angels,* then, David combined the motifs of long-standing and very popular strains in early Netherlandish painting, and added to them his own contemporary flavor.

The Virgin's imminent coronation as Queen of Heaven refers not only to her Assumption and triumph over death, but also to the fulfillment of her relationship with Christ as his bride, a concept that is stressed in the Song of Solomon.[42] Beyond the

suggestion of this relationship between the Virgin and Child, which is reflected in the gentle embrace of the two, are other indications. Eithne Wilkens connects the prayer beads, which are carried by the Christ Child in the Van Eyck painting but here have become a rosary, to betrothals and weddings in medieval Europe, when they were presented by the bridegroom to the bride as a sign of respect and trust.[43] In this context the rosary beads further echo

248. Attributed to Adriaen Isenbrant, *Virgin and Child in a Shrine*, ca. 1520. Oil on panel, 22.8 × 17.4 cm. Private collection, Germany

the poetry of the Song of Solomon, in which Christ was understood in contemporary exegeses as the bridegroom and the Virgin as his bride. The rosary beads carried by the Child allude to the opening phrase recited on them, "Ave Maria, gratia plena," or "Hail Mary, full of grace," the words uttered by Gabriel at the Annunciation to the Virgin, and therefore recall the moment of Christ's Incarnation and entry into the world. The Child looks out at the viewer, inviting the meditation that accompanies the recitation of the rosary, a practice initiated by the Carthusians but one that had become widespread

249. Workshop of Robert Campin, *Virgin and Child in an Apse*, ca. 1475. Oil on panel transferred to canvas, 45.1 × 34.3 cm. Rogers Fund, Metropolitan Museum of Art, Rogers Fund, 1905 (05.39.2)

in the last quarter of the fifteenth century, after the cult of the rosary was established at Douai by a Dominican, Alanus de Rupe, in 1470.[44]

David has converted the traditional *hortus conclusus* into a naturalistic garden, where a Carthusian monk strolls in the background reading a book. The Carthusian monastery of Genadedal, formerly located just beyond the city walls of Bruges,[45] is most likely intended here, since the locally identifiable churches of Sint Jakobs[46] and Onze-Lieve-Vrouwe (in its state before the alterations to the tower in 1519)[47] are visible just beyond the wall to the left and right of the Virgin's head.[48]

Seemingly casually planted, the garden nonetheless provides clues to the specific meaning of the painting, that is, the redemption of humanity and the Virgin's participatory role as coredemptor with Christ, a concept discussed extensively by Carthusian authors, especially Denis the Carthusian, who wrote to augment and elucidate the texts of Ludolph the Carthusian of nearly a hundred years before him.[49] Prominently placed just beyond the porch to the left of the Virgin is the iris (or sword lily), which signifies the prophecy of Simeon in the Gospel of Luke (2:35) of the sword that would pierce through the heart of the Mother of God as she experienced the rejection of her son by mankind. To the right is the columbine, symbolizing the Virgin's sorrow, as its name in French, *ancolie,* was thought at the time to be related to the word for "melancholy."[50] Joining these flowers, near the iris, is the strawberry plant, whose five-petaled blossoms represent the five wounds endured by Christ on the cross and whose tripartite leaves stand for the Trinity.[51] These flowers traditionally are emblematic of the Seven Sorrows of the Virgin, by which Mary expressed her compassion with certain events of Christ's suffering. IHESUS [RE]DEMPT[OR] on the cloth under the Christ Child underscores this meaning, as do the angels' headbands with crosses and the Virgin's cloak in red, the color of Christ's Passion.

By sharing the Virgin's compassion through meditation on the suffering of Christ, the devout sought the intercessory powers of the Virgin Mary for their own salvation. Through fervent prayer, the most sought-after experience was a vision of the holy personage come alive, an experience that is directly intended by this painting.[52] In David's composition the Virgin is literally only a step away.

Whether the original model for this motif of the Virgin and Child in the Metropolitan painting was an icon *de la façon de Grèce* of the type Philip the Good collected (as seems likely, given its derivation ultimately from the Pelagonitisa Virgin), or a contemporary painting that was consecrated and endowed with indulgences, or both, David made specific reference to a model close at hand. This is Jan van Eyck's version, which he copied exactly in pen and ink on paper (Figure 35). As has been discussed in chapter 1, David must have had access to Van Eyck's panel,[53] or an exact copy of it (such as Figure 244), for the pen-and-ink sketch trails off with incomplete forms at the edges of the design where the original painting meets its engaged frame, slightly cutting off the draperies of the angels and the left edge of the fountain basin (compare Figures 242 and 35).

From this small drawing, David may have produced a larger-scale design, working out the forms in considerable detail, thus eliminating the need for the type of more fully worked-up underdrawing

250. IRR detail of Virgin and Child in Figure 241

that is routinely found in David's paintings.[54] It is equally likely, however, that he simply copied the drawing by eye with brush and ink onto the

251. IRR detail of Virgin and Child in Figure 241

252. X-radiograph detail of heads of Virgin and Child in Figure 241

grounded panel, making slight adjustments in the contours of forms and at the lower edge of the draperies in order to coordinate the fall of the folds with the stone ledge of the porch (Figures 250 and 251). Incised lines demarcate the archway, a summary underdrawing lays out the basic forms of the landscape and buildings and the music-making angels, and slightly more detailed work in brush and pen shows indications for the modeling of the draperies of the angels above.[55]

The X-radiograph provides more revealing information about David's considerations during the evolution of this painting (compare Figures 251 and 252). The detail of the Virgin and Child shows quite clearly that David originally followed the Eyckian model exactly, both in the underdrawing and in the initial paint layers; that is, the Virgin with her hair pulled in tightly at the nape of her neck and the profile view of the Christ Child's head. In the upper paint layers, he re-formed Van Eyck's Virgin into his

own familiar type, adding loose, flowing hair with golden highlights, and turned the head of the Christ Child outward (as he did in the Metropolitan Museum *Rest on the Flight into Egypt,* Figure 234) to address the viewer directly. These modifications and the afterthought of the boldly Italianate columns and capitals with putti heads painted over the completed archway, as well as the view to the Bruges cityscape and vast distance in the landscape beyond, transformed Van Eyck's *Virgin and Child at the Fountain* into a vision of the Virgin and Child taking place in contemporary Bruges.

Just as in the Metropolitan Museum version of the *Rest on the Flight into Egypt,* David demonstrates here an advanced understanding of the balance of color and light, including the delicate chiaroscuro treatment of the music-making angels and the subtle sfumato effects for the modeling of the heads of the

253. X-radiograph of Figure 241

Virgin and Child, and thereby achieves a convincing integration of the figures within the space, not simply before it. Attention lavished on the details—the gold strings of the harp, the sumptuous golden-tiled floor, the *couleur changeante* effects for the lute-playing angel's robe—is not at the expense of the greater whole, which encompasses not only the city of Bruges, but also the mountainous landscape of the world beyond. Undoubtedly an important commission (for an unknown client) painted by David at the peak of his creative talents, the *Virgin and Child with Four Angels* must date from about 1510–15.[56] This painting, then, was not in any sense a standard copy or replica of Van Eyck's Antwerp panel, but an inspired statement of Carthusian doctrine delivered through the vehicle of a venerated icon (to which Van Eyck's painting probably also refers) in a purposefully

arranged, contemporary setting with which the viewer could identify.

The fascination with Byzantine-inspired icons led to their assimilation into the mainstream of Netherlandish painting in the form of small devotional diptychs. Among these are a series of works by David of the Virgin and Child and Christ Taking Leave of His Mother (Figures 256, 257, 261, and 262), probably originally framed to be opened and closed like a book, which focused on the mystery of Christ's Incarnation and his purpose on earth. Found in the tracts of Pseudo-Bonaventure's *Meditationes vitae Christi* and Ludolf of Saxony's *Vita Christi,* the essence of the theological discussions prompting such images was that one could approach Christ and receive salvation through participation in and imitation of his life, particularly by personal identification

254. Unknown Sienese painter, *Cambrai Madonna*, ca. 1340. Oil on panel. Cathedral of Cambrai (Photo Copyright IRPA-KIK, Brussels)

255. Dieric Bouts, *Virgin and Child*, ca. 1455–60. Oil on panel, 21.6 × 16.5 cm. The Metropolitan Museum of Art, Theodore M. Davis Collection, Bequest of Theodore M. Davis, 1915 (30.95.280)

256a,b. Gerard David, *Virgin and Child* and *Christ Taking Leave of His Mother*, ca. 1490–95. Oil on panel, each 9.7 × 7.5 cm. Alte Pinakothek, Munich

257a,b. Gerard David, *Virgin and Child* and *Christ Taking Leave of His Mother*, ca. 1490–95. Oil on panel, 11.5 × 8 cm and 11.5 × 7 cm. Öffentliche Kunstsammlung, Basel

258. Gerard David, *Virgin and Child*, ca. 1490. Oil on panel, 7.6 × 5.1 cm. Serra de Alzaga Collection, Valencia

259. Workshop of Gerard David, *Virgin and Child*, ca. 1510. Detail. Oil on panel, 15.9 × 11.4 cm. The Metropolitan Museum of Art, Robert Lehman Collection, 1975 (1975.1.118)

with his suffering. The Virgin is a chief exemplar of empathic response to her son's anguish, and the visual emphasis of these small devotional diptychs is placed on this aspect of her being as well as on her vital role in both the Incarnation and Christ's sacrifice for humanity's redemption. The recurring interlocking themes here are the Virgin's compassion and the constancy of her faith.

Modeled on Byzantine prototypes probably encountered through Italian or Bohemian examples (such as Figure 243),[57] these diptychs are yet another manifestation of the interest in eastern icons of the type that were apparently popular with the dukes of Burgundy. Their increased production and acquisition by a wider audience may suggest their importance not only as devotional objects but also as a reflection of courtly taste.

The formal evolution of these paired images represents subtle shifts in the emphasis placed on time-honored themes. The diptychs in Munich and Basel[58] of the 1490s (Figures 256 and 257) ultimately

reflect the ongoing popularity of the *Cambrai Madonna* (Figure 254). But David probably knew the intimate motif of the Virgin and Child through an intermediate source, namely that of Dieric Bouts (Figure 255), who along with his workshop produced a number of variants of the *Cambrai Madonna*.[59] In particular, David assimilated Bouts's more human and tender embrace (with Christ's right arm around the Virgin's neck).[60] Painted like miniatures on panel, David's diptychs join together the conventions of portraiture—for example, in the cast shadows evident behind the figures in the Munich version—with Byzantinizing effects of holy icons, such as the gold backgrounds. In effect, they present "living icons."

As a previously unknown panel by David and the somewhat larger example from his workshop show (Figures 258 and 259), such images were produced also as tiny independent panels (about 7.6 × 5.1 cm

260. IRR detail of Christ and Mother in Figure 257 (Photo Peter Berkes)

and 15.9 × 11.4 cm, respectively) that could be carried as talismans or aids for private devotion.[61] Increased demand for such images required simplified methods of producing them. Initially these miniature paintings were worked up in paint from detailed pen- or brush-and-ink underdrawings, as in the Basel *Christ Taking Leave of His Mother* (compare Figures 257 and 260) probably copied from workshop patterns.[62] In the first decade of the sixteenth century, the considerable popularity of these small diptychs, as well as a greater interest in the more narrative explication of the theme, necessitated a change in the details of the production of these paintings. In the Metropolitan Museum *Christ Taking Leave of His Mother,*[63] the

addition of Mary Magdalene and Martha to the Virgin and Christ required a reworked design, one that David made directly on the panel in a loose black chalk sketch (Figures 262 and 264). The likely candidate for the left half of the diptych is a *Virgin and Child with Musical Angels* that, like the Metropolitan panel, has been elaborately reframed and now hangs in the Bearsted Collection, Upton House, Banbury (Figure 261).[64] It shows a different motif for the Virgin and Child found in later works by David, namely in the *Virgin and Child with Four Saints* (Figure 59). The painted portions of the Metropolitan and Bearsted panels (except for the cut edges of the former) are equivalent in size, and the gilded

261. Gerard David, *Virgin and Child with Musical Angels*, ca. 1500–1510. Oil on panel, 15.7 × 11.8 cm. Upton House, Banbury (Photo © Upton House, The National Trust Photo Library, London)

262. Gerard David, *Christ Taking Leave of His Mother*, ca. 1500–1510. Oil on panel, 15.6 × 12.1 cm. The Metropolitan Museum of Art, Bequest of Benjamin Altman, 1913 (14.40.636)

background decoration of each matches with its stippling and feathered strokes emanating from the holy figures; the reverses are marbled, providing a decorative embellishment when the diptych was closed. The *Virgin and Child,* which has suffered in its condition and has been restored, especially in the head of the Child,[65] follows a pattern that has been transferred to the panel by pouncing (Figure 263)— a fact that indicates that by the first decade of the sixteenth century, the demand for these diptychs had increased to the point where it was cost-effective and labor efficient to develop streamlined working procedures for more easily and quickly supplying the demand. As was typical of David's workshop method, it was the new or adjusted design that was carried out in a free sketch in black chalk directly on the panel, and the repeated composition—here of the

Virgin and Child—that was directly transferred from an existing cartoon, in this case by pouncing.

The Beginning of Mass Production

The developments that took place in David's production after the turn of the century that suggest new marketing strategies for his paintings are a direct result of interwoven social, political, and economic events occurring in Bruges. The strong presence of the extravagant court life of a succession of Burgundian dukes had fostered the growth of a market for luxury goods. Although the dukes themselves did not regularly commission paintings (preferring tapestries, illuminated books, and precious metalwork instead), their wealthy court functionaries ordered works from the leading painters of the day. This was not solely to

263. IRR detail of Figure 261

264. IRR detail of Figure 262

address their spiritual needs, but also to enhance their status through a conspicuous show of wealth.[66]

Jean Wilson suggests that it may have been the unexpected death of Mary of Burgundy, and a growing concern among merchants of luxury goods about their future livelihood with the possible shift of locations of the court under the Hapsburg Maximilian of Austria, that prompted the establishment in Bruges of the *pandt,* or marketplace, for luxury goods including paintings. The *pandt* came into being in 1482, only a few months after Mary's death, at the request of the Guild of Saint Nicholas, which was responsible for the sale of luxury items.[67] Unfortunately, there are no records of stall rentals for the period 1482 to 1512, leaving open the question of the relative success of the *pandt* during those early years of its operation. However, Wilson's survey of the participation of painters in the Bruges *pandt* thereafter shows that in the second and third decades of the sixteenth century business was thriving. After 1511, with the weakening of the guild rules prohibiting painters

from exhibiting in more than one place, artists were encouraged to participate in the *pandt* as well as to display their products in the windows of their shops.[68]

Meanwhile, the *pandt* in Antwerp on the grounds of the Onze-Lieve-Vrouwekerk was by 1484 exclusively devoted to paintings and selected luxury objects. Thus Antwerp and Bruges simultaneously had competing markets, and certain artists, including David and Jan Provost, must have seen the advantage of belonging to the guild in both locations in order to participate fully in both markets. Although names of such leading artists as Provost, David, Isenbrant, and Blondeel do not appear on the lists of those who rented stalls at the Bruges or the Antwerp *pandt,* these painters may have worked through dealers who would represent their works at the market.[69]

It is in the context of these developments that key paintings from David's later production should be considered. Among these are the frequently repeated themes of the Rest on the Flight into Egypt and the Virgin and Child with the Milk Soup. The localization

277. Attributed to Simon Bening, *Virgin and Child*, ca. 1520. Oil on panel, 24.4 × 21 cm. The Metropolitan Museum of Art, The Friedsam Collection, Bequest of Michael Friedsam, 1931 (32.100.53)

chin; short, thin eyebrows); the formulaic brushwork in the highlights of the Virgin's wavy hair; the more generalized depiction of the hands. Above all, the landscape is uncharacteristic for David but particularly close to the art of Simon Bening, the great innovator in landscape depiction in contemporary Ghent–Bruges book illumination, who may indeed be the author of this painting.[91] Bening might well have integrated David's popular figural motif into his own landscape conception in a period when the arts of panel painting and manuscript illumination were particularly closely affiliated in Bruges. Whether by Bening or not, this charming composition moves away from the purely religious content of its model and toward the developing secular genres that became so popular in seventeenth-century Flanders and Holland.

278. Virgin and Child in central panel of Sedano Triptych (Figure 150)

Gerard **DAVID** vers 1460±1523 (École flamande)
La Vierge et l'Enfant Jésus
entre le donateur Jan de Sedano et sa femme

279. IRR of Figure 278

At least one other contemporary painting indicates the use of some form of pattern transfer that is no longer visible. This is most evident in the case of the relationship between the motif of the Virgin and Child in the Sedano Triptych in the Louvre with that in the Philadelphia Museum of Art *Virgin and Child Enthroned with Two Angels* (compare Figures 278 and 280).[92] The former, dating from the 1490s, shows a meticulous pen- or brush-and-ink underdrawing of the type redrawn or copied over from a carefully

worked out preliminary design on paper (Figure 279). The latter, contemporary with the *Rest on the Flight into Egypt* paintings of the first decades of the sixteenth century, reveals the type of free sketch in black chalk that we traditionally associate with a new design in the process of being worked out directly on the

280. Gerard David, *Virgin and Child Enthroned with Two Angels*, ca. 1510. Oil on panel, 99.7 × 65.5 cm. John G. Johnson Collection, Philadelphia Museum of Art

281. IRR of Figure 280

panel (Figure 281). Tracings made from the corresponding motif of the Virgin and Child in the Louvre
and Philadelphia paintings, however, show that the
same pattern has been employed for both, only
reversed for the later version. Close examination of
the underdrawing in the Philadelphia example reveals
that the positions of the Virgin's right hand and the
Child's feet correspond exactly to the Sedano painting
and that David altered these features in the painted

layers. This use of a standard pattern transferred to
the grounded panel to establish the basic form, which
subsequently was further worked up and altered in
its various details through reworking with black chalk
over it, is a practice that can be identified in the
working methods of other early-sixteenth-century
artists after David, such as Dirk Vellert and especially
Adriaen Isenbrant.[93] More obvious indications of
the transfer of the exact same motif of the Virgin and

282. Ambrosius Benson?, *Virgin and Child with Musical Angels*, ca. 1525. Oil on panel, 99 × 75.5 cm.
Hessisches Landesmuseum, Darmstadt

Child from the Sedano Triptych and the Philadelphia *Virgin and Child* are revealed by the underdrawing of the Darmstadt *Virgin and Child Enthroned with Musical Angels* (Figures 282 and 283), a painting from David's workshop that is sometimes attributed to his assistant Ambrosius Benson. Here the rigid lines of the draperies have been transferred by the tracing or pouncing, gone over with brush, of a pattern closely corresponding in size and most of its details

(with adjustments to the left side of the Virgin's cloak) to the Philadelphia version.[94]

These examples show that a method of pattern transfer for major motifs, especially of the Virgin and Child, was already being employed by David as a matter of routine workshop practice, certainly by the first decade of the sixteenth century. In the period directly following, apparently as a result of increased demand for paintings such as the *Rest on the Flight*

283. IR photo detail of Virgin and Child in Figure 282

into Egypt, workshop methods were further stream-lined by the introduction of pounced cartoons. This enabled a painter of even modest skills to exactly reproduce the desired composition for sale. The known variants of David's *Rest on the Flight into Egypt,* which are connected with the production of Adriaen Isenbrant, have been discussed by Jean Wilson. Her conclusions reinforce those suggested here: that market factors in Bruges and Antwerp provided an impetus for changes in how art was produced in the first decades of the sixteenth century.[95] About this time David clearly realized the advantage of affiliat-ing himself with the more active art-market center of Antwerp, and joined the Antwerp painters' guild in 1515, even though he continued to maintain his residence in Bruges.

It is David's production of the paintings of the *Virgin and Child with the Milk Soup* (Figures 284–287) that establishes him as fully in tune with the market opportunities of the day. Astutely assessing the popular appeal of more secular representations of the Virgin and Child and the growing taste for models derived from Italian art, David perhaps tried to corner the market with what he anticipated would be a best-seller. In this way, he may have attempted to create, rather than simply to respond to, new tastes in art.[96]

Although the Aurora Trust painting (Figure 284) is the most finely executed and elaborate of at least seven known versions in terms of slight additions to the standard pattern, and certainly the best preserved, all of the examples surprisingly reveal a pounced underdrawing (gone over with brush and black pigment in order to form an easily readable and uniform linear design; compare Figures 288 and 292).[97] Unlike the various examples of the *Rest on the Flight into Egypt,* they appear to have been created contemporaneously.[98]

There are slight changes from painting to painting. We can reasonably assume, however, that all of them originated from the same cartoon or from cartoons produced from the same template, for they agree in size and details of drapery folds, pose, facial features, and so forth. Therefore, though it is no longer extant, we know that there must have been a drawing in David's atelier that was pricked for transfer to make these paintings at a time when streamlined production was effected for marketing purposes.

From our twentieth-century viewpoint we are intent upon identifying the prototype and replicas of like compositions.[99] In the case of the *Virgin and Child with the Milk Soup,* scholars have argued that the prototype is lost because no painting exists in which there is the type of freehand, creative underdrawing expected in the original, or first example, in a series of like design. Contrary to this view, I would propose, given David's likely intentions from the outset, that there was no original to begin with, in this traditional sense of the term.

In a further consideration of the question of original and copy, however, are additional details of technique and execution in the various versions of the *Virgin and Child with the Milk Soup.* Despite the fact that all of the versions are derived from the same cartoon, there is a varied approach in both execution and subtle shifts of meaning that separate a customized or individualized painting, as in the Aurora Trust picture, from more routine workshop production, as found in the others (for example, those in Genoa, Brussels, and Rancho Santa Fe). Whether the Aurora Trust picture was singled out in this way in compliance with a particular commission or simply produced as a model to be shown, perhaps in the artist's shopwindow, to attract further orders cannot be determined.

Differences in working method in the Aurora Trust picture in relation to the other versions are evident from the ground up to the final painted layers and probably indicate workshop participation in the latter. In the Aurora Trust painting, David began as in the other versions with the pounced cartoon, but in going over it with the brush to connect the dots of the pouncing he made certain further adjustments to the design. The left edge of the foreground table, which originally passed through the middle of the knife, was moved farther to the left (Figure 290); the background tree was brushed in (in a manner similar to the trees in the middle stage of the Mauritshuis landscape wings, see chapter 5) with several lower branches that were edited out in the upper painted layers (compare Figures 228 and 284); and the Virgin's head was painted in fully with a headband and visible ear before the veil was painted over it (Figure 289). As the final form was followed in the other paintings (Figures 285–287 and 291, 292), the Aurora Trust picture must have been the first within an intended series of paintings.

At the middle stage of working up the design into the painted layers, differences in execution may also be observed. The flesh tones of the heads of the Virgin and Child in the Aurora Trust painting are densely worked up and the highlights prominently placed on the forehead, bridge of the nose, and neck, as the X-radiograph shows (Figure 293). The evidence available of at least one of the other versions, for example the Brussels painting, reveals that a whitish application

285. Gerard David, *Virgin and Child with the Milk Soup*, ca. 1515. Oil on panel, 41 × 32 cm. Genoa, Palazzo Bianco

for the flesh areas was more generally applied in a broadly brushed-on base tone (see X-radiograph, Figure 294). In this case the modeling of the features of the face was accomplished not with built-in contrasts in the preliminary lead white layer, but only at a later stage in the painting process with the

284. Gerard David, *Virgin and Child with the Milk Soup*, ca. 1515. Oil on panel, 33 × 27.5 cm. Aurora Trust, New York

application of glazes in the uppermost layer. This difference in handling the flesh tones of the latter group shows the kind of abbreviated technique used for accelerated production, as has been noted in other contemporary examples that were produced in multiple copies.[100] The result of the buildup of the preliminary flesh tones in the separate paintings is evident on the surface where the texture of the paint in the Aurora Trust picture has a rather densely

286. Gerard David, *Virgin and Child with the Milk Soup*, ca. 1515. Oil on panel, 35 × 29 cm. Musées Royaux des Beaux-Arts de Belgique, Bruxelles de Belgique—Koninklijke Musea voor Schone Kunsten, Brussels

modeled, buttery quality, and the other versions appear flatter and more thinly painted.

The stimuli that prompted the production in general of the *Virgin and Child with the Milk Soup* are varied, having to do both with increasing interest in a more secular treatment of themes in art and with the new popularity of Italian art (specifically the influx of Leonardesque models). Like the Metropolitan Museum version of David's *Rest on the Flight into*

Egypt, the Aurora Trust painting is indebted to Italian models—not just to the influence of the sfumato and chiaroscuro effects of Leonardesque works, but to specific compositions originating in Lombardy.

The influx of Italian art into the mainstream of south Netherlandish painting had been slow but steady, certainly since the middle of the fifteenth century. Its incipient stages can be seen in Rogier van der Weyden's work as a passing interest[101] and

287. Workshop of David, *Virgin and Child with the Milk Soup*, ca. 1520. Oil on panel, 37.5 × 32.5 cm. Deutz collection, San Diego, California

perhaps with more enduring effect in the paintings of Petrus Christus in his consistent interest in the application of the rules of perspective and in certain Italian conventions such as the *sacra conversazione* of his Frankfurt *Virgin and Child with Saints Francis and Jerome.*[102] Memling may have been particularly attuned to the Italian portrait type, a result of the prevailing influence of his many foreign clients. He also began to incorporate Italian Renaissance architectural elements

and putti with swags in his paintings, an effect that David used in his *Justice of Cambyses* panels and thereafter. But the greatest manifestation of the interest in Italian art came in Antwerp in the first decades of the sixteenth century with the apparent introduction of examples in the style of Leonardo and his followers, and in Brussels with the impact of the art of Raphael. In particular, Quentin Massys and Joos van Cleve were influenced by Leonardesque models

288. IRR of Figure 284

for paintings that they produced mostly in the 1520s.[103]

David introduced his own version of the Italianate Madonna somewhat earlier, at the forefront of this movement. His exposure to possible prototypes was probably the result of his travels to northern Italy but could also have come through the use of composi-tions, motifs, and painting techniques by Italian artists working in the north. His Lombard apprentice,

Ambrosius Benson, who was in David's atelier at least by 1519, came too late to have inspired either the *Rest on the Flight into Egypt* or the *Virgin and Child with the Milk Soup*.

Here it is important to consider a Lombard com-position that was circulating in the north in the form of both paintings and drawings. This is Bernardino de' Conti's *Madonna Suckling the Child* (Figure 295), signed and dated 1501, from which a number of

289. IRR detail of Figure 284

copies and variants were made by both Italian (Figure 296)[104] and northern artists, as well as at least one attributed to Benson himself.[105] The parallels between the de' Conti painting and David's *Virgin and Child with the Milk Soup* are not incidental. They include the basic composition with the Virgin facing right and holding the Christ Child (albeit in a different pose), this grouping making up roughly three-quarters of the composition; the view in the upper right corner out to the landscape beyond of houses on a lake bordered by trees; even the vase with the same type of pansy and stock flowers sitting on a table beneath the window (in the Aurora Trust version). In addition, the particular angle of the Virgin's head in a nearly profile view, with sharply defined facial features (especially the prominent, straight nose), and her hair flowing loosely beneath a headdress of ribbons or veil appear distinctly similar in both the Italian example and David's *Virgin and Child with the Milk Soup*. In theme they are also related—one nurses the Christ Child, the other feeds him the milk from a bowl.

Wilhelm Suida suggested that the original on which the de' Conti painting is based was a lost work by Leonardo of before 1499.[106] This may well be the case, as copies in Leonardo's style by his Milanese followers indicate (Figure 296). Moreover, there are the various versions, many of which show the Virgin in a similar pose, of Leonardo's drawings for the *Madonna and Child with the Cat* of about 1478–81 (Figure 297), and the *Madonna and Child with a Bowl of Cherries* of about 1478 (Figure 298), all leading up to the *Benois Madonna* of about 1478 (Hermitage, Saint Petersburg).[107] Drawings or paintings after the *Benois Madonna* must have been circulating in the north in the early decades of the sixteenth century, for Flemish imitations of it exist, at least one of which has been associated with a follower of Joos van Cleve.[108]

When these sketches by Leonardo are compared directly with David's Virgin and Child in the Milk Soup paintings, in certain details they are closer to each other than David's figures are to the de' Conti example. David appears to have assimilated not only the pose of Leonardo's Virgins, but also that of the Child in the particular position of the legs (see Figure 298)—the right leg extended and the left leg pulled up at an angle closer to the body. The studies for the *Madonna and Child with the Cat* were among Leonardo's earliest uses of wash over an ink drawing, and if David directly saw them, they must have been influential for his own technique in the underdrawing for the *Virgin among Virgins* of 1509.[109] Finally, Leonardo's drawing of the *Madonna and Child with a Bowl of Cherries* provides a connection to David's

290. IRR detail of Figure 284

291. IRR detail of Figure 285

painting in both its figures and its theme, as the Aurora Trust painting shows the Child holding a branch of cherries. The presumably lost Leonardo painting of this subject had a great following among Leonardo's pupils, especially Giampietrino, and was extremely popular with Antwerp painters, notably Joos van Cleve and Quentin Massys, but probably not until the 1520s.[110] The connection between David's *Virgin and Child with the Milk Soup* and these Leonardesque designs at an earlier date

292. IRR of Figure 286

strongly indicates his forward-looking and modern approach.

Now returning to the series of the Virgin and Child with the Milk Soup paintings to examine the meaning of these genrelike subjects for the contemporary viewer, we find, just as in their technique, subtle differences in the presentation of the Aurora Trust and the other versions, perhaps as a result of a client's request for an individualized product or one whose religious content was more prominently

293. X-radiograph of Figure 284

294. X-radiograph of Figure 286

295. Bernardino de' Conti, *Madonna Suckling the Child*, ca. 1501. Oil on panel, 61 × 44 cm. Accademia Carrara di Belle Arti, Bergamo

296. Milanese follower of Leonardo da Vinci, *Madonna Suckling the Child*, ca. 1520. Oil on panel, 68 × 49 cm. Alte Pinakothek, Munich

expressed. Among the details evident in the Aurora Trust painting that are missing in the others are a figure of Adam carved into the door of the cupboard directly behind the Virgin; the three pears on the top of the cupboard; the branch of cherries held by the Christ Child instead of a spoon; the vase of flowers prominently displayed on the table by the window instead of on the top of the cupboard (holding iris, columbine, pink, pansy, dame's rocket, and stock); the rolled-up cloths revealed in the uncovered basket; and a fully naked Christ Child, not wearing the diaphanous shirt of most of the other examples.

Considered together, these details present the keys to the meaning of this painting, which in general concerns Christ's Incarnation and Redemption of humanity. The Virgin, turning her back on the carved figure of Adam on the cupboard door, is the new Eve; Christ is the new Adam, who in the

nakedness of his human nature holds the fruit of paradise, the cherries, in his right hand. That the path to Redemption comes through sacrifice and sorrow is indicated by the flowers in the vase denoting the Virgin's sorrows and compassion with Christ, and the cloths in the basket, which may signify the winding cloths for Christ's crucified body. A precious devotional book, whose purse cover rests nearby, emphasizes devotional practice as the means by which one achieves salvation.

The message of salvation and redemption is conveyed above all through the imagery of nourishment—the nourishment of the Child by the Virgin and, in turn, of mankind by Christ with his own Body and Blood. For women saints and mystics of the Low Countries, food was a metaphor for interaction with the divine, and it was central to religious practice. The *vitae* of these women are replete with references to the substitution of holy food (the Eucharist) for ordinary eating.[111] They used scriptural passages, especially from the Song of Solomon, to provide the imagery of food and eating that expressed the soul's desire for God; bread, apples, milk—prominently placed in the *Virgin and Child with the Milk Soup* paintings—were symbolic of the Eucharist.

The meaning of the *Virgin and Child with the Milk Soup* appears to be further associated with themes encountered in the writings of women theologians of the later Middle Ages, from Hildegard of Bingen and Elizabeth of Schönau to Catherine of Siena and Julian of Norwich, who used women to symbolize humanity,[112] and mothering "as a description for the nurturing and loving . . . that the soul receives from God. . . ."[113] Mechteld of Magdeburg "treats Mary and Christ as parallel figures, each nursing the soul (with milk and blood respectively),"[114] and the activity of nursing or providing sustenance is a metaphor for the love of God flowing to the soul of man.[115] As Carolyn Walker Bynum expresses it: "What is

new in Julian [of Norwich] is the idea that God's motherhood, expressed in Christ, is not merely love and mercy, not merely redemption through the sacrifice of the cross, but also a taking on of our physical humanity in the Incarnation. . . ."[116] And again, "Thus human nature, fallen in Adam, is taken on, *married,* and redeemed by Christ the bridegroom in Mary's body. It [human nature] is the bride; it is symbolized by the female."[117]

While the Aurora Trust painting appears to express fully the religious, including mystical, fervor of the time, the other versions of the *Virgin and Child with the Milk Soup* are stripped down to the essential details of the everyday and commonplace nourishment of a child by his mother. Gone are the references to the old and new Adam, to the cherries of paradise, to the flower symbolism that denotes the Virgin and her suffering with Christ's Passion. The

297. Leonardo da Vinci, *Madonna and Child with the Cat,* ca. 1478–81. Pen and ink with wash, 12.5 × 10.5 cm. Gabinetto dei Disegni e delle Stampe, Galleria degli Uffizi, Florence (Photo Scala/Art Resource, NY)

298. Leonardo da Vinci, *Madonna and Child with a Bowl of Cherries,* ca. 1478. Pen and ink and over metalpoint, 35 × 25 cm. Musée du Louvre, Paris (Photo © RMN)

child is now modestly clothed and regards his spoon (not underdrawn in any version but added only in the painted layers) with a sense of playful innocence. Although the same meaning discussed above for the Aurora Trust painting may also be implied here, the tone of these other versions is altered. It is less religious and more secular in nature, probably more in keeping with a mass-market interest.

Recently, Susan Ross has argued convincingly that the paintings of the *Virgin and Child with the Milk Soup* and the *Rest on the Flight into Egypt* "represent the secularization of Mary [as] the result of an evolution in the psychological function of Mary as a symbol."[118] Not discriminating between the various versions of the two main themes, she notes that in these paintings toward the end of his career David depicts the Virgin "engaged in her most human function as mother," a deliberate change in mode whose purpose was to "substantiate the evolving order of life on earth." To support her thesis, Ross notes the transitions in the beginning of the sixteenth century in Flanders from a society that "could be described as agrarian, rural and based on a sense of collectivity," to "one which was based on capitalism, urbanization, and . . . individualism." These transitions had a major impact on the family and particularly on the role of women, and the time was one when the Holy Family and especially the loving and nurturing relationship between the Virgin and Child were held up as models for living. Contemporary writings, such as those of Erasmus, More, and Vives, supported the new idea that marriage and a virtuous family life were superior to the formerly highly acclaimed state of celibacy.

David was not alone in expressing this epitome of the virtuous mother by the relationship between Mary and Christ. Joos van Cleve, Quentin Massys, Joachim Patinir, Adriaen Isenbrant, and others developed this theme along similar lines. In this respect David was not only a participant, but also a trendsetter. He moved easily from the tradition of religious painting to the new interest of the clients in more secular depictions, ones that addressed everyday concerns and underscored the fulfillment available to those who embraced family life as a part of good Christian living. As in his novel depiction of landscape in the Mauritshuis panels and the Baptism Triptych, David again anticipated here the rich development of the theme of Mother and Child that became a genre of its own in seventeenth-century Dutch and Flemish painting.

NOTES

1. Friedländer 1924–37, vol. I (1924); Ridderbos 1995, pp. 225–31.

2. Wilson 1991, p. 202.

3. Friedländer 1967–76, vol. XI (1974), p. 47.

4. On the terminology of copies, see Mund 1983, pp. 19–31; for a summary discussion of the issues involved with copies in early Netherlandish painting, see Mund 1994, pp. 125–41, and bibliography on pp. 631–32. For an overview and bibliography concerning the recent investigations into socioeconomic factors relating to the production of art in the Netherlands, see Montias 1990, pp. 358–73, and Montias 1993, pp. 1542–63; for the established south Netherlandish markets, see Wilson 1983, pp. 474–79; Wilson 1986, pp. 1759–66; and Wilson 1990b, pp. 621–27; Ewing 1990, pp. 558–84; Jacobs 1998, pp. 149–65; and Wilson 1998, pp. 163–87.

5. Dijkstra 1990.

6. Toussaert 1963, p. 280.

7. Duclos 1910, pp. 285–88.

8. For a review of the religious institutions of Bruges and their particular devotional practices, see M. P. J. Martens 1992.

9. Sanderus 1641–44, vol. II (1642), pp. 78 ff., listed these relics among those in the collection of the Sint Donaaskerk (see also Toussaert 1963, p. 292).

10. Harbison 1993, p. 106.

11. C. Thelliez, *La merveilleuse image de Notre-Dame de Grâce de Cambrai: Cinq siècles d'histoire* (Cambrai, 1951); A. Begne, *Histoire de Notre-Dame de Grâce, patronne du diocèse de Cambrai* (Cambrai, 1910); Ainsworth 1993b; Belting 1994, pp. 438–41.

12. For a discussion of this and further copies made by other artists and the literature on the subject, see Mund 1994, pp. 125–41.

13. Belting 1994, p. 268.

14. Wilson 1995c, pp. 132–46.

15. Ainsworth 1994c, pp. 72–78.

16. For examples, see Shorr 1954, Type 3, pp. 20–23. In the Netherlandish versions the orb replaces the Greek rotulus held by the Child.

17. The documents were first published by L. van Hasselt, "Het necrologium van het Karthuizer-Klooster Nieuwlicht

of Bloemendaal buiten Utrecht," *Bijdragen en mededeelingen van det historisch Genootschap, gevestigd te Utrecht* 9 (1886), pp. 201–2; H. J. J. Scholtens, "Jan van Eyck's 'H. Maagd met den Kartuizer' en de Exeter-Madonna te Berlijn," *Oud Holland* 55 (1938), pp. 49–62, esp. p. 51; Ainsworth 1994c, pp. 72–78.

18. For the most recent discussion, bibliography, and illustration, see Ainsworth 1994c, pp. 102–6.

19. Ainsworth 1994c, pp. 126–30, n. 18; van Asperen de Boer in Ainsworth 1995, pp. 115–21; D. Martens 1995b, pp. 29–31; and *Sammlung Stroganoff Leningrad,* Rudolph Lepke's Kunst-Auctions-Haus, Katalog 2043 (Berlin, 1931), pp. 10–11, cat. no. 17.

20. For the identification of the Master of the André Madonna as the Master of the Évora Altarpiece, a Bruges follower of David's, see D. Martens 1995c, pp. 211–22; this master replaces the orb in the Christ Child's hand with an apple, probably as a result of subtle changes in meaning already introduced in the Budapest version by Petrus Christus, in which Adam and Eve appear as sculptures in the arch surrounding the new Adam and Eve, i.e., the Virgin and Christ Child.

21. Eisler 1989, pp. 146–50.

22. The provenance of the painting is private collection, Madrid; Abelardo Linares, S.A., Madrid, ca. 1940; Charles B. Wrightsman collection, New York, 1962; donated to the MMA in 1977. For discussion and related bibliography, see van Miegroet 1989, pp. 246, 251, 254, 304, cat. no. 38.

23. For many examples, see Shorr 1954, pp. 38–44. Recently, I have benefitted from discussions with Stanton Thomas and Hugo van der Velden, who are both working on the influence of Byzantine icons in Netherlandish painting. For initial discussions of this, see Harbison 1991, pp. 158–67, and Harbison 1993, pp. 157–66; see also Silver 1983, pp. 95–104.

24. Lasareff 1938, pp. 42–46; Belyaev 1930, pp. 386–94.

25. Shorr 1954, esp. pp. 38–44, for the *Eleousa* type; see also the entries on this type by K.-A. Wirth in *Reallexikon zur deutschen Kunstgeschichte* (Stuttgart, 1958), vol. IV, cols. 1297–1307, and by M. Restle in *Lexikon der Marienkunde* (Regensburg, 1967), vol. I, cols. 1550–1554. A provocative article suggests that Netherlandish artists precisely copied not only the motifs, but also the style of Byzantine icons (C. Périer-d'Ieteren, "Une Copie de Notre-Dame de Grâce de Cambrai aux Musées Royaux de Belgique à Bruxelles," *Bulletin des Musées Royaux des Beaux-Arts de Belgique* 3–4 [1968], pp. 111–14).

26. Silver 1983, p. 101.

27. Harbison 1993, pp. 158–59, referring to Toussaert 1963, p. 272.

28. Comte de Laborde, *Les Ducs de Bourgogne: Étude sur les lettres, les arts et de l'industrie pendant le XVe siècle et plus particulièrement dans les Pays Bas et le Duché de Bourgogne* (Paris, 1851), vol. II, p. 240, no. 4079, and p. 265, no. 4249.

29. See Purtle (1982, pp. 157–67) on the interpretation of this image.

30. Contemporaneous with Van Eyck's painting, to judge by its technique (studied recently at I.R.P.A., Brussels) and its early dendrochronological date, estimated by Peter Klein as sometime after the tree's felling date of 1419 (published in

P. Sutton et al., *Prized Possessions: European Paintings from Private Collections of Friends of the Museum of Fine Arts, Boston,* no. 50 [Boston, 1992], pp. 152–53), and unlikely to be from the Bouts group in the 15th century, as Silver suggests (1983, pp. 95–104).

31. See C. W. Dutschke et al., *Guide to Medieval and Renaissance Manuscripts in the Huntington Library,* vol. 2 (San Marino, 1989), p. 410, where the image accompanies a text of the Fifteen Joys of the Virgin.

32. Gemäldegalerie, Berlin, no. 525B, on oak, 57 × 41 cm.

33. The copy is now in a private collection in Portugal (or possibly Spain), having been sold at Sotheby's, London, Dec. 14, 1977, lot no. 155A (72.5 × 46.5 cm). I am particularly indebted to Mme Gothgebergh at the Institut Royal du Patrimoine Artistique, Brussels, who shared with me the results of the examination of this painting in May of 1997.

34. Sold at Christie's, New York, Jan. 11, 1995, lot 43 (22.8 × 17.4 cm), Galerie Edel, London, German collection; for shrine Madonnas and the emphasis on pilgrimage travel, see Falkenburg 1988.

35. For the relationship between David's *Virgin and Child with Four Angels* and the Master of the André Madonna *Madonna Standing in an Arch,* see Eisler 1989, pp. 146–50, no. 17, and esp. D. Martens (1995a, pp. 33–46), who refutes the common assumption that the André Madonna must derive from David's painting. Indeed, it is possible, because of the details of the architecture depicted, that the two derive not one from the other but from a common model (D. Martens 1995a, p. 45) available in Bruges. Martens has not referred to the information from the technical investigation of the paintings (see Eisler 1989, p. 148, for the Thyssen painting), which shows that the angels in the Thyssen picture were added on top of the completed floor, perhaps as an afterthought, rather than planned at the outset, as in the case of David's painting. In addition, David added the Renaissance columns and capitals on top of the archway in a further development beyond the André Master's painting. Didier Martens (1995c, pp. 211–22) has identified the André Madonna Master as the Master of the Évora Altarpiece, perhaps an artist working in David's workshop. If this was the case, the two paintings may well have been produced side by side from a common model for the setting, in order to accommodate two clients who wanted different Madonna icons in the same locally recognizable setting.

36. See M. P. J. Martens 1992, pp. 331–32, for a review of patronage there.

37. Scholtens 1938, as in note 17 above.

38. On the issue of archaism in early Netherlandish painting, see Panofsky 1953, vol. I, pp. 350–51, 351 n. 7; Silver 1983, pp. 95–104; Blacksberg 1991, pp. 57–66; Belting 1994, pp. 432–42; Koerner 1993, p. 122 ff.; and van Miegroet 1989, pp. 95, 100, 102, 103, 105, 110, 139 nn. 1 and 2, 140 nn. 44–47 and 51.

39. Herzog (as in Purtle 1982, p. 146) cites numerous examples in which Mary in a niche is represented as the personification of the church. David may have intended to allude to this tradition, as he added a column at each side of the composition, perhaps further equating the Virgin with

the columns that uphold the church. This comes from the exegesis of Honorius of Autun on Ecclesiasticus 24:15, who says: "Sion is referred to as a tower, and is the Church, in which the Mother of God is established as a column by its writings and preaching: For on her life, most worthy of praise, the entire Church rests supported." (Honorius of Autun, *Sigillum B. Mariae* [Migne PL, vol. 172, col. 498], quoted in Purtle 1982, p. 147).

40. Lievens–de Waegh 1991, vol. 1, pp. 106–27, and Ainsworth 1996, pp. 149–58.

41. See Friedländer 1967–76, vol. VIb (1971), pl. 37, no. 10; pl. 41, no. 11; pl. 102, no. 59; pl. 104, no. 60; pl. 105, no. 61; pl. 108, no. 65; pl. 128, no. 104.

42. Purtle 1982, p. 152; Panofsky (1953, p. 415) notes that the connection between the Coronation of the Virgin and the espousal imagery of the Canticle was further formalized by the text of the Vulgate.

43. Wilkens 1969, p. 53.

44. On the development of the cult of the rosary, see T. Esser, *Unserer lieben Frauen Rosenkranz* (Paderborn, 1889), and H. Thurston, "Our Popular Devotions: II, The Rosary," *The Month, A Catholic Magazine* 96 (1900), pp. 403–18, 513–27, 620–37, and ibid., 97 (1901), pp. 67–79, 172–88, 286–304, 383–404; and Wilkens 1969.

45. Destroyed by the iconoclasts in 1578; for a brief history and references, see M. P. J. Martens 1992, pp. 331–42.

46. Previously thought to be Sint Donaaskerk, by A. Janssens de Bisthoven (letter of Oct. 22, 1968, in the files of the European Paintings Department, MMA), an opinion that was repeated in the literature until now. D. Martens (1995a, pp. 29–55, esp. pp. 39–45) has convincingly argued for the identification of Sint Jakobskerk instead.

47. M. Comblen-Sonkes, *Les Musées de l'Institut de France,* Les primitifs flamands, I: Corpus de la peinture des anciens Pays-Bas méridionaux au quinzième siècle 15 (Brussels, 1988), p. 131.

48. This is not a geographically accurate view but one composed of important known architecture in Bruges, perhaps relating to the details of the commission. On the meaning of identifiable architecture in paintings, see Harbison 1995b, pp. 21–34, and response by M. P. J. Martens in Ainsworth 1995, pp. 44–46, and D. Martens, as in note 46 above.

49. Von Simson 1953, pp. 9–16, esp. pp. 11–14; Hedeman 1995, p. 196.

50. Levi d'Ancona 1977, p. 105.

51. K. Lipffert, *Symbol-Fibel* (Kassel, 1964), p. 57.

52. On visions, see Camille 1989, pp. 233–35; Harbison 1993, pp. 157–66; and D. Freedberg, *The Power of Images* (Chicago, 1989), pp. 283–316.

53. The painting appears in the 1523 inventory of the possessions of Margaret of Austria, where it is described as "fort antique." This intriguing notation raises the question of whether "fort antique" meant an ancient motif, as in the case of Byzantine icons. For a discussion of the inventory, see Eichberger 1996, pp. 258–79.

54. See discussion in chap. 1. A similar minimal underdrawing, mostly restricted to the contours of the main figure

of Saint Michael, exists in David's Saint Michael Altarpiece (Kunsthistorisches Museum, Vienna), which appears to have been modeled after a print source or manuscript illumination.

55. The underdrawing for the crowning angels here (illus. in Ainsworth 1985, pl. 20) is very similar to the underdrawing of the Virgin in the Frankfurt *Annunciation* (see Sander 1993, p. 239; fig. 150) of ca. 1506.

56. The attribution to David of this painting has not been uniformly accepted. Previously, objections have been raised by Colin Eisler, Julius Held, and Charles Sterling (letters in the archive files of the European Paintings Department, MMA). The date suggested here is not in conflict with the dendrochronological results; Peter Klein has determined that the earliest possible felling date of the tree used for the panel here is 1492 (see Appendix B).

57. On exchanges between Bohemian and Netherlandish artists, see M. S. Frinta, "Bohemian Painting vis-à-vis Southern Netherlands," in *Flanders in a European Perspective: Manuscript Illumination Around 1400 in Flanders and Abroad,* M. Smeyers and B. Cardon, eds. (Leuven, 1995), pp. 74–91.

58. Van Miegroet 1989, pp. 282–83, no. 11.

59. Ainsworth 1993b.

60. Ringbom 1984, pp. 29–30.

61. The former is illustrated here by the kindness of a private collector in Spain. The latter is in the Robert Lehman Collection; see Wolff 1998, cat. no. 22 (including an illustration of the underdrawing), and Ainsworth and Christiansen 1998, cat. no. 77.

62. Thanks to Peter Berkes, chief restorer at the Öffentliche Kunstsammlung, Basel (letter of Sept. 12, 1995), and to Peter Eikemeier, curator of paintings at the Bayerische Staatsgemäldesammlungen, Munich (letter of Sept. 25, 1995), for information concerning these paintings in the Basel and Munich collections. In the Munich examples, in a few places, the underdrawn lines have beaded up here and there, looking like pouncing, although the strokes are certainly continuous.

63. The provenance of this painting is as follows: Spain; Otto H. Kahn, New York; Duveen, New York; Benjamin Altman, New York. For a review of the pertinent literature, but confusion about the relationship of the left and right position of the paintings in the diptych, see van Miegroet 1989, pp. 102–3; 282–83, no. 11b; see also Ainsworth and Christiansen 1998, cat. no. 76.

64. Ainsworth and Christiansen 1998, cat. no. 76, and Upton House, *The Bearsted Collection: Pictures* (London, 1964), pp. 46–47.

65. See the report of Renate Woudhuysen-Keller, *The First Ten Years: The Examination and Conservation of Paintings, 1977 to 1987, The Hamilton Kerr Institute Bulletin* 1, pp. 112–13; see fig. 3 for state after cleaning and before restoration. I am very grateful to Sarah Staniforth and Oliver Lane for permission and help in studying the *Virgin and Child* painting at Upton House in Sept. 1995.

66. See Wilson 1998, pp. 13–84.

67. Ibid., p. 168.

68. Ibid., p. 174.

69. Ibid., p. 195. Isenbrant may have sold his paintings through the Antwerp salesman Marc Bonnet, who rented stalls at the Bruges *pandt* during the period 1520–21 and 1531–32 (Wilson 1995a, p. 2).

70. By Friedländer 1967–76, vol. VIb (1971), pp. 107–8, nos. 212, 214 (without discussion); by Mundy 1981–82, pp. 211–22, and van Miegroet 1989, pp. 301–3.

71. On the art market in the southern Netherlands, esp. in Bruges and Antwerp, see Van Houtte 1967, pp. 77–92; Wilson 1990b, pp. 621–27; Wilson 1983, pp. 476–79, Wilson 1998; Ewing 1990, pp. 558–84; for an overview, see Campbell 1976, pp. 188–98; Montias 1990, pp. 358–73; Montias 1993, pp. 1541–61.

72. Campbell 1976, pp. 188–98; see also Montias 1990, pp. 368–69, for a review of these issues.

73. See Montias 1990, p. 369; see also Goddard 1985, pp. 401–17, and Jacobs 1989, pp. 207–29.

74. See Campbell 1976, p. 198; Wilson 1995a, p. 2.

75. Campbell 1976, p. 194; Wilson 1983, pp. 476–79.

76. Suggested by Dirk De Vos 1988, p. 142, and Ainsworth 1990, p. 652.

77. Ainsworth 1993a, pp. 20–26 and chap. 1.

78. Wilson 1990a, pp. 523–27; Wilson 1991, pp. 191–206; Wilson 1995a, pp. 1–17; and Wilson 1998, pp. 105–10.

79. To my knowledge, no previous author has suggested other than that these versions were all made at the same time. In the date of the Rest paintings, van Miegroet (1989, pp. 242–46, 301–4) must either be used with extreme caution or disregarded, as the discussions in the text and entries are confused as far as the versions are concerned, and many of the accompanying illustrations are misidentified.

80. This suggested date is not incompatible with the results of dendrochronological studies carried out by Peter Klein, which indicate that the earliest felling date of the tree used for the painting is 1490; storage and seasoning of the wood before painting may account for another ten years (see Appendix B).

81. Thanks to John Hand, Catherine Metzger, and Kristi Dahm for their kind assistance and permission to study the Washington painting and record the underdrawing in it.

82. Molly Faries noted this in the course of her examination of the painting for the National Gallery, Washington, systematic catalogue, Hand and Wolff 1986, p. 63.

83. Wilson 1983, pp. 60–64, 212–13; these are listed in Hand and Wolff 1986, p. 67, n. 13; Wilson 1998, pp. 104–10.

84. I studied these in July 1991 through the kind permission of Marina Cano and with the assistance of Ronda Kasl. Illustrated in Friedländer 1967–76, vol. XI (1974), pl. 132, no. 174a, and pl. 136, no. 183a. Infrared reflectography results are housed in the Sherman Fairchild Paintings Conservation Department, MMA.

85. For permission to study and to document the underdrawing in these paintings in the Alte Pinakothek, Munich, I am very grateful to Peter Eikemeier, curator of early Netherlandish painting, and to Hubert von Sonnenburg, then director of the Doerner Institute.

86. Dendrochronology by Peter Klein indicates a felling date for the tree from which the panel for the painting came of 1499, with an additional ten years added for storage and seasoning of the wood (see Appendix B).

87. At an earlier point in researching this question, I described the ends of loaded pen or brushstrokes here as indications of pouncing (Ainsworth 1985, p. 54). Further examination of this issue has shown no evidence whatsoever of pouncing in this example.

88. Acc. nos. 47 and 1904–CE, respectively.

89. Wilson noted this in 1991, pp. 191–206, and Wilson 1998, pp. 93–103.

90. Wilson (1998, pp. 102, 202) has identified four other related variants of this half-length *Virgin and Child*.

91. Discussed by M. Ainsworth at Colloque 12 of "Le dessin sous-jacent dans la peinture" (publication forthcoming 1999).

92. More fully discussed in Ainsworth 1997a, pp. 103–8.

93. Ibid., for discussion of Isenbrant's *Mass of Saint Gregory* in the Getty Museum. See also Wilson 1998, pp. 110–11, 129.

94. My sincere thanks to Dr. Theo Jülich and A. Wiesman Emerling for checking the details of the Darmstadt painting with a tracing of the Philadelphia version.

95. Wilson 1991, pp. 191–206, and Wilson 1998, pp. 163–87.

96. See Wilson 1990b, p. 626, for theories about artists' motivations and aims in creating their products for sale.

97. For a review of the literature on this series and earlier discussion of the technical results of the study, including the discovery of a cartoon transfer in all known versions, see Comblen-Sonkes 1974–80, pp. 29–42. In addition to the examples cited by Comblen-Sonkes are ones in Seville (A. M. Mendoza et al., *Museo de bellas artes de Sevilla* [Seville, 1984], p. 91, cat. no. 83); in the Accademia Carrara, Bergamo (inv. 1041); in an unknown location, but available in a photo in the Getty Archive, Los Angeles (Douwes Photo Archive, under "Gerard David"); in the Musée des Beaux-Arts, Strasbourg; one formerly in the collection of Dr. Joseph Uyttenhove of Koekelaere (sold at auction, Palais Royal des Beaux-Arts, Brussels, Oct. 26–27, 1983). For the opportunity to study and document the underdrawing in the examples of the Aurora Trust in Genoa and in Brussels, I am very grateful to the following curators or owners in charge of these works: Gerald Stiebel, Laura Tagliaferro, Eliane de Wilde, and Françoise Robert-Jones, and certain others who wish to remain anonymous.

98. Unfortunately, dendrochronology has not yet been carried out on any of the known versions of the *Virgin and Child with the Milk Soup*.

99. For useful discussions about attitudes toward the copy, see *Studies in the History of Art* 20 (1989), devoted to questions of originals, copies, and reproductions. A case study for 15th-century depictions, namely Dieric Bouts's *Virgin and Child*, is found in Ainsworth 1993b.

100. See Stroo and Syfer-d'Olne 1996, pp. 165–73, esp. p. 170, for an example of the Bruges School that copies a prototype of a Virgin and Child by Rogier van der Weyden. More recently, I have observed this same phenomenon in a copy (probably contemporary) from a private collection in South America of the MMA *Virgin and Child* by Jan Gossaert (I am grateful to Otto Naumann, Ltd., for an opportunity to

study this painting in August 1997). N.B. The X-radiograph of the Genoa version of the *Virgin and Child* does not reveal clear information about its technique because of the marbleized reverse, which blocks the X-rays.

101. For example, in the Uffizi *Lamentation,* modeled after a composition by Fra Angelico; see Davies 1972, p. 212.

102. Ainsworth 1994c, pp. 60–62 and chap. 4.

103. For Massys's art, see Silver 1984, pp. 78-79, 177–88; for Joos van Cleve, see Hand 1978, pp. 192–215 passim, esp. pp. 212–15, and Scailliérez 1991, pp. 44–61, esp. pp. 57–61. For general remarks on the influence of Leonardo's art in Antwerp, see Sulzberger 1955b, pp. 105–11, and Marlier 1967, pp. 25–27.

104. Inv. no. 68 in the Galleria Lochis, illustrated in G. Frizzoni, *Le gallerie dell'accademia Carrara in Bergamo* (Bergamo, 1907), p. 131; and in F. Rossi, *Accademia Carrara Bergamo: Catalogo dei dipinti* (Bergamo, 1979), p. 95.

105. The most thorough discussion may be found in H. Pauwels, "Een nieuwe toeschrijving aan Ambrosius Benson," in *XLIII Congres Sint-Niklaas-Waas 1974 Annalen* (Sint-Niklaas, 1975), pp. 291–96, with illustrations of seven versions, of which four are attributed to Netherlandish artists in the first decades of the 16th century. To these may be added a drawing in Kupferstichkabinett (KdZ 12315), attributed to a 16th-century Netherlandish master (see E. Bock, Berlin, and J. Rosenberg, *Staatliche Museen zu Berlin: Die niederländischen Meister,* vol. I, text [Frankfurt am Main, 1931], pp. 64–65). See also a mention of a Lombardesque copy after de' Conti's painting in S. Sulzberger, "L'Influence de Leonard de Vinci et ses repercussions à Anvers," *Arte Lombarda* 1 (1955), pp. 105–11,

esp. p. 109 and fig. 4, and other northern versions in the catalogue of the Walker Art Gallery, Liverpool, 1977, p. 142, ill.; and C. M. Woodward and F. Robinson, ed., *A Handbook of the Museum of Art, Rhode Island School of Design* (Providence, R.I., 1985), p. 181.

106. Suida, 1929, p. 272.

107. The Benois Madonna is illus. in K. Clark, *Leonardo da Vinci,* M. Kemp, ed. (London and New York, 1988), fig. 14, p. 61.

108. Schmidt 1910, p. 316, and Reinach 1912, pp. 358–59.

109. See discussion in chap. 2.

110. See Marlier 1967, pp. 25–27; L. Campbell, *The Early Flemish Pictures in the Collection of Her Majesty the Queen* (Cambridge, 1985), pp. 29–30, cat. no. 18, and Hand 1978, pp. 213–15; for versions by Massys, see P. Pieper, *Die deutschen, niederländischen und italienischen Tafelbilder bis um 1530* (Aschendorff Münster, 1986), pp. 506–08. For Joos van Cleve, see Friedländer 1967–76, vol. IXa (1972), pl. 73, no. 58 and pls. 78, 79, nos. 63a–k; for Massys, see Silver 1984, pp. 230–31.

111. Bynum 1987, p. 117.

112. Ibid., p. 264.

113. Ibid., p. 266.

114. Ibid., p. 411, n. 61.

115. Franklin 1978, pp. 101–55, esp. pp. 143–44.

116. Bynum 1987, p. 266.

117. Ibid., p. 268.

118. Read in manuscript; to be published as S. Ross, "Gerard David Models for Motherhood" in *Rutgers Art Review* (forthcoming).

Early Netherlandish painting is generally viewed as conservative in theme and treatment—a period of art that placed little premium on originality, but rather assiduously maintained the status quo. While it is true that the subject matter of art produced at this time demonstrates an adherence to standard themes, certain artists, Gerard David in particular, applied their creative talents to inventing more effective ways to engage the viewer in an impassioned dialogue with the work of art. Such creative impulses could not always be given free rein; painters were, after all, often bound by the patron's specific requirements of theme and presentation. But by David's time, at the end of the fifteenth century, the sale of works of art less often involved an individual contractual agreement between a patron and a painter than it did the artist's accommodation of a diverse and wealthy group of clients who bought paintings on the open market.

This study takes into account changes in the production and marketing of paintings at the turn of the sixteenth century, changes that resulted from a variety of important social and economic factors. A close look at the work of art itself provides a unique opportunity to encounter this development directly, for it is in an artist's working procedures that the first signs of change are evident and that the extent of his departure from traditional approaches can be assessed. It is only logical that these indications should be revealed on the most personal or fundamental level of the artist's endeavor, especially in an age when the final product had to comply with the aesthetics and often conservative taste of the times.

Artistic innovation and progress are not measured here by the end product alone but also by the way in which David arrived at that point. In this regard, shifting tastes, new methods of marketing art, and the changing nature of workshop practice—factors that encouraged artists to introduce new themes and treatments in their paintings—are inextricably bound together in a progressive development that redefined the artist and his role at the turn of the sixteenth century. David's career spans this transitional period, in which the making and the meaning of art were in a state of flux. A significant part of the story of his achievement lies in the way he maneuvered through this time, not as a willing follower, but as an innovative leader.

This book takes up as a challenge Friedländer's assumption that, given "that David's art is set by the co-ordinates of time and place, as well as by individual endowment, itself colored by time, place and ethnic origin, . . . there is no possible way in which this complex of forces at work can be unravelled."[1] An examination of the historical and visual facts that takes into account David's working practices has now attempted to do just that—to unravel the complex forces at work in David's notable career.

A premise of this investigation is that the fundamental character of Gerard David's artistic development and progressive tendencies may be rediscovered through the details of his working methods. A close look at his extant drawings and a comparison of them with his approach to a given painting—its emerging form—have yielded new information. The drawings themselves provide keys to the essential nature of his art. David was, above all, interested in the power of various types of physiognomy and individual expression to convey the mood and meaning of a painting, and he intended to involve the viewer in his subject matter by portraying locally familiar types and sites. The drawings he made of heads and hands attest to his reliance on life studies to imbue his work with a sense of contemporary experience. David added to these studies images he recorded from the paintings of his revered predecessors, notably Jan van Eyck, not to copy certain motifs slavishly and to incorporate them into his own compositions, but to study more intimately the vision of the art of his north Netherlandish predecessors with whom he shared a certain aesthetic bond. David also gave equal importance to the settings for his scenes and made drawings after nature as source material for the realistic environments he created for his paintings. These lifelike renderings were merged with standard compositional formulas that could be instantly recognized by the viewer, thus effecting immediate rapport with the image.

The fortuitous survival of some twenty drawings by Gerard David and his workshop allows for this first in-depth analysis of the function they served. Given the paucity of extant sheets by the leading early Netherlandish painters, this investigation provides a unique opportunity to study the habitual working methods of at least one of these artists. The comparison of these drawings with the underdrawings in David's paintings shows the co-existence, on a routine basis, of repeated motifs and new designs. This phenomenon is exemplified in David's underdrawings, where meticulous, fixed renderings in pen or brush of stock-figure types stand side by side with free sketches in black chalk of new design elements. The employment of set patterns for paintings indicates not only an efficient use of the artist's energies for repeated themes, but also the initial stages of strategies to increase the production of paintings for the open market in a period when individual commissions were decreasing. At the end of David's career, pricked cartoons for the transfer of entire compositions came into use for the first time, offering a clear sign of the accelerated production of certain "best-sellers" that were in high demand.

Case studies of David's two most securely documented works—the *Justice of Cambyses* of 1498 and the *Virgin among Virgins* of 1509—indicate the poles of his style rather than provide the common features of the artist's working technique. The *Justice* panels must have presented a considerable challenge not simply in the initial representation of this unusual theme but also in the substantial revisions that became necessary, probably owing as much to the request of the client as to David's own initiative. The seamless intermingling of the chief protagonists of the Cambyses narrative with portraits of Bruges's city

aldermen provides a realistic sense of the contemporary relevance of the ancient tale and its admonition. Certain modifications of the two *Cambyses* panels were dictated by an apparent interest in keeping the meaning of the work current—especially by depicting locally identifiable sites and probably newly elected aldermen. Indeed, David further updated the panels to include the coats of arms of Philip the Handsome and his new wife, Joanna the Mad, in order to show the city's allegiance to the new rulers of the Netherlands. A close look at other revisions in these pictures clearly indicates the progress of David's stylistic change during the last decade of the fifteenth century, as he turned for inspiration from Dieric Bouts to Hans Memling at a time when David may have hoped to fill the prominent position vacated by Memling at his death in 1494. The work on the *Justice* panels is one of the first manifestations of David's keen entrepreneurial sense in attempting to garner his share of Bruges's business and to develop his reputation through high-profile civic projects.

David's interest in making current, approachable, and timely the communication of an age-old theme must have been among the primary motivations for his novel treatment of the *Virgin among Virgins*. In the tightly cropped and densely packed image of the virgins for the high altar of the Convent of Sion, David eliminated all sense of narrative or conventional setting, instead merging the picture space with the viewer's own space. Moreover, in his efforts to make this a living scene—a kind of tableau vivant—he individualized the virgins in a way that, if they are not portraits of actual sisters in the convent, they appear to be. David further blurred the line between sacred and secular by including his own image and that of his wife as donors fully present as part of the assembly of holy figures, albeit at the fringes of the composition. The interrelationship of the making and the meaning of his work is unmasked by a technical examination of this painting, which shows David's plan, through the underdrawing of the figures, both to experiment with a new type of undermodeling in the creation of ever more dramatic lighting effects and to focus the strongest illumination on his own image. This subtle contrivance boldly asserts his own presence, not so much to underscore his spiritual connection to the holy figures present as to highlight his prominent standing within the elite society that had close connections to the Convent of Sion. A hint of the change in David's self-awareness as an artist is evident by a comparison of his tentative, unobtrusive presence looking out at the observer from the far left edge of the *Arrest of Sisamnes* to his bold, self-confident demeanor nearly a decade later in the *Virgin among Virgins*.

The route from David's origins in the north Netherlands to his mature phase in the community of Bruges artists can be traced through his early works, key panels of which are in the Metropolitan Museum's collection. An investigation into the production of David's early paintings has revealed his consistent reliance through the turn of the century on the lessons of the art of Dieric Bouts, not of Hugo van der Goes, as has been previously supposed. To some extent visually apparent in the final product, the signs of Bouts's influence are even more obvious in the underdrawings of David's paintings, as demonstrated in the Budapest *Nativity*, the *Arrest of Sisamnes* panel in the *Justice of Cambyses* of 1498, and even in the Frick *Deposition* of about 1500. All suggest that David worked for a period of time in Bouts's Leuven workshop before arriving in Bruges as a master in 1484. Although David often started with Bouts's lessons in mind, he never imitated his models but instead reworked them during the painting process, thereby converting them into his own idiom.

Apart from David's most important commission of his first period in Bruges, the *Justice of Cambyses* panels, which must have taken a long time to complete, there was a certain amount of rather routine work. Except for examples such as the *Adoration of the Magi* or the Sedano Triptych, the extant paintings show little sign of having been commissioned works. From this we might draw the conclusion that David was still in the process of building his reputation and artistic presence in Bruges, an effort that ultimately led to a number of important commissions in the first decade of the sixteenth century.

The routine output of these early years comprises mostly small-scale works, which are rather conservative in their treatment of standard themes. Certain subjects—the Nativity and the Lamentation among them—were especially popular, and David apparently produced multiple versions, which were available for ready sale directly from his workshop or on the open market. At this point David had an efficient working procedure that combined the use of standard patterns along with newly introduced modes of representation, a fact evident in the underdrawings of his paintings, where meticulously rendered, fixed designs are juxtaposed with David's free sketches in black chalk for his more experimental additions.

Some of the works from this initial phase reveal David's willing accommodation of his patron's wishes—for example, to paint in the style of Hugo van der Goes (as in his copy of Hugo's *Adoration of the Magi*) or of Jan van Eyck and Hans Memling (as in the Sedano Triptych). Occasionally, he put aside his nascent interest in landscape painting in order to accommodate a triptych perhaps originally conceived with a sculpted centerpiece (as in the Lehman Passion wings). David continued on a course to develop and adopt new methods of working. Instead of using the traditional tüchlein technique for his great *Deposition*, he proceeded with the paint-layer structure as if working on panel, thereby contributing an early example of oil technique on canvas. In paintings from the turn of the century David began to use broader brushstrokes and washes in his underdrawing for the undermodeling of his figures, as in the *Resurrection* panel of the Passion wings, and he increasingly sought ways to include aspects of the visible world to elicit viewer response to the theme at hand.

By the last decade of the fifteenth century David was well aware of the substantial economic power of the foreign community of merchants and bankers in Bruges and the business advantage to be gained by catering to them. The keen taste of Italian and Spanish nationals for Netherlandish painting had been well established early on, when the rulers of the southern European territories sought out the paintings and the painters of the north to decorate their palaces and villas in emulation of the extravagant court life of the Burgundian dukes.

As a number of David's paintings of this decade—several of the Lamentation and the Nativity, and possibly the Frick *Deposition*—have an Italian or Spanish provenance, it is most likely that David produced paintings for export during his early days in Bruges. This clearly developed into a specialized production in which he catered to this group by adapting his style to their expectations and specifications, namely in the Sedano Triptych, the Saint Anne Altarpiece, and the Cervara Altarpiece.

This is a stylistically diverse group of works ranging from the 1490s to 1506, and their individual variations or departures from David's standard practice can probably be explained by the stipulations of the commission, the details of which in each case are lost to us today. It is in the technical investigations of these works that David's particular means of accommodating his clients becomes more apparent.

David's overture to the Sedano Triptych on its exterior wings—copies of Adam and Eve from the Ghent Altarpiece—was distinctly Eyckian, as was the Virgin and Child panel on the interior, which is borrowed from Jan van Eyck's *Virgin and Child with Saints and Canon van der Paele*. These models were studied from the originals and carried over in the underdrawing in David's meticulous rendering of fixed designs, while the saints and the donors were prepared with a free-hand sketch in black chalk. Evidence of reworking in the head of the Virgin shows David's attempts to approximate the Virgin type of Jan van Eyck, a type quite unlike his own from those same years. This "Van Eyck" was brought up to date by the addition of swags and putti à la Memling. Whether or not by specific request of the client (which is most likely the case given the considerable popularity of works by Van Eyck in the client's native Castile), this conflation of Van Eyck and Memling also served David's purpose. In not too subtle a fashion, he suggested, by emulating his great predecessors in Bruges, his own candidacy as their successor.

Close examination of other paintings made for export, namely the Saint Anne Triptych and the Cervara Altarpiece, helps us to differentiate a less prestigious commission, produced with workshop participation (the Saint Anne Altarpiece), from one that was tailor-made to fit the site and liturgical requirements of a renowned Benedictine abbey. The study of these two commissions reveals a variable quality of execution within a single workshop at roughly the same time, probably as a result of the details of the commission, the available information about the destined site, and the amount to be paid for the job at its completion. On the one hand, in the Saint Anne Altarpiece David relied on stock patterns available in the atelier that could be executed by assistants under his guidance. The Cervara Altarpiece, on the other hand, was considerably more complex in its format, involving a conflation of northern and Italian modes. Its production required careful planning and execution and the development of new motifs. In its final form, the Cervara Altarpiece is the crowning achievement of David's career, a testimony to the extent to which he would satisfy his client's demands.

An added benefit of the commission for the Cervara Altarpiece was David's probable first hand acquaintance with Italian art, which he incorporated into this altarpiece and which he continued to assimilate into his work before its widespread introduction into Netherlandish painting. David's adoption of Italianate motifs and modes of representation was subtle; he took inspiration from them and merged them with his own northern sensibility. Lombard types, such as Bernardino de' Conti's *Virgin and Child*, are not exactly copied for David's *Virgin and Child with the Milk Soup*. Instead, the essence of the Italian model's setting and the poses and modeling of the figures were taken over and transformed. In this way David's introduction of Italian art in the north was less conspicuous than the later efforts of Massys, whose insertion of Leonardo's grotesque types into his paintings was a more direct and obvious borrowing.

Concurrent with David's attempts to fulfill his client's requirements were endeavors of his own to advance effective communication of the theme of his paintings to the viewer. A principal area of this effort was in landscape painting, a genre dramatically advanced by David's startling new conception. The interior, naturalistic setting of the splendid Baptism Triptych, which takes the viewer's position into account, was only a prelude to David's most novel achievement in this genre on the outside wings of the Nativity Triptych. The idea of presenting a lush forest view devoid of human presence was unprecedented in panel painting at the time. However, it was not without its roots, and David may be considered as both the inheritor of this genre and a product of his own times in its representation.

The concept of pure landscape or the dominance of landscape in northern painting had its origins where David's artistic career likely began, in the region around Haarlem. There is a direct line of descent from its incipient stages in the fourteenth century through the art of Aelbert Ouwater, Geertgen tot Sint Jans, and Dieric Bouts in the latter part of the fifteenth century. Whatever David's early exposure to these artistic strains was, his interest in landscape must have been reawakened as he became acquainted with its form in the Ghent Altarpiece by the Van Eyck brothers and with examples from the Leuven workshop of Dieric Bouts. At the same time, following on certain pioneering efforts of such artists as Simon Marmion, artists of the Ghent-Bruges school of manuscript illumination began to experiment increasingly with the expressive possibilities of landscape in miniatures. David's close connection to both north Netherlandish panel painters and south Netherlandish manuscript illuminators provided a solid foundation for his own development of the genre.

In David's preoccupation with the effective communication of the theme, he did not give in to nature's raw, unkempt side but instead developed a well-ordered presentation, exploiting the symbolic possibilities of individual species, along with the power of nature to express a serene environment for spiritual renewal and meditation. He adopted an integral approach in which he combined patterns of plants from model-book sources (herbals, perhaps) and his own nature studies. His unique achievement was the creation of a natural environment that, if not real, seemed real. David took pains to represent the indigenous forms of nature in the environs of Bruges—not the world-view landscapes of Patinir in nearby Antwerp—so that his viewers would find immediate rapport with the image, thus facilitating their participation in the religious theme. The type and specific form of these landscapes were familiar from painting to painting, so that the contemporary viewer could continue with the Holy Family from the Nativity to the Rest on the Flight into Egypt as a kind of pilgrimage of life, empathizing completely (as was the mode of the Devotio Moderna) with the trials and tribulations of Christ.

These novel depictions of standardized themes created a certain product identity for David and his workshop at a time when there was increasing demand for paintings to be mass-produced for sale on the open market. Such products, however, must be differentiated from other copies that were made on commission as replicas of a revered icon believed to have been endowed with special powers, such as the *Virgin and Child with Four Angels*. The close study of various copies produced by David and his workshop allows us to place them in the context of individual commissions or for the purpose of the marketplace. Previously considered as equivocal by Friedländer, and all those of a given composition to have been produced at the same time, it is now possible with closer scrutiny (including technical investigation and dendrochronology) to distinguish one painting from another as to their purpose and moment of creation. This, in turn, provides additional information for rediscovering the impetus behind David's production.

The increasing demand of the open market caused David to alter his working methods and to introduce ways of streamlining the production of his most popular themes, namely the Rest on the Flight into Egypt and the Virgin and Child with the Milk Soup. This was a gradual process that can be traced by a close examination of the paintings themselves. The treatment of the Washington *Rest on the Flight into Egypt*, in its planar spatial construction, restricted depiction of landscape, and emphasis on an isolated event within the narrative, indicates that it was created about 1500 to 1505, a date supported by dendrochronology. The Metropolitan Museum version, however, and the Madrid copy, with their further development of the depth and precise description of landscape (which is now considered as part of a continuous narrative from painting to painting), represent a variation on this theme of about a decade later. The Madrid panel already shows signs of a reduction of form for streamlined manufacturing and the further restriction of the sacred essence of the painting in favor of a more profane—and perhaps more marketable—thematic treatment. It was this latter version that served as the model for the mass-production of paintings by David's followers. In these cases, the increased use of pounced underdrawings demonstrates an intensified mode of pattern standardization and duplication.

It was a short step to the implementation of streamlined production methods in David's own atelier. In moving from the religious to the more secular in theme, David produced a series of the *Virgin and Child with the Milk Soup*, each from the same cartoon (or a similar template). Although one in the series, the Aurora Trust version, provides a particular combination of motifs for a more sacred reading, the others of the group pare down the composition to the bare essentials, producing an idealized image of a mother nurturing her child, not necessarily the Virgin feeding the Christ Child. These newly altered features of both the making and the meaning of David's art respond to the increasingly powerful impetus of the open market.

Far from being exemplary of the "last flowering of the [Flemish] tradition," as Panofsky had labeled him,[2] David was an innovator of his time. He introduced new themes for paintings and new treatments of traditional subjects in advance of his contemporaries, such as Quentin Massys and Joos van Cleve, who, in certain respects, followed David's lead. Moreover, David employed labor-efficient techniques, thus paving the way for the mass production of paintings motivated by the active sixteenth-century art markets. Herein lie the seeds of development for what would become the standard images and methods of manufacture in seventeenth-century Dutch and Flemish painting.

NOTES

1. Friedländer 1967–76, vol. VIb (1971), p. 98.
2. Panofsky 1953, vol. I, p. 352.

CHRONOLOGY OF DRAWINGS AND PAINTINGS BY GERARD DAVID

This list includes the core works by David, not those by workshop assistants or followers. The numbers in the column at the right correspond to catalogue numbers in van Miegroet 1989, where alternative dates by various authors are discussed. "NI" indicates that the work is not included in his book.

Drawings (ca. 1490–1510)

Paintings

DENDROCHRONOLOGICAL ANALYSES OF PANELS ATTRIBUTED TO GERARD DAVID

by Peter Klein

The dendrochronological analysis of wood panels[1] is an important dating tool in art history, for it allows us to arrive at a *terminus post quem* for a panel painting by indicating the felling date of the tree from which the board or boards that make up the painting were cut. Furthermore, a comparison of the growth-ring series from individual boards often enables us to determine whether or not they come from the same tree. If they do, it may be possible to make an attribution to a particular workshop. Information gathered from the nearly complete oeuvre of a painter may supply art historians with corroborative evidence for issues of attribution and dating.

The methods used in dendrochronological analysis involve measuring the width of the annual rings on a board and comparing the growth-ring curve resulting from this measurement with various dated master chronologies. A fairly precise dating of the panel can be determined on the basis of the specific characteristics of the growth-ring curve and on the geographic origin of the wood.

In preparing oak boards for paintings, panel makers would usually make a radial cut, which produces a cross section of the tree (Figure 1). The bark and the light, perishable sapwood would be cut off, thereby eliminating evidence of the latest growth rings and making a determination of the exact felling year impossible, as only the latest measured growth ring of a board can be used to indicate the exact year.

The estimated number of sapwood rings cut off (and hence to be added in making a calculation of age) may be derived from statistical evaluation. The provenance of the oak[2] is significant in establishing such a statistical basis. The number of sapwood rings varies: a range from seven to fifty rings can be found in trees grown in western Europe, whereas the range is only nine to thirty-six in eastern Europe. This information is significant here, because most of the wood used for Netherlandish panels from the fifteenth century to the middle

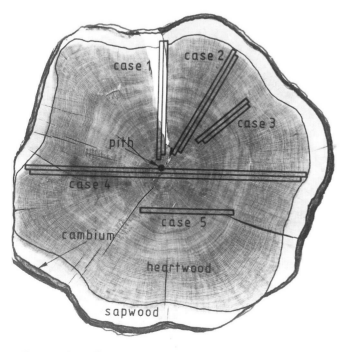

1. Cross section of a tree

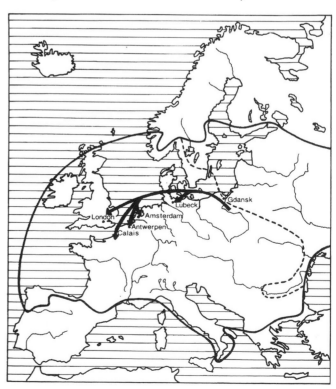

2. Map of Europe indicating sources of oak for panels used by Netherlandish painters

of the seventeenth century originated in the Baltic region (Figure 2).

The number of sapwood rings found in about three hundred oak trees from northern Poland was analyzed, and the result showed a median value of fifteen rings. Fifty percent of all trees had thirteen to nineteen sapwood rings, with a minimum of nine and a maximum of thirty-six. The number of sapwood rings also depends on the age of the tree—that is, a three-hundred-year-old tree generally has more sapwood rings than a tree of one hundred years.

In order to determine the earliest possible felling date, one must add at least nine sapwood rings to the latest growth ring found on a board. Because Netherlandish panel makers normally used trees more than two hundred years old, it is more accurate to add the median number of rings rather than the minimum. Thus, if some of the sapwood is still preserved on the board, the felling date of the tree can be estimated if one adds the median figure of fifteen growth rings to the last heartwood ring, taking into account a span of only minus-two or plus-four years. If a panel is made exclusively of heartwood, however, the felling date of the tree cannot be determined as precisely, because an unknown number of heartwood rings in addition to the sapwood rings may have been cut off the board during the preparation of the panel. Therefore, only the youngest heartwood ring can be determined.

The next step is to determine how much time elapsed between the felling of the tree and the painter's use of the panel. Signed and dated panels of the sixteenth and seventeenth centuries show that most panels were used two to eight years after the tree was cut down. The few signed and dated early Netherlandish paintings from the fifteenth century indicate an average of ten years' seasoning time, but this figure can differ widely from one instance to another.

In spite of these variables, dendrochronological analysis often helps us to date and locate a painting geographically. The examination of Gerard David's panel paintings demonstrates this process clearly (see table). Although the use of sapwood in fifteenth-century panels is very rare, sapwood rings are found on three of the David panels: the *Rest on the Flight into Egypt* (The Metropolitan Museum of Art, New York), the *Lamentation* (Philadelphia Museum of Art), and the *Virgin and Child* (Gemäldegalerie, Berlin). Unfortunately, the two securely dated works by David—the Bruges *Justice of Cambyses* (1498) and the Rouen *Virgin among Virgins* (1509)—have not yet undergone dendrochronological analysis. For those panels studied, one must

therefore apply seasoning times typically used by painters who worked during this period to account for the seasoning times that may have been employed by David.

A series of growth rings for each board is measured and plotted on a graph, creating a unique fingerprint for each tree. Different boards can then be compared and matched to a tree with a similar fingerprint, which permits an attribution to a particular panel workshop. From this information art historians may find corroborative evidence for temporal attributions. For example, while it is impossible to draw specific conclusions about boards from the same tree, the information may suggest that panels could have been available in an artist's workshop simultaneously, which gives further support to similar production dates for different paintings. Keep in mind, however, that different artists may have purchased panels from the same panel workshop and that panels from the same tree may not all have been painted in the same studio. Panels could also sit in an artist's studio for an unspecified period of time before they were used. By evaluating the data from the boards of different panels, one can determine, for example, that board III of the wings depicting the *Archangel Gabriel* (50.145.9a) and the *Virgin* (50.145.9b) in the Metropolitan Museum were cut from the same tree as the board of the Frankfurt *Annunciation* (FFM, 1095), although boards I and II of *Gabriel* and the *Virgin* come from different trees. The boards of the Metropolitan's *Saint John the Baptist* (32.100.40b) and *Saint Francis Receiving the Stigmata* (32.100.40c) come from the same tree.

The panels of the Metropolitan wings depicting *Christ Carrying the Cross* and the *Resurrection* (1975.1.119) come from the same tree. This, of course, means that the versos of those wings, which were cut apart at the beginning of the twentieth century and are also in the Metropolitan, come from the same tree.

Board II of the left wing and boards I and II of the right wing from the Washington Saint Anne Altarpiece were cut from the same tree, although the four boards used in the central panel and the remaining boards I and III from the left wing and board III from the right wing come from different trees.

Furthermore, it can be proved that some boards in other paintings can be attributed to the same tree: boards I and II from the *Adoration of the Magi* (Metropolitan Museum); both boards from the *Rest on the Flight into Egypt* (National Gallery of Art, Washington); all boards from *Saint Anthony, Saint Christopher, Saint Francis,* and *Saint Jerome* (Gemäldegalerie, Berlin);

boards I and III from the *Lamentation* (Art Institute of Chicago,), and boards I and II from *Christ Nailed to the Cross* (National Gallery, London).

The study and evaluation of a large number of panels used by one artist allow evidence for typical workshop practices to emerge. By the statistical analysis of a number of dated and signed paintings, one can establish the period between the felling date of the tree and the creation of a painting. The different regional master chronologies in Europe often permit the determination of the provenance of the trees and, consequently, the origin of the panels. Finally, the information gathered can be compared to dates based on traditional art-historical analysis to provide additional support or contradictions to those conclusions.

NOTES

1. For further information about dendrochronological analysis, see D. Eckstein et al., "New Evidence for the Dendrochronological Dating of Netherlandish Painting," *Nature* 320 (1986), pp. 465–66; and P. Klein, "Dendrochronological Analyses of Panels of Hans Memling and His Contemporaries," in *Memling Studies: Proceedings of the International Colloquium, Bruges, 10–12 November 1994,* edited by H. Verougstraete, R. van Schoute, and M. Smeyers (Leuven, 1997), pp. 287–95.

2. At this time, oak, beech, and some conifers (fir and spruce) can be dated. Linden and poplar cannot be dated because of the lack of reference chronologies.

GERARD DAVID AND FOLLOWERS

Paintings/ Museum, inv.no	wood species	boards	growth rings heartwood/ sapwood	youngest growth ring	earliest felling date	origin of wood/ remarks
Virgin and Child Berlin, B, 573A	Oak	I	149/3	1466	1472	Baltic
Four boards:	Oak					Baltic
Saint Antony		I	127	1452		all boards = same tree
Saint Christopher		I	127	1463		
Saint Francis		I	97	1446		
Saint Jerome Berlin, B, S. 17		I	131	1467	1476	
Bishop and Donor Cambridge, CAM, 1906.6B	Oak	I	290	1468	1477	Baltic
Lamentation Chicago, CHI, 1933.1040	Oak	I	200	1466		Baltic
		II	125	–		I, III = same tree
		III	203	1467	1476	
Portrait of a Monk Cleveland, CLE, 42.632	Oak	I	111	1549	1558	Baltic
Christ Taking Leave of His Mother Dublin, DUB 13	Oak	I	87	1437		Baltic
		II	88	1437		
		III	81	1453	1462	
Saint Jerome Frankfurt, FFM, 1091	Oak	I	180	1443	1452	Baltic
Annunciation Frankfurt, FFM, 1095	Oak	I	228	1475	[1494]	Baltic see NY 50.145.9a
Virgin with the Dead Christ Kreuzlingen, KRE	Oak	I	161	1485	1494	Baltic
The Holy Family Kreuzlingen, KRE	Oak	I	210	1489	1498	Baltic
Canon Bernardinus de Salviatis and Three Saints London, LN, 1045	Oak	I	244	1454		Baltic
		II	176	1472	1481	
		III	163	1461		
		IV	140	1414		
Christ Nailed to the Cross London, LN, 3067	Oak	I	263	1456	1465	Baltic
		II	252	1455		I, II = 1 tree
Crucifixion Madrid, THY, 85	Oak	I	179	1455	1464	Baltic
		II	180	1448		
Adoration of the Magi Munich, MP, 715	Oak	I	224	1475		Baltic
		II	291	1477		
		III	110	1475		
		IV	165	1478	1487	
Virgin and Child Munich, MP, 1080	Pear					wood identification

Paintings/ Museum, inv. no	wood species	boards	growth rings heartwood/ sapwood	youngest growth ring	earliest felling date	origin of wood/ remarks
Crucifixion New York, NY, 09.157	Oak	I II	187 51	1480 –	1489	Baltic
Nativity New York, NY, 32.100.40a	Oak	I	243	1468	1477	Baltic
Saint John the Baptist New York, NY, 32.100.40b	Oak	I	189	1417	[1427]	Baltic see NY 32.100.40c
Saint Francis Receiving the Stigmata New York, NY, 32.100.40c	Oak	I	187	1418	1427	Baltic I, NY 32.100.40b = 1 tree
Rest on the Flight into Egypt New York, NY, 49.7.21	Oak	I	167/5	1495	1499	Baltic
Gabriel New York, NY, 50.145.9a	Oak	I II III	128 231 60	1465 1485 1375	1494	Baltic III, NY 50.145.9b (III), FFM 1095 = 1 tree
Virgin New York, NY, 50.145.9b	Oak	I II III	167 155 84	1475 1474 1315	[1494]	Baltic see NY 50.145.9a
Virgin and Child New York, NY, 1975.1.118	Oak	I	82	1433	1442	Baltic
Christ Carrying the Cross (left wing)	Oak	I	222	1477	[1496]	Baltic NY 1975.1.119, NY 1975.1.120 = 1 tree
Resurrection (right wing) New York, NY, 1975.1.119		I	118	1487	1496	Christ + Angel and Resurrection + Mary = front and reverse side
Gabriel (left wing) Virgin (right wing) New York, NY, 1975.1.120	Oak	I I	231 179	1487 1487	1496 1496	Baltic see NY 1975.1.119
Virgin and Child with Saint Joseph New York, NY, 1975.1.121	Oak	I	160	1321	1330	Baltic
Virgin and Child with Four Angels New York, NY, 1977.1.1	Oak	I II	206 83	1483 1416	1492	Baltic
Adoration of the Magi New York, NY, 1982.60.17	Oak	I II	255 254	1484 1485	1494	Baltic I, II = 1 tree
Pietà Philadelphia, PHI, 54	Oak	I	112	1443	1452	Baltic
Lamentation Philadelphia, PHI, 328	Oak	I II	230/5 176	1471 1464	1475	Baltic I, II = 1 tree
Virgin and Child Enthroned with Two Angels Philadelphia, PHI, 329	Oak	I II	188 247	1467 1454	1476	Baltic
Head of Christ Philadelphia, PHI, 330	Oak	I	155	1463	1472	Baltic
Crucifixion Philadelphia, PHI, 395	Oak	I	95	1476	1485	Baltic
Virgin and Child in a Landscape Rotterdam, ROT, 2446	Oak	I	144	1475	1484	Baltic
Mocking of Christ priv. coll.	Oak	I II III	59 236 45	– 1471 –	1480	Baltic
Saint Anne Altarpiece Washington, WNG, 613 central panel	Oak	I II III IV	113 253 172 158	1477 1478 1481 1353	1490	Baltic l. wing (II), r. wing (I, II) = 1 tree
left wing		I II III	190 218 79	1480 1387 –		
right wing		I II III	187 204 210	1380 1363 1375		
Rest on the Flight into Egypt Washington D.C., WNG, 1937.1.43	Oak	I II	280 271	1481 1480	1490	Baltic I, II = 1 tree
The Night Nativity Vienna, W, 904	Oak	I II	236 100	1478 1476	1487	Baltic
Portrait of a Goldsmith Vienna, W, 970	Oak	I	154	1472	1481	Baltic
Saint Michael Altarpiece Vienna, W, 4056	Oak	I II	– 394	1468	1477	Baltic

Adhémar, H.
1954 *Le Dessin français au XVIe siècle*. Paris.
1962 *Le Musée National du Louvre, Paris. Les primitifs flamands, I: Corpus de la peinture des anciens Pays-Bas méridionaux au quinzième siècle*, 5. Brussels.

Ainsworth, M. W.
1982 "Bernard van Orley as a Designer of Tapestry." Ph.D. diss., Yale University.
1983 "Underdrawings in Paintings by Joos van Cleve at the Metropolitan Museum of Art." In *Le dessin sous-jacent dans la peinture, Colloque IV, 1981*, edited by R. Van Schoute and D. Hollanders-Favart, pp. 161–67. Louvain-la-Neuve.
1985 "Gerard David's Working Methods: Some Preliminary Observations." In *Le dessin sous-jacent dans la peinture, Colloque V, 1982*, edited by R. Van Schoute and D. Hollanders-Favart, pp. 53–60. Louvain-la-Neuve.
1988 "Gerard David's Drawings for the *Justice of Cambyses* Once Again." *Burlington Magazine* 130, pp. 528–30.
1989a "Reassessing the Form and Function of Gerard David's Drawings and Underdrawings." In *Le dessin sous-jacent dans la peinture, Colloque VII, 1984*, edited by R. Van Schoute and D. Hollanders-Favart, pp. 131–36. Louvain-la-Neuve.
1989b "Northern Renaissance Drawings and Underdrawings. A Proposed Method of Study." *Master Drawings* 27, pp. 5–38.
1990 Review of *Gerard David*, by Hans J. van Miegroet. *Art Bulletin* 72, pp. 649–54.
1992 "Implications of Revised Attributions in Netherlandish Painting." *Metropolitan Museum Journal* 27, pp. 59–76.
1993a "Gerard David's Workshop Practice—an Overview." In *Le dessin sous-jacent dans la peinture, Colloque IX, 1986*, edited by R. Van Schoute and H. Verougstraete-Marcq, pp. 11–33. Louvain-la-Neuve.
1993b *Facsimile in Early Netherlandish Painting: Dieric Bouts's "Virgin and Child."* Exh. cat. New York: The Metropolitan Museum of Art.
1994a "Gerard David." In De Patoul and Van Schoute 1994, pp. 482–93.
1994b "Hans Memling as a Draughtsman." In De Vos 1994b, vol. 2, pp. 78–87.
1994c [with contributions by M. P. J. Martens] *Petrus Christus, Renaissance Master of Bruges*. Exh. cat. New York: The Metropolitan Museum of Art.
1995 [as editor]. *Petrus Christus in Renaissance Bruges: An Interdisciplinary Approach*. New York and Turnhout.
1996 "The *Virgin and Child in an Apse*: Reconsidering a Campin Workshop Design." In *Robert Campin: New Directions in Scholarship*, edited by S. Foister and S. Nash, pp. 149–58. Turnhout.
1997a "Old Assumptions Reconsidered Through Revised Methodologies." In *Le dessin sous-jacent dans la peinture, Colloque XI, 1995*, edited by R. Van Schoute and

H. Verougstraete-Marcq, pp. 103–8. Louvain-la-Neuve.
1997b "The Mocking of Christ: A Hitherto Unknown Painting by Gerard David." *Städel Jahrbuch* 16, pp. 159–70.
1998 "An Unfinished Landscape Painting Attributed to the Master LC and Sixteenth-Century Workshop Practice." In *Herri Met de Bles: Studies and Explorations of the World Landscape Tradition*, edited by J. Marrow, B. Rosasco, and N. Miller, pp. 117–27. Turnhout.

Ainsworth, M. W., and K. Christiansen
1998 [as editors] *From Van Eyck to Bruegel*. Exh. cat. New York: The Metropolitan Museum of Art.

Alexander, J. J. G.
1992 *Medieval Illuminators and Their Methods of Work*. New Haven and London.

Alizieri, I.
1870 *Notizie dei disegno in Liguria dalle origini al secolo XVI*, I. Genoa.

Antwerp
1930 *Exposition internationale Coloniale Maritime et d'Art Flamand. Section d'Art Flamand Ancien, I: Peinture—Dessins—Tapisseries*. Antwerp.

Arndt, K.
1961 "Gerard David *Anbetung der Könige* nach Hugo van der Goes." *Münchner Jahrbuch der bildenden Kunst*, 3d ser., 12, pp. 153–75.

Aschenheim, C.
1899 *Der italienische Einfluss in der vlämischen Malerei der Frührenaissance*. Strasbourg.

van Asperen de Boer, S., J. Dijkstra and R. Van Schoute, with C. M. A. Daldenup and J. P. Filedt Kok
1992 *Underdrawing in Paintings of the Rogier van der Weyden and Master of Flémalle Groups*, vol. 41 of *Nederlands Kunsthistorisch Jaarboek* [1990].

van Asperen de Boer, S. et al.
1997 *Jan van Eyck: Two Paintings of Saint Francis Receiving the Stigmata*. Philadelphia.

Baes, E.
1899 "Gerard David et l'élément étranger dans la peinture flamande du XVe au XVIe siècle." *Annales de la Société d'archéologie de Bruxelles* 12, pp. 377–431.

Balbi, G. P.
1996 *Mercanti e "nationes" delle Fiandre: i genovesi in età bassomedievale*, Piccola Biblioteca Gisem 7. Pisa.

Baldass, L. von
1918 "Die Niederländschaftsmalerei von Patinir bis Bruegel." *Jahrbuch der Kunsthistorischen Sammlungen des Allerhöchsten Kaiserhauses* 34, pp. 111–57.
1936 "Gerard David als Landschaftsmaler." *Jahrbuch der Kunsthistorischen Sammlungen in Wien*, n.s. 10, pp. 89–96.
1937 "Die niederländischen Maler des spätgotischen Stiles." *Jahrbuch der Kunsthistorischen Sammlungen in Wien*, n.s., 11, pp. 117–38.

Baldini, U.
  1991 "La Grande 'Incompiuta'" *Critica d'Arte* 56, no. 7,
      pp. 22–37.
Balis, A., et al.
  1993 *Les Chasses de Maximilien*. Paris.
Barthélemy, C.
  1854 [as translator] *Rational ou manuel des divins offices de
      Guillaume Durand*, 5 vols. Paris.
Bauman, G.
  1984 "Attributed to Gerard David: *The Adoration of the
      Magi*." In *Notable Acquisitions 1983–84, The Metropolitan
      Museum of Art*, pp. 50–51. New York.
  1986 "Early Flemish Portraits, 1425–1525." *Metropolitan
      Museum of Art Bulletin* 43, no. 4.
Becherucci, L.
  1985 "L'Adorazione dei Magi." In *Leonardo la pittura*, by
      M. Alpatov et al., pp. 39–44. Florence.
Behling, L.
  1967 *Die Pflanze in der Mittelalterlichen Tafelmalerei*. Weimar.
Belting, H.
  1994 *Likeness and Presence: A History of the Image before the Era
      of Art*. Translated by E. Jephcott. Chicago and London.
Belting, H., and C. Kruse
  1994 *Die Erfindung des Gemäldes: Das erste Jahrhundert der
      niederländischen Malerei*. Munich.
Belyaev, N.
  1930 "L'Image de la sainte vierge Pelagonitisa." *Byzantino-
      slavica* 2, pp. 386–94.
Benesch, O.
  1957 "Die grossen flämischen Maler als Zeichner." *Jahrbuch der
      kunsthistorischen Sammlungen in Wien* 53, n.s. 17, pp. 9–32.
Benjamin, L. W., III
  1973 "The Empathic Relation of Observer to Image in
      Fifteenth-Century Northern Art." Ph.D. diss.,
      University of North Carolina, Chapel Hill.
Bermejo, E.
  1973 "Un nuevo *Descendimiento* de Gerard David." In *Actas
      del XXIII Congreso internacional de historia de arte* 1,
      pp. 309–11. Granada.
  1975a "Nuevas pinturas de Adrian Isenbrant." *Archivo español
      de arte* 3, pp. 1–25.
  1975b "Gerard David y Ambrosius Benson, autores de dos
      pinturas ineditas de la Virgen con el Niño." *Archivo
      español de arte* 3, pp. 259–63.
van Biervliet, L.
  1991 *Leven en werk van W. H. James Weale: Een Engels kunst-
      historicus in Vlaanderen in de 19de eeuw*. Verhandelingen
      van de Koninklijke Academie voor Wetenschappen,
      Letteren en Schone Kunsten van België 53, no. 55.
      Brussels.
Blacksberg, L. A.
  1991 "A Painting of the Godhead by Jan van Eyck and
      Gérard David: A Study of Influence and Effect." In
      *Le dessin sous-jacent dans la peinture, Colloque VIII,
      1989*, edited by H. Verougstraete-Marcq and R. Van
      Schoute, pp. 57–66. Louvain-la-Neuve.
Blockmans, W.
  1995 "The Creative Environment: Incentives to and
      Functions of Bruges Art Production." In Ainsworth
      1995, pp. 11–20.

Boccardo, P., and C. Di Fabio
  1997 [as editors] *Pittura Fiamminga in Liguria secoli XIV–XVII*.
      Genoa.
Bodenhausen, E. Freiherr von
  1905 *Gerard David und seine Schule*. Munich.
Bodenhausen, E. Freiherr von, and W. R. Valentiner
  1911 "Zum Werk Gerard Davids." *Zeitschrift für bildende
      Kunst*, n.s., 22, pp. 183–89.
Boon, K. G.
  [1946] *Gerard David*. Amsterdam, n.d.
  1947 "De erfenis van Aelbert van Ouwater." *Nederlands
      kunsthistorisch jaarboek*, pp. 33–46.
  1964 *Gids voor het Rijksprentenkabinett: een overzicht van de
      verzamelingen met naamlijsten van graveurs en tekenaars*.
      Amsterdam.
  1978 *Netherlandish Drawings of the Fifteenth and Sixteenth
      Centuries*. The Hague.
Borchert, T. H.
  1997 "Rogier's *St. Luke*: The Case for Corporate Identifi-
      cation," in Purtle 1997, pp. 61–86.
Botvinick, M.
  1992 "The Painting as Pilgrimage: Traces of a Subtext in
      the Work of Campin and His Contemporaries." *Art
      History* 15, pp. 1–18.
Brandenbarg, T.
  1995 "Saint Anne: A Holy Grandmother and Her Children."
      In *Sanctity and Motherhood: Essays on Holy Mothers in
      the Middle Ages*, edited by A. B. Mulder-Bakker,
      pp. 31–65. New York and London.
Brans, J. V. L.
  [1959] *Vlaamse schilders in dienst der Koningen van Spanje*.
      Leuven, n.d.
Brinkmann, B.
  1997 *Die Flämische Buchmalerei am Ende des Burgunderreichs:
      Der Meister des Dresdener Gebetbuchs und die
      Miniaturisten seiner Zeit*. Turnhout.
Brown, C. M.
  1972 "An Art Auction in Venice in 1506." *L'Arte* 18–20,
      pp. 121–36.
Bruges
  1949 *Gerard David*. Exh. cat. Bruges: Groeningemuseum.
Bruijnen, Y.
  1997 "Celebrating the Reunification of Gerard David's
      Triptych." In *Art on Wings: Celebrating the Reunification
      of a Triptych by Gerard David*, pp. 11–23. Exh. cat. The
      Hague: Mauritshuis.
Brussels–Delft
  1957–58 *Dieric Bouts*. Exh. cat. Brussels: Palais des Beaux-Arts;
      Delft: Museum Prinsenhof.
Bueren, T. van, and M. Faries
  1991 "The 'Portraits' in Geertgen tot Sint Jans' Vienna
      Panels." In *Le dessin sous-jacent dans la peinture, Colloque
      VIII, 1989*, edited by H. Verougstraete-Marcq and R.
      Van Schoute, pp. 141–50. Louvain-la-Neuve.
Buijsen, E.
  1997 "Considering the Ox and the Ass in Search of an
      Interpretation for Gerard David's *Forest Scene*." In *Art
      on Wings: Celebrating the Reunification of a Triptych by
      Gerard David*, pp. 24–38. Exh. cat. The Hague:
      Mauritshuis.

Butler, M.
  1976 "A Technical Investigation of the Materials and
       Techniques Used in Two Flemish Paintings." *Museum
       Studies* 7, pp. 59–71.
Butzkamm, A.
  1990 *Bild und Frömmigkeit im 15. Jahrhundert: Der Sakraments-
       altar von Dieric Bouts in der St. Peterskirche zu Löwen.*
       Paderborn.
Bynum, C. W.
  1987 *Holy Feast and Holy Fast: The Religious Significance of
       Food to Medieval Women.* Berkeley.
Cahn, W.
  1991 "Medieval Landscape and the Encyclopedic Tradition."
       In *Contexts: Style and Values in Medieval Art and Literature,*
       pp. 11–24. Yale French Studies, edited by D. Poirion
       and N. F. Regaldo. New Haven.
Camille, M.
  1989 *The Gothic Idol: Ideology and Image-Making in Medieval
       Art.* Cambridge.
Campbell, L.
  1976 "The Art Market in the Southern Netherlands in
       the Fifteenth Century." *Burlington Magazine* 118,
       pp. 188–98.
  1981a "Early Netherlandish Painters and Their Workshops."
       In *Le dessin sous-jacent dans la peinture, Colloque III,
       1979,* edited by D. Hollanders-Favart and R. Van
       Schoute, pp. 43–61. Louvain-la-Neuve.
  1981b "Notes on Netherlandish Pictures in the Veneto in the
       Fifteenth and Sixteenth Centuries," *Burlington
       Magazine* 123, pp. 467–73.
  1991 Review of *Gerard David* by Hans J. van Miegroet.
       Burlington Magazine 133, pp. 624–25.
  1994a "L'organisation de l'atelier." In De Patoul and Van
       Schoute 1994, pp. 89–100.
  1994b "Rogier van der Weyden and His Workshop."
       Proceedings of the British Academy 84, pp. 1–24.
  1995 "Approaches to Petrus Christus." In Ainsworth 1995,
       pp. 1–10.
Campbell, L., S. Foister, and A. Roy
  1997 "The Methods and Materials of Northern European
       Painting, 1400–1550." *National Gallery Technical Bulletin*
       18, pp. 6–55.
Canfield, B. F.
  1995 "The Reception of Flemish Art in Renaissance
       Florence and Naples." In Ainsworth 1995, pp. 35–39.
Carmel: Its History, Spirit, and Saints
  1927 Compiled from approved sources by the discalced
       Carmelites of Boston and Santa Clara. New York.
Carus-Wilson, E. M.
  1932–34 "The Origins and Early Development of the Merchant
       Adventurers." *Economic History Review* 4, pp. 147–76.
Castelfranchi Vegas, L.
  1984 *Italie et Flandre dans la peinture du XVe siècle.* Translated
       by A. C. Ippolito and C. D. Rotelli. Milan.
Castelnovi, G. V.
  1952 "Il Polittico di Gerard David nell'Abbazia della
       Cervara." *Commentari* 3, pp. 22–27.
Cennini, C. d'A
  1960 *The Craftsman's Handbook: The Italian "Il libro dell'arte."*
       Translated by D. V. Thompson. New York.

Châtelet, A.
  1973 "Geertgen tot Sint Jans dessinateur: Une proposition."
       In *Album Amicorum J. G. Van Gelder,* pp. 79–82. The
       Hague.
  1981 *Early Dutch Painting: Painting in the Northern
       Netherlands in the Fifteenth Century.* Translated by
       C. Brown and A. Turner. New York.
  1996 *Robert Campin: Le Maître de Flémalle.* Antwerp.
Châtelet, A., and D. Vanwynsberghe
  1996 "Simon Marmion," in Nys and Salamagne 1996,
       pp. 151–79.
Clark, K.
  1972 *Landscape into Art.* New York and London.
Clayton, M.
  1996 *Leonardo da Vinci: A Singular Vision. Drawings from the
       Royal Collection at Windsor Castle.* Exh. cat.. London:
       Queen's Gallery, Buckingham Palace. New York,
       London, Paris.
Cleven, E.
  1990 "'Ach, was ist der Wald schön grün': Gerard David,
       das 'bosgezicht' und sein (Miss-)Verständnis." *Akt* 46,
       pp. 2–14.
Collett, B.
  1985 *Italian Benedictine Scholars and the Reformation: The
       Congregation of Santa Giustina of Padua.* Oxford.
Collier, J. M.
  1975 "Linear Perspective in Flemish Painting and the Art of
       Petrus Christus and Dirk Bouts." Ph.D. diss., University
       of Michigan, Ann Arbor.
Comblen-Sonkes, M.
  1974–80 "À propos de la *Vierge et enfant à la soupe au lait:*
       Contribution à l'étude des copies." *Bulletin des
       Musées Royaux des Beaux-Arts de Belgique* 1–13,
       pp. 29–42.
  1979 "Le Dessin mécanique chez les primitifs flamands." In
       *Le dessin sous-jacent dans la peinture, Colloque I–II, 1975,
       1977,* edited by H. Verougstraete-Marcq and R. Van
       Schoute, pp. 44–45. Louvain-la-Neuve.
  1996 *The Collegiate Church of Saint Peter Louvain.* 2 vols.
       Translated by J. Cairns. Corpus of Fifteenth-Century
       Painting in the Southern Netherlands and the
       Principality of Liège, 18. Brussels.
Conway, W. M.
  1882 "A Picture by Rogier van der Weyden and one by
       Dierich Bouts." *Academy* 21, pp. 212–13.
  1884 *The Gallery of the Royal Institution.* Liverpool.
  1908 "Drawings by Gerard David." *Burlington Magazine* 13,
       p. 155.
  1916 "Gerard David's *Descent from the Cross.*" *Burlington
       Magazine* 29, pp. 309–10.
  1921 *The Van Eycks and Their Followers.* London.
Cornell, H.
  1924 *The Iconography of the Nativity of Christ.* Uppsala.
Crowe, J. A., and G. B. Cavacaselle
  1872 *The Early Flemish Painters: Notices of Their Lives and
       Works.* 2d ed. London.
Cuttler, C. D.
  1968 *Northern Painting from Pucelle to Bruegel: Fourteenth,
       Fifteenth, and Sixteenth Centuries.* New York. Reprint
       ed., New York, 1973.

Davies, M.

1953 *The National Gallery, London.* 2 vols. De Vlaamse primitieven I: Corpus van de vijftiende-eeuwse schilderkunst
in de zuidelijke Nederlanden, 3. Antwerp.

1955 "A Reminiscence of Van Eyck by Gerard David."
Bulletin des Musées Royaux des Beaux-Arts de Belgique
4, pp. 173–75.

1970 *The National Gallery, London, Volume III.* Les primitifs
flamands, I: Corpus de la peinture des anciens Pays-
Bas méridionaux au quinzième siècle, vol. II. Brussels.

1972 *Rogier van der Weyden: An essay with a critical catalogue
of paintings assigned to him and to Robert Campin.*
London.

Delmarcel, G., and E. Duverger

1987 *Bruges et la tapisserie.* Bruges.

De Patoul, B., and R. Van Schoute

1994 [as editors] *Les primitifs flamands et leur temps.* Louvain-
la-Neuve.

Destrée, J.

1913a "Les Portraits de Gérard David." In *L'Art flamand et
hollandais,* pp. 1–5.

1913b "De Portretten van Gerard David." *Onze Kunst*
23–24, pp. 153–57.

Detroit

1960 *Flanders in the Fifteenth Century: Art and Civilization.*
Exh. cat. Detroit Institute of Arts.

Devisscher, H.

1992 "Die Entstehung der Waldlandschaft in den Nieder-
landen." In *Von Bruegel bis Rubens: Das goldene
Jahrhundert der flämischen Malerei,* pp. 191–202. Exh.
cat. Cologne: Wallraf-Richartz-Museum.

De Vos, D.

1971 "De Madonna-en-Kindtypologie bij Rogier van der
Weyden en enkele minder gekende Flemalleske voor-
lopers." *Jahrbuch der Berliner Museen* 13, pp. 60–161.

1982 *Brugge Musées Communaux: Catalogue des Tableaux 15e
et 16e siècles.* Bruges.

1987 "David, Gerard, Schilder." In *Nationaal Biografisch
Woordenboek,* vol. 12, cols. 208–20. Brussels.

1988 "Gerard David's House." *Art Bulletin* 70, pp. 141–42.

1992 "Bruges and the Flemish Primitives in Europe." In
Vermeersch 1992, pp. 319–57.

1994a *Hans Memling.* 2 vols. Exh. cat. Bruges: Groeningemuseum.

1994b *Hans Memling: The Complete Works.* Antwerp and Ghent.

Dhanens, E.

1980 *Hubert and Jan van Eyck.* New York.

Di Fabio, C.

1992 *La Galleria di Palazzo bianco Genova,* pp. 38–43.
Milan.

1997 "Gerard David e il Polittico di San Gerolamo dell'
Cervara." In *Pittura Fiamminga in Liguria secoli XIV–
XVII,* edited by P. Boccardo and C. Di Fabio,
pp. 59–81. Genoa.

Dijkstra, J.

1990 "Origineel en kopie: Een onderzoek naar de navolging
van de Meester van Flémalle en Rogier van der
Weyden." Doctoral thesis, Universiteit van Amsterdam.

1991 "Methods for the Copying of Paintings in the
Southern Netherlands in the 15th and Early 16th

Centuries." In *Le dessin sous-jacent dans la peinture,
Colloque VIII, 1989,* edited by H. Verougstraete-Marcq
and R. Van Schoute, pp. 67–76. Louvain-la-Neuve.

Douglas, R. L.

1946 "*La Vierge à la soupe au lait* by Gerard David."
Burlington Magazine 88, pp. 289–92.

Dubiez, F. J.

1947 "Een vroeg zelfportret van Gerard David." *Oud
Holland* 62, pp. 209–11.

Duclos, V.

1910 *Bruges histoire et souvenirs.* Bruges.

Dufey-Haeck, M.-L.

1979 "Le thème du repos pendant la fuite en Égypte dans
la peinture flamande de la seconde moitié du XVe au
milieu du XVIe siècle." *Revue belge d'archéologie et
d'histoire d'art* 48, pp. 45–76.

Dunkerton, J., et al.

1991 *Giotto to Dürer: Early Renaissance Painting in the
National Gallery.* London.

Duverger, J.

1955 "Brugse schilders ten tijde van Jan van Eyck." *Bulletin
koninklijke Musea voor schone kunsten van België* 4,
pp. 83–120.

1980 "Margareta van Oostenrijk (1480–1530) en de
Italiaanse renaissance." In *Relations artistiques entre les
Pays-Bas et l'Italie à la renaissance: Études dédiées à
Suzanne Sulzberger,* pp. 127–42. Brussels and Rome.

Ebbinge-Wubben, E., C. Salm, C. Sterling, and R. Heinemann

1969 *The Thyssen-Bornemisza Collection.* Castagnola, Ticino.

Ehresmann, D. L.

1982 "Some Observations on the Role of Liturgy in the
Early Winged Altarpiece." *Art Bulletin* 64, pp. 359–69.

Eichberger, D.

1996 "Margaret of Austria's Portrait Collection: Female
Patronage in the Light of Dynastic Ambitions and
Artistic Quality." *Renaissance Studies* 10, pp. 258–79.

Eisler, C.

1963 *Drawings of the Masters: Flemish and Dutch Drawings.*
New York.

1989 [as editor] *Early Netherlandish Painting: The Thyssen-
Bornemisza Collection.* London.

Emond, C.

1961 *L'Iconographie carmélitaine dans les anciens Pays-Bas
méridionaux.* Brussels.

Ewing, D.

1978 "The Influence of Michelangelo's Bruges Madonna."
Belgisch tijdschrift voor oudheidkunde en kunstgeschiedenis
57, pp. 77–105.

1990 "Marketing Art in Antwerp, 1460–1560: Our Lady's
Pand." *Art Bulletin* 72, pp. 558–84.

1994 "An Antwerp Triptych: Three Examples of the
Artistic and Economic Impact of the Early Antwerp
Art Market." Lecture delivered at the symposium
"Antwerp: Artworks and Audiences," held at Smith
College, Northampton, Mass., November 11 and 12.

Fahy, E.

1969 "A Madonna by Gerard David." *Apollo* 90,
pp. 190–95.

1972 "Gerard David, Flanders's Last Medieval Master."
Metropolitan Museum of Art Bulletin 30, pp. 242–43.

Falkenburg, R. L.

1988 *Joachim Patinir: Landscape as an Image of the Pilgrimage of Life.* Translated by M. Hoyle. Amsterdam and Philadelphia.

1994 *The Fruit of Devotion: Mysticism and the Imagery of Love in Flemish Paintings of the Virgin and Child, 1450–1550.* Amsterdam and Philadelphia.

Faries, M.

1997a "The Underdrawing of Memling's Last Judgment Altarpiece in Gdansk," in *Memling Studies: Proceedings of the International Colloquium, Bruges, 10–12 November 1994,* edited by H. Verougstraete-Marcq, R. Van Schoute, and M. Smeyers, with the collaboration of A. Dubois, pp. 243–59. Leuven.

1997b "Infrared Studies of Rogier van der Weyden's *St. Luke Drawing the Virgin*: Stages of Investigation and Perception," in Purtle 1997.

1998 [forthcoming] *Discovering Underdrawings: A Guide to Method and Interpretation.* Turnhout.

Farmer, D.

1976 "Gerard David's *Lamentation* and an Anonymous *St. Jerome.*" *Museum Studies* 8, pp. 38–58.

Ferrari, G. E., M. Salmi, and A. Grote

1973 *Breviarium Grimani.* Berlin.

Fierens-Gevaert, H.

1908 "Le Clair-obscur dans la peinture des XVe, XVIe, et XVIIe siècles." In *Mélanges Godefroid Kurth,* pp. 439–47. Liège.

Floerke, H.

1905 *Studien zur niederländische Kunst- und Kulturgeschichte: Die Formen des Kunsthandels, des Atelier und der Sammler in Niederländen vom 15. 18. Jahrhundert.* Munich and Leipzig.

Förster, E.

1869 "Gerard David aus Brügge." *Jahrbuch für Kunstwissenschaft* 2, pp. 43–47.

Folie, J.

1963 "Les Oeuvres authentifiées des primitifs flamands." *Bulletin koninklijk Instituut voor het kunstpatrimonium* 4, pp. 183–256.

Fourcaud, L. de

1911 "La fin de l'art primitif à Bruges: Gerard David." *Revue de l'art ancien et moderne* 30, pp. 337–52, 421–34.

Francis, H. S.

1958 "*The Nativity* by Gerard David." *Bulletin of the Cleveland Museum of Art* 6, no. 10, pp. 227–36.

Franklin, J. C.

1978 *Mystical Transformations: The Imagery of Liquids in the Work of Mechthild von Magdeburg.* London.

Franz, H. G.

1969 *Niederländische Landschaftsmalerei im Zeitalter des Manierismus.* 2 vols. Graz.

Freeman, M. B.

1952–53 "Shepherds in the Fields." *Metropolitan Museum of Art Bulletin* 9, pp. 108–15.

Friedländer, M. J.

1903 "Die Brügger Leihausstellung von 1902." *Repertorium für Kunstwissenschaft* 26, pp. 66–91, 147–75.

1904 "Hugo van der Goes: Eine Nachlese." *Jahrbuch der preussischen Kunstsammlungen* 25, pp. 108–18.

1924–37 *Die altniederländische Malerei.* 14 vols. Berlin and Leiden.

1927–28 "Drei Niederländische Maler in Genoa." *Zeitschrift für bildende Kunst* 61, pp. 273–79.

1937 "Ein vlämischer portraitmaler in England." *Gentse bijdragen tot de kunstgeschiedenis* 4, pp. 5–18.

1947 *Essays über die Landschaftsmalerei und andere Bildgattungen.* The Hague.

1949 *Landscape, Portrait, and Still-life: Their Origin and Development.* Translated by R. F. Hull. Oxford.

1967–76 *Early Netherlandish Painting.* 14 vols. in 16. Translated by H. Norden. New York.

Frinta, M. S.

1966 *The Genius of Robert Campin.* The Hague.

Fuchs, A. S.

1977 "The Netherlands and Iberia: Studies in Netherlandish Painting for Spain, 1427–55." Ph.D. diss., University of California at Los Angeles.

van Gelder, J. G.

1949 "The Gerard David Exhibition at Bruges." *Burlington Magazine* 91, pp. 253–54.

Genaille, R.

1986 "Le paysage flamand et wallon au XVIe siècle." *Jaarboek van het Koninklijk Museum voor Schone Kunsten Antwerpen,* pp. 59–82.

Gibson, W. S.

1989 *"Mirror of the Earth": The World Landscape in Sixteenth-Century Flemish Painting.* Princeton.

Glacken, C. J.

1967 *Traces on the Rhodian Shore: Nature and Culture in Western Thought from Ancient Times to the End of the Eighteenth Century.* Berkeley.

Glavimans, A.

1946 "Notities bij de primitieven in het Mauritshuis: Nederlandsche kunst van de 15^e en 16^e eeuw." *Phoenix* 1, pp. 46–57.

Goddard, S. H.

1985 "Brocade Patterns in the Shop of the Master of Frankfurt: An Accessory to Stylistic Analysis." *Art Bulletin* 67, pp. 401–17.

Goedde, L.

1990 Review of *Joachim Patinir: Landscape as an Image of the Pilgrimage of Life* by R. L. Falkenburg. *Art Bulletin* 72, no. 4, pp. 655–57.

Gombrich, E. H.

1985 "The Rise of the Theory of Art." In *Norm and Form: Studies in the Art of the Renaissance,* vol. I, pp. 107–21. London and New York.

Gould, C.

1981 "On the Direction of Light in Italian Renaissance Frescoes and Altarpieces." *Gazette des Beaux-Arts* 97, no. 123, pp. 21–25.

Guicciardini, L.

1567 *Descrittione di m. Lodovico Guicciardini, patritio fiorentino, di tutti i Paesi Bassi, altrimenti detti Germania inferiore, Con piu carte di geographia del paese, & col ritratto naturale di piu terre principali.* Antwerp.

Guldan, E.

1966 *Eva und Maria: Eine Antithese als Bildmotiv.* Graz and Cologne.

Haasse, H.

1989 "Gerard David, Bosgezicht." In *Gezicht op het Mauritshuis: Poëtische visies op een uitzonderlijk museum,* edited by H. R. Hoetink, pp. 63–67. The Hague.

Hänschke, U.

1988 *Die flämische Waldlandschaft, Anfänge und Entwicklungen im 16. und 17. Jahrhundert.* Worms.

Härting, U.

1995 "Bilder der Bibel: Gerard Davids 'Waldlandschaften mit Ochsen und Esel' (um 1509) und Pieter Bruegels 'Landschaft mit wilden Tieren.'" *Niederdeutsche Beiträge zur Kunstgeschichte* 34, pp. 81–105.

Hall, J.

1979 *Dictionary of Subjects and Symbols in Art.* New York, rev. ed.

Hand, J. O.

1978 "Joos van Cleve: The Early and Mature Paintings." Ph.D. diss., Princeton University.

1992 *The Saint Anne Altarpiece by Gerard David.* Exh. brochure, Washington, D.C.: National Gallery of Art.

Hand, J. O., and M. Wolff

1986 *Early Netherlandish Painting.* Collections of the National Gallery of Art: Systematic Catalogue. Washington, D.C.

Hand, J. O., et al.

1986 *The Age of Bruegel.* Exh. cat., Washington, D.C.: National Gallery of Art.

Harbison, C.

1976 *The Last Judgment in Sixteenth-Century Northern Europe: A Study of the Relation Between Art and the Reformation.* New York.

1990 "The Northern Altarpiece as a Cultural Document." In *The Altarpiece in the Renaissance,* edited by P. Humfrey and M. Kemp, pp. 49–75. Cambridge.

1991 *Jan van Eyck: The Play of Realism.* London.

1993 "Miracles Happen: Image and Experience in Jan van Eyck's *Madonna in a Church.*" In *Iconography at the Crossroads,* edited by B. Cassidy, pp. 157–66. Princeton.

1995a *The Mirror of the Artist: Northern Renaissance Art in Its Historical Context.* New York.

1995b "Fact, Symbol, Ideal: Roles for Realism in Early Netherlandish Painting." In Ainsworth 1995, pp. 21–34.

Haverkamp-Begemann, E.

1957 *Vijf eeuwen tekenkunst. Tekeningen van Europese meesters in het Museum Boymans te Rotterdam.* Rotterdam.

Haverkamp-Begemann, E., and A. Chong

1985 "Dutch Landscape and Its Associations." In *The Royal Picture Gallery, Mauritshuis,* edited by H. R. Hoetink. Amsterdam, New York, The Hague.

Hedeman, A.

1995 "Rogier van der Weyden's Escorial *Crucifixion* and Carthusian Devotional Practices." In *The Sacred Image East and West,* edited by R. Ousterhout and L. Brubaker, pp. 191–203. Urbana and Chicago.

Heil, W.

1929 "The Jules Bache Collection." *Art News* 27, pp. 4–7.

Held, J. S.

1949 "Ambroise Benson et le Maître de Flémalle." *Les Arts plastiques (Les Carnets du Seminaire des arts)* 3, pp. 196–202.

Herzog, E.

1956 "Zur Kirchenmadonna van Eycks," *Berliner Museen* 6, pp. 2–16.

Hills, P.

1980 "Leonardo and Flemish Painting." *Burlington Magazine* 122, pp. 609–15.

Hoffmann, W. J.

1997 "The *Gospel of Nicodemus* in Dutch and Low German Literatures of the Middle Ages." In *The Medieval Gospel of Nicodemus: Texts, Intertexts, and Contexts in Western Europe,* edited by Z. Izydorczyk, pp. 335–60. Tempe, Arizona.

Hoogewerff, G. J.

1912 *Nederlandsche schilders in Italië in de XVIe eeuw.* Utrecht.

1935 *Vlaamsche kunst en Italiaansche Renaissance.* Malines and Amsterdam.

1953 "A proposito del polittico di Gerard David nell'Abbazia della Cervara." *Commentari* 4, pp. 72–73.

1954 *Het landschap van Bosch tot Rubens.* Antwerp.

1961 "Pittori fiamminghi in Liguria nel secolo XVI (Gherardo David, Giovanni Provost, Joos van der Beke, Giovanni Massys)." *Commentari* 12, pp. 176–94.

Hugh of St. Victor

1961 *The Didascalicon of Hugh of St. Victor: A Medieval Guide to the Arts.* Translated by J. Taylor. New York

Huizinga, J.

1996 *The Autumn of the Middle Ages.* Translated by R. J. Payton and U. Mammitzsch. Chicago.

Hulin de Loo, G.

1902 *Exposition de tableaux flamands des XIVᵉ, XVᵉ, et XVIᵉ siècles: Catalogue critique, précédé d'une introduction sur l'identité de certains maîtres anonymes.* Ghent and Bruges.

1931 "Quelques œuvres d'art rencontrées en Espagne." *Bulletin van de Koninklijke Academie voor Wetenschappen, Letteren, en Schone Kunsten van België, Klasse der Schone Kunsten* 13, pp. 39–43.

1939 "La Vignette chez les enlumineurs gantois entre 1470 et 1500." *Bulletin van de Koninklijke Academie voor Wetenschappen, Letteren en Schone Kunsten van België, Klasse der Schone Kunsten* 21, pp. 158–80.

Humfrey, P.

1993 *The Altarpiece in Renaissance Venice.* New Haven and London.

Hyde, H. M.

1994 "Early Cinquecento 'Popolare' Art Patronage in Genoa, 1500–1528." 2 vols. Ph.D. diss., Birkbeck College, University of London.

1997 "Gerard David's Cervara Altarpiece—An Examination of the Commission for the Monastery of San Girolamo della Cervara," *Arte Cristiana* 85, no. 781, pp. 245–54.

Jacobs, L. F.

1986 "Aspects of Netherlandish Carved Altarpieces: 1380–1530." Ph.D. diss. New York University, Institute of Fine Arts, New York.

1989 "The Marketing and Standardization of South Netherlandish Carved Altarpieces: Limits on the Role of the Patron." *Art Bulletin* 71, pp. 207–29.

1994 "The Commissioning of Early Netherlandish Carved
   Altarpieces: Some Documentary Evidence." In *A
   Tribute to Robert A. Koch: Studies in the Northern
   Renaissance*, pp. 83–114. Princeton.
1998 *Early Netherlandish Carved Altarpieces, 1380–1550:
   Medieval Tastes and Mass Marketing.* Cambridge.

Janssens de Bisthoven, A.
1981 *Stedelijk Museum voor schone kunsten (Groeningemuseum),
   Brugge.* De Vlaamse Primitieven, I: Corpus van de
   vijftiende-eeuwse schilderkunst in de Zuidelijke
   Nederlanden. Brussels.

de Jongh, E.
1974 "Grape Symbolism in Paintings of the 16th and 17th
   Centuries." *Simiolus* 7, pp. 182–99.

Jungmann, J. A.
1951 *The Mass and the Roman Rite: Its Origins and Development,*
   2 vols. Translated by F. A. Brunner. New York.

Justi, C.
1886 "Altflandrische Bilder in Spanien und Portugal: III.
   Gerard David." *Zeitschrift für bildende Kunst* 21, pp.
   133–40.

Kann, A. G.
1997 "Rogier's *St. Luke:* Portrait of the Artist or Portrait of
   the Historian," in Purtle 1997, pp. 15–21.

Keith, L., and A. Roy
1996 "Giampietrino, Boltraffio, and the Influence of
   Leonardo," *National Gallery Technical Bulletin,* vol. 17,
   pp. 4–19.

Kemp, M.
1989 [as editor] *Leonardo on Painting: An Anthology of Writings
   by Leonardo da Vinci with a Selection of Documents Relating
   to His Career as an Artist.* New Haven and London.

Kemperdick, S.
1997 *Der Meister von Flémalle: Die Werkstatt Robert Campins
   und Rogier van der Weyden.* Turnhout.

Kirschbaum, E., and W. Braunfels
1968–76 *Lexikon der Christlichen Ikonographie.* Vols. 1–8. Rome,
   Freiburg, Basel, Vienna.

Klein, P.
1991 "The Differentiation of Originals and Copies of
   Netherlandish Panel Paintings by Dendrochronology."
   In *Le dessin sous-jacent dans la peinture, Colloque VIII,
   1989,* edited by H. Verougstraete-Marcq and R. Van
   Schoute, pp. 29–42. Louvain-la-Neuve.

Koch, R. A.
1951 "Geertgen tot Sint Jans in Bruges." *Art Bulletin* 31,
   pp. 259–60.
1965 "La Sainte-Baume in Flemish Landscape Painting of
   the Sixteenth Century." *Gazette des Beaux-Arts* 66,
   pp. 273–82.
1968 *Joachim Patinir.* Princeton.
1985 "A Reflection in Princeton of a Lost Epiphany by
   Hugo van der Goes." In *Tribute to Lotte Brand Philip,*
   pp. 82–87. New York.

Koerner, J. L.
1993 *The Moment of Self-Portraiture in German Renaissance
   Art.* Chicago and London.

Kofuku, A.
1990 "Landscape with Virgin and Child or Rest on the Flight
   into Egypt—Patinir and Early Netherlandish Painting."

In *Bruegel and Netherlandish Landscape Painting from the
   National Gallery, Prague,* pp. 37–47. Exh. cat. Tokyo:
   National Museum of Western Art; Kyoto: National
   Museum of Modern Art. Tokyo.

Koreny, F.
1985 *Albrecht Dürer and the Animal and Plant Studies of the
   Renaissance.* Boston.
1991 "Ein unbekanntes Aquarell mit Pfingstrosen von
   Martin Schongauer: Rogier van der Weyden–Martin
   Schongauer–Albrecht Dürer und die Entwicklung der
   neuzeitlichen Naturstudie." In *Le Beau Martin Études
   et Mises au Point,* Actes du Colloque organisé par le
   musée d'Unterlinden à Colmar, edited by A. Châtelet,
   pp. 77–90. Colmar.

Korevaar-Hesseling, E. H.
1947 *Het landschap in de Nederlandse en Vlaamse schilderkunst.*
   Amsterdam.

Kren, T.
1983 "Flemish Manuscript Illumination, 1475–1550," in
   *Renaissance Painting in Manuscripts: Treasures from the
   British Library,* pp. 3–85. Exh. cat. New York: Pierpont
   Morgan Library.
1992 [as editor] *Margaret of York, Simon Marmion, and* The
   Visions of Tondal: *Papers Delivered at a Symposium
   Organized by the Department of Manuscripts of the J. Paul
   Getty Museum in Collaboration with the Huntington
   Library and Art Collections, June 21–24, 1990.* Malibu.

Kren, T., and J. Rathofer
1987–88 *Flämischer Kalender / Flemish Calendar / Simon Bening.*
   Facsimile ed. 2 vols. Commentary, pp. 203–73. Lucerne.

Krönig, W.
1936 *Der italienische Einfluss in der flämischen Malerei im ersten
   Drittel des 16. Jahrhunderts.* Würzburg.

Kwakkelstein, M. W.
1994 *Leonardo da Vinci as a physiognomist: Theory and drawing
   practice.* Leiden.

Landau, M., and P. Parshall
1994 *The Renaissance Print 1470–1550.* New Haven and
   London.

Lane, B. G.
1975 "Ecce Panis Angelorum: The Manger as Altar in
   Hugo's Berlin *Nativity.*" *Art Bulletin* 57, pp. 477–86.
1984 *The Altar and the Altarpiece: Sacramental Themes in Early
   Netherlandish Painting.* New York.

Langton, R. L.
1946 "Gerard David: The Blessed Virgin as Queen of
   Heaven." *Art in America* 34, no. 3, pp. 161–63.

Lasareff, V.
1938 "Studies in the Iconography of the Virgin." *Art
   Bulletin* 20, pp. 26–65.

Lavalleye, J.
1949 "Les Peintres flamands du XVe siècle en Italie
   (en marge de deux expositions)." *Arts plastiques* 3,
   pp. 171–80.
1953 *Les Collections d'Espagne.* Vol. I of Les primitifs
   flamands II. Repertoire des peintures flamandes des
   quinzième et seizième siècles. Antwerp.
1956 "La Peinture et l'enluminure des origines à la fin du
   XVe siècle." In *L'Art de Belgique, du moyen âge à nos
   jours,* edited by P. Fierens, pp. 101–60. Brussels.

Lawrence, C. H.
  1989 *Medieval Monasticism: Forms of Religious Life in Western Europe in the Middle Ages.* 2d edition. London and New York.
Leeflang, H.
  1998 "Dutch Landscape: The Urban View of Haarlem and Its Environs in Literature and Art, 15th–17th Century." *Nederlands Kunsthistorisch Jaarboek* 48 (1997), pp. 52–115
Lees, F.
  1913 *The Art of the Great Masters.* London.
Lehman, R.
  1928 *The Philip Lehman Collection, New York: Paintings.* Paris.
  1998 *Fifteenth- to Eighteenth-Century European Paintings. France, Central Europe, The Netherlands, and Great Britain.* The Robert Lehman Collection, II. New York.
Leonardo da Vinci
  1956 *Treatise on Painting.* Translated and annotated by A. P. McMahon. Princeton.
Leprieur, P.
  1910 "De quelques dessins nouveaux au Musée du Louvre." *Revue de l'art ancien et moderne* 28, pp. 161–75.
Levi D'Ancona, M.
  1977 *The Garden of the Renaissance: Botanical Symbolism in Italian Painting.* Florence.
Lievens-de Waegh, M.-L.
  1991 *Le Musée National des Carreaux de Faience de Lisbonne.* 2 vols. Les primitifs flamands, I: Corpus de la peinture des anciens Pays-Bas méridionaux au quinzième siècle, 16. Brussels.
Liverpool
  1977 *Walker Art Gallery: Foreign Catalogue* . Liverpool.
Lobelle-Caluwé, H.
  1997 "Hans Memling: A Self-Portrait?" In *Memling Studies,* Proceedings of the International Colloquium, Bruges (1994), edited by H. Verougstraete, R. Van Schoute, and M. Smeyers, pp. 43–53. Leuven.
Lugt, F.
  1968 *Inventaire général des dessins des écoles du nord: Maîtres des anciens Pays-Bas nés avant 1550,* pp. 19–21. Paris.
MacBeth, R., and R. Spronk
  1997 "A Material History of Rogier's *St. Luke Drawing the Virgin:* Conservation Treatments and Findings from Technical Examinations," in Purtle 1997, pp. 103–34.
Maegawa, I. N.
  1959 "La Doctrine de Jean Gerson sur Saint Joseph." *Cahiers de Josephologie* 7, pp. 181–94.
  1960 "La Doctrine de Jean Gerson sur Saint Joseph." *Cahiers de Josephologie* 8, pp. 9–39, 251–92.
Manchusi-Ungaro, H. R.
  1971 *Michelangelo: The Bruges Madonna and the Piccolomini Altar.* New Haven and London.
van Mander, K.
  1604 *Het Schilderboeck waerin voor eerst de leerlustighe lueght den grondt der edel vry schilderconst in verscheyden deelen wort voorghedraghen . . .* Haarlem.
  1994 *The Lives of the Illustrious Netherlandish and German Painters, from the First Edition of the* Schilderboeck *(1603–4).* Introduction and translation, edited by H. Miedema. 4 vols. Doornspijk.

Marceau, H.
  1941 *The John G. Johnson Collection. Catalogue of Paintings.* Philadelphia.
Maréchal, J.
  1951 "Le Départ de Bruges des marchands étrangers (XVe et XVIe siècle)." *Handelingen van det genootschap "Société d'émulation" te Brugge* 88, pp. 26–74.
  1963 "De betrekkingen tussen de Karmeliten en de Hanzeaten te Brugge van 1347 tot 1523." *Handelingen van het genootschap "Société d'émulation" te Brugge* 100, pp. 206ff.
Marijnissen, R. H., and G. Van De Voorde
  1986 "The X-rays of Gerard David's *Legend of Cambyses and Sisamnes.*" *Academiae Analecta* 47, pp. 65–70.
Marijnissen, R. H., and H. J. van Miegroet
  1988 "Early Netherlandish Canvases." *Academiae Analecta,* 2nd ser., pp. 95–114.
Marlier, G.
  1952 "Ein Männerbildnis des Gerard David." *Weltkunst* 22/24, p. 5.
  1957 *Ambrosius Benson et la peinture à Bruges au temps de Charles-Quint.* Damme.
  1967 "Joos van Cleve—Fontainebleau and Italy." *The Connoisseur* 165, no. 663, pp. 25–27.
Marrow, J.
  1979 *Passion Iconography in Northern European Art of the Late Middle Ages and Early Renaissance.* Kortrijk.
  1986 "Symbol and Meaning in Northern European Art of the Late Middle Ages and Early Renaissance." *Simiolus* 16, pp. 150–69.
  1997 "Artistic Identity in Early Netherlandish Painting: The Place of Rogier van der Weyden's *St. Luke Drawing the Virgin,*" in Purtle 1997, pp. 53–59.
Martens, D.
  1993 "La 'Madone au trône arqué' et la peinture brugeoise de la fin du Moyen Âge." *Jahrbuch der Berliner Museum,* n.s., 35, pp. 129–74.
  1995a "Identification de deux 'portraits' d'église dans la peinture brugeoise de la fin du Moyen Âge." *Jaarboek van het Koninklijk Museum voor Schone Kunsten (van) Antwerpen,* pp. 29–55.
  1995b "La 'Madone à l'arcade' de Petrus Christus et ses Doubles." *Revue Belge d'Archéologie et d'Histoire de l'art* 64, pp. 25–30.
  1995c "La Vierge en majesté de l'ancien retable de la sé d'Évora: Une Oeuvre brugeoise des années 1500." *Gazette des Beaux-Arts,* 6th ser., 126, pp. 211–22.
Martens, M. P. J.
  1992 "Artistic Patronage in Bruges Institutions, c. 1440–1482." Ph.D. diss., University of California at Santa Barbara.
  1994 "La clientèle du peintre." In De Patoul and Van Schoute 1994, pp. 142–47, 632–33.
  1995 "Het onderzoek naar de opdrachtgevers." In *"Om iets te weten van de oude meesters": De Vlaamse Primitieven—herontdekking, waardering en onderzoek,* edited by R. Ridderbos and H. van Veen, pp. 349–93. Nijmegen.
  1997 "Hans Memling and His Patrons: A Cliometrical Approach." In *Memling Studies: Proceedings of the International Colloquium, Bruges, 10–12 November 1994,* edited by H. Verougstraete, R. Van Schoute, and M. Smeyers, pp. 35–41. Leuven.

Martín González, J. J.
    1995 "L'Art Flamand en Castilla y León," in *Vlaanderen en Castilla y León Op de drempel van Europa*, pp. 106–10. Exh. cat. Antwerp: Cathedral of Our Lady.

Mather, F. J.
    1938 "An Epiphany by Van der Goes Finished by Gerard David." *Art in America* 26, pp. 64–72.

Mayer, A. L.
    1920 "Ein unbekanntes Triptychon von Gerard David." *Zeitschrift für bildende Kunst* 55, p. 97.
    1930 "Die Sammlung Jules Bache in New York." *Pantheon* 6, pp. 537–42.

Mayo, J.
    1980 *A History of Ecclesiastical Dress.* New York.

Meder, J.
    1908 *The Mastery of Drawing.* 2 vols. Translated by Winslow Ames. New York, 1978.

Metzger, C.
    1992 "Restoration and Reconstruction of Gerard David's *St. Anne Altar.*" In *AIC Paintings Specialty Group Postprints.* Papers presented at the twentieth annual meeting of the American Institute for Conservation of Historic and Artistic Works, Buffalo, New York (1992), compiled by M. C. Steele, pp. 52–63. Buffalo.
    1995 "The Washington *Nativity.*" In Ainsworth 1995, pp. 167–74.

Michiels, E.
1964–66 *Iconographie der Stad Brugge.* Vols. I, II. Bruges.

Miegroet, H. J. van
    1986 "More News About Gerard David, Gerard Loyet, and the Enigmatic Antheunis Huyghe." *Academiae Analecta* 47, pp. 77–107.
    1987 "New Documents Concerning Gerard David." *Art Bulletin* 69, pp. 33–44.
    1988a "Early Netherlandish Canvases: Bouts in Perspective." *Academiae Analecta* 49, pp. 95–106.
    1988b "Gerard David: Patronage and Artistic Preeminence at Bruges." Ph.D. diss., University of California at Santa Barbara.
    1988c "Gerard David's House: Reply." *Art Bulletin* 70, pp. 142–43.
    1988d "Gerard David's *Justice of Cambyses*: Exemplum Justitiae or Political Allegory?" *Simiolus* 18, pp. 116–33.
    1989 *Gerard David.* Antwerp.

Montias, J. M.
    1990 "Socio-Economic Aspects of Netherlandish Art from the Fifteenth to the Seventeenth Century: A Survey." *Art Bulletin* 73, no. 3, pp. 358–73.
    1993 "Le Marché de l'art aux Pays-Bas, XVe et XVIe siècles." *Annales Économies, sociétés, civilisations* 6, pp. 1541–63.
    1996 *Le Marché de l'art aux Pays-Bas, XVe–XVIIe siècles.* Paris.

Morassi, A.
    1946 *Mostra della Pittura Antica in Liguria dal Trecento al Cinquecento.* Milan.
    1947 *Trittico fiammingo a San Lorenzo della Costa.* Florence.
    1951 *Capolavori della pittura a Genova.* Milan and Florence.

Mund, H.
    1983 "Approche d'une terminologie relative à l'étude de la copie." *Annales d'histoire de l'art et d'archéologie* 5, pp. 19–31.
    1994 "La copie." In De Patoul and Van Schoute, pp. 125–41.

Mundy, E. J.
    1980a "Gerard David Studies." Ph.D. diss., Princeton University.
    1980b "A Preparatory Sketch for Gerard David's *Justice of Cambyses* Panels in Bruges." *Burlington Magazine* 122, pp. 122–25.
    1981–82 "Gerard David's *Rest on the Flight into Egypt:* Further Additions to Grape Symbolism." *Simiolus* 12, pp. 211–22.
    1985 *Painting in Bruges, 1470–1550: An Annotated Bibliography.* Boston.

Musper, H. T.
    1968 "Die Suppenmadonna des Gerard David in der Musées Royaux des Beaux-Arts de Belgique in Brüssel." *Bulletin des Musées Royaux des Beaux-Arts de Belgique* 17, pp. 11–14.

Neale, J. M., and B. Webb
    1893 [as translators] *The Symbolism of Churches and Church Ornaments, a Translation of the First Book of the Rationale Divinorum Officiorum Written by William Durandus.* New York.

Nieburg, P.
    1946 "Twee boschgezichten van Gerard David." *Constghesellen* 1, pp. 16–17.

Nieuwdorp, H.
    1993 *Antwerp Altarpieces 15th–16th Centuries.* Vol. I, *Catalogue.* Exh. cat. Antwerp: Museum voor Religieuze Kunst.

Nieuwland, J.
    1995 "Motherhood and Sanctity in the Life of Saint Birgitta of Sweden: An Insoluble Conflict?" In *Sanctity and Motherhood: Essays on Holy Mothers in the Middle Ages,* edited by A. B. Mulder-Bakker, pp. 297–329. New York and London.

Nijmegen
    1986 *Tussen heks en heilige. Het vrouwbeeld op de drempel van de moderne tijd, 15de/16de eeuw.* Nijmegen.

Noe, S. P.
    1930 "Flemish Primitives in New York." *American Magazine of Art* 21, pp. 30–38.

Nuttall, P.
    1989 "Early Netherlandish Painting in Florence: Acquisition, Ownership and Influence, c. 1435–1500." Ph.D. diss., University of London.
    1992 "Decorum, Devotion, and Dramatic Expression: Early Netherlandish Painting in Renaissance Italy." In *Decorum in Renaissance Narrative Art,* edited by F. Ames-Lewis and A. Bednarek, pp. 70–77. Papers delivered at the Annual Conference of the Association of Art Historians, London, 1991. Birkbeck College, London.

Nys, L., and A. Salamagne
    1996 *Valenciennes aux XIVe et XVe siècles: Art et histoire.* Valenciennes.

Oldenberger-Ebbers, C. S.
    1974 "The 'Scientific' Study of Nature Reflected in the Composition of the Vegetation in Late-Medieval Paintings." *Janus: Revue internationale de l'histoire des sciences, de la médecine, de la pharmacie et de la technique* 60, pp. 59–73.

Onghena, M. J.

1959 *De iconografie van Philips de Schone.* Verhandelingen der Koninklijke Academie van België, klasse der schone kunsten, 10. Brussels.

von der Osten, G., and H. Vey

1969 *Painting and Sculpture in Germany and the Netherlands, 1500–1600.* Translated by M. Hottinger. Harmondsworth.

d'Otrange, M. L.

1951 "Gerard David at the Metropolitan, New York." *Connoisseur* 128, pp. 206–11.

Pächt, O.

1948 *The Master of Mary of Burgundy.* London.

1960 "The *Avignon Diptych* and its Eastern ancestry." *De artibus opuscula,* vol. XL: *Essays in Honor of Erwin Panofsky,* edited by M. Meiss. Zurich.

1978 "La Terre de Flanders." *Pantheon* 36, no. 1, pp. 3–16.

1994 *Van Eyck and the Founders of Early Netherlandish Painting.* Translated by D. Britt. London.

1997 *Early Netherlandish Painting from Rogier van der Weyden to Gerard David.* Translated by D. Britt. London.

Panofsky, E.

1953 *Early Netherlandish Painting: Its Origin and Character.* 2 vols. Cambridge, Mass. Reprint ed., New York, 1971.

1959–60 *Chefs-d'œuvres—dessins et gravures—du Cabinet Edmond de Rothschild.* Exh. cat. Paris: Musée du Louvre.

Parmentier, R. A.

1937 "Bescheiden omtrent Brugsche schilders in de 16de eeuw: I. Ambrosius Benson." *Handelingen van het genootschap "Société d'émulation" te Brugge* 80, pp. 89–129.

1942 "Bronnen voor de geschiedenis van het Brugsche schildersmilieu in de XVIe eeuw: 21. Gerard David." *Revue belge d'archéologie et d'histoire de l'art,* pp. 5–19.

Pauli, G.

1924–25 *Zeichnungen alter Meister in der Kunsthalle zu Hamburg.* 3 vols. Frankfurt-am-Main.

Périer-d'Ieteren, C.

1982–83 "Dessin au poncif et dessin perforé: Leur utilisation dans les anciens Pays-Bas au XVe siècle." *Bulletin koninklijk Instituut voor het kunstpatrimonium* 19, pp. 79–94.

1984 "Précisions sur la technique d'exécution des peintures de G. David." In *Preprint de la 7e réunion triennale de l'ICOM à Copenhague* 1, pp. 38–43. Paris.

1985a "Technique du dessin sous-jacent des peintres flamands des XVe et XVIe siècles: Nouvelles hypothèses de travail." In *Le dessin sous-jacent dans la peinture, Colloque V, 1983,* edited by R. van Schoute and D. Hollanders-Favart, pp. 61–69. Louvain-la-Neuve.

1985b *Colyn de Coter et la technique picturale des peintres flamands au XVe siècle.* Brussels.

1987 "Précisions sur le dessin sous-jacent et la technique d'exécution de la Nativité de Gérard David du musée de Budapest." *Annales d'histoire d'art et d'archéologie* 60, pp. 95–106.

1990 "Le marché d'exportation et l'organisation du travail dans les ateliers brabançons aux XVe et XVIe siècles." In *Fabrication et consommation de l'œuvre.* Artistes, artisans, et production artistique au Moyen Âge 3, edited by X. Barral I Altet, pp. 629–45. Paris.

1991 "Les Volets peints malinois du Retable de la Passion d'Elmpt (Rhénanie) et ceux du Retable des Templiers de Vienne." *Annales de la société d'archéologie de Bruxelles* 61, pp. 91–117.

1994 "La Technique de Memling et sa place dans l'évolution de la peinture flamande du XVe siècle." In De Vos 1994a, pp. 67–77.

Philadelphia

1972 *The John G. Johnson Collection: Catalogue of Flemish and Dutch Paintings.* Philadelphia.

Philippot, P.

1957 "À propos de la 'Justice d'Othon' de Thierry Bouts," *Bulletin des Musées Royaux des Beaux-Arts de Belgique* 6, pp. 55–80.

1962 "La fin du XVe siècle et les origines d'une nouvelle conception de l'image dans la peinture Pays-Bas." *Bulletin koninklijke Musea voor schone kunsten van België* 11, pp. 3–38.

1966 "Les grisailles et les 'degrés de réalité' de l'image dans la peinture flamande des 15ème et 16ème siècles." *Bulletin des Musées Royaux des Beaux-Arts de Belgique* 4, pp. 225–46.

1970 *Pittura fiamminga e Rinascimento italiano.* Turin.

1979 "La Conception des retables gothiques brabançons." *Annales d'histoire de l'art et d'archéologie* 1, pp. 29–40.

Pirenne, H.

1902–32 *Histoire de Belgique.* Vols. 1–4. Brussels.

Plummer, J.

1975 *The Hours of Catherine of Cleves.* New York.

Poeschke, J.

1993 [as editor] *Italienische Frührenaissance und Nordeuropäisches Mittelalter.* Munich.

Popham, A. E.

1926 *Drawings of the Early Flemish School.* London.

1932 *Catalogue of the Drawings by Dutch and Flemish Artists Preserved in the Department of Prints and Drawings in the British Museum.* 5 vols. London and Oxford.

1994 *The Drawings of Leonardo da Vinci.* Revised with introductory essay by M. Kemp. London.

Popham, A. E., and K. M. Fenwick

1965 *European Drawings (and two Asian drawings) in the Collection of the National Gallery of Canada.* Toronto.

Prevenier, W., and W. Blockmans

1986 *The Burgundian Netherlands.* Translated by P. Kin and Y. Mead. Cambridge.

Price, N. M., M. K. Talley Jr., and A. M. Vaccaro

1996 [as editors] *Readings in Conservation: Historical and Philosophical Issues in the Conservation of Cultural Heritage.* Los Angeles.

Pugin, A. W.

1868 *Glossary of Ecclesiastical Ornament and Costume,* 3d ed. London.

Purtle, C.

1982 *The Marian Paintings of Jan van Eyck.* Princeton.

1997 [as editor] *Rogier van der Weyden, St. Luke Drawing the Virgin: Selected Essays in Context.* Turnhout.

van Puyvelde, L.

1947 *Les Primitifs flamands: Catalogue.* 2d. ed. Paris. First published 1941.

Ragghianti, L. C.
1990 *Dipinti fiamminghi in Italia, 1420–1570: Catalogo.* Bologna.

Réau, L.
1955–59 *Iconographie de l'art chrétien.* 3 vols. in 6 parts. Paris.

Reel, W.
1985 "Exploring New Applications for Infrared Reflectography." *Bulletin of the Cleveland Museum of Art* 72, no. 8 (December 1985), pp. 390–412.

Reinach, S.
1912 "Flemish Imitations of the *Benois Madonna.*" *Burlington Magazine* 21, pp. 358–59.

Reiset, F.
1878 *Notice des Dessins, Cartons, Pastels, Miniatures, et Émaux exposés dans la salle du 1er et du 2e étage au Musée National du Louvre.* Paris.

Reynolds, C.
1997 "Memling's Landscapes and the Influence of Hugo van der Goes." In *Memling Studies,* pp. 163–70. Proceedings of the International Colloquium, Bruges (1994). Leuven.

Reznicek, E. K. J.
1968 "Enkele gegevens uit de vijftiende eeuw over de Vlaamse schilderkunst in Florence." In *Miscellanea Josef Duverger.* Vol. I, pp. 83–91. Ghent.

Rice, E. F.
1985 *St. Jerome in the Renaissance.* Baltimore and London.

Ridder, J. De
1979–80 "Gerechtigheidstaferelen in de 15de en 16de eeuw voor schepenhuizen in Vlaanderen." *Gentse bijdragen tot de kunstgeschiedenis* 25, pp. 42–62.
1986 "De Gerechtigheidstaferelen voor schepenhuizen in Vlaanderen in de 15de en 16de eeuw." Ph.D. diss., Rijksuniversiteit, Ghent.

Ridderbos, B.
1995 "Objecten en vragen." In *"Om iets te weten van de oude meesters": De Vlaamse Primitieven—herontdekking, waardering en onderzoek,* edited by B. Ridderbos and H. van Veen, pp. 15–133. Nijmegen.

Rietstap, J. B.
1972 *Armorial Général de Belgique . . .* Baltimore.

Ring, G.
1913 *Beiträge zur Geschichte der niederländischen Bildnismalerei im 15. und 16. Jahrhundert.* Leipzig.

Ringbom, S.
1962 "Maria in Sole and the Virgin of the Rosary." *Journal of the Warburg and Courtauld Institutes* 25, nos. 3–4, pp. 326–30.
1984 *Icon to Narrative: The Rise of the Dramatic Close-up in Fifteenth-Century Devotional Painting.* First published 1965. Doornspijk.

Roehl, R.
1972 "Patterns and Structures of Demand." In *The Middle Ages.* Vol. I of *The Fontana Economic History of Europe,* edited by C. M. Cipolla, pp. 107–42. London.

Röthel, H. K.
1956 "Ein Paliotto Gerard Davids aus der Abtei von Cervara." *Die Kunst und das schöne Heim* 54, pp. 361–65.

Rohlmann, M.
1993 "Zitate flämischer Landschaftsmotive in Florentiner Quattrocentromalerei." In *Italienische Frührenaissance und nordeuropäisches Spätmittelalter: Kunst der frühen Neuzeit im europäischen Zusammenhang,* edited by J. Poeschke, pp. 235–47. Munich.

Rombouts, P., and T. Van Lerius
1961 *Liggeren en andere historische archieven der Antwerpse Sint-Lucasgilde.* Vol. 1. Amsterdam.

Rubin, M.
1991 *Corpus Christi: The Eucharist in Late Medieval Culture.* Cambridge.

Rubin, P.
1990 "What Men Saw: Vasari's Life of Leonardo da Vinci and the Image of the Renaissance Artist." *Art History* 13, no. 1, pp. 34–46.

Salinger, S.
1951 "An *Annunciation* by Gerard David." *Bulletin of The Metropolitan Museum of Art* 9, pp. 225–29.

Salvini, R.
1984 *Banchieri fiorentini e pittori di Fiandra.* Modena.

Sander, J.
1993 *Kataloge der Gemälde im Städelschen Kunstinstitut Frankfurt am Main.* Vol. 2, *Niederländische Gemälde im Städel, 1400–1500.* Mainz am Rhein.
1995 *Die Entdeckung der Kunst: Niederländische Kunst des 15. und 16. Jahrhunderts in Frankfurt.* Exh. cat. Mainz: Städelisches Kunstinstitut und Stadische Galerie.

Sanderus, A.
1641–44 *Flandria Illustrata, Sive Descriptio comitatus istius per totum terrarum orbem celeberrimi.* Vols. 1–2. Cologne.

Scailliérez. C.
1991 *Joos van Cleve au Louvre.* Exh. cat. Paris: Musée du Louvre.
1992 "Entre enluminure et peinture: À propos d'un *Paysage avec Saint Jérôme Pénitent* de l'École Ganto-Brugeoise récemment acquis par le Louvre." *Revue du Louvre* 42, no. 2, pp. 16–31.

Scheller, R. W.
1985 "Gallia Cisalpina: Louis XII and Italy, 1499–1508." *Simiolus* 15, pp. 5–60.
1995 *Exemplum: Model-book Drawings and the Practice of Artistic Transmission in the Middle Ages, ca. 900–ca. 1470.* Translated by M. Hoyle. Amsterdam.

Schiller, G.
1969 *Ikonographie der Christlichen Kunst.* 2 vols. Cassel.

Schmidt, P. F.
1910 "Sammlungen, Magdeburg, Das Kaiser Friedrich Museum." *Der Cicerone* 2, pp. 316–17.

Schönbrunner, J., and J. Meder
1896–1908 *Handzeichnungen alter Meister aus der Albertina und anderen Sammlungen,* 12 vols. Vienna.

Schöne, W.
1937 "Ueber einige altniederländische Bilder vor allem im Spanien." *Jahrbuch der Preussischen Kunstsammlungen* 58, pp. 153–81.
1938 *Dieric Bouts und seine Schule.* Berlin.
1954 *Über das Licht in der Malerei.* Berlin.

Schryver, A. de
1955–56 "Hugo van der Goes' laatste jaren te Gent." *Gentse bijdragen tot de kunstgeschiedenis* 16, pp. 193–211.

Scillia, D. G.
1975 "Gerard David and Manuscript Illumination in the Low Countries, 1480–1509." Ph.D. diss., Case Western Reserve University

Scott, M.
1980 *Late Gothic Europe, 1400–1500: The History of Dress.* London.

Servais, M.
1955 *Wapenboek van de provinciën en gemeenten van België.* Brussels.

Shorr, D. C.
1954 *The Christ Child in Devotional Images in Italy During the XIV Century.* New York.

Shübert-Soldern, F. von
1903 *Von Jan van Eyck bis Hieronymus Bosch: Ein Beitrag zur Geschichte der niederländischen Landschafts-malerei.* Strasbourg.

Silver, L.
1977 "Power and Self: A New-Found *Old Man* by Massys." *Simiolus,* 9, no. 2, pp. 63–92.
1983 "Fountain and Source, A Rediscovered Eyckian Icon." *Pantheon* 41, no. 2, pp. 95–104.
1984 *The Paintings of Quentin Massys with Catalogue Raisonné.* Montclair, N.J.

Simson, O. G. Von
1953 "*Compassio* and *Co-redemptio* in Roger van der Weyden's *Descent from the Cross.*" *Art Bulletin* 35, pp. 9–16.
1977 "Gerard Davids Gerechtigheitsbild und der spätmittelalterliche Humanismus." In *Festschrift Wolfgang Braunfels,* pp. 349–56. Tübingen.

Siret, A.
1837 "Gérard David à Bruges." In *Biographie nationale de Belgique,* vol. 4, pp. 711–21.
1869 "Journal d'un archéologue de Bruges: M. M. Förster, James Weale et les tableaux de Gérard David." *Journal des Beaux-Arts et de la Littérature* 9, no. 7, pp. 51–53.

Smeyers, M., and J. Van der Stock
1996 *Flemish Illuminated Manuscripts, 1475–1550.* Ghent and New York.

Smits, K.
1933 *De iconografie van de Nederlandse primitieven.* Amsterdam.

Snyder, J.
1960a "The Early Haarlem School of Painting, I: Ouwater and the Master of the Tiburtine Sibyl." *Art Bulletin* 42, pp. 39–56.
1960b "The Early Haarlem School of Painting: II. Geertgen tot Sint Jans." *Art Bulletin* 42, pp. 113–34.
1971 "The Early Haarlem School of Painting: III. The Problem of Geertgen tot Sint Jans and Jan Mostaert." *Art Bulletin* 53, pp. 445–58.
1985 *Northern Renaissance Art: Painting, Sculpture, and the Graphic Arts from 1350 to 1575.* New York.
1996 "Geertgen tot Sint Jans." In *The Dictionary of Art,* edited by J. Turner, vol. 12, pp. 230–33. London and New York.

Sonkes, M.
1969a "Note sur des procédés de copie en usage chez les primitifs flamands." *Bulletin de l'Institut Royal du Patrimoine Artistique* 11, pp. 142–52.
1969b *Dessins du XVe siècle, groupe van der Weyden: Essai de catalogue des originaux du maître, des copies et des dessins anonymes inspirés par son style.* Les primitifs flamands, III: Contributions à l'étude des primitifs flamands. Brussels.

1970 "Le dessin sous-jacent chez les primitifs flamands." *Bulletin koninklijk Instituut voor het kunstpatrimonium* 12, pp. 197–201.

Sosson, J.-P.
1966 *Les primitifs flamands de Bruges, apports des archives contemporaines, 1815–1907.* Les primitifs flamands, III: Contributions à l'étude des primitifs flamands, 4. Brussels.
1970 "Une Approche des structures économique d'un métier d'art: La corporation des peintres et selliers de Bruges (XVe–XVIe)." *Revue des archéologues et historiens d'art de Louvain* 3, pp. 91–100.
1990 "L'Impact socio-économique du mécénat ducal: Quelques réflections à propos des anciens Pays-Bas bourguignons." In *Actes des journées internationales Claus Sluter* (1990), pp. 305–9. Dijon.

Stechow, W.
1966 *Dutch Landscape Painting in the Seventeenth Century.* London.

Sterling, C.
1957 "Expositions Musée de l'Orangerie: La collection Lehman." *La revue des arts* 7, no. 3, pp. 133–42.

Stroo, C., and P. Syfer-d'Olne
1996 *The Flemish Primitives,* I. *The Master of Flémalle and Rogier van der Weyden Groups: Catalogue of Early Netherlandish Painting in the Royal Museums of Fine Arts of Belgium.* Brussels.

Strubbe, E.
1956 "Rond David's Oordeel van Cambyses." Unpublished study, conference at the Groeningemuseum, Bruges (1956), as summarized on pp. 102–29 of A. Janssens de Bisthoven, *Stedelijk Museum voor schone kunsten (Groeningemuseum), Brugge.* Vol. I of *De Vlaamse Primitiven I. Corpus van de vijftiende-eeuwse schilderkunst in de Zuidelijke Nederlanden.* Brussels, 1981.

Sulzberger, S.
1949 "Gerard David a-t-il été à Venise?" *Mededelingen van het Rijksbureau voor kunsthistorische documentatie* 4, pp. 2–3.
1955a "Autoportraits de Gérard David." *Bulletin koninklijke Musea voor schone kunsten te Brussel* 4, pp. 176–78.
1955b "L'Influence de Léonard de Vinci et ses répercussions à Anvers." *Arte Lombarda* 1, pp. 105–11.

Summers, D.
1987 *The Judgment of the Sense: Renaissance Naturalism and the Rise of Aesthetics.* Cambridge.

Szabo, G.
1975 *The Robert Lehman Collection: The Metropolitan Museum of Art.* New York.

Taubert, J.
1956 "Zur kunstwissenschaftlichen Auswertung von naturwissenschaftlichen Gemäldeuntersuchungen." Ph.D. diss., Universität Marburg.
1959 "*La Trinité* du Musée de Louvain: Une nouvelle méthode de critique des copies." *Bulletin de l'Institut Royal du Patrimoine Artistique* 2, pp. 20–33.
1975 "Pauspunkte in Tafelbildern des 15. und 16. Jahrhunderts." *Bulletin koninklijk Instituut voor het kunstpatrimonium* 15, pp. 387–401.
1975 "Beobachtungen zum schöpferischen Arbeitsprozess bei einigen altniederländischen Malern." *Nederlands kunsthistorisch jaarboek* 26, pp. 41–71.

Teasdale Smith, M.
  1959 "The Use of Grisaille as a Lenten Observation."
      Marsyas 8, pp. 43–54.
Testa, J.
  1986 *The Beatty Rosarium. Studies and Facsimiles of
      Netherlandish Illuminated Manuscripts*, vol. I.
      Doornspijk.
  1992 "The Stockholm-Kassel Book of Hours: A
      Reintegrated Manuscript from the Shop of Simon
      Bening." *Arta Bibliotheca Regiae Stockholmiensis,*
      vol. 53, pp. 7–84. Stockholm.
Thomas, A.
  1974 "Die Weintraubenmadonna." In *Die Muttergottes:
      Marienbild in Rheinland und Westfalen,* edited by
      L. Küppers, vol. I, pp. 185–95. Recklinghausen.
Tietze-Conrat, E.
  1931 "Flemish School 15th Century (Perhaps Gerard
      David)." *Old Master Drawings* 6, pp. 50–51.
Timmers, J. J. M.
  1947 *Symboliek en iconographie der Christelijke kunst.*
      Roermond, Maaseik.
Torresan, P.
  1981 *Il dipingere di Fiandra: La pittura neerlandese nella letter-
      atura artistica itialiana del quattro e cinquecento.* Modena.
Toussacrt, J.
  1963 *Le sentiment religieux en Flandre à la fin du Moyen Âge.*
      Paris.
Urbach, S.
  1987 "Contribution à l'étude de la Nativité de Gérard
      David à Budapest." *Annales d'histoire d'art et d'archéologie*
      60, pp. 83–94.
  1991 "Research Report on Examinations of Underdrawings
      in Some Early Netherlandish and German Panels in
      the Budapest Museum of Fine Arts." In *Le dessin sous-
      jacent dans la peinture, Colloque VIII, 1989,* edited by
      R. Van Schoute and H. Verougstraete-Marcq, pp. 77–93.
      Louvain-la-Neuve.
Valentiner, W. R.
  1913 *Catalogue of the collection of paintings and some art objects.*
      Vol. II. *Flemish and Dutch Painting. The John G. Johnson
      Collection.* Philadelphia.
  1926–27 "The *Annunciation* by Gerard David." *Bulletin of the
      Detroit Museum of Art* 8, pp. 92–98.
Van Belle, R.
  1981 "Iconographie en symboliek van de beschildende
      grafkelders en memorietaferelen." *Handelingen van de
      geschied—en Oudheidkundige kring van Kortrijk,* n.s., 48,
      pp. 10–85.
Van Buren, A. H., J. H. Marrow, and S. Pettinati
  1996 *Heures de Turin-Milan.* Turin.
Van den Bergen-Pantens, C.
  1966 "L'Héraldique au service de l'étude d'un tableau des
      Musées royaux." *Bulletin des Musées Royaux des Beaux-
      Arts de Belgique* 4, pp. 243–46.
Vandenbroeck, P.
  1985 *Catalogus schilderijen 14de en 15de eeuw. Koninklijk
      Museum voor Schone Kunsten te Antwerpen.* Antwerp.
Van der Wetering, C.
  1938 *Die Entwicklung der niederländischen Landschaftsmalerei vom
      Anfang des 16. Jahrhunderts bis zur Jahrhundertmitte.* Berlin.

Vandewalle, A., and N. Geirnaert
  1992 "Bruges and Italy." In *Bruges and Europe,* edited by
      V. Vermeersch, pp. 183–204. Antwerp.
Van Houtte, J. A.
  1940 "La Genèse du grand marché international d'Anvers
      à la fin du Moyen Âge." *Revue belge de philologie et
      d'histoire* 19, pp. 87–126.
  1952 "Bruges et Anvers, marchés nationaux ou interna-
      tionaux du XIV au XVI siècle." *Revue du Nord* 34,
      pp. 89–108.
  1953 "Les Foires dans la Belgique ancienne." In *La Foire,*
      pp. 175–205. Recueils de la société J. Brodin 5.
      Brussels.
  1966 "The Rise and Decline of the Market in Bruges."
      The Economic History Review, 2nd ser., 19, pp. 29–47.
  1967 *Economische en sociale geschiedenis van de Lage Lande,*
      pp. 77–92. Antwerp.
  1977 *An Economic History of the Low Countries.* London.
  1982a *Bruges, Essai d'histoire urbaine.* Paris, 1967. Zeist.
  1982b *De geschiedenis van Brugge.* Tielt.
Van Molle, F., J. Folie, H. Verhaegen, P. Philippot, R. Sneyers,
      J. Thissen
  1958 "La Justice d'Othon de Dieric Bouts." *Bulletin Institut
      royale du patrimoine artistique,* 1, pp. 7–69.
Van Schoute, R.
  1958 *La Chapelle Royale de Grenade.* De Vlaamse Primitieven
      I: Corpus van de vijftiende-eeuwse schilderkunst in
      de Zuidelijke Nederlanden, 6. Brussels.
Vasari
  1906 *Le vite de' più eccellenti pittori, scultori, ed architettori scritte
      da Giorgio Vasari, pittore aretino, con nuove annotazioni e
      commenti di Gaetano Milanesi.* 9 vols., based on the 2d
      ed. of 1568. Florence, 1878–85. Reprint, Florence.
Velden, H. van der
  1995a "Cambyses for Example: The Origins and Function
      of an *exemplum iustitiae* in Netherlandish Art of the
      Fifteenth, Sixteenth and Seventeenth Centuries."
      Simiolus 23, no. 1, pp. 5–39.
  1995b "Cambyses Reconsidered: Gerard David's *exemplum
      iustitiae* for Bruges Town Hall." *Simiolus* 23, no. 1,
      pp. 40–62.
Verjans, M.
  1949 "Het franciscana in de kunst van Gerard David en
      zijn school." *Franciscana* 4, pp. 89–95.
Vermaseren, B.
  1950–51 "De Carmel van Brugge en de buitenlandse
      kooplieden." *Carmel* 3, pp. 19–31.
Vermeersch, V.
  1992 [as editor] *Bruges and Europe.* Antwerp.
Verougstraete, H., and R. Van Schoute
  1997 "Les Petites *Pietàs* du groupe van der Weyden:
      Mécanismes d'une production en série." *Techne* 5,
      pp. 21–27.
Verougstraete, H., R. Van Schoute, and M. Smeyers
  1997 [as editors] *Memling Studies: Proceedings of the International
      Colloquium (Bruges, 10–12 November 1994).* Leuven.
Veys, A.
  1952 "Portrait of an Ecclesiastic." In *Album English: Studies
      over de kerkelijke en de kunstgeschiedenis van West-
      Vlaanderen,* pp. 423–32. Bruges.

Voll, K.
1906 *Die altniederländische Malerei von Jan van Eyck bis Memling. Ein entwicklungsgeschichtlicher Versuch.* Leipzig.

Voragine, J. de
1969 *The Golden Legend.* Translated and adapted by Granger Ryan and Helmut Ripperger. New York.

Waagen, G. F.
1866–67 *Die vornehmsten Kunstdenkmäler in Wien,* vol. II. Vienna.

Walle de Ghelcke, T. van de
1949 "Gerard David." Ph.D. diss., Université Catholique de Louvain.
1950 "Le Présumé Portrait de Jacques Cnoop le jeune, orfèvre brugeois." *Handelingen van het genootschap "Société d'émulation" te Brugge* 87, pp. 155–62.
1952 "Y a-t-il un Gérard David miniaturiste?" In *Album English: Studies over de kerkelijke en de kunstgeschiedenis van West-Vlaanderen,* pp. 399–422. Bruges.

Walsh, R.
1982 "Relations Between Milan and Burgundy in the Period 1450–1476." In *Gli Sforza, a Milano e in Lombardia e I loro rapporti con gli Stati italiani ed europei (1450–1535),* pp. 369–94. Milan.

Warburg, A.
1902 "Flandrische Kunst und florentinische Frührenaissance." *Jahrbuch der Königlich Preussischen Kunstsammlungen* 23, pp. 247–66.

Weale, W. H. J.
1861 *Catalogue: Notices et descriptions avec monogrammes, etc.* Groeningemuseum, Bruges.
1862 *Bruges et ses environs; Description des monuments, objets d'art, et antiquités précédée d'une notice historique.* Bruges.
1863a "Albrecht Cornelis: Hiérarchie des anges." *Le Beffroi* 1, pp. 1–22.
1863b "Inventaire des chartes et documents appartenant aux archives de la corporation de Saint Luc et Saint Eloi à Bruges." *Le Beffroi* 1, pp. 201–22.
1863c "Gerard David." *Le Beffroi* 1, pp. 223–34.
1863d "Triptych du Baptême du Christ conservé au musée de l'académie de Bruges." *Le Beffroi* 1, pp. 276–87.
1864–65 "Gerard David" and "Documents inédits sur les enlumineurs de Bruges." *Le Beffroi* 2, pp. 288–319.
1866a "Gerard David, Sa vie et ses oeuvres authentiques." *Gazette des Beaux-Arts* 20, pp. 542–53.
1866b "Gerard David: Sa vie et ses oeuvres authentiques." *Gazette des Beaux-Arts* 21, pp. 489–501.
1866–70a "Le Couvent des sœurs de Notre-Dame, dit de Sion à Bruges." *Le Beffroi* 3, pp. 46–53, 76–93, 214–30.
1866–70b "Gerard David." *Le Beffroi* 3, pp. 334–46.
1872–73 "Documents inédits sur les enlumineurs de Bruges." *Le Beffroi* 4, pp. 11–119, 238–337.
1895 *Gerard David: Painter and Illuminator.* London.
1905 "The Shutters of a Triptych by Gerard David." *Burlington Magazine* 7, pp. 234–37.

Wescher, P. R.
1946 "Sanders and Simon Bening and Gerard Horenbout." *Art Quarterly* 9, no. 3, pp. 191–211.

Wilhelmy, W.
1993 *Der altniederländische Realismus und seine Funktionen.* Münster and Hamburg.

Wilkens, E.
1969 *The Rose-Garden Game: The Symbolic Background to the European Prayer-Beads.* London.

Wilson, J.
1983 "The Participation of Painters in the Bruges 'Pandt' Market, 1512–1550." *Burlington Magazine* 125, pp. 476–79.
1986 "Marketing Paintings in Late Medieval Belgium." In *Artistes, artisans, et production artistique au Moyen Âge: Rapports provisoires,* vol. 2, pp. 1759–66. Paris.
1990a "Workshop Patterns and the Production of Paintings in 16th Century Bruges." *Burlington Magazine* 132, pp. 523–27.
1990b "Marketing Paintings in Late Medieval Flanders and Brabant." In *Artistes, artisans, et production artistique au Moyen Âge: Fabrication et consommation de l'œuvre,* vol. 3, pp. 621–27. Paris.
1991 "Connoisseurship and Copies: The Case of the Rouen Grouping." *Gazette des Beaux-Arts,* 6th ser., 117, pp. 191–206.
1995a "Adriaen Isenbrant and the Problem of His Work." *Oud Holland* 109, pp. 1–17.
1995b "Enframing Aspirations: Albrecht Dürer's *Self-Portrait* of 1493 in the Musée du Louvre." *Gazette des Beaux-Arts* 126, pp. 149–58.
1995c "Reflections on St. Luke's Hand: Icons and the Nature of Aura in the Burgundian Low Countries During the Fifteenth Century." In *The Sacred Image East and West,* edited by R. Ousterhout and L. Brubaker, pp. 132–46. Urbana and Chicago.
1998 *Paintings in Bruges at the Close of the Middle Ages: Studies in Society and Visual Culture.* University Park, Pa.

Winkler, F.
1895 *Gerard David: Painter and Illuminator.* London.
1913 "Gerard David und die brügger Miniaturmalerei seiner Zeit." *Monatshefte für Kunstwissenschaft* 6, pp. 271–80.
1929 "Das Skizzenbuch Gerard Davids." *Pantheon* 3, pp. 271–75.
1964 *Das Werk des Hugo van der Goes.* Berlin.

Winter, P. M. de
1981 "A Book of Hours of Queen Isabel la Católica." *Bulletin of the Cleveland Museum of Art* 66, pp. 342–422.

Wolfthal, D.
1989 *The Beginnings of Netherlandish Canvas Painting: 1400–1530.* Cambridge.

Wyld, M., A. Roy, and A. Smith.
1979 "Gerard David's *The Virgin and Child with Saints and a Donor.*" *National Gallery Technical Bulletin* 3, pp. 51–65.

INDEX

C.I.N.O.A. Member Associations

Australia
The Australian Antiques Dealers' Association, Ltd.

Austria
Bundesgremium des Handels Mit Juwelen, Gold-, Silberwaren,
    Uhren, Alter und Moderner Kunst, Antiquitäten, Sowie
    Briefmarken und Numismatike

Belgium & Luxembourg
Chambre Royale des Antiquaires de Belgique

Canada
Professional Art Dealers' Association of Canada

Czech Republic
Asociace Starozitníkû

Denmark
Dansk Antikvitetshandler Union

France & Monaco
Chambre Syndicale de L'Estampe, du Dessin et du Tableau
Syndicat National des Antiquaires Négociants en Objets d'Art
    Tableaux Anciens et Modernes

Germany
Bundesverband des Deutschen Kunst- und Antiquitätenhandels
    E.V.

Great Britain
The British Antique Dealers' Association
London and Provincial Art Dealers' Association
The Society of London Art Dealers

Ireland
The Irish Antique Dealers' Association

Italy & San Marino
Associazione Antiquari d'Italia
Federazione Italiana Mercanti d'Arte

The Netherlands
Vereeniging van Handelaren in Oude Kunst in Nederland

New Zealand
The New Zealand Antique Dealers' Association

Norway
Norges Kunst – og Antikvitetshandleres Forening

Poland
Stowarzyszenie Antykwariuszy Polskich

Portugal
Associaçao Portuguesa Anticuarios

Spain
Asociacion de Profesionales en Arte Antiguo y Moderno

Sweden
Sveriges Konst och Antikhandlareforening

South Africa
The South African Antique Dealers' Association

Switzerland
Association des Commerçants d'Art de la Suisse
Verband Schweizerischer Antiquare und Kunsthändler / Syndicat
    Suisse des Antiquaires et Commerçants d'Art

The United States of America
Art and Antique Dealers League of America, Inc.
Art Dealers Association of America, Inc.
The National Antique & Art Dealers Association of America, Inc.
Private Art Dealers Association

C.I.N.O.A. Prize Recipients

1977 Penelope Eames, England, *Furniture in France
and England from the Twelfth to the Fifteenth
Century*

1978 Claire Lindgren, U.S.A., *Classical Art Forms and Celtic
Mutations*

1979 Bertrand Jaeger, Switzerland, *Essai de classification et datation
des scarabèes Menkhéperre*

1980 Norman Bryson, England, *Paintings as Signs: Word and
Image in French Painting of the Ancien Régime*

1981 Geneviève Aitken, France, *Les Peintres et le Théâtre de 1900 à
Paris*

1982 Marianne Roland Michel, France, *Jacques de Lajoue et l'Art
Rocaille*

1983 C. Edson Armi, U.S.A., *Masons and Sculptures in
Romanesque Burgundy*

1984 Nicola Gordon Bowe, Ireland, *The Life and Work of Harry
Clarke*

1985 Dr. Johannes R. ter Molen, The Netherlands, *Van Vianen—
Een Utrechtse Familie van Silvermeden met een internationale Faam*

1986 Jörg Martin Merz, Germany, *Pietro da Cortonas Entwicklung
zum Maler des römischen Hochbarock*

1987 Dr. Roland Dorn, Germany, *Vincent van Gogh's Werkreihe
für das Gelbe Haus in Arles*

1988 Mrs. Baby-Papion, France, *Les Retables nicois des XVe et
XVIe siècles peints par Louis Brea*

1989 Walter Liedtke, U.S.A., *The Royal Horse and Rider*

1990 Dr. Ulrich Leben, Germany, *Bernard Molitor, 1775–1833*

1991 Tom Crispin, England, *The Windsor Chair*

1992 Lucy Wood, England, *The Lady Lever Art Gallery: Catalogue
of Commodes*

1994 Miss Anne Crookshank and Mr. Desmond Fitzgerald,
Ireland, *The Watercolours of Ireland*

1995 Prof. Alvar Gonzales Palacios, Italy, *Il Gusto dei Principi*

1996 Geoffrey Beard, England, *Upholsterers & Interior Furnishing
in England, 1530–1840*
Honorable Mention: Christina Ordinez, Spain, *Il Mobile:
Conservazione et Restauro*

1997 Steven A. Mansbach, U.S.A., *Modern Art in Eastern Europe*

1998 Maryan W. Ainsworth, U.S.A., *Gerard David: Purity of Vision
in an Age of Transition*
Honorable Mention: Robert Keil, Austria, *Die
Portraitminiaturen der Habsburger — eine Sammlung von 600
Miniaturen*